Jacksonland

ALSO BY STEVE INSKEEP

Instant City:
Life and Death in Karachi

Jacksonland

President Andrew Jackson, Cherokee Chief
John Ross, and a Great American Land Grab

STEVE INSKEEP

PENGUIN PRESS

NEW YORK

2015

PENGUIN PRESS
An imprint of Penguin Random House LLC
375 Hudson Street
New York, New York 10014
penguin.com

Photographs by the author appear on insert pages one (top), three,
four (bottom), seven (right), and eight.

Interior map illustrations by Jeffrey L. Ward

ISBN 978-1-59420-556-9

Printed in the United States of America
1   3   5   7   9   10   8   6   4   2

DESIGNED BY AMANDA DEWEY

To Carolee, Ava, and Ana

Those who profess inviolable truthfulness must speak of all without partiality and without hatred.

Tacitus

CONTENTS

PART THREE

Old Hickory, 1815–1818

PART FOUR

Young Prince, 1820–1828

Interlude: Hero's Progress, 1824–1825

PART FIVE

Inaugurations, 1828–1829

PART SIX

State of the Union, 1829–1830

PART SEVEN

Checks and Balances, 1830–1832

Jacksonland

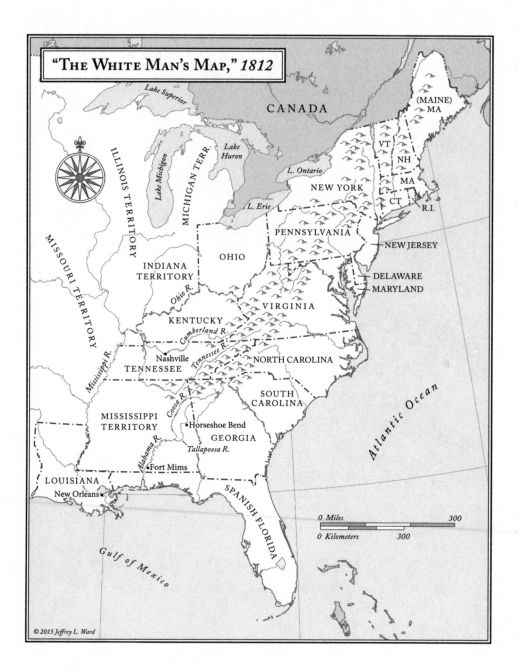

"THE WHITE MAN'S MAP," *1812*

Lake Superior

CANADA

Lake Huron

(MAINE)
MA

VT

NH

MA

Lake Michigan

L. Ontario

NEW YORK

CT

R.I.

ILLINOIS TERRITORY

MICHIGAN TERR.

L. Erie

PENNSYLVANIA

NEW JERSEY

MISSOURI TERRITORY

INDIANA TERRITORY

OHIO

DELAWARE
MARYLAND

Ohio R.

VIRGINIA

KENTUCKY

Cumberland R.

Mississippi R.

Nashville

Tennessee R.

NORTH CAROLINA

TENNESSEE

Coosa R.

SOUTH CAROLINA

MISSISSIPPI TERRITORY

Horseshoe Bend

Alabama R.

GEORGIA

Tallapoosa R.

Fort Mims

LOUISIANA

New Orleans

SPANISH FLORIDA

Atlantic Ocean

Gulf of Mexico

0 Miles   300

0 Kilometers   300

© 2015 Jeffrey L. Ward

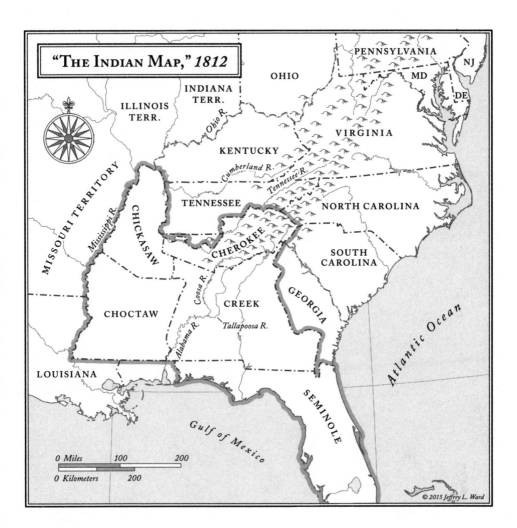

"THE INDIAN MAP," *1812*

ILLINOIS TERR.

INDIANA TERR.

OHIO

PENNSYLVANIA

NJ

MD

DE

Ohio R.

KENTUCKY

VIRGINIA

MISSOURI TERRITORY

Cumberland R.

Tennessee R.

CHICKASAW

TENNESSEE

NORTH CAROLINA

Mississippi R.

CHEROKEE

SOUTH CAROLINA

Cooia R.

CREEK

GEORGIA

CHOCTAW

Alabama R.

Tallapoosa R.

Atlantic Ocean

LOUISIANA

SEMINOLE

Gulf of Mexico

0 Miles 100 200

0 Kilometers 200

© 2015 Jeffrey L. Ward

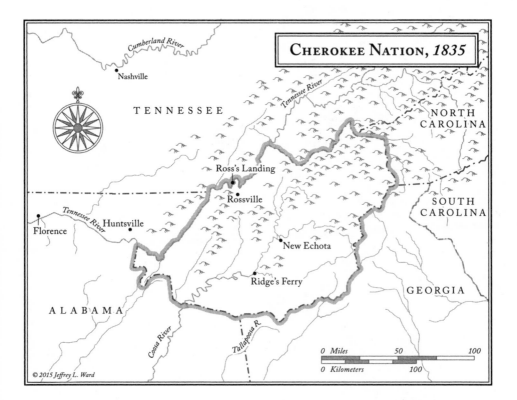

CHEROKEE NATION, *1835*

Cumberland River

Nashville

TENNESSEE

Tennessee River

NORTH CAROLINA

Ross's Landing

Rossville

SOUTH CAROLINA

Tennessee River

Huntsville

Florence

New Echota

Ridge's Ferry

GEORGIA

ALABAMA

Coosa River

Tallapoosa R.

0 Miles	50	100

0 Kilometers	100

© 2015 Jeffrey L. Ward

Prologue:

The Indian Map and the White Man's Map

This story follows two men who fought for more than twenty years. They fought over land in the American South, which is where they lived, though some said it wasn't big enough for the two of them.

One man was Andrew Jackson, who became a general, then president, then the man on the twenty-dollar bill. Those honors merely hint at the scale of his outsize life. The other man was John Ross, who was Native American, or Indian as natives were called. He became principal chief of the Cherokee Nation, though this title, too, fails to capture his full experience.

Before he was chief, and before he met Jackson, Ross was a young man navigating his complex and perilous world. That is how we first encounter him. At the age of twenty-two, he bought a boat. It was a wooden flatboat, essentially a raft with some housing on the deck. And on that boat, near the end of 1812, he set out on the Tennessee River. Starting somewhere around the site of present-day Chattanooga, the boat and its crew floated westward with the current, a speck on the water, dwarfed by riverside cliffs that marked the river's passage through the Appalachians.

Ross was traveling several hundred miles, toward a band of Cherokees living west of the Mississippi. He intended to sell them the cargo on his boat: calico, gingham, buttons, beaver traps, and shotguns. But the westward course of the Tennessee River had a way of testing travelers. Ross struggled to navigate currents so perilous that they had ominous names such as Dead Man's Eddy and the Suck. He grew so frustrated after days on the water that he stopped at a riverside settlement to sell his boat, trading for a keelboat that was narrower and more maneuverable. His crew heaved their cargo from one boat to the other. Then Ross and crew crashed through forty miles of whitewater known as Muscle Shoals, scraping on shallows and passing islands piled with driftwood. At last the water calmed, and the boat followed the river's great bend northward toward the Ohio.

Anyone covertly studying the boat would have seen four men on board. Ross was black-haired, brown-eyed, slight but handsome. Each of his three companions could be described in a phrase (a Cherokee interpreter, an older Cherokee man named Kalsatee, and a servant), but Ross was harder to categorize. He was the son of a Scottish trader, whose family had lived among Cherokees for generations in their homeland in the southern Appalachians. Ross was an aspiring trader himself. Yet he also had a solid claim to his identity as an Indian. A man of mixed race, he had grown up among Cherokee children and, in keeping with Cherokee custom, received a new name at adulthood: Koowe-skoowe, said to be a species of bird.

Whether he was a white man or an Indian became a matter of life and death on December 28, 1812. In Kentucky, as Ross later recorded in a letter, "we was haled by a party of white men." The men on the riverbank called for the boat to come closer.

Ross asked what they wanted.

Give us the news, one called back.

Something bothered Ross about the men. "I told them we had no news worth their attention."

Now the white men revealed their true purpose. One shouted that they had orders from a garrison of soldiers nearby "to stop every boat descending the river to examin if any Indians was on board as they were not permitted to come about that place." Come to us, the men concluded. Or we'll come to you.

Ross didn't come.

"Damn my soul if those two are not Indians," one of the men shouted, referring to two of Ross's crew. The man added that he would gather a company of men to pursue and kill them.

Ross came up with an answer: "These two men are Spaniard," he called back.

The white men demanded the "Spaniards" prove their identity by speaking Spanish. Peter, the servant, actually could, but the white men still "insisted it was an Indian boat & mounted their horses & galloped off."

Ross had to assume the white men were serious. The United States had declared war on Britain that year, and some native nations had joined the British side, killing white settlers, fighting alongside British troops, and throwing the frontier into turmoil. The white horsemen would not pause to find out that Ross's Cherokees were loyal to the United States. The Cherokees could travel in only one direction, and would have little chance to escape if the men on horseback arranged an unpleasant reception downstream.

Ross decided on a precaution: he whitened the boat. He had told the horsemen there were no Indians on board, and the best chance of safety was to make this claim appear true. He modified the racial composition of his crew, leaving only those who could pass as non-Indian. Ross could pass, as could the Cherokee interpreter, who like Ross was an English speaker and a "mixed-blood," parlance for part white and part Indian. The servant, who may have been a black man, would be ignored. Only old Kalsatee was a full-blooded Cherokee with no chance to fool anybody. His mere presence might even cause the others to be perceived as Indians. This, apparently, was Ross's thinking, because as he confided later, "we concluded it was good policy to let Kalsatee out of the boat." The old man would have to set off overland and meet the craft later. The remaining crew put their poles in the water and shoved the keelboat toward whatever lay ahead.

Ross spent two anxious days on the water, and Kalsatee had "a disagreeable walk of about thirty miles," probably along the bank opposite from where they'd seen the horsemen. Finally the old man rejoined the boat downstream, and they all floated to a safe haven, Fort Massac on the Ohio River, manned by professional soldiers who could tell friend from foe. The horsemen never reappeared. Reflecting on this afterward, Ross said he was "convinced" that "the independent manner in which I answered" the horsemen had "confounded their apprehension of it being an Indian boat." Indians were supposed to be children of the woods, in a common phrase of the era: dangerous but not too bright, and expected to address white men respectfully as elder brothers. Ross had talked back to the men in clear and defiant English. The future leader of the Cherokee Nation had passed as white.

That was John Ross: careful with his language, resourceful, willing to do what was necessary to survive. Also persistent, because after leaving Fort Massac, he made it to his destination west of the Mississippi as planned, offering his gingham and shotguns for sale to the band of Cherokees living there. When he finished trading in 1813, he made the long journey back to the southern Appalachians, the ancient homeland of the bulk of the Cherokee Nation. It is upon his return that our story truly begins, because that is when he first encountered Andrew Jackson.

Jackson was a soldier at the time. He was a longtime Tennessee state militia general, recently elevated into federal service to help fight the British and hostile Indians in the War of 1812. The government in Washington authorized him to recruit Tennessee volunteers to serve under his command. Though his force initially consisted of twenty-five hundred white frontiersmen, it was expanded to meet an emergency in the fall of 1813. Jackson accepted the services of several hundred friendly Indians, mostly Cherokees, who organized their own regiment under the command of a trusted white officer. The Cherokee Regiment included John Ross, and from the moment he enrolled, his destiny and Jackson's were linked. They were fighting on the same side, at least at first, but they were bound for a historic collision. Each man rose to supreme leadership of his nation, and struggled for control of millions of acres.

Their story is a prequel to the Civil War, and a prelude to the democratic debates of our era. It established the physical landscape and defined the political culture for much that followed. At the time they met, the United States was very different from what it soon became. Reading about it today feels like falling into a dream, exploring territory at once foreign and familiar. The nation was barely a generation beyond its founding. The chief executive was one of the original Founding Fathers: President James Madison, a member of a small governing elite. From a capital under construction, Madison presided over eighteen states with only a handful of notable cities. The population of the entire United States was about seven million, smaller than the modern-day populace of greater metropolitan Chicago. The future site of Chicago was a lonesome military post called Fort Dearborn, which had recently been burned by Potawatomi warriors. Immense territories from the Appalachians westward were native domains, as they had been since long before Europeans arrived. But settlers were pushing westward, and the War of 1812 spurred greater change, weakening natives and strengthening the movement of white farmers, who often brought along black enslaved laborers. In the decades after that war, young men such as Jefferson Davis, Abraham Lincoln, and Stephen Douglas were coming of age on the frontier, while the United States was swelling into the form they would inherit by the time of the Southern rebellion in 1861. This was the era when Jackson and Ross became national figures. They rose with the country and the country with them.

Jackson emerged from the War of 1812 as a hero, a full-time army general, and later the founder of the Democratic Party, whose election to the presidency came in 1828. No man of such a humble background—an orphan from an Appalachian valley—had ever risen so far. Proclaimed to be a champion of common people, he smashed what he considered elitist institutions and permanently altered American politics. Throughout his career he also constantly pressed Indians to surrender land. He used reason, intimidation, bribery, duplicity, and force. As president he codified a policy known as Indian removal, saying both races would benefit if natives moved westward to make room for white settlement. Ross rose in opposition to Jackson. He emerged from the war as a veteran officer, who soon became a Cherokee diplomat, and in 1816 temporarily blocked one of Jackson's great land acquisitions. Later, hoping to halt Cherokees' constant losses of land, Ross presided over the creation of a Cherokee constitution, which declared that the boundaries of the Cherokee Nation "shall forever hereafter remain unalterably the same." His election as Cherokee principal chief in 1828 required him to obey that mandate never to cede another foot of land.

In theory this duty was straightforward. Treaties with the United States had affirmed the Cherokees' sovereignty. They were not regarded as U.S. citizens, but as citizens of an independent nation that had every right to control its remaining territory. Yet the same treaties placed the Cherokee Nation under the "protection" of the federal government. In practice Cherokees were under U.S. authority and dependent on Washington's good faith. The Cherokee government relied on annual payments from the federal government—annuities that had been earned through past land sales, but that made Washington the Cherokees' paymaster. Cherokees were overseen by a federal "Indian agent" who lived among them and wielded great influence, like an ambassador from a colonial power. Ross, like every Cherokee, was caught in the United

States' embrace—and his innovation was to embrace it back. He never followed the example of native leaders who rose in hopeless rebellion. "We consider ourselves as a part of the great family of the Republic of the U. States," he wrote, "and we are ready at any time to sacrifice our lives, our property & every thing sacred to us, in its cause." His strategy was to insist on Cherokee rights within the great family. He fought Jackson within the democratic system just as that system was taking shape. Each man came to personify a basic democratic value: Jackson, the principle of majority rule; Ross, the principle of minority rights.

Many excellent histories describe the early nineteenth century from Jackson's point of view, with Indians as ill-fated minor characters. Many powerful works explore the same period from the vantage of Ross or other natives, with Jackson as a terrible destructive force. Weaving the stories of both men together casts them in a different light. When we judge them as players on a democratic stage, it becomes easier to understand their actions, even when we disapprove. Jackson, sometimes portrayed as a hot-tempered man of narrow intelligence, deeply understood strategy and power. Ross, often criticized for his epic stubbornness, was also creative and subtle. The Cherokees were more than mere victims: they were skilled political operators who played a bad hand long and well. Their resistance to Indian removal forced much of the nation to take sides, foreshadowed modern movements for the rights of racial minorities, and added to our democratic tradition.

This book follows the story in the order it unfolded. Titanic figures step onto the stage. They range from Jackson's great rival Henry Clay of Kentucky to his steady ally Lewis Cass of Michigan, and from the storytelling frontiersman Davy Crockett to the crafty Supreme Court chief justice John Marshall. Other characters are less famous today than they deserve to be: Elias Boudinot, a Cherokee newspaper editor; Major Ridge, his wealthy and powerful Cherokee uncle; George Troup, a ruthless Georgia governor; and Catharine Beecher, who helped to organize the first mass political campaign by women in American history.

. . .

The tangible thing over which all of them fought was real estate. We already have the land in sight, because the Tennessee River on which Ross was traveling in 1812 was a major highway through it. Our story will take us many times past the white water at Muscle Shoals. Other times we will pass the riverside settlement that today is Chattanooga: in Ross's time it was a Cherokee settlement that he developed as a ferry crossing called Ross's Landing.

Whenever land is discussed in this book, it will be vital to keep in mind that in the early nineteenth century, the same place could be represented on two different and mutually exclusive maps. There was a white man's map and an Indian map. The white man's map, the map of the United States, divided the region into states and territories, often bounded by straight and imaginary lines. The Indian map divided much of the same landmass into native nations, commonly bounded by landmarks such as rivers or ridgelines. On the U.S. map, for example, Ross lived in a house in north Georgia, within a moment's walk of the Tennessee line. By the Indian map the same house was in the heart of the Cherokee Nation, an enclave that spread across parts of several states. On the U.S. map his 1812 river journey wound several times in and out of Tennessee; on the Indian map it passed the Cherokee, Creek, and Chickasaw nations. Each map was like a parallel universe, though both were recognized by the government in Washington, which had its reasons to embrace ambiguity.

I call this book *Jacksonland* because Jackson strove to make the map his own. "The object of the Govt," he wrote once while serving as a major general, "is to bring into markett this land & have it populated." He did that in more ways than one. This book documents, perhaps more fully than before, Jackson's personal dealings in real estate that he captured as a general. While still in military service he bought and operated slave plantations on former Indian land that he had opened to white settlement using doubtful means. He worked in concert with friends who bought even more land than he did, and colonized the newly acquired territory. The names of Jackson, his friends, and his relations appeared on the purchase records for at least forty-five thousand acres sold in the Tennessee River valley from 1818 onward. Jackson mixed public and private business in ways that would be considered scandalous today, and were criticized even in the nineteenth century, when notions of ethics were different and not all details of his acts were known.

Jackson, more than any other single person, was responsible for creating the region we call the Deep South. In a larger sense Jackson was filling out the wider American South, which has persisted ever since as a powerful cultural and political force. Maybe it all would have grown the same way without him—great historical forces were at work—but his contemporaries understood that Jackson *did* the work, and did it his way. Not for nothing did they bestow his name on Jackson, Mississippi, Jacksonville, Florida, and Jackson County as well as Jacksonville, Alabama. Those were the three states he did the most to establish.

On the Indian map, of course, the future Deep South was mostly Cherokee land, or Creek land, or Choctaw or Chickasaw or Seminole land. These were the five large tribal groups remaining in the region in Jackson's day. They would become known as the Five Civilized Tribes because they were adapting their ancient cultures to white society. Despite internal resistance, many Cherokees changed their clothing, their agriculture, their religion, and the relationship between men and women. They embraced literacy and written laws, and even adopted the practice of owning slaves. They acted like immigrants assimilating to a new country, except that the new country was coming to them. Just as John Ross altered the appearance of the people on his boat in 1812, Cherokees were altering their nation in ways they considered necessary for their safety and well-being. It was also to ensure their safety that they turned for leadership to a man with the skills of John Ross. Maybe the Cherokee story would have read the same way without him—here too great forces were in motion—but when the crisis arrived, he chose a different path than other native leaders, and even other Cherokee leaders. Right or wrong, his choices are part of what makes the Cherokee story so meaningful and moving. Ross wanted to stay on the map, and find an enduring place for his people in Jacksonland.

PART ONE

———◆———

Horseshoe

1814

One

Every Thing Is to Be Feared

O n March 14, 1814, General Andrew Jackson began to compose a letter. He did it at his headquarters, an open-sided tent, or marquee, at a camp called Fort Strother in what is now Alabama. The letter was addressed to a man in the same camp. Jackson could have easily summoned the man for a talk, but wanted his message to be written for posterity.

This letter omitted the flourishes of courtesy that were common in his writing and characteristic of the age. Even when he sent a note filled with vituperation, Jackson might sign off humbly as "Respectfully your Most Obedient Servant." He began letters to his close friend and military subordinate John Coffee by addressing him as "Sir," and signed his first *and* last name when writing home to his wife, Rachel, but his note on March 14 wasted no ink on a show of respect. He did not call the recipient "Private," which was his rank in the Tennessee militia, nor even check the spelling of his name, which other documents recorded as John Wood.

John Woods,

You have been tried by a court martial on the charges of disobedience of orders, disrespect to your commanding officer, & mutiny; & have been found guilty of all of them.

Andrew Jackson was supreme commander at this camp, and Wood was at that moment the very lowest of his lowly soldiers.

The court which found you guilty of these charges has sentenced you to death by shooting

A firing squad from the Thirty-Ninth Regiment was awaiting the order to carry out the sentence.

Any soldier who glimpsed Jackson working with his aides that morning might have seen the general's gold epaulettes, with gold fringe, covering the shoulders of his blue shirt. His cold, steady eyes were set beneath bushy eyebrows in a narrow face; his gray hair was so unruly it could have been a fur hat. He was six feet two inches, 145 pounds, so thin that according to an old story his gaunt frame once saved his life in a duel, when his antagonist misjudged the narrow target inside Jackson's bulky overcoat. A stick man in uniform.

He surely wasn't any thicker after the events of the past five months. In the fall he'd ridden with his army from their homes in Tennessee, fording rivers and bypassing mountains to establish Fort Strother in the woods. Jackson made that punishing journey with his left arm in a sling, having been shot in a gunfight in a hotel in the center of Nashville. The lead ball was still in his body. Since the southward march, supplies had arrived so rarely that his army had little food; one soldier recalled later that they "lived on any thing we could get from meat and Bread down to Acorns nutts herbs & some dry cowhide." Jackson gave his soldiers his own food, which he could hardly eat. His stomach gave him constant trouble. He did contortions to ease the pain, sometimes draping his body over a sapling that had been knocked sideways for the purpose.

He was using Fort Strother as his base of operations against a rebellious faction of the Creek Nation, the largest and most important Indian confederation in the region. The Creek rebels had risen up against their own nation's leaders as well as against the United States, fighting on the same side as the British in the War of 1812. Fort Strother was near the northeast corner of a vast region known as the Mississippi Territory—present-day Mississippi and Alabama lumped together into one—though this territory was mostly a notion. Some of its borders had not even been surveyed. In reality, Fort Strother was on the Indian map, facing tens of thousands of square miles of Creek territory where virgin forest reached toward the sky and wet leaves carpeted the hillsides. The main signs of civilization near Fort Strother were Creek towns and plantations, and many of those were lifeless piles of ashes, since Jackson's troops had been ranging out to burn them. At the fort most of the men lived in tents, arranged beside parade grounds like the one where General Jackson's letter would soon be read aloud to John Wood.

The offenses of which you have been found guilty are such as cannot be permitted to pass unpunished in an army, but at the hazard of its ruin.

He went on writing for several pages. This was "the second time" that Wood had committed mutiny, Jackson claimed. The private violated "all the principles of honor," had a mind "totally dead, to every honorable sentiment," and was "perversely & obstinately bent on spreading discord." Wood's actions betrayed

an incorrigible disposition of heart—a rebellious and obstinate temper of mind, which, as it cannot be rectified, ought not to be permitted to diffuse its influence amongst others—
*   An army cannot exist where order & subordination are wholly disregarded.*

Order and subordination were on the general's mind, for his army was as undisciplined as a bear rug with the bear still in it. Only one portion of his force consisted of regular army troops: the few hundred professional soldiers of the Thirty-Ninth Regiment, established the previous year. They were Jackson's reliable men—the ones he could count on to form a firing squad, for instance. This regiment included a charismatic and theatrical young officer named Sam Houston. The rest of Jackson's force of three thousand or so had done nothing in their lives to put them in the habit of following orders. Hundreds were friendly Indians, including the Cherokee Regiment, some of whom came and went as they pleased—one, John Ross, until recently had been away on business in the Cherokee Nation. The Cherokees were prepared to fight for Jackson, but had a tradition that a warrior could refuse to go to war if he did not want to. The white men who formed the remainder of Jackson's force were also independent thinkers. These were Tennessee volunteers, who neither acted nor looked the part of professional soldiers.

Jackson, no professional soldier himself, had only begun recruiting his force in late 1812. He had offered to enroll Tennesseans and organize them to fight for the United States, and the War Department in Washington had accepted. The federal government needed states like Tennessee to help generate soldiers, having declared war at a time when the regular army had only a few thousand men. Without the resources to equip his volunteers, Jackson told them to bring their own weapons and even their own uniforms: "dark blue or brown," his orders said, "homespun or not, at the election of the wearer." One private was later described, perhaps a bit fancifully, as "a tall delicately framed youth . . . habited in a hunting shirt of some dark hue, set off with a fringe of yellow, a belt around the waist—in which he carried a dirk knife and tomahawk, and with his hat—these formed his equipment." That youth, Richard K. Call, had walked out of his studies at a boys' school called Mount Pleasant Academy to join a company being formed in his neighborhood. The bulk of the volunteers were frontier farmers. For a time the force had included Davy Crockett, a hunter and storyteller with a beloved if neglected wife at home.

It was a wildly unrealistic way to raise an army. Jackson's white men had enlisted for specified terms as short as three months, nowhere near the time his campaign required. Proud citizens of a republic, jealous of their rights and with business back home, they agitated to return as soon as their enlistments expired. Back in December Jackson had prevented a mass of troops from marching away only by having artillery aimed in their direction. Later he wrote the Tennesseans a letter saying they were free to go home if they were craven enough to abandon duty and country. Most, including Crockett, shrugged off this effort to shame them and departed, leaving Jackson with a small and motley collection of loyalists, including his friend John Coffee and Richard K. Call, that "delicately framed youth" with the tomahawk. Eventually fresh recruits arrived from Tennessee, Private Wood among them. But Coffee declared that the new men were "very clamorous and I fear will not do much good." With such a raw force "it was not to be expected," in the words of another Jackson aide, "that any thing short of the greatest firmness in its officers could restrain that course of conduct and disorder, which had hitherto so unhappily prevailed."

Then a man arrived at General Jackson's tent to inform him of Private Wood's crime. Wood ignored an officer's order to pick up some bones that other militiamen had thrown on the ground after breakfast. When the officer shouted at him, the private became enraged, and brandished his rifle before submitting to arrest. No one was hurt. Days later, the swiftly convened court-martial sentenced Private Wood to the maximum penalty allowed under the Articles of War, U.S. military law. As Jackson's aide later put it, the arrest of John Wood offered "a fit occasion" to set an example and subdue the army's "mutinous spirit." It was nevertheless a hard case. It was rare that American soldiers were executed. Wood had been with the army only a few weeks. What made the situation even more extraordinary was that Wood was believed to be underage, a little short of eighteen. In the three days following his conviction his fellow soldiers had asked the general to spare his life. Jackson's letter provided his answer.

This is an important crisis; in which if we all act as becomes us, every thing is to be hoped for towards the accomplishment of the objects of our

government; if otherwise, every thing is to be feared. . . . Between
[the] law & its offender, the commanding General ought not to be
expected to interpose, & will not where there are not circumstances of
alleviation. There appear to be none such in your case; & however as a
man may deplore your unhappy situation, he cannot as an officer,
without infringing his duty, arrest the sentence of the court martial.

Andrew Jackson
Major Genl.

Jackson's secretary wrote out a copy of the text in a letter book before sending the original on its way. The execution was scheduled for noon. Jackson and his aides completed other work that morning, appointing an assistant topographical engineer for the campaign Jackson was planning to launch against the Creeks. He also received news that one of his soldiers had died that morning, as men often did in this place with its temporary shelter, sketchy hygiene, and uncertain supplies. Jackson's staff gave orders to bury the man "with the honors of war" at two o'clock in the afternoon. Maybe by then the gravediggers would be done with John Wood.

The bushy-haired general may not have known that he was making a signal decision of his life that day, but he knew his act would be scrutinized. The proof lay in his letter to John Wood. It was Jackson's justification for an exceptional act, including its statement that the militiaman was condemned after committing mutiny for "the second time." A copy of the letter soon made it to Nashville, where it became, in effect, a press release printed in newspapers.

After the war General Jackson's supporters added to this account. Two Jackson aides authored a biography of the general that praised the execution. No doubt reflecting Jackson's view, his aide John Eaton said the death of John Wood was a "sacrifice, essential to the preservation of good order," and that it worked as intended. "A strict obedience afterward characterized the army," producing "the happiest effects."

Years later, when Jackson was running for president, the story resurfaced in far less flattering form. His political opponents tracked down former members of Private Wood's unit. These men did not talk of Andrew Jackson imposing control on his army, but of Jackson losing control of himself. In their version of the story, the general heard that Wood was defying an order and emerged from his tent screaming, "Shoot the damned rascal! Shoot the damned rascal! Shoot the damned rascal!" Although he paused long enough for the formality of a hasty court-martial, Jackson plunged ahead with his brutal impulse, having resolved in advance that "by the Eternal God" he would not pardon the youth. The execution became the subject of political pamphlets and newspaper articles, pursuing Andrew Jackson throughout his career and even staining his legacy beyond the grave.

So there were two competing interpretations of events. Historians have been left to pick and choose between them ever since, which is unfortunate, because the evidence shows that neither version is true.

Jackson was wrong to call it Wood's second mutiny. There had been an earlier altercation involving Wood's unit, but before he joined it, according to his comrades.

Jackson's critics were wrong to suggest that the general lost control of himself. If he had truly screamed to "shoot the damned rascal," one of his loyalists surely would have done it. A surviving fragment of the court-martial record contains a far more plausible statement. Upon learning that Wood was defying arrest, Jackson gave instructions that would "make it easy" to end the standoff: tell Wood a final time to give up, and "shoot him if he does not." This threat was justified, since Wood was armed and defiant, and it also worked, since Wood surrendered peacefully. Jackson had a fierce temper, but also the ability to channel it toward his goals.

More important was the context of the confrontation. Jackson was engaged in a contest of wills over Private Wood, one that apparently involved other members of the young man's unit. By the admission of one of Wood's close comrades, General Jackson offered the offender a way to save himself: "He could have the opportunity of enlisting," joining the regular army, which would bind him to service for some time. His fellow militiamen were outraged, struggling as they were with Jackson over how long *they* should serve. "Without any apprehension of the sad catastrophe which was to follow," they urged Wood to call Jackson's bluff and refuse. They did not believe Jackson would execute a teenage militiaman. When Wood briefly seemed ready to enlist, his friends "opposed it violently." Once the young man declined the offer of clemency, General Jackson surely understood the seriousness of the threat to his authority. Jackson showed he was not bluffing, but his resolve did not end the conflict, and "a strict obedience" did not afterward characterize the army. On the very day of Wood's execution, Jackson's staff ordered a court-martial for another soldier accused of mutiny. Eight days later he ordered yet another court-martial for mutiny. Later in the year, as fresh recruits kept arriving, entire units fell apart: sixty-two of a hundred men from a single company were marked as having deserted, and several men were accused of mutiny and executed.

Jackson was fighting simultaneously against the Creeks, against his own army, and against his political enemies back home in Tennessee. He was certain that the troops who'd marched home against his wishes were telling nasty stories about him. Having come from all over the state, they were spreading back to their homesteads like an infectious disease. "I have no doubts but you hear a great deal of stuff about Tyranny, etc., etc.," his friend and subordinate John Coffee wrote home to his wife, urging her to be patient until the public learned the truth. Jackson, whose regular job as major general of militia was an elected one, also served with an elected governor, and he could not ignore the risk of losing public support. He had been documenting his military victories, assuring Coffee that proof of success would "*kill dead* our enemies," adding in his uncertain spelling, "The snarling *curs* may grin—lie—and falsely swear but the[y] will die with their own bit[e]—all we have to do is perform our duty, and they are politically doomd." That, at least, was his confident prediction in mid-February, although the language and timing of his letter—he scrawled it at "12 oclock at night," by the light of some flickering flame at Fort Strother—suggested how much the topic gnawed at him.

And so on March 14 Jackson threw down a marker. He would not send home another complaining soldier, nor would he let his army fall apart. At midday the general had his entire force assemble "on an elevated piece of ground, in front of the fort," as an eyewitness reported, and the prisoner was led before them. Jackson's letter was read aloud, followed by "the performance of divine service." The firing squad took one step forward. They shot Private Wood on schedule. Understanding at the end that he truly would be killed, Private Wood had dictated a farewell message to his parents, which a fellow soldier took down for him; perhaps young Wood had never learned to write. According to the soldier who wrote and mailed it, Wood's farewell was composed in rhyme.

Jackson was beginning to impose his will on a new democratic society. He was channeling the energy of that society toward a great goal that even he probably did not yet fully see: the complete reorganization of the southern United States. Natives in that region had been on the defensive for centuries, but in 1814 five southern Indian nations still held their heartlands. The parade ground at Fort Strother, at noon on March 14, was where Andrew Jackson first demonstrated how far he would go to change that. Neither his enemies nor his own men would be allowed to stand in his way.

Two

Urge On All Those Cherokees

T he burial of John Wood was a last bit of business for Jackson's troops to complete before the army began to move. If his men were still "clamorous," most would for now march in the direction he ordered. He intended to leave Fort Strother and follow the southward course of a nearby river, the Coosa, one of several streams that radiated out from Mobile Bay like the gnarled fingers of an old man's hand. Jackson was far out on this finger, and now pointed his army in the direction of the palm.

Jackson was concentrating his scattered forces for this move. A messenger had gone to summon Jackson's friend John Coffee, who often kept his horsemen to the north. Other messengers searched out the six hundred or more Cherokees and friendly Creeks who were serving as part of Jackson's army. At least one messenger departed the Mississippi Territory, traveling northeastward up the Coosa and into the northern part of the state of Georgia. This was Cherokee country, where the courier found Second Lieutenant John Ross, an adjutant, or assistant to a senior officer, in the Cherokee Regiment.

When the summons arrived, the first thing Ross did was to pass on the news. He sat down to compose a note. He wrote to Return J. Meigs, the federal Indian agent—the government's representative to the Cherokee Nation, as well as Ross's elderly friend and patron.

Sir

    I have this moment received by Express a letter from Colo.
Morgan dated Ft. Armstrong 1st March—intimating that he had just
recd. Marching orders & would march this morning for Fort Strother
with all the Cherokees with him.

A detail of this letter suggests that Ross, like so many in Jackson's army, insisted on doing his duty in his own way. The summons said the march had already begun, meaning Ross must be needed urgently, but Ross informed Meigs without apparent concern that he did not intend to leave Chickamauga for three or four days. It's not certain what business detained him. He could have been performing the time-consuming rituals that Cherokee tradition required before going to war, although it is just as likely that Ross had more prosaic concerns. He had a wife at home, Quatie, who later that year would bear their first child. He may also have had a duty to gather supplies, which the army was so terrible at providing. Ross, after all, was a trader, and his trading firm had signed a contract to supply the Cherokee Regiment with everything from blankets to corn. There was no doubt, however, that Ross would go. He was hoping Meigs would send reinforcements from among the Cherokee Nation.

    All those who wish to signalize themselves by fighting & taking
revenge for the blood of the innocent will now step forward & you will
be good enough to urge on all those Cherokees that have been delayed . . .
I am Sir yrs respectfully

Jno Ross.

When he was ready, Ross started back toward his unit.

John Ross was twenty-three years old. He was a good deal shorter than many Cherokee men, and was almost certainly wearing white men's clothes. Traveling with his brother Lewis and perhaps other Cherokees, Ross began the ride of a little over a hundred miles, likely heading south until they struck the Coosa. They would have followed its winding course toward the army. Somewhere along the Coosa they crossed the border from Georgia to the Mississippi Territory—it was impossible to know just where, for the state line imagined by white men had never been marked.

The Cherokee Regiment they rejoined included Pathkiller, the tribe's aged principal chief, but in practice a white officer gave the orders. Colonel Gideon Morgan—well known to Cherokees through his Cherokee wife—was the commander who had sent the message to summon Ross. Morgan in turn was under Jackson's command, and the regiment was on the federal payroll. General Jackson had promised that the Cherokees would receive the same pay and benefits as white soldiers, including benefits to their families if they were killed.

Here among the gathering regiment was a man named George Guess, known to fellow Cherokees as Sequoyah. Here were other Cherokee men who, in accordance with custom, were known by names that reflected their exploits, attributes, or a wry sense of humor: the Mouse, the Broom, Club Foot, Old Turkey, Old Brains, Whiteman Killer. Before long John Ross would be recording some of these names on a list of the wounded and dead. Here also was a great fighter known in Cherokee as Tahseekeyarkey, and in English as Shoe Boots, after the high European-style boots he wore. He was a company commander, and also a free spirit. Sometimes on the march he would stop, crow like a cock, and continue on his way. It was alleged that he met Jackson once, and told the general that while he crowed like a cock, he was not a "chicken heart." Jackson was not segregated from the Indians: at least one, known as Tobacco Juice, was among a unit of "spies," or scouts, who had been detailed to serve as General Jackson's bodyguard. In such a small army it is reasonable to think that Ross, as an officer, had his first conversation with General Jackson; even if not, he would certainly have spotted the general on his horse, his face grim and wrinkled either from determination or from pain, and would have come to know the hint of a brogue in Jackson's voice.

Why was Ross fighting on Jackson's side, the side of the United States? Things had not always been so. Within living memory, the Cherokees' fathers and grandfathers had been at war against the very sort of white settlers who made up the bulk of Andrew Jackson's army. When the American colonists declared their independence in 1776, the Cherokees of the Appalachian interior remained loyal to Britain. John Ross's grandfather, a Scottish trader, helped to arm and organize the Cherokees to fight on the British side against the new United States. The Cherokee conflict against their white neighbors continued even after the American War of Independence ended in 1783. They were still at war when John Ross was born in 1790.

All that had changed by the time the Cherokee Regiment was formed in 1813. Cherokees had a new outlook, which was visible as the regiment prepared to move south with the army. There were, for example, the white man's clothes favored by John Ross, and the famous footwear of Shoe Boots. Much of the nation had adopted European-style clothes, or mixed white and native styles. It was still possible to find a man dressed in the old style, his ears slit and weighed down by heavy earrings, as well as a breastplate and wampum around his neck if he was a man of authority, but many another man would wear a buckskin hunting jacket, once disdained as a symbol of white settlers. John Ross, among others, was sometimes spied wearing a Middle Eastern–style turban. Cherokee women, for whom it was once socially acceptable to walk about half-naked, now commonly wore modest full-length dresses, the cloth for which they had often spun themselves. This outward change in clothing reflected deeper changes in Cherokee society. Despite the resistance of traditionalists, many Cherokees had been adapting to the culture of the great white tribes that increasingly surrounded them. They had been encouraged to do so ever since a peace treaty was signed in 1791 between the Cherokees and President George Washington's administration. Washington vowed that he would respect the rights and borders of Indian nations, and his approach was enshrined in a series of laws known as the Indian Intercourse Acts. The federal government, not states or individuals, would manage relations with the tribes. Government trading posts would sell Indians the goods required for civilization—whether plows for modern agriculture, or books, or boots for Shoe Boots. This was all part of Washington's sophisticated effort to keep the peace, which he considered "honorable to the national character" as well as "sound policy." Cherokees were particularly adept at seizing the advantages offered.

The very same Cherokee leaders who advocated change were the ones who went on to establish the Cherokee Regiment. These leaders included the most imposing man in the regiment, who was known as the Ridge. Barrel-chested, thick-faced, with curly hair that was starting to go gray, the Ridge was in his mid-forties. He had grown up in the old Cherokee ways, without the slightest formal education and with an early introduction to the rituals of hunting and war. More than a few men had died by his hand. Yet as he matured, the Ridge had chosen another way. He began to rise in Cherokee leadership in the 1790s when he spoke against the tribal law of revenge, which called for a family to respond in kind when one of its members was killed. The law was eventually abolished. The Ridge also took up agriculture. Now he was a planter, ferry operator, store owner, and slave owner. He never learned to speak English well, but was a powerful advocate for modernizing his nation.

It was the Ridge who, with two other leaders, promoted the idea that Cherokees should raise a force to defend the United States in the War of 1812. Ridge argued before the Cherokee leadership council that they *must* fight to ensure their own survival. If Cherokees remained neutral, they inevitably would be seen as enemies, because trigger-happy white men would categorize all Indians as either with them or against them. The leadership council agreed. By then Meigs, the old Indian agent, had already recommended that the army enroll Cherokees: "They are real horsemen, they are remarkable for the ease with which they ride . . . they are like blank stationery on which may be written anything." General Jackson soon filled in the blank. The Ridge was given the rank of lieutenant and later promoted to the rank by which he would always afterward be known—Major Ridge.

When John Ross joined this unit, he could give different meanings to his service depending on how he defined his identity. As a white trader's son who was close to the Indian agent, Ross could think of himself like his loyalist grandfather during the Revolution—a white man organizing friendly Indians to put down a rebellion. But as the descendant of Cherokee women, he could also think of himself as a Cherokee who risked his life for the United States in order to ensure his rights within it. This latter meaning is the one Ross voiced after the war was over.

Now, in March 1814, Ross and other men of the Cherokee Regiment were departing Fort Strother along with Jackson's main force—Coffee's horsemen, the Thirty-Ninth Regiment, and the clamorous Tennessee militiamen. Somewhere in the crowd was Jackson himself, wild-haired, high on his horse, and soon to be overcome with frustration. So long as the troops had been spread out, they were easier to feed, since smaller units could live off the land, but when several thousand were concentrated, the specter of starvation returned. Army contractors had sent Jackson a letter announcing their success in depositing food at an outpost of friendly Creeks called Talladega, but the army found no supplies when it arrived. Jackson wrote the contractors, and the courtesy of his wording barely contained his rage: "What could have occasioned you to the erroneous belief on which you felicitate yourselves . . . I am quite at a loss to conjecture." He would have eight days' rations for the troops' next move, barely enough to reach their ultimate destination and return if nothing went wrong.

Straight downriver, roughly midway between the army and Mobile Bay, was the heart of the Creek Nation, although Jackson was in no rush to get there. It was far more important to destroy Creek forces, so the general planned a detour. The men left the Coosa behind, marching eastward through the woods. They approached a river called the Tallapoosa, the next finger on that gnarled hand of rivers running down to

Mobile Bay. The rude path his army was following was familiar to Jackson. Back in January, learning of a large Creek encampment, he had raced along this same route toward the enemy with nine hundred newly arrived militiamen, only to realize that the Creeks were so numerous, and so well fortified, that if he attacked, he would fail. He chose instead to back away—and then the Creeks attacked him. Dozens of his men were killed before he drove off the assault. Now Jackson was returning with his enlarged force, including a couple of small artillery pieces, determined to finish the job.

Sometimes along the march, the general stopped and climbed down from his horse. A subordinate would hack down a sapling and Jackson would drape himself over it in the only pose that relieved his abdominal pain. Then he'd mount again, hardly more than a cadaver on a horse, with his bodyguard eyeing him. They continued toward the enemy's camp, tucked in a curve of the Tallapoosa River. It was a place the Creeks called Tohopeka, and white men called Horseshoe Bend.

Three

Stamping His Foot for War

R oss and Jackson were alike that late winter of 1814 in that they were not yet figures of legend. Jackson was a Tennessee politico with a checkered reputation. Had his precarious health collapsed on March 15, his forty-seventh birthday, he would have been buried somewhere near John Wood without a single achievement that later generations would recall. Ross was hardly more than a youth, slim of both stature and achievement, probably known even within the Cherokee Nation mainly as a descendant of notable traders. Now the two men were about to begin their long engagement with history. To understand how the country changed during their time, it is useful to glimpse the United States as they found it.

In 1814 the American frontier, the farthest western point of consistent white settlement, was roughly where Jackson lived. It was Middle Tennessee. Farther west than that the Indian map was the governing map, and the map of the United States became more imaginary with every mile. In fact Middle Tennessee formed a salient, a peninsula of settlement. Other parts of the frontier were not so far west. In 1803 the Louisiana Purchase extended the nation beyond the Mississippi, but except for a few cities such as New Orleans and St. Louis, the Purchase too was almost entirely the domain of Indians. Thus when Americans spoke of "the West" in Jackson's day, they usually referred not to

Oregon or the Rockies, but to Nashville, or Lexington, Kentucky, or "the Ohio country." That was the frontier.

This early version of the West was attracting migrants. The national population was exploding—from about four million in 1790 to more than seven million in 1810—and many were shifting westward. New roads and technology encouraged their movement. A traditional westward route led by horse or stagecoach over the Alleghenies to Pittsburgh, at the headwaters of the Ohio River, from which the Mississippi Valley became accessible by boat. It could take many weeks to float with the current to New Orleans, and it was challenging to return, but in September 1811, associates of Robert Fulton completed a steamboat at Pittsburgh and sent it downriver and back again. Trade was increasing on many rivers, such as the Cumberland, on the banks of which Andrew Jackson for years operated a store offering supplies such as butcher knives, cotton hoes, coffee, "Segars," chocolate, brimstone, and pink ladies' hats. The store was near the Hermitage, the farm he bought in 1804, which would remain his home and headquarters for the rest of his life. On the cash-poor frontier, farmers often paid Jackson with cotton, which he shipped downriver toward New Orleans and the wider world.

Industry was growing as the nation spread. A census report in 1810 found that manufacturers were forging so much out of iron—wagon wheels, stoves, firearms, machinery, hammers, steam engines—that they were desperate for miners to produce more iron ore. Pennsylvania each year was making "nine pounds of nails for each person in the state." Since nails were used to fasten everything else, the production of seven million pounds of nails in a single year by a single state suggested the scale of construction and manufacturing. Southern states were expanding cotton production so rapidly that it would soon become "the most considerable of our manufactures," often woven into cloth on "family looms," for the greatest of the New England textile mills had yet to be built. The cotton was grown largely on plantations run with slave labor. Slavery, though gradually disappearing in the North, was increasing in importance below the Ohio. Many westbound settlers brought the slave economy with them. Some Indians adopted the practice of slave owning. White owners also complained that escaped slaves found refuge within Indian nations.

Farmers in every state produced distilled spirits—rye whiskey, corn whiskey, applejack, rum—a total of 25,804,792 gallons of hard liquor in a year: more than three and a half gallons for every man, woman, and child. It was such a hard-drinking nation that the census report gently promoted the health benefits of beer, ale, and malt liquor, said to be more "moralizing" and "salubrious" than the hard stuff. Few people followed this advice, the report admitted. It was hard to find a "foaming" cold beer in the summer. Many a man, Andrew Jackson among them, found it "salubrious" instead to mix a little gin with the water he was drinking. And when Jackson mortally wounded a man in a duel in 1806, there was only one thing to do for his antagonist as he lay dying: to comfort the man in his final hours, Jackson sent a bottle of wine.

Some percentage of alcohol sales went to Indians. They were said to be especially susceptible to drink. Accounts of alcoholism among white men in that era suggest that natives may not have handled their liquor worse than anybody else. (The Choctaws noticed this, and when they imposed prohibition on themselves, they wryly noted in a public letter that "ardent spirits have been banished from among us, and have been compelled to take up their abode among our civilized white neighbors.") But there was no doubt that when Indians drank, it was a curse. Drunkenness led to violence and allowed white men to cheat Indians out of trade goods or land. The federal government banned the sale of alcohol on Indian territories, which merely caused natives to travel to the nearest white towns. The trade grew so pernicious that in 1808 President Thomas Jefferson urged state governors to crack down on white sellers. The long-term effectiveness of his appeal can be measured by a French traveler's account from 1825. Spending the night in a white settlement at the edge of the Creek Nation in Alabama, the traveler found the town "almost entirely inhabited" by "avaricious wretches" who had "assembled from all parts of the globe" to "poison the tribes with intoxicating liquors, and afterwards ruin them by duplicity and overreaching."

General William Henry Harrison, the governor of the Indiana Territory in the early years of the century, noticed a difference between Indians in close contact with white people and those who were not. The man from a more distant tribe "is generally well-clothed, healthy, and vigorous," while an Indian nearby was more likely "half-naked, filthy, and enfeebled by intoxication." The tribes closest to Harrison were "the most depraved wretches on earth." Harrison's awareness that Indians were suffering from their interaction with white society did not change his view of his duty. Rounding up some "depraved wretches," he negotiated treaties in 1804, 1805, and 1809, purchasing millions of acres of Indiana land at nominal prices.

These land cessions set off a chain of events that reverberated for years, eventually helping to spark Andrew Jackson's military campaign in 1813–14. An eloquent and idealistic Shawnee, Tecumseh, used the injustice of Harrison's 1809 treaty to build opposition to the white man's land grabs. With his brother, said to be a prophet, he was uniting western tribes in a great confederation. He said the United States must never sign another treaty unless it was with all the tribes, for the land belonged in common to all. Harrison's army drove off Tecumseh's men in an early-morning battle at Tippecanoe, Indiana, in 1811, but Tecumseh missed the fight. He was off to the south, on a journey to find allies among the Creeks of the Mississippi Territory.

Tecumseh's speeches, or talks as they were called, caused a sensation in the Creek Nation. The most prominent Creek leader, known as Big Warrior, warned his people that "it was easier to begin a war than to end one." But there were fault lines in the Creek Nation, caused by the federal policy of encouraging Indians to civilize. Some Creeks resisted adopting white culture, and their resistance meshed with

Tecumseh's call to defend their ancient hunting grounds. Although Tecumseh failed to win the allegiance of the divided nation, he left the Creeks with a memorable prediction. As one Creek writer recalled, Tecumseh said he would "ascend to the top of a mountain . . . and raise his foot and stamp it on the earth three times. By these actions he could make the whole earth tremble," and all the nations of the earth would feel the power of his cause.

What happened next can be seen through the eyes of a very young witness. Margaret Eades Austill was probably under ten years old, but had an eye for detail that she wrote down years later. In 1811, the same year that Tecumseh made his disappointing visit to the Mississippi Territory, Miss Austill arrived. Her family had moved westward from Augusta, Georgia, in just the kind of migration that was beginning to transform the region. They joined two other families in a westward journey with "about one hundred slave men, women and children," including a servant named Hannah, who was "black or rather blue black, with clear blue eyes." (If Margaret contemplated the sort of master-slave relationship that may have produced a woman with such a "peculiar appearance," she did not mention it.) On the way to Mississippi, the families passed by Cherokees, who "were kind and friendly," then entered domains that seemed more threatening. "As soon as we entered the Creek or Muskogee Nation, we could see the terrible hatred to the whites. . . . At night the wagons were all fixed around the encampment, the women and children and negroes in the center, the men keeping guard with the guns, so we made a formidable appearance of defense." Indians trailed the wagon train as it lumbered across the landscape.

> One night after a fearful day, the Indians had followed us for miles [and] we camped in an old field. Just as supper was announced, a most terrific earthquake took place, the horses all broke loose, the wagon chains jingled, and every face was pale with fear and terror. The Indians came in numbers around us looking frightened, and

grunting out their prayers, and oh, the night was spent in terror by all but the next day some of the Indians came to us and said it was Tecumseh stamping his foot for war.

It was the New Madrid earthquake of December 1811, which shook the whole Mississippi Valley and beyond with such force that the great river briefly flowed backward. Tecumseh had just received a divine endorsement.

When the war finally came in the summer of 1812, it would not end well for Tecumseh. After a stunning early success—he helped British troops capture the American fort at Detroit—he was killed by William Henry Harrison's troops at the Battle of the Thames. But he had put a jolt into a faction of the Creeks, who rose in revolt, first against their nation's leaders and then against white men. The traditionalists became known as the Red Sticks, apparently because of the red war clubs held by their prophets. A Creek writer of the era said the traditionalists formed encampments where they conducted "fanatical riots of shaving their heads and painting them red for distinction." By July 1813 the Creek Nation was in a state of "civil war," according to John Ross. The Cherokee trader heard news of the trouble when traveling in the Mississippi Territory, and wrote a federal Indian agent with "intelligence" that "this present crisis is very serious," and the whole Creek Nation could be conquered by "the Superior force of the rebels." Some of the rebels were traveling to Spanish-controlled Florida for gunpowder. Local white forces tried to intercept the gunpowder shipment, fighting an inconclusive battle that only seemed to increase the Red Sticks' resolve.

By now the family of Margaret Eades Austill had made a homestead in the Mississippi Territory, north of Mobile Bay. "One morning," she recalled, "mother, sister and myself were alone except [for] the servants. Father had gone to the plantation when a man rode up to the gate and called to mother to fly for the Creek Indians had crossed the Alabama [River] and were killing the people. Mother said 'where shall I fly to, in God's name?'" The man advised the family to retreat to a place called Carney's Bluff, where settlers, "all hands, negroes and whites," were building a makeshift fort.

> When we arrived at the river it was a busy scene, men hard at work chopping and clearing a place for a Fort, women and children crying, no place to sit down, nothing to eat, all confusion and dismay, expecting every moment to be scalped and tomahawked . . . I went to mother and told her I was tired and sleepy she untied her apron and spread it down on the ground and told me to say my prayers and go to sleep. So I laid down but could not go to sleep the roots hurt me so badly. I told mother I had rather jump in the river [than] lie there. She replied "Perhaps it would be best for us all to jump in the river."

Carney's Bluff was not attacked, though the settlers were not wrong to worry. They were fortunate the Red Stick leaders were choosing a different target.

The Creek uprising was not Andrew Jackson's business at first. He was occupied elsewhere on fool's errands. When he first organized twenty-five hundred volunteers in the snow at Nashville in December 1812, they were placed at the disposal of the War Department in Washington for service wherever in the country they might be needed. It was presumed that their enemy would be British invaders, not Indians, and Jackson was ordered to move toward New Orleans in case a British fleet appeared at the mouth of the Mississippi. His little army made it as far as Natchez, Mississippi, before falling victim to the administrative chaos that characterized the war. He received orders from the War Department saying his force was no longer needed. He was told to disband his unit immediately, leaving the men to find their way home to Tennessee by themselves.

Inexplicable though the order was to Jackson, it fit a pattern: Americans were learning how to fight a war, and it showed. The United States had sent undersized and undertrained forces on grandiose missions, such as invading British Canada, with predictable results. A progression of disasters (with some heroic interruptions) would continue right up to August 1814, when British forces strolled into Washington and set the president's house and the Capitol on fire. That Jackson would be ordered to disband his force in the middle of such a war was no worse than might be expected. Jackson's response to this order proved him to be very much like the men he struggled to control, from Private John Wood to Adjutant John Ross: he would not follow an order that made no sense to him. Considerably modifying his instructions, Jackson kept his unit together long enough to march them back to Tennessee. Only then did he send them to their homes, and even then he left an expectation that he might call on them again. It was said to be during this march that Jackson acquired the nickname Old Hickory, representing his toughness.

He returned to his wife, Rachel, at their house at the Hermitage, and awaited developments. Waiting must have been difficult for such an energetic personality, because he passed the time by working his way into a complicated and pointless quarrel with Thomas Hart Benton, his own military aide. This was the dispute that led to a gunfight inside a Nashville hotel in the summer of 1813, which is why, days later, he was in bed with a lead ball in his shoulder when news came that it was time to return to the war.

Reclining in pain at the Hermitage, Jackson read the news: an improvised white fortification, similar to the one at Carney's Bluff, had been overwhelmed by Creek attackers. The whole Mississippi Territory seemed to be in danger. Reinforcements for the beleaguered Mississippians must now come from several directions, and they would include Jackson's own Tennessee troops. Determined to command in person, Jackson drew up a proclamation calling both federal and state volunteers to duty, though he had to be helped onto his horse at the appointed time. Richard K. Call, he of the yellow-fringed hunting shirt, left his family a romanticized though plausible description of Jackson on the first part of the road south from Nashville, "with his arm in a sling looking pale and emaciated suffering from wounds recently received," but still with an air of command as he rode alongside troops who'd stopped to rest. His wife, Rachel, arrived in a carriage from Nashville, having brought several ladies to observe the troops and see off her husband. After a short visit, Jackson bade her good-bye and turned his horse southward, toward the land where his destiny lay.

Four

It Was Dark Before
We Finished Killing Them

The massacre that drew Jackson and Ross into the Mississippi Territory was a special act of brutality. When John Ross left behind his note about "taking revenge for the blood of the innocent," he was probably referring to blood spilled at Fort Mims, near Mobile Bay. Several hundred white settlers and friendly Creeks had taken the Red Stick threat seriously enough to cluster inside this privately built stockade, but their citadel was amateurishly designed and defended. The commander did not believe slaves in nearby fields who reported seeing Indians. It may have been hard to imagine that Creeks would attack a fort defended by well over a hundred members of the territorial militia. What the commander did not realize was that the Red Sticks had assembled an overwhelming assault force of 726 men, including escaped slaves and some of the Creeks' own slaves. They were near enough to watch white scouts patrolling the area, and could even hear the white men talking.

The Red Stick leaders included a man known among whites as William Weatherford, and among Creeks as Lamochattee. Like Robert E. Lee in a later war, Weatherford doubted the wisdom of the rebellion but fought to the fullest. Contradictory legends came to surround him, but a Creek historian who lived through the war (and who was Weatherford's brother-in-law) left a credible account. The Creek historian wrote that it was Weatherford who persuaded a Red Stick council that Fort Mims could be overwhelmed. After the Red Stick force drew near Fort Mims on August 29, Weatherford slipped through the night with two confederates to examine the white men's stockade. He peered through one of the portholes the defenders had cut in order to shoot through the wall. He realized the attackers could use the same openings to fire into the compound. When the Creeks attacked the next day, they were under orders to race across the surrounding fields without firing a shot in order to seize possession of the gun holes. Instead of sheltering gunmen aiming out, the stockade now sheltered gunmen aiming in.

The defenders retreated to their buildings and kept up a devastating defensive fire. Of four attackers assured by the Red Sticks' spiritual leader that they would be invulnerable to white men's bullets, three were quickly killed. In all, 202 Creeks were killed and many wounded. Finally the attackers set the buildings on fire, forcing the defenders into the open. Ten days later, when white troops arrived to bury the dead, their commanding officer described "Indians, negroes, white men, women and children," lying "in one promiscuous ruin. All were scalped, and the females of every age were butchered in a manner which neither decency nor language will permit me to describe."

News of the massacre proved to be a powerful motivational tool for General Jackson. His proclamation calling his troops to battle urged that Tennesseans respond to the "horrid butcheries" with a "spirit of revenge." The men who answered included David Crockett, who in 1813 was a young hunter, indifferent farmer, and talented storyteller. Crockett attended a militia recruitment meeting over the protests of his wife, who said if he marched off to war "she and our little children would be left in an unhappy situation." Crockett replied that someone had to fight or "we would all be killed in our own houses. . . . Seeing I was bent on it, all she did was cry a little, and turn about to her work. The truth is, my dander was up, and nothing but war could bring it right again."

Crockett enlisted with a unit of mounted volunteers—a paramilitary force might be a more descriptive modern phrase. Under the command of Jackson's friend John Coffee they ranged across Creek territory. Creeks slipped away as they approached, and Coffee had to satisfy himself with scorched earth. "I burnt three towns but never saw an Indian," the commander complained in a letter to his wife. Crockett participated in at least one of these raids, in which the hungry troops cleared out the village corncribs and then "burned the town to ashes." The food wasn't enough to sustain the troops for long. Crockett gained Coffee's permission to wander away from his unit and hunt deer, and once discovered a deer that an Indian must have killed and skinned only minutes before. Crockett hoisted it on his horse and brought it back to camp. If the militiamen were staggering on the edge of starvation, so were the Creeks, for whatever food the white men consumed came out of the mouths of the locals.

In October the mounted men finally took a village by surprise. Some Creeks surrendered as the assault began on the village of Tallushatchee, but others seemed to expect no quarter. Crockett said that dozens of people retreated into a single house, and a woman in the door fired an arrow and killed a militiaman. This enraged his comrades, Crockett said: "We now shot them like dogs; and then set the house on fire, and burned it up with the forty-six warriors in it."

Only a handful of whites were killed in the battle, which John Coffee laconically called "a small scirmish with the Indians" in a letter to his wife. Crockett's account described the gruesome death of a boy, perhaps twelve years old, in the flames by the side of the house. He also reported what happened the day after the battle, when the ashes of the house had cooled:

It was, somehow or other, found out that the house had a potatoe cellar under it, and an immediate examination was made, for we were all as hungry as wolves. We found a fine chance of potatoes in it, and hunger compelled us to eat them, though I had a little rather not, if I could have helped it, for the oil of the Indians we had burned up on the day before had run down on them, and they looked like they had been stewed with fat meat.

Andrew Jackson was not served a portion of this victory meal. He was not present. But a few days later, the army commander came away with a memento. Eighty prisoners had been taken in the village, among them an infant boy found in the arms of his dead mother. Some Creek women were of the opinion that the child should be killed, as his parents were dead, but the tiny orphan was brought to Fort Strother and shown to Jackson. The general decided that *he* would keep the baby. "When I reflect that he as to his relations is so much like myself I feel an unusual sympathy for him," the general wrote at the time. Jackson and the baby were both members of the brotherhood of orphans: Jackson had never met his own father, and lost his mother to disease when he was a boy during the Revolution. The general decided the infant should become a playmate for Andrew Jackson Jr., the white son he and Rachel had adopted from relatives. "I send on a little Indian boy for Andrew," Jackson wrote to Rachel, in a letter that was meant to accompany the child as he was transported to the Hermitage in Nashville. "All his family is destroyed."

Here John Ross begins to play a larger role in our story, for the Cherokee Regiment joined in the campaign to torch villages. In November 1813 the regiment joined a force of Tennesseans approaching a Creek town called Hillabee. The attackers apparently did not know, and did not pause to find out, that the Creeks of Hillabee had already resolved to give up the war, and had sent a peace envoy to General Jackson at Fort Strother. The Creeks were completely surprised by white and Cherokee attackers who slaughtered many villagers without losing a man. This massacre may have persuaded other Creeks that they would never be permitted to surrender. Many, their villages burned and their food destroyed, were concentrating at a fortified camp in a sharp curve of the Tallapoosa River, the curve called Horseshoe Bend. This was the encampment that Jackson's army approached on the morning of March 27, 1814.

Jackson gave orders to position his troops on the battlefield. The Cherokees would not charge directly at the Creek encampment; the general had a more suitable purpose in mind for them. Instead, some of Jackson's white troops faced the camp, taking possession of a small hill overlooking it. The hill was no more than thirty to forty feet higher than the camp, but high enough for the soldiers to behold the obstacle that awaited them. The river bend "resembles, in its curvature, that of a horseshoe, and is thence called by that name among the whites," Jackson wrote afterward. The Creeks had built their camp inside the peninsula:

> *Nature furnishes few situations as eligible for defence; and barbarians have never rendered one more secure by art. Across the neck of land which leads into it from the north, they had erected a breastwork of the greatest compactness and strength, from 5 to 8 feet high, and prepared with double rows of port-holes very artfully arranged.*

From these portholes, Jackson declared, the Creek defenders could fire outward "in perfect security," defending an area inside the wall that Jackson estimated at eighty to a hundred acres. The wall was constructed of two rows of heavy logs, placed about four feet apart. Between the logs the Creeks had packed clay. Jackson hoped to blast a hole in this barrier with two cannons his troops had dragged through the forest all the way from Fort Strother. Their crews rolled them up to the little hill, just 125 yards from the nearest portion of the wall. The guns jerked backward on their wheels, white smoke rolled out of the muzzles, and the sound of their fire echoed across the river valley, but the first shots either buried themselves in the wall or bounced off.

And yet Jackson's letter about the impressively defensible territory, and "barbarians" who "never rendered" a position "more secure by art," was misleading. He wrote those words after the battle, in a letter that newspapers reprinted and that historians have quoted ever since. In truth Horseshoe Bend was an appalling choice of locations to defend. The whole history of warfare argued against it. To walk the Horseshoe Bend battlefield today is to be horrified by the small distance between the battle lines: Jackson's artillerymen could look down on the defensive wall from higher ground. More important, the outnumbered Creeks drew themselves into a confined location where they could be targeted and killed whenever Jackson could gather a large enough force. They might instead have survived for years as guerrilla fighters (as Creeks who did not concentrate in the Horseshoe went on to do, working out of sanctuaries in Spanish Florida). The hit-and-run attack was a customary Indian style of warfare, yet these determined traditionalists broke with tradition. Possibly hoping to protect women and children from the white horsemen, they performed a fatal imitation of the white man's art of war. If confronted by a superior force, they would be trapped for a massacre as surely as the white settlers at Fort Mims.

Not only that. The Red Sticks inside the Horseshoe were a nearly spent force, desperate members of a society near collapse. Men, women, and children had gathered there seeking shelter from marauding horsemen. It was less a citadel than a refugee camp for survivors of Andrew Jackson's ruthlessly effective warfare—those who had not yet been set on fire atop a potato cellar, for instance. The Indians' condition would still be evident generations after the battle, when archaeologists digging up the Creek village inside the fortress found artifacts that were scarce and poor, not much beyond "gun parts and ammunition" as well as "ceramics and glass." Their trade with the outside world had been disrupted, and their meager possessions reflected "the destitute condition of a people whose homes had been recently burned." These were the people who peered through the portholes of their wall and saw Jackson's two cannons open fire.

Where were Ross and the Cherokees as the cannonade began? They were sealing the trap. Jackson sent John Coffee's horsemen, along with the Cherokee Regiment and other friendly Indians, to move *behind* the Horseshoe, on the far side of the river. If the Creeks should attempt to retreat across the river, they would be shot as they paddled their canoes across. Here the Cherokees and white horsemen waited as the bombardment began, but after two hours, some could wait no longer. Three Cherokees, led by a man known as the Whale, swam across the Tallapoosa and into the Creek camp. The Whale was wounded and unable to return; the other two Cherokees stole Creek canoes tied up by the waterside and paddled them across to their comrades—who swiftly filled the canoes and paddled them back, forming a party of marauders behind the enemy lines. There is no evidence that Ross crossed the river, although the party is known to have included Major Ridge, the upscale planter who was in time to become Ross's vital ally and mentor. The Cherokees fought courageously and caused confusion in the Creek camp.

Jackson, perceiving from the high ground that his Cherokees were inside the Horseshoe, still refrained from ordering his white troops against the obstacle of the wall, but "when I found those engaged in the interior of the bend, were about to be overpowered, I ordered the charge." The regulars of the Thirty-Ninth Regiment, including the young ensign Sam Houston, raced across the little patch of open ground between them and the wall. They fired inward through the Indian portholes—apparently just as badly designed as the portholes at Fort Mims—and scaled the wall to begin brutal hand-to-hand combat. Struck by a barbed arrow in the thigh, Houston compelled a comrade to yank it out and continued fighting. Many Creeks were killed where they stood. Others retreated toward their second line of defense, a tangle of felled trees inside the Horseshoe. Still others fled toward the river, taking shelter beneath the bluffs below the white men. When Jackson sent a man down a bluff to demand their surrender, the Creeks fired on the emissary. Jackson's men set fire to the underbrush, and then shot Red Stick fighters as they fled the flames. Creeks who tried to swim away across the Tallapoosa became target practice for the Cherokees and Coffee's horsemen on the far shore.

Decades later, John Ross would write a letter to Andrew Jackson, reminding him of the day they served together in arms against the "unfortunate and deluded red foe," a "portentous day" that was "shrouded by a cloud of darkness, besprinkled with the awful streaks of blood and death. It is in the hour of such times that the heart of man can be truly tested and correctly judged." Perhaps Ross was right that it was a moment to judge the hearts of men. But Andrew Jackson had no time for such poetic thoughts. Shortly after the engagement he described the slaughter of the Indians in a letter to his wife, Rachel:

> *It was dark before we finished killing them—I ordered the dead bodies of the Indians to be counted, the next morning, and exclusive of those buried in their watry grave, who were killed in the [river] and who after being wounded plunged into it, there were counted, five hundred and fifty seven.*

To ensure precision and avoid double counting, white soldiers cut off the noses of dead Indians as they went. It was harder to count those Indians dead in the river, but some of John Coffee's men affixed their signatures to a statement guessing that beyond the 557 bodies on land, an additional 300 Creeks were "buried in their watry grave." Given the exaggeration that has always attended body counts of enemies in wartime, this guess was almost certainly too high. Some Creeks were known to have escaped, including Menawa, a wounded Creek leader, but a great many Creek males were slaughtered at Horseshoe Bend, leaving 350 women and children to be taken prisoner with only 3 men. An American soldier said the Tallapoosa had become a "River of blood," writing that it was "very perceptably bloody" even at "10 O'clock at night." It seems unlikely that a river of the Tallapoosa's volume could truly have been so affected, but the letter did reflect the soldier's state of mind.

It fell to John Ross, as one of the few literate Cherokees, to compile a report on the Cherokee Regiment's wounded and dead. He listed the injuries company by company, such as the men of "Capt Speirs Company."

Capt. Jno. Speirs	*Severely*
Thos. Proctor	*Killed*
The Mouse	*Killed*
The Broom	*Killed*
The Squirrel	*Do.*
The Woman Killer	*Killed*
Jno. Helterbrand	*Killed*
Tolonah	*Killed*
Wachakeskee	*Do.*
Club Foot	*Slightly*
Whiteman Killer	*Mortally*
Black Prince	*Severely*
The Seed	*sleightly.*

"Do." was a common abbreviation for "ditto," which Ross used when the word "killed" became tiresome to repeat. He noted a total of eighteen Cherokees killed and thirty-six wounded. About one of every twelve Cherokees was injured or dead, a significant toll for a single day's fight, which underlined their vital role. The toll among the much larger white force—26 killed, and up to 107 wounded, depending on the count—was comparatively light, although it is still jarring to read the final two sentences of a letter that John Coffee wrote after the battle to his wife:

> *Having now nearly compleated our business here, I shall soon turn me towards home when I hope to enjoy the remainder of my life with you in quiet—my love to our little daughter—and all friends—*
>
> *Lemul Montgomery was killed in battle at the charge against the breast works by a ball through his head—*

The blunt way the soldiers discussed death in letters to their families suggests that violence, particularly involving Indians, was an ordinary feature of frontier life—and also that in their campaign of vengeance men had become desensitized. Years afterward, historians recorded the memories of elderly veterans, like the one who testified that "many of the Tennessee soldiers cut long strips of skin from the bodies of the dead Indians and from these made bridle reins." Another veteran said that "when the Horse Shoe village was set on fire," a very old Indian continued pounding corn on a mortar as if oblivious to the battle around him, until a white soldier "shot him dead, assigning as his reason for so doing that he might be able to report when he went home that he had killed an Indian." Another soldier struck a boy "five or six years of age" with the butt of his rifle, later explaining that he killed the child because he "would have become an Indian some day."

What did Jackson think of such atrocities? The soldiers' commanding general would become known in later years as an "Indian hater," though the evidence suggests Jackson's views were more complex. It was true that Jackson's army killed almost everyone they could in the Horseshoe. It was also true that he depended on natives as part of his army, and that some, like Major Ridge, gave him the greatest respect. When the fighting was over, Jackson remembered his promise to give Indians the same pay and benefits as white soldiers. Three years after the war, learning that widows of Cherokee soldiers were not receiving death benefits, he appealed on their behalf to the War Department: "I did believe they were to be considered in every respect on the same footing with the militia . . . I made this promise believing it was Just," he said, insisting that the families of the Cherokee dead must now be "placed in the same situation of the wives & children of our soldiers who have fell in Battle." The contradictions are breathtaking. He wrote this remarkable letter urging equal benefits for a racial minority while visiting the Cherokee Nation in 1817, during an attempt to negotiate a treaty obtaining substantial Cherokee land for nothing. Even that treaty contained contradictions; profoundly unfair as it was, it included a provision offering individual farms along with U.S. citizenship to some Cherokees who wished to claim it. Three hundred eleven heads of families took the offer. Though he was deeply prejudiced, it is more relevant to say that Jackson was violently opposed to anyone who stood in his way. When people posed no threat to his interests, he allowed himself to act on impulses of fairness that he otherwise suppressed.

It was the Red Sticks' misfortune to stand in Jackson's way, and Jackson showed no regret for the devastation he had inflicted. Days after Horseshoe Bend, one of his letters made its way to the public, becoming in effect a press release. It was published in the *National Intelligencer,* an influential Washington newspaper. As printed, Jackson's account of the battle only briefly mentioned the Cherokees, noting their casualties but not the Cherokee attack that triggered the final assault. The letter did include Jackson's testimony that the Creeks fought bravely, but were "cut to pieces" until the battlefield was "strewed with the slain," including a Creek spiritual leader who had been "shot in the mouth by a grapeshot, as if heaven designed to chastise his impostures by an appropriate punishment."

Jackson would soon demonstrate that he had a punishment in mind that was far more important to him than blood.

Within a few weeks after the battle Jackson had sealed his conquest by marching to the Creek heartland. He occupied the ruins of a fort there, which was renamed Fort Jackson in his honor, and brusquely demanded the unconditional surrender of Creek chiefs who came professing peace. He also demanded that they bring him William Weatherford, the rebels' war leader, as a prisoner. Weatherford saved them the trouble by boldly marching into Jackson's camp alone, gaining an audience with the general, and frankly admitting that he was surrendering only because he had no troops left. Jackson was so impressed that he let Weatherford go free.

Weatherford's surrender became part of the mythology of the Creek War, a moment of closure in the later style of Lee at Appomattox. The reality was different. The comparison would be better if, after General

Lee surrendered in 1865, other Confederate soldiers retreated into the hills and fought on for many years. That was roughly what happened with the Red Stick rebels in 1814. They were devastated at the Horseshoe but not eliminated. Weatherford was virtually the only rebel leader who surrendered. Others fled southward through the woods, crossing the border to Spanish Florida, where they were soon receiving arms and supplies from British ships offshore. These rebels would emerge to conduct raids on white settlers for many years.

The refusal of most Red Sticks to give up caused some awkwardness when Jackson organized peace talks in July, at Fort Jackson, under the shade of his marquee. The Creeks were dignified and had no reason to be hostile. Nearly all were Jackson's allies, for the enemies had not come. This proved no obstacle for Jackson. He demanded land from all the Creeks, enemies and allies alike. The cession he dictated was roughly in the shape of the letter "L." The horizontal leg ran along the whole length of the border with Florida, and cut off the Creeks from any possible contact with Spanish territory. The vertical leg rose through the center of what is now Alabama, and cut off the Creeks from tribes and white settlers farther west. Aside from strategic considerations, the region to be surrendered consisted of twenty-three million acres of saleable real estate.

One account records the Creek leader Big Warrior rising to remind Jackson that he had gone into battle *against* the Red Sticks. "I made this war, which has proved so fatal to my country, that the treaty entered into a long time ago with father Washington might not be broken. To his friendly arm I hold fast." But Washington's friendly arm was long gone, and Jackson had instructions from Washington, DC. The chiefs could accept his terms or flee to Florida. When, on August 6, Big Warrior appealed for a settlement to be delayed until the Red Sticks were actually defeated, Jackson wrote the Creek leaders a letter. He said his land grab was necessary to separate loyal Creeks from Red Sticks.

> *Brothers—You say, that when they are all conquered, we will settle—*
> *that the war is not over. I answer—we know the war is not over—and*

that is one reason why we will run a line between our friends and our
enemies. . . . The safety of the United States and your nation requires,
that enemies must be separated from Friends. . . . Therefore we will
run the line—our friends will sign the treaty.

Jackson was making peace not with enemies but with friends, and
was warning Big Warrior that if he failed to sign, he would cease to *be* a
friend. The chiefs yielded, marking Jackson's first great step in the
removal of the Indians from the Southeast. The Creeks once had been
the most powerful and most centrally located of the region's native
nations. Now they were isolated, and their power was destroyed.

After the sad Creek chiefs approved the Treaty of Fort Jackson on
August 9, 1814, their war was largely over. Jackson's would continue.
Rewarded for his victory with a permanent major generalship in the
U.S. Army, he rebuilt his force again over the summer, accepting more
recruits, putting down more mutinies, and having more soldiers shot.
Running desperately short of funds to supply his troops, he wrote for
help to friends in Nashville, who appealed to a bank for $50,000. He
briefly invaded Spanish Florida, chasing British troops, and then
arrived at New Orleans in time for the main British invasion that winter. But John Ross would not be among the defenders at the Battle of
New Orleans at the start of 1815, for by then he and the Cherokee
Regiment had gone home. There was a divide in Jackson's forces,
between the men who became his absolute loyalists and remained with
him to the end, and those whose loyalty was conditional—who followed
him into battle when they felt it was right, but also insisted upon their
right to leave. John Ross was among the conditional men. He left a few
weeks after the carnage of Horseshoe Bend. He was home well before
the signing of the Treaty of Fort Jackson, though as a reader of newspapers and gatherer of intelligence, he followed the negotiations and
grasped their importance. The next time Ross came to the attention of
history it would not be in the service of General Jackson, but in defiance
of him—and in defense of Cherokee lands.

PART TWO

———⟶◆⟵———

Origins

1767–1814

Five

Send a Few Late
Newspapers by the Bearer

O nce in a letter, John Ross referred to the boundary of the
Cherokee Nation. He called the area beyond the Cherokee
border the "whiteside." He wrote that compound word as if it
was in common use, as it might have been for a man like Ross, who
lived on the dividing line between two worlds. Part white and part
Cherokee, he grew up crossing and recrossing a border between races.
Not until well into his adult life did he definitively signal where he
would come to rest.

Ross was the son, grandson, and great-grandson of white traders
who had lived in the Cherokee Nation since British colonial times,
though the word "trader" did not really describe the compass of their
influence. They acted as vital links between the Indian and white
worlds. Traders bought furs and other items, exchanging them for cloth,
guns, beads, and whiskey. Often they married native women, which
explained Ross's Cherokee blood. His prosperous family built homes in
Cherokee places that would later become famous landmarks of the Civil
War, like Chickamauga and Lookout Mountain.

From his earliest days Ross felt the tug of competing identities. Born October 3, 1790, he spent his early years surrounded by Cherokees who visited his father's store. Cherokee children were his friends. One year his mother made plans to take her children to the annual Green Corn Festival, one of the celebrations around which the Cherokee year was organized. She expected him to dress like a white child, but the boy didn't want to appear before his friends that way. She let him change into traditional Indian dress—which, for a small boy, might not be very much clothing at all.

Kooweskoowe, the bird's name he received at adulthood, appropriately honored his ancestry in the Cherokee Bird Clan. His great-grandmother had been a full-blooded Indian, a woman named Ghigooie, whose clan was one of seven into which the nation was divided. She married a Scottish trader and bore children, including Ross's maternal grandmother. That grandmother—half white, half Indian—grew up to marry another Scottish trader. He was John McDonald, an outsize character whose personal experience with shifting loyalties foreshadowed Ross's own.

McDonald was among generations of northern Britons who flooded the American colonies throughout the eighteenth century. From Ireland, Scotland, and northern England came roughly a quarter-million people, a migration that played an enormous role in shaping the early American identity. While most of these migrants settled among colonists like themselves, the traders found opportunity beyond the frontier, on the Indian map. McDonald learned the Cherokee language and became an adviser to Cherokee leaders. He was also a sort of diplomat representing the interests of the British crown. When other colonists revolted in 1775, McDonald remained loyal to his king, as did the Cherokees, who saw the distant king as their protector against the land-grabbing white men who lived nearby. Enrolled as a British soldier, McDonald organized Cherokees to fight the American rebels. He became the sort of overseas operator the British Empire used for centuries, Lawrence-of-Arabia types who learned local tongues and motivated native armies to fight in the British cause. In McDonald's case it was a lost cause. When the British gave up in 1783, they abandoned their Indian allies as well as Tories like McDonald. He became American by force of circumstance rather than by choice.

The Tory trader did not embrace his new identity easily. He became a one-man nation with his own foreign policy. He continued living among the Cherokees, but as they negotiated for peace with the new United States, McDonald maintained ties with Britain and even with Spain, which controlled Florida and New Orleans to the south. He was not alone in hedging his bets with the Spanish. James Wilkinson, the commander in chief of the U.S. Army, received barrels of Spanish coins in payment for intelligence and advice. Farmers and traders had to swear allegiance to Spain to ship goods down the Mississippi. Generations later, a historian discovered the astounding news that Andrew Jackson himself took a secret oath to the Spanish crown. These oaths were mostly a farce; westerners got the access to New Orleans that they needed, and never got around to delivering the interior United States to Spanish control. But nobody was certain where John McDonald's loyalties lay. In 1792 he went on the Spanish payroll, earning $500 a year, a substantial sum on the cash-poor frontier.

One day the trader learned of two other white men in danger. They were traveling by boat down the Tennessee River when a band of Cherokees seized them. The leader of the Cherokee band, known as Bloody Fellow, was angry at the white men for giving a ride to a native who was out of favor. But McDonald arrived in time to smooth over the dispute, managing the affair so adroitly that Bloody Fellow changed his mind about the white travelers and welcomed them to trade with the Cherokees. One, Daniel Ross, settled near McDonald. He was yet another Scotsman, and married McDonald's daughter Mollie, who was one-fourth Cherokee. Of their nine children, John Ross was the third, and the oldest son.

. . .

Nothing about his ancestry made it impossible for Ross to be regarded simply as Cherokee. Cherokee society was matrilineal, with ancestry traced through mothers rather than fathers, and Ross could follow his Cherokee blood directly through his mother, grandmother, and great-grandmother. All those white men were less relevant. It was expected that a woman would marry outside her clan, and common to marry outside her nation. The idea that Ross was only "one-eighth Cherokee" would not have made much sense in Cherokee culture.

Many white people, far more focused on racial purity, would not have accepted a man with Ross's genealogy as white. But Ross could pass as white among those who did not know his family. His upbringing made this possible. He grew up in an English-speaking household, which the Ross family made a little outpost of white civilization. They kept the house stocked with books, maps, and the most recent newspapers available on the frontier; Daniel Ross wanted his children to read. (John Ross returned the favor on at least one occasion in later life, helping to keep the house stocked with reading material; his 1813 letter to the federal Indian agent warning about the Creek rebellion ended with a friendly postscript: "Grand Father & Father presents their respects to you & will be very thankful if you will send a few late newspapers by the bearer.") Young John began his formal education around age nine, when his father hired a tutor. He went on to study at a private academy established for the benefit of Indians, and emerged well educated by the standards of the frontier. As an adult Ross would come to look striking in the European-style clothing that had made him uncomfortable as a boy. His best-known portrait showed him in a formal dark suit with a vest, his hair carefully trimmed and combed back, his large eyes focused on the artist, looking every bit the youthful statesman with his right hand holding a piece of paper. He moved about the Cherokee Nation in boots and a jacket, sometimes topped by a broad-brimmed, flat-crowned planter's hat. Because he could have passed as a white man, his leadership skills and eloquence might well have led him to prominence, given the widening opportunities for white men in Andrew Jackson's America. Yet something drew Ross away from the whiteside and closer to his Indian identity. Given the ability to claim membership in one of two different groups, Ross gradually strengthened his ties to the group that was smaller, more vulnerable, and seemingly destined to lose.

He certainly prospered as a Cherokee, because he was an entrepreneur. He developed real estate in both the Cherokee and white senses of the term. Although Cherokee land was owned in common by the nation, plots could be improved by individuals, as Ross did with houses and fields and the Tennessee River settlement called Ross's Landing. On the whiteside, Ross speculated in land as allowed by white custom, purchasing remote tracts in hopes that spreading settlement would increase their value. Ross also purchased people as slaves. Decades after Ross's death, a ninety-six-year-old man testified to an oral historian: "My grandfather, father and Auntie were bought by John Ross." Ross later sold the father in a trade for real estate. Ross's slaves, like his wife and children, were very rarely discussed in his letters, although we can occasionally glimpse them. When Ross referred to "the bearer of this letter" or sending "newspapers by the bearer," it is reasonable to imagine that the papers were carried across the Cherokee Nation in a black hand.

Ross was wealthy enough that when he became a Cherokee leader, his political opponents questioned how he made his money. They never proved their suspicions of corruption, and the modern-day editor of Ross's papers found no sign that Ross had dipped into the Cherokee treasury. When Ross emerged as a leading defender of Indian rights, his white critics made a darker allegation. Ross wasn't a true Indian, they charged, but part of a mixed-blood elite who misled simple-minded Cherokees to maintain positions of personal wealth and privilege. It was certainly correct that some elites of native nations proved to be excessively self-interested, although it is challenging to classify Ross among them. Corruptible elites commonly worked *with* white men rather than against them, trading away communal land if the government paid bribes or granted plots of land in their names. John Ross himself was granted 640 acres as part of a treaty with the United States in 1819. But if the land grant was meant to peel him away from the Cherokee Nation, it didn't work. He grew more steadfast in defense of the people he regarded as his own. He persisted even after his house was taken away from him and occupied by white settlers.

If Ross ever explained his choice, the explanation has not survived. He might have been the last to know, given the human tendency to choose a course in life and find the reasons afterward. Once he became a Cherokee leader it would have been politically awkward to admit that he ever had a chance to assume a different allegiance. But in pondering his eventual stand on the Cherokee side of the line, it is worth considering the cumulative effect of Ross's experiences. This book began with Ross's journey down the Tennessee River in 1812, when he was challenged from the riverbank by white horsemen. Prudence required Ross to obscure his Cherokee heritage and pass as white. This was probably not the only time he ever had to do so. He certainly encountered many people over the years who would have treated him differently depending on whether they perceived him as a white man in a statesman's black clothes, or a suspicious character on a boat with red men. Ross would have taken their view of Indians personally: it was an affront to him and to his family, particularly his mother. A man in frontier America was expected to seek redress for insults. Though Ross never challenged other men to duels, as Andrew Jackson did, he was equally jealous of his honor. Ross's answer could have been the life he chose. Maybe he remembered the behavior of the white horsemen who confronted him along the bank of the Tennessee River. Maybe he didn't want to be one of them.

Six

I Am Fond of Hearing
That There Is a Peace

R oss knew his Cherokee history, or at least a version of it. The
Green Corn Festival, the annual event at which he had wanted
to dress like an Indian as a boy, was where the history was
passed from one generation to the next. Old men offered dramatic ren-
ditions of tales that they had first heard as boys.

Until the 1790s, the Cherokee oral tradition included a migration
story. The tale suggested that many generations past, the Cherokee, or
Tsalagi, people had lived outside the Appalachians, but had been driven
by some calamity into the mountains. Cherokee elders were still repeating their story around the time of Ross's birth, but soon stopped. It's not
clear why, although Cherokees may have noticed that white men could
use such tales of past migration to suggest Indians were nomads and not
really attached to their land. Ross, as an adult, simply said that Cherokees had held their land since "time immemorial."

This was true enough. Cherokees had lived in the southern Appalachian highlands since long before white men arrived. Their homeland
centered on the Great Smoky Mountains, known for a wondrous blue
haze that tinted the view of the higher slopes. A traditional Cherokee
story said the mountains were created in the distant past, when the

earth was new and soft, and a great buzzard flew so low that it created hills and valleys as its wings beat the ground. From these mountains, Cherokee hunting grounds stretched out as far as modern-day South Carolina, Virginia, and Kentucky. They were a powerful nation, often at war with the Creeks to their southwest and various nations to the north.

Because early Cherokees were not literate, much of what is known about their history came from their encounters with Europeans. The earliest known contact came in 1540, when the Spanish explorer Hernando de Soto found them well established in a string of towns. Failing to discover the gold he was seeking, de Soto and his Spanish soldiers moved on. Later the Cherokees encountered French explorers and traders, who moved inland from the Gulf Coast or down the river systems from the Great Lakes in search of furs. The most sustained contact with white settlers began after 1670, when the British established Charles Towne, or Charleston, as the capital of their new Carolina colony. The British crown granted the Carolinians a sphere of influence including most Cherokee territory.

Day-to-day British contact with the Cherokees came through soldiers and through traders such as Ross's Scottish ancestors. Of all the colonial traders, the most famous may have been James Adair, who lived for forty years among southern tribes before publishing a book drawn from his experience in 1775. Adair's eyewitness observations were only partly diminished by his motivation for offering them: he wanted to demonstrate that Indian customs were similar to Jewish customs, proving the popular theory that the Indians were descendants of a lost tribe of Israel. In fairness to Adair, he could never have embraced this outlandish notion unless he had been willing to see Indians as human beings like himself. Native "persons, customs, &c. are not singular from the rest of the world," Adair wrote. "Their notions of things are like ours." He was a sympathetic observer. Adair recalled the Cherokees in the first part of the 1700s as a nation of considerable reach and power. He knew of sixty-four towns and villages, "populous, and full of women and children." He believed that if provoked the nation could bring six thousand warriors into the field, a force that would dwarf anything the British colonists could muster. Later the population was devastated by European diseases, and may have been cut in half by a single smallpox epidemic in 1738.

Cherokees were attracted by the opportunities of trade with the British. The British were attracted by the possibility of gaining powerful allies against less cooperative natives. In 1711 the colonists of Charles Towne supplied guns to the Cherokees on condition that they help to fight the Tuscaroras, who were being displaced from their homes near the coast. Cherokees joined British forces in an early version of Indian removal, driving the Tuscaroras so far away they were forced to find refuge among the Iroquois of upstate New York. Soon enough, however, the British encroached on Cherokee land, leading to outbreaks of violence. In 1760 the British unwisely massacred twenty-two Cherokee members of a peace delegation, and triggered a powerful response. Standing Turkey, a Cherokee leader, laid siege to Fort Loudon, which had been built in the Appalachians to keep an eye on the Cherokees. The starving garrison was forced to surrender, and though offered a safe passage out, they were attacked once outside the walls. Many British were killed or captured. Retaliating for this retaliation, the British sent an army that burned fifteen Cherokee towns.

When peace was reestablished, the British agreed to send a young officer, Lieutenant Henry Timberlake, to live for several months among the Cherokees. Timberlake produced a memoir filled with details of Cherokee life and diplomacy. Today it is not unusual to see Cherokees of the Appalachians sporting elaborate tattoos in Cherokee script or traditional patterns; Timberlake saw something similar in 1761 and 1762: "The Cherokees are of a middle stature, of an olive color, tho' generally painted, and their skins stained with gun-powder, pricked in very pretty figures." Cherokee women grew their hair "so long that it generally reaches the middle part of their legs," and wore it "club'd," or folded back upon itself. Generations of interaction with outsiders had already influenced their clothing styles, which were growing closer to those of Europeans.

Each Cherokee town had a town house for public meetings, next to the public square where games were played. The town house was a building in the shape of a dome, framed with logs and roofed over with bark. People sat around the fire according to their membership in the seven Cherokee clans, divided like slices of pie, as they discussed questions facing the town or the nation. Timberlake described Cherokee government as a "mixed aristocracy and democracy," with chiefs or headmen being chosen "according to their merit in war and policy at home." The system was aristocratic because a chief or village headman might serve for life and could be succeeded by members of his family if they had earned the people's respect. It was democratic because the chiefs had limited power. Timberlake said the chiefs led only "the warriors that chuse to go, for there is no laws or compulsion on those that refuse to follow, or punishment to those that forsake their chief: he strives, therefore, to inspire them with a sort of enthusiasm, with the war-song, as the ancient bards did in Britain." Not only was there freedom to dissent, and even to sit out war; there was no punishment for any crime short of murder. Murder required the victim's family to seek revenge, although even an accused killer could find safe haven in specially designated "towns of refuge," much as hunted men in other cultures sought refuge in churches or mosques.

The freedom to ignore leaders could trigger instability. One Cherokee story, recorded in 1828, describes a chief leading an expedition of thirty men to explore western land. The chief encountered four strange men of an unknown tribe, made friends with them, and exchanged gifts. But when he informed his thirty confederates, they cast aside his diplomacy and chased down the strangers as presumed enemies, killing two. The exploring party itself then came under attack. In other cases, this loose style of governance produced positive results. In the 1760s Lieutenant Timberlake was impressed by the Cherokees' diplomacy. Though they depended on trade with the British to their east, they maintained ties with the French from New Orleans and Canada. Timberlake realized the Cherokees were playing one colonial power against another, preserving independence from each. "Their alliance with the French seems equal . . . to our most masterly strokes of policy; and yet we cannot be surprized at it, when we consider that merit alone creates their ministers, and not the prejudices of party, which often create ours."

Very soon after Timberlake's visit it grew harder to play outside powers against one another. The British drove away the French in 1763, and the Americans drove away the British in 1783. The Spanish still controlled Florida to the south, but the Americans were the dynamic power. All the American Indian nations put together might number 600,000 or 700,000 people against the United States' irrepressible millions. Cherokees needed other ways to guard their sovereignty, and Cherokee leaders embraced the civilization program when it was extended by President Washington in the 1790s.

Washington had developed respect for natives through personal experience. During the colonial period, when he was a military officer charged with defending the frontier of Virginia, he found Indians to be such formidable opponents that only other Indians could defeat them. He urged Virginia to seek help from natives, including Cherokees. Once he became president, he tried to avoid fighting Indians at all. This required him to protect Indian land from white encroachment. It wasn't that he opposed western settlement (which he saw as his nation's future) nor even that he opposed real estate speculation in Indian lands (which he had done on a grand scale himself). He simply opposed white land grabbers' triggering wars his government could not afford. Washington's policy explicitly recognized the two dissonant maps of America— the Indian map of nations with great blotches of land, and the U.S. map of straight lines dividing states and territories. He even took the side of the Indian map: the authority of states would only extend to the point where they reached Indian borders.

It was true that this benevolent approach contained its measure of self-interest. Washington expected that the colors of the Indian map would fade. Natives would need less land for modern agriculture than for hunting, raising the hope that civilizing tribes might sell surplus territory. Indians might even need to sell land to pay their bills at federal trading posts. In an 1803 letter marked "unofficial and private," President Thomas Jefferson described the policy in terms that make him sound to modern ears like a drug dealer promoting the controlled substance of consumer capitalism. "We shall push our trading houses," Jefferson wrote, "and be glad to see the good and influential individuals among [the Indians] run in debt, because we observe that when these debts get beyond what the individuals can pay, they become willing to lop them off by a cession of lands." In a message for public consumption, Jefferson expressed the same idea more elegantly: Indians trading land for goods would discover "the wisdom of exchanging what they can spare and we want for what we can spare and they want." Jefferson did not think he was doing any harm. Though he knew Indians might be compelled to move west, he felt they might someday grasp a better alternative: they could "incorporate with us as citizens of the United States."

Whatever its long-term intentions, the civilization program formally recognized Indian rights and offered real opportunities. The program also created certain political strengths for Cherokees. The most striking example of this came with the spread of Christianity. From 1800 onward, Cherokee leaders allowed Moravian and other missionaries to set up schools, spreading literacy and training for skills such as carpentry. When exposed to the new faith, many Cherokees embraced it and blended it with ancient beliefs, as Christians around the world have always done. (Once I sat with a Cherokee man who knew the generations of his family back to the early 1800s; he observed that his lineage included biblical names such as Solomon, David, and Adam— "meaning they were Christianized"—even though some were also "conjure men," using ancient methods to read minds, give strength to warriors, and influence events.) But if the missionaries did not succeed as purely as they might have liked, the spread of Christianity increased popular sympathy for Cherokees. Many Americans equated the Christian religion with civilization itself. In 1819 a mission in the Cherokee Nation received a visit from President James Monroe. John Ross understood the political value of his nation's Christianized image, and though never overtly religious, he joined a church in 1829, just as his nation was under severe pressure.

A significant part of the civilization program was the promotion of Ross himself. By traditional standards he was an unlikely leader, who had fought in the Creek War but came away with no particular exploits to extol. But as an educated English speaker, he had the skills for an age in which sovereignty must be defended by words instead of bullets. He was rewarded with positions of increasing prominence. By the 1820s, the aging leader Charles Hicks was providing Ross with tutorials on tribal history in order to prepare him for a future position of leadership.

One more change in Cherokee culture reflected all the others. It was the change in the role of women. The women affected may have included John Ross's wife. She was believed to be half Cherokee (though some stories said otherwise), and was known by both a Christian name, Elizabeth, and a Cherokee name, Quatie. She bore six children. But the most important thing to know about her is that almost nothing is known. She is, alongside Ross, nearly invisible.

Cherokee women were not always so. Because it was a matrilineal society, a husband joined his wife's family rather than the reverse. When they divorced, the wife kept her property. During his stay among the Cherokees in the 1760s, Lieutenant Timberlake realized that participation in war and governance was not exclusive to men. There were "war-women" whose exploits made him think of Amazons, and some were "as famous in war, as powerful in the council." It was more common that women were delegated tasks such as growing food, but at least one "warwoman" did turn up when Cherokees met U.S. negotiators to conclude the Treaty of Hopewell in 1785. According to a contemporary news account, "The War-Woman of Chota" delivered one of the speeches. She said she spoke for herself and all the young men of Chota, her town.

> I am fond of hearing that there is a Peace; and I hope you have now taken us by the hand in real friendship. I have a Pipe and a little Tobacco to give the Commissioners to smoke in friendship. I look on you and the Red People as my CHILDREN.

This warwoman did not refer to white men as her elder brothers. She was confident enough to position *herself* as a wise parent and the men of both races as her offspring. She was probably Nancy Ward, who reportedly lived to a great age and became a "beloved woman," or revered elder, whose advice was greatly influential.

Women did not entirely lose their influence in later years, but the civilization program altered the status of some women, and certainly the elites. The customs of inheritance, in particular, seemed problematic to white advisers; the possessions of deceased men and women alike were spread among their respective clans, and so were diffused. It would be so much better if sons inherited from their fathers, so that families could accumulate wealth. In an earlier century, women routinely went as bare-breasted as men. Now long dresses were the custom, reflecting the modesty expected of Christian women. As the economy shifted from hunting to agriculture and home manufacturing, women undertook labor that men would not. John Ridge, the son of Major Ridge, recalled in 1826 that it was women who "were first prevailed to undertake" the work of spinning and weaving. They would make "white or striped homespun" cloth, woolen blankets, coverlets, and stockings. It was, to be sure, valuable work: "I can only say that their domestic cloths are preferred by us to those brought from New England." But it was a different life than that of a "warwoman." There is no record showing that women joined the Cherokee Regiment at Horseshoe Bend in 1814. The closest thing to women on the force were soldiers who went by a Cherokee name translating as "The Good Woman," who according to a modern scholar were men.

John Ross's wife, Quatie, must have been a formidable figure or at least a durable one. As her husband rose in politics and diplomacy, and came to spend several months a year in Washington, she was at home with an expanding family. She may have had help from the slaves John Ross accumulated, but she did not often have her husband. Though Ross wrote enough letters that his correspondence fills two thick volumes, there is not a single surviving letter that he ever addressed to his wife. Ross's biographer speculates that Quatie might have been illiterate, which would explain the absence of letters but would also underline the distance between his status and hers. For all the restrictions on women in white society, Andrew Jackson's wife wrote letters that showed her to be a sharp observer and an influence on her husband. No one knows how Quatie influenced Ross. Hers was an existence hidden from view.

Seven

Every Thing That Was
Dear to Me

The same mass migration that brought John Ross's Scottish forebears to America also brought the parents of Andrew Jackson.

Jackson's mother and father were Scots-Irish immigrants. Beginning in the 1600s, the British government encouraged these Protestants to move from Scotland to the north of Ireland, where they helped to control the rebellious Catholic island. Later many made the leap across the ocean, where they helped take control of a continent. Unlike some migrants, drawn to America by religious freedom or dreams of riches, the Scots-Irish, also known as Scotch Irish, made no high pretense. Many were poor, proud, and seeking to make a slightly better living. They were the "hoosiers," or rough backwoodsmen, who settled much of the American interior. Their descendants became so numerous in the southern Appalachians that when one of Jackson's early biographers traveled the region in the 1850s, he made a discovery. "The features and shape of [the] head of General Jackson, which ten thousand sign-boards have made familiar to the people of the United States, are common in North Carolina and Tennessee," he reported. "I saw more than twenty well-marked specimens of the long, slender, Jacksonian head, with the bushy, bristling hair."

The same biographer described the Scots-Irish as a "tough, vehement, good-hearted race" who were "formed to grapple with practical affairs" and displayed a "curious" dry sense of humor. They also tended to seek conflict, to "*contend* for what they think is right with peculiar earnestness. . . . Hot water would seem to be the natural element of some of them." This combative image was plainly a stereotype, but remains useful to us because Jackson's famous life story probably went far to enshrine the stereotype. "I was born for a storm," Jackson once said, "and calm does not suit me." Scots-Irish culture was adaptable to the violent frontier. If the westward movement brought them in conflict with Indians, so their ancestors had fought Irish Catholics or rival branches of the Protestant church. And if frontier living was harsh and remote, so were their ancestors' lives near the Irish Sea. Many immigrants hacked out farms in the fertile valleys of the Appalachians, such as the valley where Andrew Jackson's parents built a home in 1765. Andrew was born in 1767, near enough to the border between North and South Carolina to prompt debate in later years about which state should claim him. Of a more important fact there was no dispute: his father died months before the infant's birth. His mother moved the remnants of the family into another family's home, where she essentially became the housekeeper.

Accounts of Andrew's childhood portray a tempestuous boy. If he was not challenged to a fight, he would start one, and if knocked down, he would never give up. These accounts, while plausible, are not entirely reliable. They were written down long after Jackson became the most famous man in America, when people would naturally recall stories about Jackson the child that confirmed the established image of the adult. It is more certain that the boy grew up as the society around him came apart. He was nine years old when the Declaration of Independence was signed in Philadelphia, and sixteen when the Treaty of Paris secured that independence in 1783. Jackson lived those years in a landscape scarred by guerrilla warfare and murder as rebels contended against loyalists. By his teenage years he was a messenger and eventually a fighter for the rebels. Captured by British soldiers along with his

brother Robert, Andrew refused a demand to clean an officer's boots.
The boy is reported to have declared that he was a prisoner of war,
meaning that he was entitled to more dignified treatment, a remark
that prompted the officer to strike him with a sword. "The sword point
reached my head," Jackson recalled years later, "and has left a mark
there as durable as the scull." The Jackson boys' mother successfully
negotiated for their release, but afterward she contracted cholera and
died while serving as a nurse for American prisoners in British hands.
Andrew Jackson would refer in later years to "the struggle for our liberties, in which I lost every thing that was dear to me."

Nothing assured that this orphan of the Revolution would rise to a
position of leadership. Before he could command his army at Horseshoe
Bend, he had to survive years of his own high-risk behavior. As a teenager, Jackson followed friends to Charleston, South Carolina, and did
little besides drink and gamble. Later he traveled back inland to Salisbury, North Carolina, and studied to become a lawyer when not occupied with entertainment. Long afterward, people in Salisbury recalled
the night that the future president and three friends ended a night of
drinking by smashing their glasses and the furniture of the tavern where
they were staying, and throwing the remnants on the fire.

Then the young lawyer—still just twenty-one, for it was 1788, the
year the Constitution was ratified by enough states to take effect—
received an offer to move west. He accepted a job as a prosecutor in the
most remote part of North Carolina, the western zone that would eventually emerge as a separate state called Tennessee. He took on the trap-
pings of a gentleman as he traveled toward his new home. Reaching the
Appalachian town of Jonesborough, he purchased his first slave. The
record of the sale noted that "Andrew Jackson Esquire" took possession
of "a Negro Woman named Nancy about Eighteen or Twenty Years of
Age." He also fought his first duel. Gentlemen were accustomed to
demand "satisfaction" when their honor was impugned, and Jackson
believed another attorney insulted him in court. "When a man's feelings and charector are injured he ought to seek a speedy redress," he

wrote his antagonist. Many men in Jackson's time spoke freely of their "feelings" and confessed to the reality that they were governed by emotions. Jackson was especially emotional, and wrote of his "feelings" throughout his life, though he also learned to control those emotions when necessary. On the day appointed for the duelists to meet with pistols drawn, they acted out a lifesaving compromise, with both men firing in the air, leaving dignity and honor preserved.

It also preserved their lives, of course. Jackson was able to continue westward to his permanent posting, a rude frontier town called Nashville. It was not even ten years old, and breathtakingly remote from the East. Not only were mountains in the way; the rivers, which were the best highways, led in the opposite direction. Nashville was on the banks of the Cumberland, which flowed northwestward to the Ohio and then down the Mississippi, where Indians and European powers had more influence than the United States. But this remoteness meant a man of energy and talent faced less competition for leadership. The vigorous young prosecutor quickly made connections with the local elite, boarding at the home of the Donelson family, whose late patriarch John Donelson was among the founders of Nashville. Before long Jackson married Rachel, one of Donelson's daughters. He became a delegate to his state's constitutional convention in his twenties, and Tennessee's first representative in Congress at age thirty. Before the age of forty he was a prominent trader and planter. His farm, the Hermitage, had the style of a rough frontier settlement, where he lived with Rachel in a two-story log house, but he steadily added to his property until he had dozens of enslaved men, women, and children tending more than a thousand acres. He ran a dry goods store and riverside boatyard that he developed into a kind of playground for men, including a tavern and a racetrack.

Controversy followed the whip-thin politician with the wiry hair. Although his ownership of slaves was unremarkable in Tennessee, he sometimes engaged in slave dealing, a business that even slave owners considered disreputable. He also endured criticism for his continuing tendency to challenge other men to duels, a practice that remained common but illegal. In 1806 Jackson let an exchange of insults with a Nashville man escalate into a duel, and resolved to kill his opponent. Jackson let the other man shoot first, took a lead ball near his heart that would remain in his body the rest of his life, yet remained standing. He took time to be sure of his aim before firing a fatal shot in return. Unfortunately for Jackson, his antagonist was a popular young man whose death stained Jackson's reputation; and that reputation was already colored by scandal. It was widely known that he had been together with Rachel for years before she completed her divorce from an abusive husband. Rachel and Andrew lived as husband and wife from 1790 or 1791 onward even though the formal decree ending her previous marriage did not arrive until 1793. They had to be remarried in 1794 to clear up doubts about their status. But having married, they cultivated a conventional family life. With no children of their own, they adopted their son Andrew Jr. from Rachel's relatives. When Jackson traveled, his miserable wife wrote him letters urging him to hurry home. He wrote back tenderly to express regret that he could not.

The muddled circumstances of his marriage proved to be characteristic of Jackson. He took counsel of what he wanted, what his friends desired, and what he felt to be right. He was guided less by the norms of society than by what he considered "Just," as he wrote in his letters, often capitalizing the word. For his marriage to Rachel, the most romantic act of his life, he was willing to endure decades of whispers and insults. A darker manifestation of this characteristic came out in Jackson's slave trading. The social convention that it was acceptable to own human beings as property, but that only low-down characters would engage in the slave trade, would have been just the sort of elaborate hypocrisy by which Jackson refused to be governed. Modern readers can wish that he resolved this hypocrisy by rejecting both practices. Instead he embraced them both when it suited his interests. His approach to slavery foreshadowed his approach to federal Indian policy:

he would reject what he saw as its false piety, and rewrite the policy in the way that suited people like himself.

He was one of many frontier leaders who made their own rules. One of the region's leading men, the Revolutionary War hero John Sevier, briefly established his own state, called Franklin. Jackson's first political mentor, William Blount, admitted that he became territorial governor of the future state of Tennessee to support his personal land speculation. Jackson, the orphan finding his way in the world, absorbed the ethos of such older men. When Aaron Burr passed through Nashville in 1805—Burr, who as vice president of the United States had killed Alexander Hamilton in a duel—he was just the sort of colorful rogue who was welcome for an extended stay at the Hermitage. Burr was on a mysterious western journey that eventually led to his arrest for some vague treasonous plot, possibly a plan to found his own independent nation. The exposure of Burr forced Jackson to denounce him and to insist that he had not known anything about Burr's plans, even after the two men talked for days and Jackson sold boats to Burr for his expedition.

Until the Battle of Horseshoe Bend in 1814, the record of Jackson's career suggests a talented man thrashing about in the dark, trying to locate a ladder that no man of his background had ever climbed. His speeches made an impression in the House of Representatives, but he left his seat. He served briefly in the Senate but resigned and went home, becoming a justice on the Tennessee supreme court. He won election in 1802 as major general in command of the Tennessee militia, but for years he found no wars to fight. Like many a westerner, he speculated in land. He bought and sold the rights to tens of thousands of acres, including land alongside the Mississippi River that eventually became Memphis. It was common for speculators to buy the rights to Indian land and then press their politicians to clear it of Indians— pressure that Jackson, as a politician himself, was well connected to apply. But he made the mistake of dealing with men more dreamy-eyed than he was, and when one of his land sales unraveled, Jackson struggled to avoid bankruptcy and the risk of debtors' prison.

That was long before the War of 1812, when his military and diplomatic triumphs opened new horizons for a man with a real estate background and business connections. During that war he was a general in command of an army. When it was over, he applied his relentless energy to the conquest of acreage.

PART THREE

Old Hickory

1815–1818

Eight

Address Their Fears and Indulge Their Avarice

Almost the whole nation celebrated Andrew Jackson after Horseshoe Bend and New Orleans. His defeat of the British at the Battle of New Orleans, especially, was the perfect American story. Throwing together regular army soldiers, Tennessee militiamen, Choctaw Indians, New Orleans militia forces including free black men, and gunners commanded by the local pirate Jean Laffite, Jackson placed his main force behind a canal and a barricade. On January 8, 1815, the British invaders ran straight at Jackson's guns. The British frontal assault was the same tactic that Jackson employed against the Creek wall at the Horseshoe, but Jackson had chosen far more defensible ground. Trapped in the open, facing the murderous fire of the Americans behind their barricade, the British assault force lost 291 redcoats killed, and more than 1,300 others wounded or captured. The Americans suffered 13 dead and a few dozen wounded or captured. The surviving British boarded ships and sailed away.

It was true that the battle took place after the War of 1812 was over—news had yet to arrive of a peace treaty signed two weeks earlier—but only the sourest critic could dismiss New Orleans as a needless fight. The triumph of New Orleans was not its strategic importance but its style. It embodied an enduring American ideal: that free citizens would come together in defense of liberty. Generations later, many American war movies would contain the same basic plot as the Battle of New Orleans: a diverse band of citizen soldiers, thrown together by their commander, overcame their differences and improvised their way to victory. Of course, the black men in Jackson's army could not vote, while his Choctaw allies were under pressure to give up their land, but few people were thinking about such things in 1815. Public adulation fell on the mélange of hardy frontiersmen and the wild-haired Tennessean who led them. Jackson would spend the remainder of his life in the brilliant light of fame.

Before 1815 ended, however, the hero was hearing a rumble of discontent. It involved his other, considerably more substantive victory. Nobody would ever debate whether Horseshoe Bend was a meaningless battle, since the general had exploited it to claim a land area larger than Scotland. Everyone knew the federal government would begin putting the land up for sale, and this knowledge lay behind a rumor that circulated around Nashville. In December 1815, Jackson's friend John Coffee heard the rumor. He wrote Jackson to warn that two men were telling stories about "some pretext or color of fraud about you and myself with some others concerning the purchase of lands in the new country."

Andrew Jackson, the longtime land speculator, was being accused of planning with his friends to speculate in the real estate he had just conquered.

Jackson seized his pen, telling Coffee of his "astonishment and surprise" at this attempt to "injure" him. "Such base ingratitude will meet its reward," he wrote.

> It is evidence of such wanton wickedness & depravity of heart that I can scarcely believe it myself, that I have huged such monsters to my boosom, called them friend, and risqued my life for the preservation of the charector & feelings of such a man.

Coffee went to confront the men on Jackson's behalf. He brought along another of General Jackson's close friends—James Jackson, unrelated to the general by blood but close to him in outlook, an Irish immigrant who had become a wealthy merchant and avid horse racer in Nashville. Coffee and James Jackson stared down one suspected storyteller and then the other. Each professed his innocence and blamed the other.

What must have made the rumor especially galling was that it was true. General Andrew Jackson really was going to buy former Indian land in "the new country." So was John Coffee. So was James Jackson. Coffee was going to play a special role, which General Jackson alluded to in the same letter in which he complained about the outrageous suggestion of a "color of fraud" in his conduct. At the end, Jackson dropped his tone of outrage and gave Coffee good news.

> *P.S. I have the express promise that you will be appointed receiver of Publick money—A.J.*

Jackson was campaigning to have Coffee hired to run the federal land office for northern Alabama. The "receiver of Publick money" would be in charge of conducting all the sales of former Creek land that were about to take place, putting him in an ideal position to pass on inside information.

Coffee didn't get the job, but Jackson engaged another agent to nose around a federal land office. "My Dear General. . . . We have succeeded in acquiring an accurate Knowledge of all the sections of good Lands to be sold," reported the agent in a letter marked "Private." He called Jackson's attention to four sections of land that "would form a most desirable establishment for your old age."

Andrew Jackson was about to participate in the biggest real estate bubble in the history of the nation up to that time. His multiple plantations in the new country would considerably exceed the acreage of the

Hermitage. Some of his closest friends and allies would colonize the new country and be installed among its leading citizens. He was nation-building. On its face there was nothing wrong with this. But to make it happen, Andrew Jackson the real estate magnate first needed help from General Jackson the federal official. He had to get the former Creek land on the market. This proved to be complicated, because some of the most valuable land was found not to be Creek territory at all. He hadn't really conquered it at Horseshoe Bend. He hadn't even taken it at the Treaty of Fort Jackson.

Andrew Jackson had a problem. General Jackson solved it. What follows is an account of what he did and how he did it.

The prize was the Tennessee Valley. Through it ran one of the great highways of the region, the river that John Ross traveled in December 1812 during his journey to trade with the Cherokees in the West. The Tennessee cut its way out of the Appalachians and spilled into the plains, flowing east to west in the shape of a jagged smile. White settlers had long ago taken control of its upper reaches and tributaries. But farther downriver, the Indian map showed that much of the valley was still the domain of Cherokees, Creeks, and Chickasaws. This was especially true at the Big Bend of the Tennessee, where the channel dipped into present-day Alabama. It was here that the currents roared through the shallows known as Muscle Shoals, forty miles that were perilous to travel downstream and often impossible to travel up.

Andrew Jackson would have known about the shoals almost as long as he was a westerner. He likely heard about them soon after his arrival in Nashville in 1788. The Donelson family, with whom he boarded, had made it to Nashville on a route that included a terrifying descent through those rapids. The Donelsons' story surely interested Jackson, because it involved the woman who became his wife.

Rachel was twelve years old in December 1779, when her father organized a convoy of settlers who started down the Tennessee. The current flowed westward, the direction they wanted to go, but everything else was against them. Boats ran aground on sandbars. Cherokees opened fire from the banks. The journal kept by Rachel's father recorded a boat shot full of holes, an enslaved man drowned while fleeing an attack, and an infant dashed on the rocks. When the survivors reached Muscle Shoals, they intended to travel overland to the planned settlement on the Cumberland River, but failed to find a message from a guide who was to give them directions. They decided to continue by water, shooting the rapids directly ahead. "The water being high made a terrible roaring," wrote Rachel's father, John Donelson, "which could be heard at some distance among the drift-wood heaped frightfully upon the points of the islands, the current running in every possible direction. . . . Our boats frequently dragged on the bottom, and appeared constantly in danger of striking." Emerging safely on the far side, the party drifted downriver to the Ohio—and then, half-starved, improvised sails to travel upriver on the Cumberland to what became Nashville.

Muscle Shoals gained a sinister reputation, as Jackson knew. He'd heard stories of a village near the bottom of the shoals, which Creeks had once used as a base for raids on white settlements, committing "ever kind of rapine & murder on our women & children." The attacks ended in 1787, when Tennessee militiamen moved south and burned the village called Coldwater. A little upriver was an elegant plantation where a white man, John Melton, lived with his Cherokee wife. Atop the riverside cliff known as Melton's Bluff, he built a sprawling farm worked by slaves and featuring a two-story house and a tavern. Local lore held that Melton was a river pirate, a legend that may have been overblown. Whatever Melton did to make his fortune, he was discreet enough that the Tennessee militia never came to burn his plantation. But he had hacked out a lucrative life in remote and beautiful country.

And it *was* beautiful, that land south of the Tennessee River. Above the bluffs stretched tableland—high ground sometimes many miles wide, in places framed by mountains and exceedingly rich in soil. The land was covered in timber, and said to carry veins of iron ore. The river made it all accessible. Crops could be shipped downstream to the Ohio River, then the Mississippi, all the way to New Orleans. True, the Muscle Shoals were an obstacle to travel farther upriver—but for a land speculator, this obstacle created an opportunity. Muscle Shoals was the head of navigation for cargo boats traveling to or from New Orleans. Journeys must start or end there. Should the valley be opened to settlement, the lower end of the shoals would require riverside towns. Street grids. Civilization. The Donelsons had hardly completed their nightmare voyage when men of means began to see that the region had great potential. In 1783 a North Carolina land company began a long-running but ultimately fruitless effort to take control of hundreds of square miles in the region that later became northern Alabama. The Muscle Shoals Company, as it was called, included the exuberant speculator William Blount, who went on to become Tennessee's territorial governor and Andrew Jackson's early political mentor.

A second effort to capture land around Muscle Shoals, by an organization called the Tennessee Company, began shortly after Jackson's arrival in Nashville in 1788. This too came to nothing, but the shoals were part of the frontier land conversation, and Jackson passed near them many times. The Natchez Trace crossed the Tennessee a few miles below the rapids. From 1789 onward Jackson traveled this road to and from Natchez frequently—herding slaves, leading troops, conducting his first marriage ceremony with Rachel in Natchez, and also famously quarreling with a federal Indian agent on the road. In 1816, General Jackson was assigned to build a new military road through the region, which would speed the journey to New Orleans. Though built for national security purposes, it would also open up previously inaccessible real estate. Jackson's engineers laid out a route that would cross the Tennessee at the lower end of Muscle Shoals.

The prize was in view, but could not be claimed unless someone gained access to Indian land.

.   .   .

The north side of the river was largely Cherokee until treaties in 1805 and 1806, under which the nation sold a swath of modern-day northern Alabama and much of Middle Tennessee. These treaties, negotiated by President Thomas Jefferson's administration, perfectly reflected his goal that Indians should trade land for American goods, exchanging "what they can spare and we want for what we can spare and they want." Under one treaty the government paid for land with "three thousand dollars in valuable merchandise" plus another $11,000 in either cash or merchandise, followed by an annual subsidy of $3,000. The second treaty gave up at least five thousand square miles for even less compensation—$10,000 plus a gristmill and a cotton gin. That treaty was a curious document entirely aside from the nominal payment. While it sold Cherokee territory for less than half a cent per acre, it exempted certain parcels from the sale, including a strip of rich land along the north shore of Muscle Shoals. This was land controlled by Doublehead, the Cherokee leader who negotiated the treaty. He was renting that land to farmers and wanted to continue profiting from it. Doublehead did not have long to enjoy this income. Other Cherokees judged his treaty so terrible that it amounted to treason, and murdered him in 1807.

The Cherokee land ceded in these treaties had drawn interest on the real estate market for years. (Speculators bought and sold the rights before the land was even available; Jackson was involved in a deal for eighty-five thousand acres that fell apart when his purchase was ruled invalid.) But because of the land reserved for Doublehead, the treaties did not yet open up the north bank of the river at Muscle Shoals.

The south bank was also closed to white settlement. Several native nations made conflicting and overlapping claims—Chickasaws and Cherokees as well as Creeks. It would take a forceful and visionary personality to alter these facts on the ground. Such a personality was available. In 1814, as we have seen, General Jackson imposed the Treaty of Fort Jackson upon his Creek allies. *"We will run the line,"* he had vowed, underlining his words. In the years that followed, Jackson set about consolidating this conquest—and expanding it. The Treaty of Fort Jackson was worded in such a way that it never explicitly declared that the south bank of the Tennessee River should become the property of the federal government. The boundary of the Creek cession in that area was simply not defined. Jackson nevertheless began to operate as if it *was* defined, and moved to "run the line" as he wanted. A surveyor had been appointed to mark the boundaries of the Creek cession, and in early 1816 Jackson repeatedly urged him to complete his work, even though it appeared the surveyor was exceeding his authority. "Do you progress with the line," Jackson instructed, as the surveyor captured real estate that was claimed by both Cherokees and Chickasaws.

Knowing that Chickasaws were complaining to the surveyor as he tugged his chains across the landscape, Jackson told him to hire "25 mounted gunmen as a guard." Jackson confessed that "I am not Legally authorised, to call for such a force," but the gunmen would be "punctually paid." His letter did not specify who would pay them. Jackson had confidence the surveyor would do as he wished, for the surveyor was John Coffee. "Go on my dear Genl," Jackson told his friend,

compleat the line & show them you are as prompt in the cabinet as in the field.

As for where the line should be drawn, Jackson added, "your own Judgt is your guide," and then he told Coffee exactly where that judgment should guide him. "Cold Water is in the Creek country," Jackson wrote. He was telling Coffee that the Creek land cession must include the property around Coldwater Creek, that little stream that flowed into the Tennessee River at Muscle Shoals.

There is no proof that General Jackson was thinking of buying land at Coldwater as he gave these instructions. He may have urged Coffee to obtain the land around Coldwater because he genuinely thought it was Creek territory. But a reading of his correspondence throughout the period makes it clear that he was always mindful of real estate interests. Two years later, when land near Coldwater finally went on the market, Jackson bid on it.

Jackson scrawled a letter to a Chickasaw leader, warning of "immediate punishment" if anyone blocked or insulted the surveyor. He assured the Chickasaws that if they disagreed with Coffee's line, they could complain to Washington after it was finished, but Jackson seemed to be altering the facts in a way that would make any protest futile. White settlers from Tennessee were coming southward to take Indian land as quickly as Coffee could run his line, and General Jackson was reluctant to perform his legal duty to evict them.

Coffee shared Jackson's spirit. The government in Washington had given him no information about where to mark one of the dividing lines. "I would be glad to be informed," he wrote, "though I shall not detain for it." He moved on with his work, but he could not move quickly enough. In the spring of 1816 a thunderbolt arrived from Washington: their superiors informed both Jackson and Coffee that the whole south bank of the Tennessee River was off-limits. It didn't belong to the Creeks. And because it didn't, it could not possibly be part of the Creek land cession. Jackson and Coffee had been improperly laying claim to two million acres.

They had been stopped, in large measure, through the efforts of John Ross. It was the only time in Andrew Jackson's career that he was ever soundly defeated by Indians.

Nine

Men of Cultivated Understandings

J ackson, the hero who destroyed the frontal assault of the British at New Orleans, discovered that on this occasion he was the victim of a flank attack. The Cherokees had gone around his defenses, making their case for ownership of the two million acres directly to Jackson's civilian superiors. On the day Jackson was urging his surveyor to "Go on my dear Genl," and telling him to hire armed guards, John Ross was in Washington, about to wreck all his plans.

Like any visitor to the capital at the time, Ross was walking among ruins. It was less than two years since the British had torched the Executive Mansion and the Capitol, doing such a thorough job that the fires left behind nothing but the blackened stone walls. These somewhat Romanesque remains, looking like the signs of a lost empire rather than a rising one, attracted gawkers and tourists long after the British were gone; at least one visitor to the capital was so distracted while gaping at "the Burnt Buildings" that he lost his "red morocko pocket Book" and had to advertise for it in the local newspaper. By 1816 the reconstruction was under way, but Congress was still meeting in a brick house across the street from its ruined chambers, and President Madison was living in a house in town. Vast open spaces yawned to the sides of Pennsylvania Avenue, the grand boulevard designed to be the city's main street. Congressmen crowded into boardinghouses on Capitol Hill, taking their meals at communal tables, while the beginnings of the new city's permanent elite invited diplomats and other distinguished guests into their fashionable homes.

Ross was in town as part of a Cherokee delegation. Although they had come to settle unrelated issues, intelligence of Coffee's surveying work reached the capital and abruptly shifted the focus of their mission. At age twenty-six Ross was not the most senior member of the group, but was a vital part of it, one of the few Cherokees who had the education and language skills to debate on equal terms with federal officials. The powerful planter Major Ridge had more influence but less English; another leading Cherokee, George Lowrey, was the delegation's designated speaker when they visited President James Madison, but was apparently not able to write his name. In the coming years Ross would travel with many delegations to Washington, and by necessity wrote many of their letters and formal documents; on joint letters he was sometimes the only one in the group who signed his name instead of making a mark. With his gracious manners and white men's clothes, Ross was probably one of the members of the delegation who made a positive impression on local newsmen. "These Indians are men of cultivated understandings," the *National Intelligencer* reported. Not only that: their recent past made it difficult to dismiss the Cherokees as hostile savages:

> [They] were nearly all officers of the Cherokee forces which served under General Jackson during the late war, and have distinguished themselves as well by their bravery as their attachment to the United States.

Their service at Horseshoe Bend may have been left vague when Jackson's initial battle report reached the *National Intelligencer* in 1814, but now the delegation managed to work this reality into the capital's conversation. It gave them credibility to speak boldly to federal officials. Ross did not assume the submissive tone that was expected of Indians, who were encouraged to think of themselves as children and of the president as their Great Father. When the government was slow to attend to their concerns, Ross wrote directly to William H. Crawford, the secretary of war, whose department oversaw Indian affairs. "Brother," he began, "thirty-two days have no[w] elapsed since we arrived at the seat of the American Government . . . we hope you will no longer delay." Though the secretary was one of the capital's imposing figures, Ross lectured him. "During the late war we availed ourselves of an opportunity to prove attachment to the Government of the United States; yet some of our White Brethren on the frontier wish to remain insensible of it." With multiple statements like this over the next twenty years, Ross laid a moral foundation for his cause. He foreshadowed the later arguments of African Americans, who in generations to come would argue that their own service in war had proven their claim to equal rights. It was during these negotiations that Ross informed an official at the War Department, "We consider ourselves as a part of the great family of the Republic of the U. States," adding that Cherokees were willing to sacrifice everything in the republic's defense.

Crawford seemed impressed. The Cherokees insisted the two million acres had long belonged to them, and said that even the Creeks had affirmed Cherokee possession of the land after Horseshoe Bend. The Cherokees knew the Appalachian landscape so intimately that Ross was able to describe their boundary line across war-scarred areas where some of the landmarks existed only in memory: "Beginning at a point where Vann's old Store formerly stood . . . and from thence continued to the Coosa River . . . from thence in a straight line, and crossing a fork of the Black Warrior River a little below the old town burnt by General Coffee." Crawford and President James Madison approved a treaty affirming the Cherokee claims, and sent the delegation home with silver-plated rifles, presents for the Cherokee veterans who first swam the Tallapoosa to capture enemy canoes and trigger Andrew Jackson's great victory.

When news reached Jackson in Nashville, he was outraged. Bypassing Secretary Crawford, he wrote directly to President Madison: "The late hasty convention with the Cherokees, is much regretted & depre-cated in this quarter," he said. The Cherokees "never had the least sem-blance of claim" to the territory. Leaving Cherokees in possession of it cut off one part of the union from another, blocked the passage of mili-tary supplies, and "wantonly surrendered" territory of "incalculable Value to the U States." The answer to Jackson came not from the presi-dent but from Crawford, who coolly knocked down Jackson's arguments one by one—military supplies, for example, were still allowed to pass through the Cherokee land, as Jackson must have known, since he was in charge of building the military road through it. Aside from that, Crawford said, the surveyor had blatantly exceeded his power.

Crawford pushed further. He instructed General Jackson to stop Ten-nessee intruders from grabbing the Cherokee lands: "The idea of resisting the authority of the government, must not be admitted for a moment." The truth was that Jackson himself seemed to be resisting the authority of the government. He dragged his feet about evicting intruders, saying they were too poor to relocate, and accused Crawford of insulting them:

Tennesseeans . . . are recorded as the worst sort of robbers, Taking from the poor Indian.

Supporting fire arrived from Nashville. A group of men from Jack-son's home county sent a "remonstrance" to Congress. Indians must be pushed farther away so that white citizens could travel without "the risk of being murdered at every wigwam by some drunken savage." The same document contained a revealing accusation against the Cherokees, calling them "so tenacious" that "they would not surrender one acre without receiving what would be the value of the land." It was, in other words, unacceptable for white men to contemplate the possibility that they could be forced to pay full price.

The pressure on Washington paid off. Jackson was given a chance to recover the land he had taken once and lost. Although President Madison remained adamant in rejecting Jackson's illegitimate capture of the Tennessee Valley, he was willing to see Jackson obtain it through more acceptable means. Jackson was appointed to talk with the Cherokees about selling it. He lost no time, bidding good-bye to Rachel and riding southeastward to Cherokee country. Two horses died on him during the trip, which he called "extra service of the most unpleasant nature."

Jackson's style of negotiating was frank and coercive. In talk after talk over the years, he told native leaders he was their friend, and that he wanted to pay for their land—but that if they failed to sell, white settlers would take their land for nothing. In that sense, the intruders constantly slipping onto Indian lands were like an army at Jackson's back. He would later describe his strategy in another negotiation with Indians by saying, "We must address ourselves to their fears and indulge their avarice." Both approaches were present when he negotiated with the Cherokees in 1816. The element of fear came from John Coffee, who rode ahead of Jackson and brought Cherokee leaders a warning that their nation might be destroyed if they bargained too hard. Once Jackson arrived, he appealed to avarice, making "some small presents to the fifteen chiefs that attended here," as Jackson said. Cherokee negotiators were each paid between $50 and $100.

The Cherokee negotiators did not include increasingly stubborn John Ross. Nor did the group include the influential planter Major Ridge, who backed out after hearing John Coffee's threats. The Cherokees who remained to face the onslaught included the Horseshoe Bend veteran known as George Guess or Sequoyah, who would be better known in a few years for developing a Cherokee syllabary, or writing system. Despite Jackson's pressure, the delegation managed to hold out for a treaty that was not the worst ever signed. Jackson knew what he wanted and was willing to deal for it. The Cherokees succeeded in retaining about seven hundred thousand acres, including land in northeastern Alabama to which they had the strongest claim. They ceded the remainder of the land for a payment of $65,000. Jackson got the southern bank of the Tennessee in the area of Muscle Shoals.

Now the whole region of the shoals was in the hands of the federal government except for isolated scraps on the north shore, the largest being the late Doublehead's former land. Doublehead's reservation became an afterthought, which Jackson was able to obtain for no payment at all when he negotiated a Cherokee treaty on other issues in 1817. Three and a half decades after investors first tried to capture Muscle Shoals, General Jackson finished the job.

Jackson and his friends would move to take advantage. The scale of their gain has rarely, if ever, been calculated. Many real estate records from the era have been lost. But records that survive show that after 1816, the names of Andrew Jackson, his relatives, and his two closest business associates appeared on the titles to more than forty-five thousand acres of newly opened Alabama land. Most was in the Tennessee Valley. The empire they created included every square foot of real estate in a new city founded along Jackson's military road at Muscle Shoals.

Ten

Let Me See You as I Pass

Conditions were now set for real estate transactions that so enriched Jackson and some of his friends that the new wealth altered their lives. Jackson's work had acquired millions of acres for the federal government. Now President James Madison's administration was expected to subdivide the land and sell thousands of desirable plots to the public. Jackson and his friends made plans to buy some of the land as private citizens. They did this at the same time Jackson continued to influence the situation in his capacity as a public official.

His motives were complex, and Jackson doubtless would have described them as pure. His official goal was the security of the United States, and the evidence shows him constantly working to strengthen the great republic's hold on the unstable frontier. But the evidence shows something more. Jackson managed national security affairs in a way that matched his interest in land development. They combined in his mind; he spoke of them together.

On November 12, 1816, he urged the secretary of war to build a series of arms depots across the region he was responsible for securing. Jackson suggested the location for a central arsenal: "I know of no situation combining so many advantages . . . as the lower end of the Muscle shoals." The same day that he urged the federal government to locate an arsenal and its employees there, he wrote the president to urge the federal government to begin surveying and selling the area's real estate. It wasn't the first time he had written the president on this subject. "In my last to you, I took the liberty of drawing your attention to the benefits that would result . . . by bringing into market those tracts of country lately acquired." He framed his argument in terms of national defense:

> *I am so deeply impressed with the importance of this subject that I*
> *cannot forego the present opportunity of again bringing it to your*
> *view . . . the land can be brought into market, within a very short time,*
> *which will immediately give to that section of the country a strong and*
> *permanent settlement of American citizens, competent to its defense.*

Alabama, Jackson knew, was about to become a separate territory as Mississippi became a state. Did the new president need a surveyor for the new territory? Jackson suggested one. John Coffee would be an excellent choice for northern Alabama, the area that included Muscle Shoals.

In a letter to Coffee six weeks later, Jackson spoke of the new country not as a bulwark of defense but as a business opportunity:

> *I wrote to Genl Parker . . . and farther added, that I was determined,*
> *to engage in purchasing or entering lands for any Individual or*
> *company, on the following terms . . . that I would . . . purchase & enter*
> *the amount, at my own expence, having one third of the land so*
> *purchased or entered.*

It appeared that Jackson was aspiring to help speculators buy land, expecting to receive a share of the real estate in return.

He could not do this right away. It would take time for President Madison's administration to assume formal possession of the Cherokee land, survey it, and establish the mechanisms to auction it. But Jackson found a way to move more swiftly than the government. Since Indians remained on the land for the time being, he dealt directly with Chero-kees to take temporary ownership of a piece of prime real estate. It was the great plantation once operated by John Melton, the reputed river pirate at Muscle Shoals.

Melton had recently died, leaving his half-Cherokee son holding the plantation, and it was from the son that Jackson and a partner bought the right to use it. Jackson was free to exploit it until federal surveyors got around to subdividing it two years later. Jackson's overseer moved into Melton's old house and used about sixty enslaved people to grow crops of cotton and corn. The writer Anne Royall visited the plantation in 1818; she described walking a field "white with cotton and alive with negroes," on high ground that seemed "suspended between heaven and earth," with a view of islands in the river that seemed like "floating meadows." The writer noticed signs of pain along with the beauty. A white boatman informed her that he had lost his Cherokee wife. When the Cherokee land cession was announced, his wife abruptly joined a group of Cherokees going to live in the west. Although as a mixed couple they probably could have remained together, she no lon-ger wanted to stay, and he was not willing to go. The boatman chased her down the river in a canoe, and gave her a final tearful embrace.

Now and again Andrew Jackson stopped by Melton's Bluff, and his letters afterward were uncharacteristically happy. "I was at the Bluff Two days & nights, Major Hutchings deserves a Meddle," he said of his overseer. "He has the finist Prospect of a good crop I ever saw, his cot-ton far excels any crop I have seen." The soil and climate of the Tennes-see Valley proved ideal for growing cotton, and world demand for cotton was soaring.

A few calculations suggest what this meant for Jackson. To make a profit, after feeding their slaves and shipping their crops to market, southern planters generally needed to sell cotton for 10–15 cents a pound. During the war cotton dropped below 12 cents, and sometimes could not be sold at all. But when peace returned, prices climbed.

Cotton reached 32 cents by late 1816. The price in some cities hit 35 cents in July 1817, the month that Jackson described his crop worth a medal.

Tennessee Valley soil could produce far more pounds of cotton per acre than land farther east. While it is not known how many acres were under cotton cultivation at Melton's Bluff that year, the sixty field hands could probably have picked six hundred acres at an absolute minimum. A conservative estimate gives a sense of the bounty: even if only three hundred of the acres were used for cotton, even if yields per acre were somewhat less than the maximum, and even if Jackson sold for some- what less than the peak price, the profit for Jackson and his overseer from that single year's cotton crop, on that single plantation, would have exceeded $35,000, which in 1817 was an income for a prince. President Monroe's salary was $25,000. Jackson was wealthy before 1817 in terms of property, but like many westerners he was cash-poor. Commanding troops in 1814, he'd scribbled a letter to his friend James Jackson in Nashville, asking him to send $300 for spending money, though he wasn't sure he had it on account. "If I have not that sum in the Bank," Jackson added, "you . . . must endorse for me." From 1817 onward, the land and the cotton of the Tennessee Valley promised to transform his financial situation. It was in 1819 that Andrew and Rachel Jackson gave up living in their two-story log house at the Hermitage. They began building the mansion that, with expansions and renovations over many years, would grow into the magnificent home that still stands today, with a white colonnaded front that awed approaching visitors. The old log house was cut down to a single floor and converted into slave quarters.

Visiting Melton's Bluff again in September 1817, Jackson contem- plated acquiring more land. He sent a letter to John Coffee, who had been appointed the federal surveyor just as Jackson recommended. "Let me see you as I pass," Jackson wrote, "and I would be glad [if] you could bring with you the survey of the 3rd. Township & 8th. range—and that including cold water or spring creak—I have but little doubt, but something can be done at the sales—on which subject I wish to see you." Federal land offices divided territory into a grid; the "3rd. Township & 8th. range" would have been near Melton's Bluff, while "cold water or spring creak" was the area he had urged Coffee to make sure was included when he "ran the line" to define the Creek land cession.

In 1818 he stopped by Melton's Bluff again to watch the harvest of another crop of cotton; prices late that year climbed a few cents higher than the year before, so the harvest meant another $35,000 if not far more. The slaves had to hurry to gather in the crop, because surveyors were busy dividing the property into city blocks for a new town. The town never amounted to much, but the land boom was only beginning.

The very best place for a town, Jackson believed, was at the foot of Muscle Shoals: the head of easy navigation, and the place where Jackson's military road crossed the river, *and* where he had urged the government to locate an arsenal. He had written his friend John Coffee back in 1817 to help spread the word. He urged the federal surveyor to send on advice to the president about possible new town sites. There should be a town at Muscle Shoals; it "will become one of the largest towns in the western country—here will capital concentrate itself—and it will become the *Nashville* of the Tennessee."

Up until that time there was only one significant white settlement in northern Alabama: Huntsville, upstream from Muscle Shoals. It was built around the Big Spring, a scenic source of fresh water, but was still a rude frontier town. John Coffee, pausing there during the war, dismissed it with a single sentence to his wife: "I am yet confined at this loathsome place."

In early 1818 Coffee rode again to that loathsome place. He found conditions even less appealing. Hundreds of men were converging on the town, overloading the local taverns—log cabins that were part bar, part restaurant, and part hotel. Food was so scarce that prices soared, and some could not find it at any price. Yet the threat of starvation could not keep men away, for Huntsville was to be the location of a federal land sale. The register of deeds noted that "many gentlemen from the Eastern States (very considerable capitalists too) have arrivd. in this Country," some accompanied by slaves.

The land office for northern Alabama occupied a log cabin in Huntsville. Until this year only a little Tennessee Valley land had gone on the market, commanding ordinary frontier prices of about $2 an acre on average. February 1818 promised to be different. The auctioneer was about to begin selling close to a million acres. Witnesses recorded signs of excitement they had never experienced before. Buyers formed coalitions to avoid bidding against each other, but when the auctions began, their efforts collapsed. Prices for some tracts soared from the minimum $2 an acre up to $50. And then $70 an acre. And then $78.

Returning from a land sale, Coffee wrote Jackson: "The prices have surpassed any ever known in the U.S. heretofore." He believed the prices also surpassed reason, and Coffee bought no property at first. In later rounds of auctions, prices subsided. The quality of land varied, the cartels regrouped to limit competition, and each new round of land sales increased the supply of available property. Yet prime land continued to sell for many times its price before the bubble, spurred by easy terms of payment and the incredible price of cotton. Millions of dollars poured into the land office. The madness for real estate even infected the receiver of public money. He was supposed to be forwarding the land payments to Washington, but fell months behind, until his superiors slowly realized he had failed to forward some $80,000. He had been making bogus sales to himself, recording phantom down payments for land in his own name.

John Coffee waited patiently through the frenzy, and settled in to steady buying when he judged the price was right. In the years that followed, the federal surveyor's name appeared on federal patents for more than fifteen thousand acres. Sometimes his name appeared alone, and sometimes with those of other men who appeared to be joint investors. Sometimes in the crowds at the auction, or in the taverns and houses around town, he did business with a familiar face from Nashville— James Jackson, long-standing associate of both Coffee and Andrew Jackson and apparently richer than either. James Jackson's name would eventually appear, singly or with others, on federal patents for twenty-two thousand acres. These were the two men who in 1816 had moved to quash rumors that they, along with Andrew Jackson, were planning to speculate in the newly won Indian lands.

Andrew Jackson's friends purchased some of their acreage with Andrew Jackson. Often one man would be recorded as the "assignee" of others, typically meaning that he was designated to purchase the land on behalf of a partner or partners. Presumably when Jackson was "assignee," he was taking a portion of land for himself as he had said back in 1816 that he would. From early 1818 onward, Coffee, James Jackson, and Andrew Jackson were all members of a business partnership "to purchase or enter lands in the Alabama Territory." Other partners included John Donelson, Andrew Jackson's brother-in-law, and a group of Philadelphia investors. It is difficult to determine exactly how much land the men bought or sold together, but an analysis of federal records suggests that an absolute minimum of 6,700 acres was bought for the partnership, and possibly much more.

Sometimes too Jackson acted on his own. When another round of sales began in November, cheers echoed through Huntsville: Jackson himself was standing in the crowd, his unmistakable figure the shape of his cane, with his mass of hair making him loom even higher over his fellow men. He was planning to bid on property around Coldwater Creek at Muscle Shoals: "Section 33, Township 3 south, Range 11 west." It was, as Andrew Jackson noted in a letter, "on the military road" that General Jackson had built. When the plot came up for sale, Jackson entered the minimum bid, and out of respect for the national hero, no one else raised his hand.

This section I bought at two dollars per acre, no person bidding against me and as soon as I bid off, hailed by the unanimous shouts of a numerous & mixed multitude—This on the eve of my retireing from all Public appointment, I am compelled to say was gratifying as it was an approval of my official acts.

Given the range of land values at the time, the square mile was instantly worth thousands of dollars more than Jackson paid for it—probably tens of thousands. He used it for some years as a farm, known as the Big Spring plantation, and sometimes lived there for a month at a time. "I am determined to push that farm for a livelihood," he wrote in 1822, while giving instructions to install a cotton gin. That same year he advertised a $50 reward for a slave who escaped from there. In 1823 he personally led the effort to capture three more escaped slaves, and had to put two of the men in irons, a step he said he regretted.

His square mile on the south side of the river was eventually expanded to include adjoining property. Jackson also bought land on the north side of the river—land under his own name at a place called Evans Spring, as well as three additional tracts in the name of Andrew Jackson Hutchings, an orphaned relative of Rachel's who had come to live at the Hermitage alongside the adopted son Andrew Jackson Jr., as well as the adopted Indian Lyncoya. Hutchings was a minor at the time of the land purchases in his name. At least one of those tracts became Jackson's third plantation in the valley, while others may have been used for farming or speculation or both.

It is hard to prove what role, if any, Jackson played in the land purchases by another relative. More than twenty-two hundred acres were purchased under the name of William Donelson, Rachel Jackson's nephew. William Donelson was also the registered name for the purchaser of thirteen town lots in Coldwater, the former Indian village at the bottom of Muscle Shoals.

Not only were Jackson and his friends and relations buying land near Muscle Shoals, his friends were colonizing it. John Coffee moved from Nashville to a new plantation just north of the Tennessee River, which he would call Hickory Hill. James Jackson relocated from Nashville to a plantation near Coffee's, which he called the Forks of Cypress. James Jackson's property became the apotheosis of southern plantation life, with a grandeur that can still be sensed amid its ruins today. His house stood on high ground, surrounded on all four sides by colonnades some thirty feet high. From the colonnades he could look down on his fields and horse track. The slaves who worked the plantation over the years included an ancestor of Alex Haley, the twentieth-century author of *Roots*, a famous narrative of slavery.

James Jackson and John Coffee also realized the potential for founding a city at Muscle Shoals. Early in 1818 they were among a group of businessmen who formed the Cypress Land Company, which purchased land near their future plantations. John Coffee arranged to lay out a street grid, which quickly became the city of Florence. The key for land speculators was to buy land from the government at an affordable price, often by collaborating with other bidders to reduce competition, and then quickly resell the land at a profit. The Cypress Land Company succeeded: it paid $85,000 for the land and quickly resold it (in half-acre town lots) for $229,000. Florence included a ferry across the Tennessee River, and it straddled Andrew Jackson's military road. In this venture Andrew Jackson was no more than a minor stockholder, but he obtained his share of tribute—buying five town lots in his own name at what appeared to be bargain prices, and gaining shares of quite a few more town lots. He remained involved in Alabama real estate for at least a decade: as late as 1829, when Jackson was about to take office as president, a document showed John Coffee acting as Jackson's "attorney in fact" in Florence, receiving security on an overdue debt by taking the title of a Florence man's home.

Having added to his fortune and his friends' fortunes while pursuing his national security goals, Jackson then relied on his friends while attending to further matters of national security. In the fall of 1818—the same year he bought Muscle Shoals land—Jackson negotiated a treaty with the Chickasaws to buy West Tennessee and the western end of Kentucky. He concluded the treaty by promising to pay a massive bribe. The payoff could not be made without proper financing, so the general's friend James Jackson provided what was necessary: he advanced $20,000 to buy a strip of land from a Chickasaw leader, hoping to keep the land for himself. A journal written by the federal negotiators described the massive payment as a "doceur," or sweetener. In the end the federal government took the land and repaid James Jackson's $20,000, but the Irish immigrant seemed to take it all in stride. He later bought some of the land yet again from the government. Once established at Florence, James Jackson was elected to the Alabama legislature, and was among the leaders throwing the new state's early and crucial support to a presidential candidate in the election of 1824: Andrew Jackson.

Jackson and his beneficiaries probably did not imagine they were doing anything more unseemly than using their resources and connections. In fairness it must be said that they paid for their land, and risked their money on the purchases. Their land lost some of its value after cotton prices crashed in 1819. But no one person had done more to create the land bubble than General Jackson, and when the sales began, no one could have had more inside information about the best land to buy than his friend and partner John Coffee, who had it surveyed at federal expense.

A surprising aspect of Jackson's real estate dealings is that he had time for them at all. His life was accelerating. A biography authored by his former military aides was published in 1817, deepening his fame. He was also continuing to direct military operations in the South, including some that led to land acquisitions even grander than those in Alabama. In 1818—in between Alabama land transactions—Jackson assembled the latest of his improvised armies and sent it southward. Its instructions were to cross outside the legal boundaries of the United States,

and chastise marauding Indians who were based in Spanish Florida—
"chastise" in the way that Jackson sometimes used the word, to mean
killing. His targets were Seminoles, a mix of Florida natives and refugees from the Red Stick rebellion. Jackson entered West Florida in
March. Then he conquered it. Ignoring written orders to concentrate
on Indians and stay away from Spanish forts, Jackson captured Pensacola, ran up the American flag, installed a governor, and started collecting taxes.

Fearing that the invasion could cause war with Spain, President
James Monroe ordered Jackson to withdraw. Congress investigated the
general for usurping the constitutional power of Congress to declare
war, but Jackson's adventure worked out brilliantly. Concerned though
they were about trampling the Constitution—"to the support of which,"
the Founding Father in the White House gently reminded Jackson, "my
public life has been devoted"—Americans really wanted Florida. Jackson's invasion helpfully demonstrated that Spain could not defend it.
Within a year the Spanish government agreed to sell the entire future
state. Not wanting Jackson's adventure to interfere with this purchase,
President Monroe doctored the official record. The president wrote
Jackson a remarkable letter, warning that the general's official reports
of his invasion could be politically damaging. He instructed Jackson to
"correct" his reports, retroactively changing his reasons for taking Pensacola so that it would seem the Spanish were to blame. "Your letters [to
Washington] were written in haste, under the pressure of fatigue &
infirmity," Monroe said, feeding Jackson the necessary excuse for making corrections.

Monroe could not protect Jackson from all criticism. A familiar
rumor spread—that Jackson and his friends were profiting from real
estate he conquered. Once again, there were facts behind the rumor. A
collection of Jackson's associates—friends, relatives, former soldiers—
had banded together to buy Pensacola real estate in the winter of 1818.
They managed to buy Florida land just *before* Jackson invaded, which
was just in time to see if its value might soar after an American

conquest. Senate investigators heard this story, and their official report included a veiled reference to it. Andrew Jackson was furious, describing one of his critics in the Senate as a "hypocritical lying puppy," and his anger was likely justified. The Senate produced no evidence that Jackson's motive for taking Florida was real estate speculation. He had seized Pensacola because he wanted it, as many Americans had for years. But if it was unlikely that General Jackson took Pensacola for his friends' real estate consortium, a subtly different scenario was plausible. It was possible that Jackson's friends knew in advance of his intention to take Florida, and adroitly positioned themselves to profit. They were certainly close enough to Jackson to learn his plans. A leader of the Pensacola enterprise was John Donelson, Andrew Jackson's business partner and brother-in-law. Donelson went to Florida to make his marvelously timed real estate investments while carrying a letter of introduction from Andrew Jackson. Jackson's friends and relations never denied what they called their "Pensacola speculation," nor did they deny that Jackson helped them. They denied only that Jackson had any financial interest in the partnership. They said he helped out of "friendly motives."

In his abiding interest in land, Andrew Jackson was a reflection of his country as well as his time. The settlement of land quite literally underlay the entire project of building the United States. But Jackson's acute sensitivity to rumors about his real estate business revealed another layer of the story. While the speculator was not necessarily immoral or corrupt—the risks he took spurred development, and left behind prosperous and lovely cities like Florence—speculation was a morally fraught enterprise. The speculator obtained land cheaply and sold it more expensively to common people. That was what made rumors about Jackson's land dealings dangerous: they threatened his developing political persona as the champion of the common man. Had all the facts been known, the public would have seen that Jackson selectively obeyed orders, pushed laws to the limit, trafficked in inside information, and took advantage of his official position and connections. He shaped his real estate investments to complement his official duties, and performed his official duties in a way that benefited his real estate interests. Jackson, with his naturally suspicious cast of mind, would have had no trouble perceiving something corrupt had he seen any rival conducting business the way he did with his friends.

Once he began running for president, Jackson's political enemies began questioning his land deals, but they never got the goods. A pamphlet during the 1828 campaign proposed to investigate the 1818 Chickasaw treaty and the $20,000 bribe, but failed to report damning evidence. Of other transactions there was no longer an original record to investigate. It was inherently hazardous to store paper records in wooden buildings on a frontier lit by fire. On December 14, 1827, just before the start of the presidential election year, fire consumed the building containing the offices of the Cypress Land Company, which built the city of Florence. Although Jackson's friends later reconstructed what they believed the accounts to be, all the original records in the office were destroyed.

PART FOUR

Young Prince

1820–1828

Eleven

This Unexpected Weapon
of Defence

Several times in his life John Ross had reason to send letters to Andrew Jackson. One occasion came in June 1820, when General Jackson was still based in Nashville, with authority over military affairs in the South. Ross wrote the letter from his home, which stood by a spring in a little settlement known as Rossville. The U.S. map would have shown the house just inside the northern boundary line of Georgia, about 150 miles southeast of Nashville. The Indian map showed that Rossville stood a few miles from the Tennessee River, the current boundary of the Cherokee Nation.

The house said a lot about Ross. While Andrew Jackson the orphan had left his hometown behind to start anew in the West, Ross had grown up surrounded by his relatives, as a kind of frontier prince. At age thirty he was living not many miles from his birthplace, in a settlement named for his family. He was sharing this solid house with his wife, Quatie, and their steadily increasing brood of children. It was a dogtrot house, meaning the first floor consisted of two large rooms separated by a breezeway. The second floor stretched the length of the house, which had the long and comfortable look of a lodge, with a

chimney at either end. The furnishings were solid. Maybe even then
Ross was sleeping in a bed like the one he was believed to use in later
years, with an elaborately carved headboard as tall as a man. Having
arrived at home late one night in June, he'd fallen into bed for a night's
rest before he turned to his correspondence.

Rossville Cherokee Nation
June 19th 1820

Sir
   I have the honor of informing you that I arrived here last evening.

Ross used up a line or two before getting around to business. He was
wise to write carefully. He was informing General Jackson of his effort
to do something that, in the long term, was the opposite of what the
general wanted: pushing white settlers off Cherokee soil.

I have been induced to accept of the command of the Cherokee Light
horse ordered into service by the Honble. Secry. of War, for the removal
of Intruders off Indian lands on the Northern frontier of this nation.

By the "Northern frontier" Ross meant the legal boundary between
Cherokee land and what he called the whiteside. Settlers were crossing
the Tennessee River into Cherokee territory—asserting the white map
and ignoring the Indian map. Cherokees had gained the federal government's agreement that it would evict these "Intruders," by force if
necessary, but the government did not act. In particular General Jackson did not act. "I have no troops within three hundred miles of the
cherokee nation," he complained when asked for help in early 1820. The
general said his orders from Washington called for him to concentrate his
troops elsewhere; the sale of Florida was not yet consummated, and he
wanted to be ready for anything.

   Having served under the general's command, Ross probably knew
what to think of Jackson's explanation. Jackson would have reinter-

preted his orders had it suited his strategic purposes. But in this matter of the intruders on Cherokee land, General Jackson declared that he must strictly follow instructions. He could do nothing except "talk big," sending a note threatening the intruders with arrest, and hoping that bluster would scare them off. Jackson's hesitation was even more awkward because the intruders had ignored a January first deadline to depart or face consequences. Jackson said he would attend to the problem as soon as he could spare troops from work on a military road. There were bridges to be repaired. Shrubbery must be cleared. The "shrubing" work was "indispensible," Jackson stressed. In the meantime, Jackson suggested that the Cherokees employ their own force to remove white settlers. This was the Cherokee Light Horse, a company of lightly armed cavalry, for which John Ross was a natural choice as commander, having military experience, a calm temperament, and the ability to speak the white man's tongue. Cherokees had the law on their side but didn't know what would happen when they turned their guns on white men.

> On the 17th inst. the Detachment was ordered out on duty under my command. The first object presented itself was a place occupied by a man (Atkinson) who had officially threatened opposition.

Atkinson was a man who had moved his family across the river to a spot within a day's ride of Rossville. There was no doubt he was encroaching. The Tennessee was an unmistakable border. Just as surely, the settler regarded the land as his own, having labored to improve it.

"There has been threats of opposition breathed from almost every quarter," Ross wrote. With that in mind, his men on horseback carefully approached the Atkinson farm, weapons at the ready. But no shots rang out.

> On our arrival to the spot, it was found evacuated. The crop was ordered to be distroyed.

Ross, the short man on horseback, signaled some of his troops to dismount. They began to set Atkinson's abandoned food stores on fire. Ross kept his eye on the edge of the woods, waiting for any sign of the "threatened opposition." Atkinson was out of sight but not necessarily gone. Ross studied the abandoned farm—the empty house, the quiet fields. The family seemed to have fled quickly, having left their live-stock behind. Sheep bleated and geese honked as the flames began to rise.

Three years of maneuvering had led up to this moment when Chero-kees tried to police their land while General Jackson stood back. Dur-ing those three years Jackson believed he was making arrangements for *Cherokees*, not white intruders, to evacuate the Cherokee Nation. His efforts did not succeed—but they helped to explain both his reluctance to protect the Cherokees and the Cherokees' increasing determination to defend themselves.

Jackson's treaty with the Cherokees in 1817—the same one that captured former Cherokee land that became Florence, Alabama, with-out making any payment for it—contained other provisions, designed to obtain still more land over time. In fact it included a mixture of incen-tives that "will give us the whole country in less than two years," as Jackson predicted in a letter to John Coffee. Individual Cherokees would be invited to relocate voluntarily, moving westward to join the small band of Cherokees who had been living across the Mississippi and up the Arkansas River since 1808. Each Cherokee who agreed to the move would receive transportation, a rifle, a blanket, assorted sup-plies, and western land. No Cherokees would remain on their ancestral land, Jackson believed, "except those prepared for agricultural persuits, civil life, & a government of laws."

It must have been frustrating for Jackson to realize as time passed that the vast majority of Cherokees weren't taking the deal. They hated his treaty. It was not "Just," a concept that meant as much to Cherokees as it did to Jackson. The deal had been negotiated with a small group of Cherokee leaders, using Jackson's customary pressure tactics, and imposed over the protest of dozens of other leading figures. In 1819, finding Cherokees still in place, the government negotiated yet another treaty, purchasing still more land, and including provisions designed to peel away individual Cherokees. Some would receive individual plots of land. Some accepted; yet both treaties intensified Cherokee debate about how they could improve their governance and avoid being sucked into such land cessions. A resolution grew among tribal leaders that the territorial concessions in the 1819 treaty should be the last they ever made.

It was also in 1819 that John Ross boldly wrote a letter to President James Monroe. Amid a few flourishes of deference toward the president (Ross appealed for "the interposition of your Fatherly hand") the rising Cherokee diplomat complained of the government's "evil" tendency to call assemblies of Indian leaders and demand territory with no notice. Ross said he hoped "the Government will now strictly protect us from the intrusions of her bad citizens and not solicit us for more land—as we positively believe the comfort and convenience of our nation requires us to retain our present limits."

This "positive belief" lay behind Ross's order in 1820 that the Cherokee Light Horse should begin its mission by torching the Atkinson farm. But another aspect of Ross's thinking shaped what happened next. He was capable of understanding his antagonist's point of view, and this empathy made him reluctant to go to extremes.

As his men set aflame the food stores at the farm, Ross had been waiting for the response—the sound of hooves, the gunshot from the woods. But when at length he saw figures approaching, it was not a party of white gunmen. It was one man, one woman, and some children.

Atkinson came across the river with his wife & family to defend it, not by the force of powder & lead, but by the shedding of tears, this

*unexpected weapon of defence had more effect on the minds of the men,
than if he had resorted to the measures threatened. . . .*

*His conviction of error & pitiful acknowledgements &c &c
induced me to permit him to recross the river to the whiteside
unmolested with a few sheep & geese—his crop was all distroyed.*

Ross watched Atkinson go away, driving his livestock before him. It was probably all he owned. Though the strategy of gaining great strips of land for white settlement was a central project of the frontier elite, illegally occupying Indian land was a job for the poor. Not just any farmer would risk his life, labor, and possessions to improve land that might be snatched back. This white farmer had probably taken Cherokee property because he couldn't afford the abundant real estate on sale nearby in Alabama. Atkinson did not even have the support of relatives or other white Tennesseans. Nobody had rallied to help defend his farm. Surely his poverty was evident to Ross as soon as his weeping family appeared.

A few years earlier, Ross had denounced "the conduct of the malitious and lawless class of our white Brethren on our frontier our property frequently stolen our lands forcibly occupied & the blood of Country people spilt all in cold blood & unprovoked." But now, finding himself with power over one such land grabber, he could summon no wrath. He showed as much mercy as circumstances allowed, and went home. Delegating a lieutenant to oversee his men's next moves, he rode away from the Light Horse for a few days, returning to Rossville, where he could write his report to General Jackson in his two-story cabin of his ancestors.

Atkinson's sorrow and submission left Ross feeling optimistic about other white intruders. "I am induced to believe they will mostly cooperate like Mr. Atkinson," he wrote, but here he was wrong. Later that summer, other settlers would resist the Cherokee Light Horse, assembling a little army of about seventy. Their force was strong enough that the Cherokee horsemen decided to hold off their assault until federal troops at last arrived. But for now Ross was able to report his mission successfully begun.

I have the honor to be Sir, yr. vry. obt. Hble. Servt.

Jno Ross.

While Jackson's reply to this note, if any, has not survived, it is easy to calculate from other letters what Jackson thought of it. He almost certainly disapproved. He would never have let Atkinson walk away. Jackson believed it was a mistake to allow white squatters to depart with their livestock. The squatters would simply wait until the troops had moved on, and then return. While Jackson showed little enthusiasm for removing white settlers, he had none at all for doing a job badly, or for giving anyone a chance to flout his will. If white settlers were to be removed at all, the job should be thoroughly and irresistibly done. Once *his* troops finally arrived, he would order them to hold white settlers and deliver them to the nearest civilian lawman for prosecution.

Here was a subtle but significant difference between the two men who would contend over the years that followed. Andrew Jackson could show mercy and respect. He could have empathy for others; he could never have succeeded as a politician otherwise. But these qualities were governed by his ruthlessness. He must never lose a fight. He must always uphold his authority. Ross, too, proved to be fiercely and stubbornly competitive. But there were moments when Ross let his stubbornness give way to generosity and, Ross hoped, to justice.

Twelve

Ominous of Other Events

Running off squatters was an accomplishment, but Ross next needed to run off an entire state. The bulk of Cherokee land lay within Georgia, which was demanding control of what it considered its own real estate. It was the Georgians above all who insisted that the old ambiguity must end, that the Indian map must vanish in favor of the white man's map. By the 1820s Georgians were beginning to get their hands around a lever that could be used to expel the Cherokees.

Georgia's leverage grew out of the strange and convoluted history of Georgia itself. It was the last of the thirteen colonies to be established, founded in 1733, more than a century after the start of British settlement in Virginia and New England. Established as a refuge for debtors, it instead became a state of slave plantations, where the number of black workers was growing so rapidly that it approached the number of free white residents. The bulk of the populace was concentrated near the Atlantic coastline and along the lower reaches of the rivers. Farther inland, the colony of Georgia was a work of imagination, defined purely by mapmakers rather than by any actual governance or development.

Georgia as first imagined had a much different shape than the Georgia that appears on maps today. The British decreed that the northern and southern borders of the colony consisted of two straight lines, which stretched westward for as far as the mind could conceive, crossing every river, valley, and mountain "in direct lines to the South seas." These lines formed a strip of land that crossed the entire continent to the Pacific, even though white men had scarcely seen the territory, other colonial powers claimed it too, and Indians controlled it. Georgia's claim was so extravagant that Georgians could not even describe it. As late as 1798 they approved a constitution declaring that the northern boundary of the state would be determined by drawing a straight line westward, starting from the point where a stream branching off from the Tugaloo River met the boundary of South Carolina, *unless the stream never touched South Carolina,* in which case the boundary would be determined another way. The border was an either/or hypothetical, made necessary by a boundary dispute. On the southern side of the state, a map from 1799 included a blank space labeled with the words "These parts are little known."

Such maps did not assure the Georgians title to the land. Even Europeans, who made the rules of colonialism, could not articulate any principle by which they should own a giant strip of a continent because they said so. Rather than strictly indicating Georgia's control of real estate, the colonial map marked off a sphere of influence where Georgia colonists were supposed to be able to trade or do business without interference from other colonies or rival European powers. The real estate within those areas was understood to be owned by the natives unless they were displaced by treaty, purchase, or war. But the maps of British territory came to mean more than that. A map made by a Virginian in 1755 showed numerous British colonies, including Georgia, stretching right across North America, each of them tinted different colors like stripes in a rainbow flag. The map became powerfully influential, inspiring Americans with the idea that a whole continent was already theirs, needing only to be occupied. It was the eighteenth-century equivalent of a doctored photograph, a projection of a notion rather than of reality.

After the Treaty of Paris secured American independence in 1783, speculators acted on the notion. They began buying and selling rights to the Georgia backcountry, the distant lands between the East Coast and the Mississippi River. Investors formed companies to deal in land that had not yet been obtained from the Indians and that in some cases was not even clearly within the United States as its boundaries were drawn at that time. Federal authorities opposed such enterprises, insisting that they would create pressure to snatch Indian land and provoke wars. "The government is determined to exert all its energy for the patronage and protection of the rights of the Indians," wrote Thomas Jefferson, the first secretary of state, in 1791. Georgians shrugged, and in 1795 sold four companies the rights to thirty-five million acres. State legislators were given shares in the mind-boggling enterprise in exchange for supporting it; this became known as the Yazoo fraud, named after a distant river in the countryside that was to be put up for sale. Chastened by such revelations, in 1802 the Georgians surrendered their western lands for good, ceding to the federal government what became the bulk of Mississippi and Alabama.

In the compact with Washington, the Georgians managed to slip in a special provision that proved decisive in the years to come. This provision said that the newly shrunken state must be cleared of Indians. The federal government undertook to "extinguish the Indian title" to all lands inside the state of Georgia as soon as the title could be "peaceably obtained, on reasonable terms." This meant that the Indians could not be removed until they agreed to it, but Georgia leaders chose to interpret the compact as a sacred commitment to move out the Indians no matter what. This commitment was imaginary, rather like the map of Georgia—but as with the map, Georgians set out to make it real. This was the lever they could use to dislodge the native population.

Georgians were so determined to remove the Indians that some regarded even Andrew Jackson as a laggard. Jackson's 1814 treaty after Horseshoe Bend had removed the Creeks from a large part of Georgia, but Georgia politicians deemed this an injustice, since Jackson allowed the Creeks to maintain a portion of their territory. "The same treaty ought to have extinguished for Georgia the Indian claims to all the lands within her limits," complained a rising Georgia politician, George M. Troup. Instead, Georgia "was not noticed in it."

In early 1824 a Cherokee delegation including John Ross visited Washington. The federal government, honoring its duty to Georgia, made an offer to buy Cherokee land. The Cherokee diplomats, honoring their duty to their people, refused to sell. Georgia's congressional representatives exploded in fury, and signed a bombastic letter to the federal government "insisting" on an "immediate fulfillment" of the government's "obligations." If the Cherokees would not sell, the government should simply "order" them out, said the Georgians. The Georgians implied that if Washington failed to act, Georgia would evict the Indians— nullifying federal authority and prompting a national crisis. A shocked President James Monroe called the letter an "insult" at the first of several cabinet meetings that were consumed in discussing it. To read accounts of those meetings is to imagine the frustrated Founding Father pushing the letter across the table for his cabinet secretaries to read for themselves. He called for "defiance" in response, although his reply became more moderate as Monroe and his aides drafted and edited. They did not want to provoke conflict with a state that described its sovereignty in terms that sounded like Georgia was an independent nation. (The governor was sometimes styled in official documents as "His Excellency, Governor and Commander in Chief of the Army and Navy of this State and of the Militia thereof.") The administration finally sent a letter that did no more than remind Georgia of federal efforts to follow what the compact actually said.

John Quincy Adams—son of President John Adams and a contender for the presidency himself—was present for these cabinet meetings in 1824, for he was secretary of state. He noted in his diary that President Monroe arrived at a moment of truth: "The President spoke of the compact as a very unfavorable bargain to the United States—as it certainly was." Georgians had received something for nothing. They'd signed away their claim to western land they had never effectively possessed. In return they'd washed their hands of the Yazoo fraud, collected a federal payout of $1.5 million, and obtained the Indian removal clause they were now using to bully the federal government. The compact was like a second Yazoo fraud.

Adams had some respect for Cherokees. They'd been working on him. John Ross, Major Ridge, and other visiting Cherokees regularly attended Mrs. Adams's Tuesday night social events. Mr. Adams found their "manners and deportment" to be no different "from those of well-bred country gentlemen. . . . They dress like ourselves," added Adams, except for a "young and very handsome man" who wore a "purfled scarf." The Cherokee leaders were prosperous, each worth $50,000–$100,000. Ridge, with his limited English, remained so quiet that Adams thought he did not speak the language at all, but Ross and others spoke well, and apparently took advantage of those Tuesday socials to feed Adams propaganda about Cherokees. "They are now, within the limits of Georgia, about fifteen thousand," Adams wrote—certainly an overestimate—"and increasing in equal proportion to the whites; all cultivators, with a representative government, judicial courts, Lancaster schools, and permanent property." Adams noted that the Cherokees "write their own State papers, and reason as logically as most white diplomatists . . . Ross is the writer of the delegation. They have sustained a written controversy against the Georgia delegation with great advantage."

Adams was present when the delegation paid a call on President Monroe. Ridge, the leader, made a few remarks in Cherokee. Ross understood enough Cherokee to interpret, with another leader, George Lowrey, there to pick up when Ross faltered. The president replied with "general expressions of kindness." Secretary Adams watched the Cherokees depart the Executive Mansion, most likely without telling them what was on his mind: Their improvement in civilization made them more threatening to the Georgians, not less, since it made them harder to dislodge. Adams had heard John C. Calhoun, the secretary of war, say as much in a cabinet meeting: "The great difficulty arises from the progress of the Cherokees in civilization," he said. Not *arises despite* Cherokee progress. Arises *from*.

The unresolved conflict made Adams uneasy, and the recalcitrant Cherokees bothered him less than the aggressive Georgians. Though the South's effort to secede from the union was decades in the future, Georgia politicians were already talking of their membership in the union as conditional, to be maintained only as long as Georgia's own definition of its sovereignty was honored. Something was happening in the South that the Massachusetts diplomat didn't fully understand, though he was prophetic enough to sense that calamity loomed. "I suspected this bursting forth of Georgia upon the Government of the United States was ominous of other events," he said.

Thirteen

The Taverns Were
Unknown to Us

Facing such powerful demands for Cherokee land, Ross knew he could not simply refuse. He must offer an alternative. Around the time of Georgia's political eruption in 1824, Ross joined with other Cherokees to write down a suggestion that contained a hint of humor, even mockery. The Cherokees said that if Georgia needed more land, it should forget about the Cherokee Nation and take over part of Florida.

He added that if the Cherokees were ever to come under state authority, it should be a state of their own. Ross proposed that Cherokees should someday "enter into a treaty with the United States, for admission as citizens under the form of a Territorial or State government." A year later, in 1825, Ross and two other leaders fleshed out this vision. If Cherokees remained where they were, "the day would arrive when a distinction between their race and the American family would be imperceptible; of such a change the nation can have no objection." Even racial distinctions could be overcome: "Complexion is a subject not worthy [of] consideration in the effectuation of this great object." The Cherokees would happily "extinguish" traditional culture "for the sake of civilization and preservation of existence. . . . The sooner this takes place the great stumbling block *prejudice* will be removed." In short they would change almost everything in order to preserve their rights to the land, and in the late 1820s they built up their political defenses with this vision in mind.

Preserving their land required a stronger Cherokee government. A stronger government required a better system of laws, so they made plans to draft a new constitution. John Ross was president of the constitutional convention, which chose to begin its work on a date whose symbolism nobody could miss: July 4, 1827. As presiding officer, Ross held the same position at the Cherokee constitutional convention that George Washington had held in the meetings that produced the U.S. Constitution forty years earlier, in 1787. Like Washington, Ross soon afterward became the first leader to be chosen under the basic law whose creation he had just overseen.

There was poetry in this parallel, since the Cherokee constitution was the ultimate achievement to grow out of Washington's civilization program. Ross and the Cherokees were committing an act of political jujitsu—taking the force of an opponent's blow and turning it against him. The Founding Fathers had offered civilization as a means to humanely pacify and displace the Indians; Cherokees accepted the offer and used it to strengthen themselves in place. The 1827 constitution claimed for Cherokees a permanent place in the American union, with inviolable borders under the auspices of the federal government, somewhat like the new territory of Florida or the new state of Alabama. When it became apparent what the Cherokees were doing, white leaders were shocked. Cherokees were acting as if federal Indian policy meant what it said, rather than what it actually meant.

The constitution was Ross's triumph, though it was also the culmination of a process stretching back before he could remember. A man who had been present for much of that process was by his side as they took the final step: Major Ridge, solid and imposing as his name. He personified a large part of the Cherokee story, for the Ridge embraced new ideas, turned them into Cherokee legislation, and enforced them over a span of decades. If anyone doubted John Ross's authenticity as an Indian leader, they could not doubt the Ridge, who was steeped in the old ways and never spent a day in a white man's school (although he also had a mixed-race ancestry). He was a veteran of old wars. He was a killer. He concluded there must be a better way, and demonstrated it.

A full-color portrait shows Major Ridge as he appeared around the years when the constitution was produced. Consciously or not, the painter rendered Ridge with the solidity and seriousness of a George Washington. Curly gray hair framed his broad face. He gazed a bit to the painter's left. He wore a coat, a vest, a high white collar, and a black cravat. He looked like a wealthy southern planter, which, by then, he was.

Ridge gave an account of his upbringing to Thomas McKenney, a federal Indian official, and the story demonstrated how far Ridge had come since his birth in 1771. His parents named him Nung-no-hut-tar-hee, roughly translated as "He who slays the enemy in the path." His father was a full-blooded Cherokee. His mother was half white and half Cherokee, though there was very little white cultural influence in the youth he described. White people were an external threat. His family lived in Tennessee, along the Hiwassee River, where white invaders were burning Cherokee villages during his youth. He was still very young when he became a refugee. His father loaded the family onto canoes and fled down the Hiwassee to the Tennessee River, and from there southwestward to safety.

His early education was accompanying his father on the hunt. Around the age of twelve he was taken to an aged war chief, who performed a ritual to dedicate the boy to the warrior's life. He scratched the boy bloody with a sharpened wolf bone, and then had him bathe in a stream. "I shall make you dreadful," the old man promised. Ridge lived up to the prediction. In 1788 Tennessee settlers murdered a beloved Cherokee chief, Old Tassel, who had approached them under a flag of truce. The atrocity prompted Cherokee raids of reprisal, and in hand-to-hand combat, the teenage Ridge killed a white man with a spear. This earned him the status of an Outacite, or man-killer. Later Ridge joined another party that attacked a white settlers' stockade, mounting such a sustained attack that the white defenders ran out of ammunition. The Cherokees slaughtered all the men and some of the women.

The name he assumed as an adult reputedly referred to something he had said while on the hunt. "I came along the top of the mountain," he informed other men when arriving in camp, and the expression evoked his lofty character. Invited in his twenties to become a representative to the Cherokee National Council, an important governing body, the Ridge gained the notice of older chiefs for his thoughtful speech. It was while serving in the council that he began the long campaign to ban the custom of blood revenge.

The Ridge championed this reform while retaining his old ferocity. After the Cherokee chief Doublehead sold tribal land north of the Tennessee River in the treaties of 1805 and 1806, the Ridge accepted the responsibility of delivering his punishment. He shot Doublehead in the jaw and left him for dead. Learning afterward that the wounded chief had slipped away, Ridge was part of a group of men who tracked him down and finished their task with a pistol, a tomahawk, and a spade. Seven years later Ridge was on the roll of the Cherokee Regiment, and was, as we have seen, among the Indians who paddled across the Tallapoosa, causing the chaos behind enemy lines that sparked Andrew Jackson's triumph at the Battle of Horseshoe Bend.

Much like Jackson, he blended his identity as a warrior with that of a gentleman farmer. A chronicler of the family speculates that his wife, known as Sehoya or Susanna, may have spurred him in this direction. She began by cultivating cotton, which allowed her, like other Cherokee women, to spin cloth. By the 1820s, the Ridge and Susanna were living on an elegant estate. Their white wood house had four brick fireplaces, verandas, a balcony, and thirty glass windows. Their orchards included apple, cherry, quince, plum, and 1,141 peach trees. Susanna no longer needed to pick cotton, since that work could be left to thirty slaves. The house was the headquarters of a business empire including a ferry, a toll road, and a popular trading post that Ridge ran as the senior partner of a young white man.

Ridge even made a profit from diplomacy. When the Creeks were forced into yet another negotiation to sell land, they asked Ridge for help. They relied on his knowledge of Washington and employed his son John Ridge as their interpreter. From the proceeds of the eventual land sale, the Creeks paid the Ridges, father and son, a breathtaking tribute totaling $25,000. Federal officials found the payment so unusual that they suspected corruption, although in a later era, the payment would simply have been described as a lobbying or consulting fee.

By the time of the drafting of the Cherokee constitution in 1827, Ridge and Ross were among the dominant political figures in the Cherokee Nation. Pathkiller, the elderly principal chief who had been the Cherokee Regiment's nominal leader, had died six months earlier. Death had also claimed Charles Hicks, his deputy, who had been tutoring Ross on Cherokee history. Of the remaining leaders, Ross and Ridge were particularly well positioned. Ross was the leader of the Cherokee National Council, or upper legislative body, while Ridge led the National Committee, or lower house. Ridge was the perfect ally for Ross—adept at the new ways but credible among those who clung to the old, and also credible among white men. Ridge was not literate in English: when he signed joint letters with Ross he affixed his mark, leaving no doubt which man had written the text. But Ross would have known that the mark was priceless. Should the two men ever part ways it would risk disaster. Ridge could turn his strengths against Ross, and make his own policy if he wanted.

Ross convened the constitutional convention at the new national capital, New Echota, which on the white man's map was in northern Georgia. It was named after an older Cherokee town that had been ceded for white settlement. Leaders first held an assembly at New Echota in 1819, and by 1825 had gone in for modern real estate development, dividing the settlement into a hundred one-acre lots. Although the nation would retain formal possession of the land, rights to its use could be bought and sold, and a map of the planned street grid did not radically differ from the principles used in John Coffee's 1818 map of Florence, Alabama. New Echota was never a grand capital—it was a village with a permanent population of fewer than a hundred, where even the main public buildings were made of wood—but among the typical log cabins of this frontier settlement was a scattering of frame houses, which according to a visitor from Connecticut "would be called respectable in Litchfield County & very decently furnished to be in any country & all new say built within 3 or [4] years." There was a main street sixty feet wide, and a public square covering two acres. A council house rose next to the square; it had two floors, one for each branch of the legislature, with simple wooden benches for the legislators. From the glass windows of the New Echota council house, it was possible to look across the square to the courthouse.

Twenty-one elected delegates and a secretary debated the constitution at New Echota. Most were mixed-bloods, whose partly white ancestry had deepened their familiarity with the white world and also, in some cases, opened doors to their education. (Mixed-bloods took disproportionate numbers of seats in the missionary schools.) The delegates had certainly been influenced by European-American legal traditions, Ross perhaps most of all. His education in republican government stretched back to his youth, when he grew up surrounded by books and newspapers acquired by his father. "From my earliest Boyhood in reading," he once recalled, he learned "reverence" for the U.S. government. "And after I advanced far enough to understand the beautiful system under which the Constitution of the United States was established, my reverence became more firmly confirmed."

The U.S. Constitution he revered included this preamble:

We the People of the United States, in Order to form a more perfect Union, establish Justice, insure domestic Tranquility, provide
for the common defence, promote the general Welfare, and secure
the Blessings of Liberty to ourselves and our Posterity, do ordain
and establish this Constitution for the United States of America.

Ross surely had this document on the table or in mind while drafting a Cherokee constitution.

We, the representatives of the people of the CHEROKEE NATION
in convention assembled, in order to establish justice, ensure tranquility, promote our common welfare, and secure to ourselves and
our posterity the blessings of liberty; acknowledging with humility
and gratitude the goodness of the sovereign Ruler of the Universe . . .
do ordain and establish this Constitution for the Government of the
Cherokee Nation.

The document completed over the next three weeks divided power
between three branches of government—the judiciary, the legislature,
and the executive. The right of a trial by jury "shall remain inviolate,"
and no citizen should be subjected to double jeopardy. Amid these
familiar provisions the drafters sprinkled nods to religion, rather as
some state constitutions did, starting with the preamble's expression of
gratitude to the "Ruler of the Universe." This was not surprising, since
Christian revivalism was sweeping the United States, and was making
additional progress among Cherokees. In 1810, one Christian mission
was at work among the Cherokees, and reported exactly one convert. In
1820, two missions reported forty-one converts. Over the next few
years, four missions—Moravian, Congregationalist, Methodist, and
Baptist—said they had won over about a thousand souls, and in the
single year of 1827, the year of the constitution's adoption, the missions
claimed six hundred more. Ross was relying on the missionaries for

another act of political jujitsu. Although they wanted to bring the word of God to Indians, Ross understood that they could transmit the views of Indians to the American people. They could educate white men about Indian progress. It was not by accident that a leading missionary, Samuel Worcester, was granted land to build a house at New Echota.

Not every Cherokee approved of a constitution that borrowed so much from white culture. As Ross strengthened the national government, local leaders lost power. As he pushed new cultural practices, traditionalists resisted. These traditionalists, under the leadership of a chief named White Path, never let their resistance fully burst into the open; a later scholar reported that they did not want to expose tribal divisions to white men. This may have been the reason that the modernists were able to meet the rebels late in June and gain their quiet acquiescence.

Maybe, also, the dissenters realized the central benefit of the constitution. Under this law there would be no repeat of 1775, when white speculators bought most of modern-day Kentucky for a houseful of trade goods; or of 1805 and 1806, when Doublehead sold much of Tennessee; or, for that matter, 1821, when some local chiefs allegedly conspired to sell Cherokee land in Alabama after corresponding with a friend of theirs, General Andrew Jackson. In each of these cases one or more Cherokee leaders freelanced agreements with outsiders. Now only one man would be in charge of Cherokee business with the United States: the principal chief, or chief executive, who had traditionally served for life but would now be elected to four-year terms by the legislature.

Whatever business the chief might conduct with the United States, it was not going to be a real estate transaction.

Article I, Sec. 1.

The boundaries of this nation, embracing the lands solemnly guaranteed and reserved forever to the Cherokee Nation by the Treaties concluded with the United States, are as follows; and

shall forever hereafter remain unalterably the same—to wit—
Beginning on the North Bank of the Tennessee River at the upper
part of the Chickasaw old fields. . . .

Surely as the delegates proofread this document, and read it aloud for
the delegates who were not literate, they must have noticed that the passage used the word "forever" twice. They must have liked the sound of
it. They left it that way.

The constitution had hardly been approved when the Cherokees had an
opportunity to test it. The men in New Echota that summer included a
representative of the federal government—General John Cocke, a Tennessee military officer and a veteran of Jackson's campaign against the
Creeks. Cocke was one of three commissioners who were bringing a
proposal from Washington. The federal government was offering to
buy half a million acres of Cherokee land in North Carolina, as well
as land for the digging of a canal. The commissioners invited Cherokee leaders to the federal Indian agency at Rattlesnake Springs, Tennessee, to discuss the government's proposal, and promised to pay "every
expense" of Indians who attended.

Ross and Ridge declined. Ross, as he had once told President Monroe, despised the federal practice of calling special meetings with little
notice. It allowed the government too much power to set the agenda.
He told the commissioners to wait until the next legislative session in
October 1827 in New Echota.

General Cocke and his fellow commissioners lost their cool.

*We are correctly informed that Mr. John Ross has used all of his
influence with the Nation to thwart the views of the United States.*

Or so they complained in a letter that was addressed to John Ross, the
very man they needed to win over. "You remark," they went on, that

you have invited our attendance on the day appointed for the meeting
of the approaching session of the General Council. Can you expect this
subterfuge will avail, when you know you have predetermined to reject
every proposition that we are authorized to make to the Cherokee
Nation?

Ross barely paused to deny the accusation, simply noting that Cocke
had failed to name his source of information. "We are sorry to discover
that you are ready to believe every unfavorable report respecting us." He
went on to answer another of the commissioners' arguments for a meeting at the Indian agency. The commissioners had said that Rattlesnake
Springs was perfectly capable of accommodating the Cherokees:

It is true there is no palace for the reception of a King or Emperor; but
there are four taverns in the vicinity of the Agency, and one at it,
where all the Committee and Council can be well accommodated, and
their expenses paid by us.

One could imagine Ross struggling to suppress a smile as he penned
his reply, professing to be mystified by the commissioners' sarcasm.

We do not understand the idea you intend to convey, in reference to a
palace for the reception of a King or Emperor, as the Cherokee Nation
are governed by neither, and we were not informed that you had
anticipated the arrival of any of the Crowned Heads from abroad.

Then came the final thrust.

As to the four taverns spoken of we assure you that they were unknown
to us.

Perhaps *you* are familiar with every shabby inn selling whiskey, Ross
was saying. *We* are not.

The commissioners had no choice but to meet the Cherokees in New Echota at the time John Ross had suggested, at which time their proposal to buy land was politely rejected.

> *In giving you this definitive reply, we do it with consideration and respect, uninfluenced by any Individual, but solely with the view of maintaining the interest of our nation.*
>
> *With great respect, we are politically your friends and brethren.*

Ross saved copies of all the correspondence. It would prove useful later.

Interlude:
Hero's Progress

1824–1825

Fourteen

Liberty, Equality, and True Social Order

T he U.S. Capitol, seat of the government Cherokees sought both to emulate and to outwit, was a different building in the 1820s than it is today. So white and perfect is the modern facade that a visitor might see no sign that the Capitol has been added to in the manner of an expanding family's rambling house. In the 1820s the white cast-iron dome was not even imagined. The architect of the Capitol had recently completed a smaller, simpler dome of copper that turned green when exposed to the weather.

The chamber of the House of Representatives was a gorgeous disaster, breathtaking to visit and terribly suited for its purpose. Redesigned after the British burned it in 1814, the room was roughly a half circle, with a high, arched roof—beautiful curvatures that complemented the semicircles of legislators' desks, and also caused the human voice to reverberate in maddening ways. A lawmaker might perfectly hear a whisper a hundred feet away, while understanding not a word of the speaker at the rostrum. An account of one speech in 1819 described a lawmaker drowned out by "walking and talking and coughing" as he "begged" in vain to be heard.

But certain events compelled people to fill the House and strain their ears. Such an event came on December 10, 1824. "At an early hour the galleries began to fill with spectators," a newspaperman reported,

> and soon after 11 o'clock, many ladies entered into the Hall, and took possession of the sofas and seats, which were appropriated for their reception.

So momentous was the occasion that women had been granted a rare dispensation, allowed not merely in the elevated gallery at the back of the hall, but on the House floor.

> A great number of additional seats soon became necessary; and, long before the hour appointed for the reception of the General, the House presented an exhibition of beauty and fassion which, we presume, has scarcely ever been equaled.

The "General" was the Marquis de Lafayette. During the American Revolution the French general had fought alongside General Washington. Wounded in battle, Lafayette fought on, and played a role at the Battle of Yorktown. Now, at age sixty-seven, he had returned to behold the country whose freedom he had helped to secure.

The House chamber was likely dim that day, as it was when Samuel F. B. Morse painted a picture of it. The future inventor of the telegraph began his career as an artist, and in 1822 rendered the House preparing for business. Lawmakers clustered near their seats, every man in a black coat and white shirt. A great brass chandelier was lowered from the ceiling so a man could set its lamps aflame. Beneath that chandelier on the day of Lafayette's 1824 visit, the House began its work by voting to invite the Senate to attend the event, though oddly it was a contested vote, 90–69. Representatives made room for senators at the desks, and then

> General La Fayette entered the House, supported on his right by
> Mr. Mitchell, the chairman of the select committee, and on his
> left by Mr. Livingston. . . . The General was then conducted to
> the sofa placed for his reception, when the Speaker addressed him.

Lafayette was in good health; he did not need to be "supported" on
either side by a member of the House. But no politician would have
missed the opportunity to be seen beside him. Cabinet secretaries and
diplomats leaned forward from their seats in the gallery, and all fell
silent to hear the welcoming remarks of the Speaker of the House, who
now stood behind the rostrum.

The Speaker was Henry Clay of Kentucky, one of the most remarkable men of the early American republic, who had been a dominant
force in Washington for more than a decade and was still well short of
fifty. Clay was born in 1777, the same year Lafayette arrived to fight
the British, and his remarks reflected Clay's place in a younger generation. "Few of the members who compose this body shared with you
in the War of our Revolution," Clay said, but everyone knew "the perils,
the sufferings, and the sacrifices which you voluntarily encountered."
This reference to generational differences fit into a generational drama
in which Clay was involved. James Monroe, the last of five Founding
Fathers to serve as president, was retiring. It was time for new leadership. Clay was a candidate in the presidential election of 1824. Since
none of the four candidates had won a majority of the electoral votes
that determined the winner, the Constitution said that the deadlock
must soon be broken, and the next president chosen, by the House—
this House, whose members sat in their semicircles facing Henry Clay.

Clay was a leader from the growing West, and author of economic
policies that came to be called the American System. He won so many
admirers during his long life that more than a dozen states across the
country would name a Clay County or Clay Township after him. But in
1824 he was not the only westerner on the ballot. Andrew Jackson was

a candidate, and though the counting was incomplete in early December, it was clear that the hero of New Orleans had amassed more electoral votes than anyone. He was poised to elbow Clay off the pinnacle of generational and sectional leadership.

Jackson was in Washington that December as a senator from Tennessee, and was almost certainly in the House chamber as Clay spoke. Of course, the two would show no sign of their confrontation. A presidential candidate was not supposed to campaign in public—but each man privately believed the other to be a menace. Their battles over many years would transfix the nation and influence its future, including its future treatment of Indians. Though the candidates did not debate Indian policy or anything else in 1824, it mattered who won. Clay had an ugly prejudice against Indians, but said they had rights and should not be removed without their consent. Jackson thought differently. He considered it a "farce" to make treaties with natives. They were subjects of the United States, who could be told what to do.

Clay missed none of the dramatic opportunities of introducing Lafayette. The French general, he said, had a chance to see what Americans had built upon his Revolutionary labor: "the forests felled, the cities built, the mountains leveled, the canals cut, the highways constructed, the progress of the arts, the advancement of learning, the increase in population—General . . . You are in the midst of posterity. Every where, you must have been struck with the great changes, physical and moral, which have occurred since you left us."

Lafayette had last seen a confederation of thirteen states along the Atlantic coast. Now the states numbered twenty-four, the United States controlled both banks of the Mississippi, and the newest state, Missouri, lay entirely west of it. Lafayette was on his way to see every one of those states, traveling by carriage and steamboat. Huge crowds met the old soldier, starting when his ship arrived in New York in August 1824. The New York crowd, estimated at fifty thousand people, was more than the entire population of the city in Revolutionary times. Now it was a metropolis swiftly approaching two hundred thousand. News of Lafayette's arrival spread to every part of the country, even frontier zones; an article on Lafayette appeared in the *Tuscumbian*, in the newly settled Tennessee Valley near Florence, Alabama.

Lafayette wanted to see everything. After arriving in New York, he dashed up to New England for a commencement at Harvard, where the library had twenty thousand books, an incredible collection for its time. Lafayette's secretary said Harvard's curriculum ranged from divinity and anatomy to "the Oriental languages"—not a surprise, since American seafarers were trading with China. Recently endowed chairs at the university focused on "Rhetoric and Eloquence," important as democratic politics developed, and the application of physical and mathematical sciences to "the useful arts," meaning business and industry. The profits generated by the useful arts were evident when Lafayette returned to New York, the commercial capital. He attended a celebration at Castle Garden, a fortress recently transformed into a place of entertainment, where hundreds danced cotillions beneath an "immense and splendid cut-glass chandelier." He moved about the eastern waterways on steamboats run by Cornelius Vanderbilt, a self-educated sailor turned ferryboat entrepreneur who was making himself the richest man in America. Vanderbilt boats and stagecoaches combined to hurry the elites between New York and Philadelphia on an early version of the route that would become the modern-day Northeast Corridor railroad line, and when Lafayette made the trip, he rode in a carriage with Vanderbilt at the reins. At Philadelphia, workers and artisans marched in parade: "three hundred weavers—one hundred and fifty rope-makers—one hundred shipbuilders—seven hundred mechanics," accompanied by "one hundred and fifty butchers" riding horses.

On a side trip up the Hudson River, Lafayette heard "the thunder of a cannon a thousand times repeated by the echoes" off the surrounding cliffs—the signal that they had arrived at West Point. The U.S. Military Academy was thriving under the leadership of superintendent

Sylvanus Thayer. Dedicated to creating a professional officer corps, the academy offered opportunity to youths like Robert E. Lee, whose prominent Virginia family was down on its luck. Farther up the Hudson, Lafayette glimpsed a portal to the expanding West: the Erie Canal, the almost-completed new route to the Great Lakes. He'd already seen a three-dimensional relief map of the canal on display in Manhattan, laid out on a table sixty feet long with water in the channel, lined by models of "houses, trees and animals."

The interior needed every connection it could get. Western life was harsh: typical was the story of Thomas Lincoln, one of many Kentuckians who lost their farmland to disputes over the title. Lincoln moved in 1816 to the brand-new state of Indiana, where establishing a farm required clearing the woods tree by tree on land that had only recently been cleared of Indians. By 1824, Lincoln's first wife was dead of an incurable disease, he was straining to support his family, and he began renting out his teenage son Abraham as a laborer. Western life was so difficult partly because of transportation: farmers struggled to ship crops to market, paid high prices for supplies, and found that any journey back East was an endurance contest. When Senator Andrew Jackson traveled to attend Congress in the fall of 1824, his route from Nashville to Washington took twenty-eight days. Traveling with Rachel, he missed the start of the session on December 6. On December 8, as the Senate conducted business, an exhausted Jackson slouched at his desk in the Senate chamber, scrawling a note to a friend. He said the journey had taken so long even though he had gone "without resting one day." He also said he was "in good health," which was untrue. Rachel wrote a friend to say, "My dear husband was unwell nearly the whole of our journey." Even after two weeks of recovery in Washington, the best Rachel could say was that her husband "is in better health than when we came."

Lafayette was planning to see the interior, accepting invitations from cities and states. As letters arrived from places with names like Cahaba, Alabama, the general may have noticed something curious.

White settlers were forming new states by displacing Indians, yet they preserved Indian names. The Alabamas were a branch of the Creeks. If the British in colonial days had bestowed many names that referred to people or places in the old country—New Jersey, Georgia, Pennsylvania—the founders of newer states preferred Tennessee, Mississippi, and Illinois. Americans even applied Indian names to social organizations. New York's Tammany Society, or Tammany Hall, had been named in the 1780s in honor of a Delaware chief. As Tammany evolved into a political organization that dominated New York for generations, its members were called braves. The leaders were sachems, or chiefs, who met in a building known as the Wigwam. If the use of native names, or the occasional donning of war paint, was not a deep or respectful reflection of native culture, it was still meaningful. European immigrants and their descendants sensed that the tribes made the United States distinct. To have a connection to Native Americans was to *be* American.

Indians slipped into literature and art. James Fenimore Cooper was at work on his Leatherstocking Tales, soon to include *The Last of the Mohicans.* When Samuel F. B. Morse painted his panorama of the House chamber in 1822, he put an Indian in it: a Pawnee chief, in full headdress, observing the proceedings from the gallery. The detail was drawn from life. The chief had been invited to the chamber to impress him with the power of the United States. There is no record of what he thought about the acoustics.

This was the America that Lafayette surveyed when he returned to be in "the midst of posterity," as Speaker Henry Clay put it. In only "one respect" could Lafayette "find us unaltered, and that is in the sentiment of continued devotion to liberty." Clay praised Lafayette for "your consistency of character, your uniform devotion to regulated liberty, in all the vicissitudes of a long and arduous life." When Clay finished his talk before the crowded House, Lafayette was "very evidently affected," according to a newspaper account. The hero remained seated for several seconds, apparently composing himself. At length he rose to reply:

"Well may I stand firm and erect, when . . . I am declared to have . . . been faithful to those American principles of liberty, equality, and true social order, the devotion to which, as it has been from my earliest youth, so it shall continue to be to my latest breath."

When newspapers printed accounts of Lafayette's emotional exchange with Clay, an irony became apparent. The praise of liberty and progress looked odd when printed alongside certain other items that made the papers. One account could be seen on Henry Clay's personal copy of the *Argus of Western America,* a Kentucky newspaper whose editor was among his political allies. The *Argus* included advertisements on its front page, which was the reason that Lafayette's description of the "American principles of liberty, equality, and true social order" appeared inches from an ad placed by one Edward O. Chambers.

$50 REWARD

RAN AWAY from the subscriber, residing in Lauderdale county, Ala on Sunday night, the 31st of October last, a negro man named

ISAAC.

The owner described the escaped slave as "26 or 27 years old," perhaps "5 feet 8 or 10 inches high," with a "down look," a tendency to call himself a doctor, and a small piece missing from his nose, "occasioned by a bite." Isaac was also "fond of spirits," according to the owner who was uncertain of Isaac's age or height.

Isaac's fate was related to that of Indians, and directly tied to the exploits of Andrew Jackson. Isaac had been living in Kentucky, a slave state, when he was sold down to Alabama in 1818. That was the same year that Lauderdale County, his new home, was founded along the north bank of Muscle Shoals. He was apparently one of the first slaves imported after Andrew Jackson's conquests and treaties opened the region and sparked the 1818 land bubble. The seat of Lauderdale County was Florence, the new city founded at tremendous profit by Jackson's friends. The area's new plantation owners would be stuck on the land for quite some time; the land market crashed along with cotton prices in 1819. The plantation owners relied on the labor of men like Isaac to slowly redeem their investments.

There was nothing unusual about the ad for the escaped slave. Other issues of the *Argus* reported on a question debated in the Kentucky legislature: If a slave was executed for committing a crime, should the owner be compensated for the loss of his property? A proposal for a tax to finance such compensation was defeated, 33–30; it wasn't clear if lawmakers objected to the principle or just disliked the tax. In a slave-based economy, such questions must inevitably arise in democratic debate.

Did no one notice the contradictions? Of course they did. Some Americans had agitated against slavery even before 1790, when Benjamin Franklin signed a petition calling on Congress to remove this "Inconsistency" from the "Character of the American People." Northern states gradually did free their small slave populations in the republic's early years. Slavery was more entrenched in the South, though some questioned it. One of the men General Lafayette encountered during his American journey was Edward Coles, a Virginian who had inherited slaves and decided that the institution was morally wrong. Coles relocated with his slaves to Illinois, granted them liberty, provided them land, and won election in 1822 as an antislavery governor. Lafayette also encountered people involved in grander schemes. Since 1816, leading citizens had been financing the American Colonization Society, which proposed that slaves should be gradually freed over time and given passage to Africa, from which they or their ancestors had come. A founding officer of the society was Speaker of the House Henry Clay.

Supporters of colonization had a variety of motives. Some worried about the nation's soul. Others were slave owners—including Clay, who traveled with a manservant and used dozens of other enslaved people to work his farm outside Lexington. Clay concluded early in life that slavery was "a great evil," but he kept slaves he acquired through inheritance and marriage. He said that until slavery was outlawed he had a right to practice it. His views made him the perfect politician for Kentucky, which had pro- and antislavery sections, and also the perfect man to support the Colonization Society. It promised to address the evil in a way that did not explicitly threaten the existing order. Gradual colonization was considered far safer than simply abolishing slavery, which would deny slaveowners' property rights and create a far larger class of free black people than many whites wanted. Clay said the society occupied the thoughtful middle ground between "rash" abolitionists and those who found slavery a "blessing."

Arguments for colonization began to resemble arguments for removing Indians across the Mississippi. African Americans, like Indians, were alleged to be incompatible with the new republican society. Even if they could assume the responsibilities of citizenship, it was said, white prejudice would prevent them from doing so in peace. Better for all, the argument went, if they were transported to some separate place.

Fifteen

Clay Is Politically Damd

At dinners and parades honoring Lafayette, few Americans talked with his traveling party about the presidential election of 1824. It would have been unseemly to bring up divisive issues. Lafayette's secretary began to think that the hero's tour had "paralyzed all the electoral ardour." He should have known better. Americans were intently focused on the contest, as were Europeans. The secretary, Auguste Levasseur, who later published a memoir of the tour, wrote that European analysts were predicting disaster for the young republic. In previous elections the United States had "been able to restrict its choice to a few individuals, rendered dear to their country by their revolutionary services," but now the nation must "open the door to the ambitious and designing."

The political moment was even more fractious than it seemed. For more than a generation, a single national political party had governed the United States. Thomas Jefferson's Democratic-Republican Party had won election in 1800 and had held the presidency ever since. Their old rivals, the Federalists, had steadily faded into oblivion, to the point that in 1816 and 1820, President Monroe hardly faced meaningful opposition. But in 1824 the dominant party did not settle on a single candidate. There was no formal convention or primary system to choose a nominee, and an old informal system—leaving the nomination to the party's members of Congress—fell apart. Each of the four contenders that fall was Democratic-Republican. The great ruling coalition was poised to split.

Lafayette seemed to encounter presidential candidates everywhere. For a time he traveled with one, Secretary of State John Quincy Adams. If Clay was driving to dominate the second generation of American leaders, Adams *was* the second generation, the son of the Revolutionary firebrand John Adams. He combined his father's stubborn adherence to principle with a quiet demeanor. When Adams traveled with Lafayette on an overnight steamboat, the Frenchman's party was stunned to see the secretary of state preparing to sleep with the common passengers on the floor of the dining room.

Adams, at fifty-seven, had pinched eyebrows, a receding hairline, and whitening sideburns. He'd been a senator and a diplomat, part of the team that negotiated an honorable end to the War of 1812. Now he was well positioned to win the presidency. The previous two secretaries of state had each won the top job. Many presumed Secretary Adams would too. But Jackson's candidacy was strong. When a visitor asked about plans for his administration, Adams got out of answering by saying that "I had never thought the probability of my election sufficient to warrant me in thinking about it at all." This was the disinterested pose required of all candidates, but Adams surely had genuine moments of doubt.

Unable to do anything but await the results, Adams passed a day in October accompanying General Lafayette on a tour of Philadelphia institutions, such as the "Pennsylvania Hospital for Sick and Insane Persons." The highlight was a visit to the penitentiary, including a new building designed so that every prisoner would live in solitary confinement, and would therefore have time to think and reform. Here was one of the few recorded instances of his visit in which Lafayette could not restrain himself from commenting on current events. The old general informed his hosts that he had *been* in solitary confinement after the French Revolution, and the experience had not reformed him in any way. Solitary confinement was torture, known to drive men mad. In his diary, Adams recorded walking with Lafayette between "convicts drawn up in double line." The brooding presidential candidate thought he saw signs of "vice and guilty lives" in the double row of faces—"desperation, malice, hatred, revenge, impudence, treachery, and scorn." Soon afterward Adams departed with Lafayette for Washington.

Lafayette checked into the Franklin House, also called Gadsby's after the owner. Gadsby's was a few blocks northwest of the White House, and Lafayette hadn't been there long when he learned that Andrew Jackson had just checked into the same hotel. Resolving to pay a call, Lafayette discovered Jackson on his way to call on him. They met at the stairs. They talked of old times. Jackson remembered spotting General Lafayette in Charleston early in the Revolution, when Jackson was only a boy. Lafayette managed to leave the impression, unlikely though it was, that he remembered seeing Jackson. Jackson's wife, Rachel, sensed that "the emotion of revolutionary feeling was aroused in them both." In the following days she took a close look at the French hero: "He wears a wig, and is a little inclined to corpulency. He is very healthy, eats hearty, goes to every party, and that is every night."

Her husband was not healthy or hearty, and not attending many parties; Mrs. Jackson, deeply religious, regarded parties and the theater as temptations to resist. The Jacksons did go to functions hosted by President Monroe's wife, Elizabeth, in the Executive Mansion. Ushered into the house where they hoped soon to live, they crossed the high-ceilinged main hall on their way to the drawing room. Later known as the Green Room, with its polished wood furnishings and portraits on the walls, it was among the smaller and more gracious of the ceremonial rooms; here the crowds might include Lafayette as well as other presidential candidates, for all four contenders were now sharing this small city and its even smaller political society. Clay and Adams might turn up anywhere. The fourth candidate, Treasury Secretary William Crawford, was nearly always at home, having suffered a stroke, but Crawford's campaign manager was moving about—Senator Martin Van Buren of New York, a deft operator who had already proved his mastery in the union's richest and most populous state. At events filled with such notables, Andrew Jackson was excellent, shaking off his health problems, trim and tall in fine clothes, courteous to ladies, the center of attention in any room. Then he went back to Gadsby's and wrote sourly about the experience. Washington social events were "nothing but shew—nothing of pure principles of friendship in these crowds—hypocrisy and hollow heartedness predominates."

Custom required hypocrisy of Jackson, who had to pretend he had no interest in his own candidacy. He tried to follow the custom, insisting even in private letters that he was not following the news. The same letters showed he *was* following the news. As soon as he arrived in Washington that December, he had promised a friend back home that "when I have . . . become a little acquainted with the views of the political knowing ones here, I will give you the speculations on the presidential question." He mentioned one of his rivals in particular—not Crawford, whose health doomed his prospects, nor Adams, but his fellow westerner Henry Clay.

This made sense. When the undecided election was thrown to the House, Clay would be in a powerful position, the man who knew how to work the personalities and rules. Even if he couldn't win, he would influence the outcome. But there was another reason for Jackson to watch Clay. Jackson hated him. Their mutual dislike dated back to a disagreement involving Jackson's dealings with Indians. The disagreement had come half a dozen years earlier, but Jackson neither forgave nor forgot.

Clay was elegant of dress and informal in manner. He drank whiskey, gambled at cards, and once ended an alcohol-lubricated dinner by dancing down the length of a banquet table. A portrait made in his youth showed a lean and lanky man staring confidently at the painter, a half smile on his face. This permanent crook of the mouth showed up in painting after painting made over the half century of his career. Late in his life, photography made it possible to capture Clay's countenance, and in these images the half smile looks more like a wry grimace, as if he cannot believe the human comedy he's been witnessing all this time.

Clay had an easier start in life than Jackson, growing up in a moderately prosperous Virginia family. Yet their similarities were considerable. Like Jackson, Clay never really knew his father, who died when Henry was four. (His mother remarried.) Also like Jackson, Clay had little formal education, served as an apprentice to lawyers before becoming a lawyer himself, moved west in his youth, and grew prosperous enough to buy an elegant farm. Margaret Bayard Smith, member of a prominent Washington family and a keen observer, said of Clay: "Whatever he is, is all his own, inherent power, bestowed by nature and not derivative from culture or fortune." Jackson too.

Elected to the Senate in 1806, Clay took his seat even though he was several months below the constitutionally mandated age of thirty. In 1811 he became a member of the House, and was elected Speaker on the first day of his first term. Ideas he supported defined federal policy for a generation—taxes on imports, federal roads, and a national bank, all of which he eventually labeled as elements of his American System, and all of which he saw enacted over opponents who said they were not authorized by the Constitution. He was forceful, eloquent, and too clever for his own good. In 1812 he led a congressional faction called the War Hawks, who pushed the United States toward conflict with Britain. He managed to avoid the destruction of his career as the war went wrong. He even redeemed himself as a member of the negotiating team that concluded an honorable peace, working alongside John Quincy Adams. But Clay's advocacy of war, like many of his political choices, had an unanticipated consequence: in this case, the rise of Andrew Jackson.

Clay's opposition to Jackson became explicit in 1819, after Jackson conquered Florida. The House considered whether to punish Jackson, and Clay delivered an hours-long speech to a House chamber packed with spectators. It was a perfect exhibition of his style. However happy Americans were to be gaining Florida, Clay said, the general was slipping away from civilian control. "Wonderful energy!" he said of Jackson's conquest. "Admirable promptitude. Alas! That it had not been an energy and a promptitude within the pale of the Constitution." Margaret Bayard Smith heard the speech while seated on some steps outside the gallery. The House had fallen so silent that she "did not lose a word." Clay needed every word. He was attacking the popular acts of a wildly popular man. Jackson was growing so famous he was mobbed in the streets. Even Clay felt obliged to say Jackson's motives were "pure," but the end did not justify Jackson's means. The general exceeded orders, and failing to condemn him would be "a triumph of the principle of insubordination." Interrupted by a Massachusetts lawmaker who defended Jackson, Clay replied, "The gentleman from Massachusetts is truly unfortunate. Fact or principle is always against him."

The Speaker went on to question the origins of the invasion of Florida. Why was Jackson chasing renegade Indians? Because Indians were rebelling. Why were they rebelling? Because Andrew Jackson imposed an unjust peace treaty after the Battle of Horseshoe Bend: illegitimate, infused with a "dictatorial spirit," and "utterly irreconcilable" with American values. Once his speech was finished, Mrs. Smith recalled, Clay "came and sat a few minutes on the steps by me, throwing himself most gracefully into a recumbent posture." This was part of the performance: his physical grace, his informality, his careful attention to an influential woman. Mrs. Smith's husband was at various times a publisher, a banker, and a federal official, making the Smiths early members of Washington's permanent governing establishment. Clay knew his business. He had, however, made a lasting enemy in General Jackson.

Jackson's defense was, in essence, that the Spanish deserved what they got. They had failed to prevent Indians in Florida from mounting raids across the border. Also, the invasion was popular. The people would sustain him. He was right: Clay himself ended his speech by acknowledging his cause was probably lost, and that the House would vote down every effort to censure Jackson. "Clay is politically damd," Jackson afterward wrote to one of his political managers in Tennessee. "You will see him skinned here" in Washington, where Jackson had gone to coordinate his own defense, "and I hope you will roast him in the West. . . . If Mr. Casidy [a Nashville newspaper editor] can be got sober I wish him to scorch him." The capital's leading newspaper, the *National Intelligencer*, published a claim that the general had been over-heard "in the public taverns and ballrooms of Washington" making threats "of personal vengeance, even to cutting off the ears of some of the members [of a Senate investigating committee] . . . and some members of the House of Representatives."

Yet as the election of 1824 approached, Jackson mastered his rage. He met Clay for dinner in Washington more than once. No ears were cut off. When the presidential election was thrown to the House, Jackson was intensely suspicious of Clay, yet evidence suggests he would have been willing to reach some accommodation. Jackson had no trouble, in later years, relying on former opponents as close advisers, including former allies of Clay. Jackson was capable of making an alliance with Clay. It was Clay who could not abide Jackson.

The presidential election of 1824 was the same as the elections of later generations in one vital respect. It was not decided by a popular vote. Under the Constitution, each state chose a small number of electors, by whatever means the state desired, and a vote by these electors selected the president. The popular and electoral votes need not turn out the same, as a later generation would learn during the disputed election of the year 2000. In 1824 there was not even a nationwide popular vote to win. Most states had only lately embraced the innovation of a popular vote for presidential electors, and several still left the choice to their state legislatures.

In 1824, there were 261 electoral votes. Gaining a majority required 131. Results rolled in over a period of weeks, mostly during those twenty-eight brutal days when Mr. and Mrs. Jackson were bouncing eastward toward Washington. Jackson did well across the South and West, winning several states including Alabama and Mississippi, which he had done so much to bring into the union. His popularity also extended as far as the big northern state of Pennsylvania. In total he had 99 electoral votes, more than anyone else. Adams, dominant in New England, had 84. Clay and Crawford won scattered victories. No one had a majority. In such a case the Constitution said the top three contenders must be voted upon by the House: it became a brand-new election, in which the popular vote was even less relevant.

Jackson would be a candidate before the House; so would Adams. Clay and Crawford were battling for the third and final slot. After Jackson arrived in Washington, he watched intently to see if his despised rival would get it.

If Louisiana has not voted for Mr Clay he is not in the house.

Clay needed Louisiana's electoral votes. It soon became clear that he didn't win them. Jackson could feel victory getting closer.

I should never have aspired to the responsibility—but, let the lords will be done.

Now, however, the Speaker of the House took on a new role. As the House prepared to break the three-way deadlock, Clay could swing the election to one of the candidates who remained.

With or without Jackson's consent, his supporters reached out to Clay. One was Sam Houston, the soldier who had climbed at General Jackson's orders over the Creek barricade at Horseshoe Bend, and who was now a Tennessee congressman. Houston met a friend of Clay's, and said Clay could end up as Jackson's secretary of state. Congressman

James Buchanan of Pennsylvania took a similar message directly to Clay. But Clay was leaning in another direction. Encountering John Quincy Adams at a dinner in honor of General Lafayette, Clay asked to have "some confidential conversation upon public affairs."

Clay told a Kentucky friend the House vote was a "choice of evils." This was not the warmest endorsement of Adams, but Clay probably believed that Adams would support the American System. It's also likely that Clay's ambition pushed him toward Adams, since Jackson was his rival for the affection of the West. But Clay's political calculus was complex, since he would pay a price in Kentucky for opposing a western man. Clay's own explanations for his decision are worth considering.

> *In the election of Mr Adams we shall not by the example inflict any wound upon the character of our institutions; but I should much fear hereafter, if not during the present generation, that the election of the General would give to the Military Spirit a Stimulus and a confidence that might lead to the most pernicious results.*

Clay said this so often that he likely believed it was true. He'd been hearing confirmation of his judgment for years. "Too much of a Soldier to be a civilian," said Return J. Meigs Jr., a former Ohio governor and U.S. postmaster general (whose father, the longtime Cherokee Indian agent, worked with Jackson in Tennessee for many years). "There is more of the Dictator—than of the Consul in his Character." A consul was a peacetime leader in ancient Rome, and the metaphor resonated in a country that dwelled on Greco-Roman precedents for its republican experiment. It was not by chance that Americans gave an ancient Roman name to the Senate, or put the Bank of the United States in a building that resembled an ancient Greek temple. Latin was taught in many schools, including those set up for Indians. Even Clay, with his limited education, was introduced to Greek and Roman writers while serving as an apprentice to a Virginia jurist. Meigs, in his letter to Clay from Marietta, Ohio, threw in two lines in Latin from the Roman poet Horace, and assumed his friend in Kentucky would be able to decipher them. Clay's 1819 speech summarized Jackson's Florida campaign with Caesar's famous phrase *"Veni, vidi, vici."* Suddenly Jackson was Caesar and Clay was Cicero, the Roman senator who tried to stand in his way.

While Clay's apprehensions were understandable, he could have viewed Jackson differently. It was true that as a general, Jackson found new and creative ways to exercise power—just as Clay found new and creative ways to exercise power as Speaker of the House. Each was a disruptive figure who unnerved conventional thinkers. Clay's brooding on history blinded him to the reality of his rejection of Andrew Jackson: The candidate Clay considered least suited for the presidency was the one who most resembled Clay.

Clay visited Adams for a long talk, and took the opportunity to complain. Representatives of all the candidates had been appealing for his support in a manner he considered "gross." Obviously, Henry Clay was not going to make a "gross" bargain to support Adams. Adams's diary noted that without requesting "any personal considerations for himself," Clay told Adams "he had no hesitation in saying that his preference would be for me." The Speaker visited Adams again on January 27, "and sat with me a couple of hours, discussing all the prospects and probabilities of the presidential election. He spoke to me with the utmost freedom," even discussing what to do about friends of Adams who seemed to be wavering in their support. With his self-confidence and ease, Clay had already assumed the position of adviser of the man he expected to make president. That was the way to gain a post in Adams's cabinet without asking for it.

Jackson was under increasing stress. He was flooded with callers at Gadsby's hotel—fifty to a hundred a day, according to Rachel. He ended a letter to one of his political managers: "Since I have sat down to write this I have been interrupted twenty times & oblige now to close it hastily—A.J." The bills Jackson received from the hotel suggested the mounting costs of entertaining. On January 11 he paid for eight bottles of port wine, a pint of whiskey, three more bottles of wine, and "2 Extra Dinners in Private Parlour." On the fourteenth he was billed for claret, cigars, brandy, whiskey, champagne, three more dinners, and three bottles of "wager wine"—this, of course, beyond the meals and lodging for himself, Rachel, three servants, and four horses. He'd arrived in Washington with $2,300 but was running out of cash. He had to write to John Coffee in Alabama, asking him to send more. His health was more precarious than his finances. "We are all well," Rachel wrote home on January 27, "except bad colds (Mr Jackson has not been very well sinc He left home) his mind has kept him Down he Longs for retirement at His own fire side I knew from the first how wrong it was, but my advise was nothing." One night after meeting a congressman, Jackson slipped on his way up Gadsby's stairs and painfully shifted one of the bullets in his body.

Despite his anxiety and pain, Jackson was writing letters to supporters that perfectly expressed his position. His ideas guided his supporters then, continued to guide them for years afterward, and would be emulated, in one form or another, down to the present day. He wrote to his old friend John Overton, a Tennessee judge:

> Let me rise or fall upon the rule that the people have the right to choose the chief executive of the nation, and a majority of their voices have a right to govern, agreeable to the declared principles of the constitution—
>
> Having been supported by the majority of the people, I can have no feelings on the occasion—If party or intrigue should prevail, and exclude me, I shall retire to my comfortable farm with great pleasure— there you know, was the height of my ambition.

It was a brilliant letter. If all its premises were accepted, there was no patriotic course for anyone to take except to salute Andrew Jackson on his way to the Executive Mansion. Jackson's vision matched perfectly with his political requirements, although it did not match with the facts.

the rule that the people have the right to choose the chief executive of their nation, and a majority of their voices have a right to govern

That was not a rule. While the Founders had respected the principle of majority rule, they found the power of the majority, like all power, to be dangerous if unchecked. Check it they did, including by the creation of the Electoral College, designed to filter the will of the people through the eminent men who would be voted into it.

Having been supported by the majority of the people

He hadn't been supported by a majority. Never mind that women and nearly all racial minorities did not vote, or that several states did not hold popular elections for president at all. In the four-way race, Jackson gained 42 percent of votes cast in the states that held a popular vote. Although Jackson led Adams's 31 percent, neither had a majority. Of ten million Americans, about 359,000 voted, of whom about 151,217 marked ballots for Jackson.

If party or intrigue should prevail, and exclude me

Here Jackson did not see himself merely as a man fighting a three-way contest in the House as required by the Constitution. It was a one-man contest. Jackson was the only person whose victory could possibly be just. Any reverse he might suffer was by definition illegitimate, a betrayal of America through elitist "intrigue."

Jackson engaged in some intrigue of his own. Letter after letter resembled the one he sent to a Philadelphia merchant, a supporter in Pennsylvania.

With regard to the Presidency, My Dear Sir, you must excuse my
inability to inform you—I know nothing of the movement of parties,
or of the combinations, which are alledged to be in secret caucus. It is
true rumors of the kind exist.

Having denied any knowledge of the news, he passed on the most
salacious news that he had: rumors of "combinations" involving Henry
Clay. His supporters pushed the rumors into the open. Late in January
a pro-Jackson newspaper in Pennsylvania published a devastating interpretation of events. An anonymous congressman claimed that the presidency had gone up for sale. John Quincy Adams was buying support
from Henry Clay, and Clay's price was to become secretary of state,
"should this unholy coalition prevail."

Just to make sure this report had the proper effect, the pro-Jackson
editor mailed a copy to Henry Clay. Clay read it. There he was, accused
of a corrupt design to become secretary of state. The top post in the
cabinet. The post that in the republic's short history had become the
surest springboard to the presidency. The posting Clay would want,
should he serve in the cabinet at all. Now it was Clay's turn to explode
in fury, publicly challenging the source of the story to a duel, and
demanding an investigation in the House. On January 29, he wrote a
long letter to a friend that reads as if its coauthor were bourbon. Insiders
in Washington

have turned upon me and with the most amiable unanimity agree to
vituperate me. I am a deserter from Democracy; A Giant at intrigue;
have sold the West—sold myself—defeating Gen Jacksons election to
leave open the Western pretensions that I may hereafter fill them
myself—blasting all my fair prospects &c &c &c. . . . The Knaves
cannot comprehend how a man can be honest. They cannot conceive
that I should have solemnly interrogated my Conscience and asked it to
tell me seriously what I ought to do?

"I perceive," Clay went on, "that I am unconsciously writing a sort of defence, which you may possibly think imp[lies] guilt."

The distraction did not keep Clay from the task to which he had set himself. He lined up the votes Adams needed, twisting arms so effectively that when the House met in its great echoing chamber, the lawmakers made John Quincy Adams the president-elect on the first ballot.

Jackson bore defeat well in public, walking into a crowded reception at the Executive Mansion and offering Adams his congratulations. Probably Lafayette was in the crowd; his secretary Levasseur was there, and found Jackson "open and sincere." In private, everything was different. Within days, Jackson supporters met the president-elect to present an ultimatum: Clay must be denied the post of secretary of state, or a "determined opposition" would be organized against Adams from the very start of his administration. Adams, refusing to be intimidated, offered Clay the State Department. Clay hesitated, sensing the danger, but accepted: yet another of his fateful choices with unintended effects.

By then Jackson had long since issued his judgment in a letter from Gadsby's hotel. The nation had never witnessed "such a bare faced corruption," wrote the general who had bullied, intrigued, and bribed Indians into surrendering tens of millions of acres of real estate. None of that was important now. What mattered was that Henry Clay had betrayed him.

So you see the Judas of the West has closed the contract and will receive the thirty pieces of silver—his end will be the same.

Sixteen

We Wish to Know Whether
You Could Protect Us

A t the time of Lafayette's visit, the federal Bureau of Indian Affairs administered native matters from offices in Georgetown, on the western edge of Washington. The bureau was run by Thomas McKenney, who was considered an expert on the tribes. McKenney's offices included a special room that was once seen by the traveling English novelist Frances Trollope. "The walls," she wrote, "are entirely covered with original portraits of all the chiefs who, from time to time, have come to negotiate with their great father, as they call the President." McKenney paid to have each visitor sit with the same painter. Some of the Indians wore expressions of "noble and warlike daring," while others were shown with "a gentle and *naïve* simplicity." At some point Major Ridge went up on the wall, as did John Ross, both of whom visited Washington in the early part of 1825.

There is no record that either man met Lafayette, though at least one visited Gadsby's while Lafayette was staying there. Major Ridge arrived at the hotel on January 10, joining the stream of visitors to see Gadsby's other famous guest, Andrew Jackson. "Our heads have become white," Ridge observed when the two veterans of Horseshoe Bend met. Ridge was around fifty-three, Jackson fifty-seven. Possibly using his English-speaking son John Ridge as interpreter, the Cherokee leader delivered a short and respectful speech. "Our hearts have been with you always," Ridge assured his former commander. Left unstated was Ridge's reason for visiting Washington. He was acting as an adviser to the Creek Nation as it tried to avoid losing more land; this was the mission that earned Ridge and his son commissions totaling $25,000.

A few weeks later John Ross arrived in the capital to join Ridge in the latest Cherokee delegation. Georgia was making another demand for Cherokee territory. It was Thomas McKenney's duty to pass on this demand to the Cherokees, even though he knew what the answer would be. He made his request in a desultory, one-sentence note.

> *Friends and Brothers: I am directed by the Secretary of War to enquire if you have authority to negotiate with the Government for a sale of your lands; and especially for that portion of them lying in the limits of Georgia.*

The answer penned by Ross walked right up to the edge of sarcasm.

> *It would seem from the enquiry that the Secretary of War is impressed with the belief that our nation may be disposed to make a cession of our lands.*

So that the secretary "may have full information," Ross said the Cherokees' refusal to sell was "unchangeable." This caused a problem for the government, since Georgia's desire for Cherokee as well as Creek land within the state was equally unchangeable.

The duty of resolving these irreconcilable demands fell on John Quincy Adams soon after his inauguration. Adams's elevation must have been a hopeful sign to the Cherokees who'd so often visited his home. But if Adams appreciated the propaganda he'd been given about the Cherokee Nation, he was not enthusiastic about their prospects. In a cabinet meeting during his first year in office, President Adams heard Henry Clay remark that Indians were an "essentially inferior" race, "not an improvable breed," and on their way to extinction. Some in the room were shocked, but Adams was not. He wrote afterward that "I fear there is too much foundation" for Clay's opinions. Indians thus depended on a president who recognized their rights but regarded them as a lost cause. Adams's resolve would promptly be tested—so soon, in fact, that when General Lafayette bid good-bye to the new president after the election and resumed his tour of all twenty-four states, he would reach the states of the emerging Deep South in time to witness a portion of the test.

The journal of Lafayette's secretary, Levasseur, recorded memorable scenes as the party moved southward. Somewhere below Norfolk, Virginia, the group stopped at a "small, solitary inn," where the owner served whiskey and bread. The owner's wife brought in their son, a toddler who, repeating after his father, thanked Lafayette for their liberty. Approaching Charleston, South Carolina, Levasseur smelled the city before he saw it. "The coolness of the night had condensed the perfumes from the orange, peach, and almond trees, covered with flowers, and embalmed the air." The city gave Lafayette "balls, displays of artificial fire-works, and entertainments" that lasted for days. While on a steamboat in the harbor, the great man was saluted with cannon fire from Fort Moultrie, which had guarded Charleston since the Revolution. Army engineers were finally planning a new fortress, to be built on a shoal in the harbor and to be called Fort Sumter.

Between the blasts of cannons and toasts to the Revolution, Lafayette's secretary noticed a pervasive emotion: "fear." South Carolina was a slave state, with a majority black population. The white minority had been terrified just three years before, in 1822, to learn that a free black man named Denmark Vesey was plotting a slave insurrection. Authorities hanged Vesey and dozens of alleged co-conspirators, and by the time of Lafayette's visit, intensified security regulations gave South Carolina the feel of a police state. One measure decreed that when ships docked at Charleston, any free black sailors on board must be jailed so they could not carry messages to black people onshore. When a Supreme Court justice found the imprisonments unconstitutional, South Carolina openly defied the ruling, saying that stopping "insubordination" was "paramount" to "all laws" and "all constitutions." Baffled by this early example of a state nullifying federal law, national officials did nothing.

In the 1820s progressive thinkers in the South were reluctant to fully endorse slavery. They defended it only as a necessary evil inherited from past generations. South Carolina's great political thinker John C. Calhoun even suggested it was a passing phase, telling a northerner in 1823 that slavery was "scaffolding, scaffolding, Sir—it will come away when the building is finished." But he neglected to specify who was going to take down the scaffolding, and Lafayette's perceptive secretary noticed that no one was available. A vote against slavery would be a vote against the personal fortunes of many leading politicians.

State officials proved active enough on issues better aligned with their interests, such as opening up the countryside for white settlement. On his way to Charleston, Lafayette had spent the night in a new settlement under construction, sleeping in the only house that had a roof, and rising in the morning to see that the surrounding forest had only recently been cleared. Developing new towns and surrounding farms required the continuing removal of the state's Indians, which in turn required the state to engage in some lobbying. Since only the federal government was allowed to do business with Indians, states pressed for federal help. In 1816, as part of a broader negotiation with the Cherokees, the government proposed to buy their South Carolina land. This was the same negotiation in which Cherokees, including John Ross, focused on preserving two million acres in Alabama threatened by Andrew Jackson. Though they won back the Alabama land, at least temporarily, they had to give up something. They sold their stake in South Carolina for $5,000.

A ship took the national guest and his party from Charleston down the coast to Savannah, Georgia, in March 1825. Waiting for Lafayette amid the crowd at the waterside was His Excellency G. M. Troup, governor and commander in chief of the armed forces of Georgia, and also Lafayette's host. He had brought along some of Georgia's troops to fire a salute to the approaching boat in the harbor. The salute was only the start; the legislature had authorized Troup to draw unlimited funds from the treasury to arrange Lafayette's travel across the state and onward to Alabama.

Governor Troup is worth dwelling on for a moment, this welcoming politician waiting by the waterside. He was a curly-haired, sideburned, cold-eyed planter's son. He had strong views about natives; he was the same man who claimed that even Andrew Jackson was laggardly in 1814 because he failed to clear all of the Indians from Georgia. And as Lafayette's boat neared shore in 1825, Troup was in the midst of an operation designed to push out many natives who remained.

He was a man accustomed to conflict. He was born in 1780, in the midst of the Revolution, to a wealthy family that apparently stayed loyal to the British crown. The family Bible recorded their flight from one loyalist safe haven to another—Mobile Bay, London, British-controlled Charleston. At the close of the war the Troups returned to Savannah and made their peace with the new order, although Troup spent his youth in a society that was still polarized and suspicious. He became a politician almost as soon as he graduated from Princeton, and developed a withering, apocalyptic, paranoid style. In 1825, thirty-six years before the Civil War, he was already telling constituents that they must prepare "to stand to your arms." Washington, he declared in a message to the legislature that spring, would "soon, very soon" be aiming for "the destruction of every thing valuable in the Southern country." Troup was a template for a certain kind of American politician who would persist in later generations. In his world, the people were besieged by radical judges, conspiracies, and imminent plots to overturn their way of life. Washington officials were not at all what they claimed to be. He predicted that Supreme Court justices and Congress would soon collude and, "discarding the mask," reveal themselves as "fanatics" who would free Georgia's slaves without even paying for them.

But there were no such nightmare visions now, for Lafayette's boat had finally come ashore. The curly-haired governor was greeting the visiting hero, and guiding him through Savannah. Horses pulled them on a kind of parade float as ladies threw flowers on the ground. "La Fayette mania," scoffed a Savannah woman, Mary Telfair. She claimed the celebrations were overblown, and reported that a friend was referring to the nation's guest as "the *nations jest.*" Her nonchalance was an act. Telfair had been just as jaded the previous fall when she was visiting Philadelphia and Lafayette arrived there, but she went to see him anyway. Most likely in Savannah too she joined the crowds that lined the streets.

Governor Troup brought Lafayette inland, to the state capital at Milledgeville, where the hero of liberty was thronged by admirers in the statehouse. The next morning his carriage was on the road. The party rolled through Macon, Georgia, "a civilized speck lost in the yet immense domain of the original children of the soil," wrote Levasseur. "Within a league of this place, we are again in the bosom of the virgin forests," surrounded by trees so enormous they "appear as records of the age of the world." Not long after that the travelers were in Creek country. Their progress slowed as the road grew worse. The track was often washed away by the spring rains, and Creeks often helped them manhandle a small carriage they'd brought along. Once the party had to cross a stream that was so swollen the water flowed over the bridge. A double line of

Indians waded out onto the submerged planking, in racing water breast-high, holding hands in order to guide Lafayette's party safely across.

Stopping at a cluster of cabins, they encountered two Creek men at a front door, "one young, the other middle aged, both remarkable for their beauty and form. They were dressed in a short frock, of light material, fastened around the body by a wampum belt. Their heads were wrapped with shawls of brilliant colours, their leggings of buck-skin reached above the knee." Lafayette and Levasseur fell into conversation with the younger man, named Hamley, who spoke English.

Lafayette had heard something about the Creeks on his way here. He'd heard that they were about to be removed from this forest. Some Creeks had agreed to sell their land in Georgia. The sellers were led by a chief known as General William McIntosh, or M'Intosh. "General" was an honorific title, given him because of his service fighting under the command of Andrew Jackson at the Battle of Horseshoe Bend. When Lafayette began asking about this sale,

[Hamley's] countenance became somber, he stamped on the ground, and, placing his hand upon his knife, murmured the name of M'Intosh in such a manner, as to make us tremble for the safety of that chief; and when we appeared to be astonished, "M'Intosh," exclaimed he, "has sold the land of his fathers, and sacrificed us all to his avarice. The treaty he has concluded in our name, it is impossible to break, but the wretch!" He stopped on making this violent excla-mation, and shortly afterwards quietly entered on some other topic of conversation.

It is possible that Hamley had personal knowledge of the treaty he despised. The treaty bore the name of a "William Hambly," an inter-preter. But even if this Hamley was not a witness, the story would have been familiar to every Creek family in Georgia. General Lafayette's host, Governor Troup, had found the way to obtain the Creek land, using McIntosh as his accomplice.

In January 1825, while Lafayette was in Washington and the capital was consumed with the presidential election, two men appeared at
the Creek Indian agency in Georgia. They said they were U.S. commissioners, empowered to negotiate a treaty with the Creeks. This was
true, but not the whole truth. They were also Georgians, and federal
officials including the president himself later concluded that the men
acted as agents for Georgia. Working in collaboration with Governor
Troup, the commissioners pressed to buy every square foot of Creek
land in Georgia. When many Creeks resisted, the commissioners dealt
with William McIntosh, who was not the principal chief, but was well
known to white leaders. He had a white father. His cousin was Governor George M. Troup.

McIntosh also had a certain reputation. In 1821, when the Creeks
signed a treaty ceding some of their land, McIntosh arranged to receive
1,640 acres for himself. He used some of the land to build an inn at
Indian Springs, where the waters were said to have healing powers. In
1823 he wrote a letter to John Ross of the Cherokees, saying he could
pass on a bribe of $2,000 from the white men if Ross would help to sell
off Cherokee land. "Nobody shall know it," McIntosh promised in the
letter. Rather than take the money, Ross had the document read aloud
at a Cherokee leadership meeting. Cherokees never trusted McIntosh
again, but for the federal commissioners in 1825 he was the man to see.

Allegations of bribery soon swirled around the federal Indian
agency. The federal Indian agent was shocked. Even the agent's brother
said he was offered $10,000 and five square miles of land in exchange
for his help. Increasingly suspicious Creek chiefs stripped William
McIntosh of his authority to speak for them—but this only drove him
into the white negotiators' arms. His faction of Creeks signed a document on February 12 that gave Georgia everything it wanted. It would
be known as the Treaty of Indian Springs, having been signed at William McIntosh's inn. The commissioners sent an exuberant message to
Governor Troup.

We are happy to inform you that the "long agony is over."

Soon after this, William McIntosh sent a letter "To His Excellency George M. Troup," giving instructions on how to send $2,000 that Troup had promised to lend him.

William McIntosh needed something besides money. McIntosh's son and other Creeks traveled to Milledgeville to have dinner with Governor Troup, and made their main concern clear in a follow-up letter, five times using the word "protect" or "protection."

If [critics of the treaty] should attempt to breed a disturbance with the friendly Indians we shall inform you for protection, and we hope you will protect us . . . we look for protection from you. . . . P.S. We wish to know from you in writing whether you could protect us, should protection be necessary.

McIntosh knew the penalty for his betrayal of the nation was death. He was unavailable to greet Lafayette as he made his way through Creek country; he may have been lying low. But his son Chilly McIntosh did come out, and welcomed Lafayette to the family's home village. Chilly offered an explanation for his father's act as they watched a game of stickball, the local variant of lacrosse: it was time to admit the inevitable. Contact with white men was destroying the Creeks, who might renew themselves farther west. Chilly McIntosh would make that journey west, and would live long enough to fight in the Civil War. His father would not. On April 30, 1825, after the Marquis de Lafayette had safely passed through the Creek Nation, two hundred Creek men surrounded the house of William McIntosh and set it on fire. He might have burned to death had not the attackers dragged him out, stabbed him to death, and shot him dozens of times.

The Treaty of Indian Springs could not stand. Newly inaugurated President Adams took a personal interest in the case, summoning the federal Indian agent to the Executive Mansion to tell his story. The treaty was so embarrassing that even John Forsyth, a Georgia congressman, sent word that he would "infinitely rather" the United States negotiate a new agreement that gave the Creeks more generous terms. Adams voided the treaty. But there was still that compact of 1802. The president still felt obliged to act as Georgia's land agent; he lacked Andrew Jackson's talent for reinterpreting his obligations when he felt them to be wrong. The Adams administration negotiated a new treaty with surviving Creek leaders who came to Washington. Negotiations grew so intense that President Adams's diary for January 18, 1826, noted that "the first chief of the deputation, Opothle Yoholo, attempted last evening to commit suicide." Finally, the Creeks consented to sell most of their land in Georgia, but the Georgians under Governor Troup refused to accept this. They wanted it all. Defying federal authority, they began surveying even the Creeks' remaining land to sell to white buyers.

U.S. Army forces under General Edmund P. Gaines were ready to move against Georgia to protect the Creeks if ordered. Had Gaines acted, it might have become a farce, or it might have turned into a civil war in 1827. President Adams couldn't know in advance. In what he called "the most momentous message I have ever sent to Congress," Adams said he had decided not to risk war with Georgia, and would instead pursue the matter in the courts. The administration was not even effective at that. Finally the federal government went to the Creeks once again, and bought what little Georgia land they had left. Georgia would soon be cleared of all natives except for John Ross's Cherokees.

When the Marquis de Lafayette departed the western edge of Creek territory, he emerged in the white-occupied lands of Alabama. From there he traveled by water—downriver to Mobile, along the edge of the Gulf of Mexico to New Orleans, and then on a zigzag course up the Mississippi Valley, stopping to visit each state he encountered along the way. Other than New Orleans, this whole section of the United States had been established within the span of a single life. At a dinner in Nashville, Lafayette met a man described as the first white settler in Tennessee.

While staying in Nashville, Lafayette climbed aboard a carriage for a trip out of town. A short distance into the countryside he arrived before the increasingly opulent farm known as the Hermitage, where Andrew Jackson stood to greet him. The failed presidential candidate had arrived home a few weeks earlier, having made his own trip west from Washington. Jackson had followed the customary route westward— up to Pittsburgh, then down the Ohio—and his acts along the way revealed his state of mind, for the defeated man did not act defeated at all. He was reaching out to political supporters. Passing through Pittsburgh, he missed connections with an iron and glass manufacturer who had passionately backed him, but the man sent a letter racing down the Ohio River after Jackson. The manufacturer, Henry Baldwin, pledged to continue his political activity, "having in view the same object—the same purpose—& the same policy which have hitherto guided all my conduct." The object, purpose, and policy were the election of Andrew Jackson to the presidency: his supporters were already thinking of a second run in 1828. Jackson remained the most popular man in America. Though his health was wrecked beyond redemption, his destiny still lay before him. When Lafayette took Jackson's hand at the Hermitage, he was touching not the nostalgic past but the American future.

Jackson was a genial host for the national guest. The two men looked around the prosperous and orderly farm, with black servants always close at hand—Lafayette portly and nearing exhaustion from his monumental tour; Jackson sticklike and white-haired but feeding on the energy of the moment. Inside the house, Jackson produced a brace of pistols and asked: Do you recognize these? Lafayette did. Many years earlier, the pistols had belonged to Lafayette. He'd made a gift of them to George Washington. Now Jackson had obtained them. "I believe myself worthy of them," he said, "if not from what I have done, at least for what I wished to do for my country."

PART FIVE

Inaugurations

1828–1829

Seventeen

We Are Politically Your Friends and Brethren

Long afterward, it became clear that the year 1828 was a watershed. It was the year of a momentous presidential election. It was a hinge point for American culture, which previously had leaned heavily on its European forebears, and increasingly afterward became its own self-confident creation. And it was the year that a Native American culture took a step toward self-empowerment and self-preservation. In a wooden house in New Echota, the capital of the Cherokee Nation, a printer rolled ink across a page of metal type. Some of the type on the page was in English. The remainder was in Cherokee, using symbols for Cherokee syllables in the system developed by Sequoyah. It was the first written language for any Native American nation. And it was the first time a native nation ran a newspaper. The printer laid a sheet across the inked type, pulled a lever to press it between two metal plates, and afterward probably hung the sheet over the rafters to dry. The inaugural issue of the *Cherokee Phoenix* was dated February 21, 1828.

Until that day natives relied on oral history, passed from one generation to another, while the wider American public mostly read accounts filtered through white observers. The speeches of famous chiefs passed through multiple hands and were likely romanticized on their way to publication. Even the Harvard library with its twenty thousand volumes would have contained few words of Indians recorded by Indians. Now some natives would add their perspectives in two languages.

No evidence shows that John Ross conceived of the newspaper, but he understood its potential. The *Phoenix* came into existence after the Cherokee legislature, where Ross was a leader, committed $1,500 toward establishing the newspaper and a National Academy. Though the academy never amounted to much, Ross valued the newspaper so highly that when its subsidy seemed insufficient in later years, he paid bills from his own pocket. Having grown up in a home stocked with the latest newspaper editions, and having spent time in Washington, he intuitively grasped the link between the media and power in a democracy.

Cherokees needed the newspaper in order to play their emerging role as part of the American body politic. Since their agreements with the federal government could no longer be backed by force, they must rely on the law, which was made, interpreted, and applied by the people's representatives. Cherokees depended on the democratic system. They worked that system even though they had no right to vote for federal officials, only for Cherokee leaders. Ross put it perfectly in the closing line of his 1827 letter telling federal commissioners that Cherokees would not sell land: "With great respect, we are politically your friends and brethren."

Ross still had a copy of that letter, along with the whole correspondence in which the frustrated federal commissioners demanded an advantageous place and time for negotiations, and accused Ross of "subterfuge," only to have Ross subtly mock them. Somehow in the spring of 1828 these letters made their way from the council house in New Echota to the printshop of the *Cherokee Phoenix*, which was only a short walk away. The editor took an interest in the letters, which the printer began to set in type.

.   .   .

The birth of the *Phoenix* reflected the era. The number of newspapers was growing. In 1775, by one count, the thirteen colonies supported 37 newspapers. This number increased until, by 1823, the nationwide total reached 598. By the presidential election year of 1828 there were 802. Some were daily papers; many more came out weekly. Within a few more years, cheap "penny papers" in major cities would vastly expand newspaper circulation. Newspapers were multiplying far more rapidly than the population, growth that coincided with expanding commerce, speedier communications, rapid urbanization, and intensifying democratic politics. The *National Intelligencer* in Washington had been the semiofficial voice of the ruling Democratic-Republican Party since the start of the century, but a more diverse political scene demanded additional voices. Politicians subsidized those voices: officeholders steered government printing contracts to friendly newsmen, and Henry Clay once loaned an editor $1,500. Andrew Jackson had supportive papers in key states, like the Philadelphia sheet that first printed claims that Clay and Adams were about to consummate a corrupt bargain for the presidency. As the 1828 election approached, Jackson's men added to their network of news outlets. Many editors saw where the future lay and shifted toward the general.

Jackson, though not known to read a great many books, was the quintessential newspaper consumer. In the 1820s he subscribed to as many as seventeen papers at a time, and did not like to throw them away. He might go through them later, seeking clippings he wanted to pass to a friend or use to smite an enemy. The papers piled up so high that his household began having them bound—huge volumes, each with a year to a year and a half's worth of issues and as oversize as the broadsheet papers it contained. The information in those volumes could be instruments of power. And Jackson the collector of newspapers was also a collector of newsmen. Once he became president, Jackson would draw newspaper editors into his circle of intimate advisors—especially Francis Blair and Amos Kendall, who came to his side even though they were from Henry Clay's Kentucky.

Since newspapers were linked to the interests of specific parties or politicians, it made sense that marginalized groups sought their own outlets. *Freedom's Journal*, widely considered the first black-owned and -operated newspaper, started in New York in 1827. To start their own paper in 1828, the Cherokees overcame numerous obstacles. There was no printing press in the Cherokee Nation, no experienced printer, and no such thing as Cherokee metal type. Fortunately the missionary in town, Samuel Worcester, was able to write to his base in New England for help in obtaining the necessary equipment. The Cherokees found a veteran printer in Tennessee, who took the job though he had trouble distinguishing the Cherokee symbols and tended to leave that part of the job to his assistant. From February onward the lone editor came and went from the shop, handing the printers editorials and the latest news.

Murder.

We are informed of a murder being committed in the neighborhood of Sumach. The name of the person killed is William Fallen, and of the murderer Bear's Paw. We have not heard of the circumstances.

Later issues of the paper accused local authorities of leaving the suspect "unmolested." Possibly stung by this unprecedented media attention, authorities finally put Bear's Paw on trial. He was acquitted.

A subscription to the *Phoenix* cost $3.50 a year, with a discount if paid in advance. "Subscribers who can only read the Cherokee language" received a greater discount—a signal that those literate in English were likely more prosperous than others. The newspaper reported that the Cherokee Nation was, as a whole, accumulating wealth. One article said that the eastern Cherokees, with a population conservatively estimated at thirteen thousand, owned sixty-two shops, fifty gristmills and saw-mills, and 7,683 horses, not to mention $200,000 worth of fencing that penned in 22,531 black cattle and 46,700 hogs. In English and in Cherokee, the *Phoenix* published the full text of the constitution ("We, the representatives of the people of the CHEROKEE NATION . . .") as well as letters debating its meaning and texts of other laws. Readers on April 24 were informed that any person who "shall lay violent hands" on a woman, "forcibly attempting to ravish her chastity contrary to her consent," would receive fifty lashes and have an ear cut off. Other laws published in the paper revealed how well the Cherokees had learned the ways of the surrounding white population. "*Resolved by the National Committee and Council,* That intermarriages between Negro slaves and Indians, or whites, shall not be lawful . . . any male Indian or white man, marrying a negro woman slave, he or they, shall be punished with thirty-nine stripes on the bare back."

The *Phoenix* also did something notable for a newspaper in the Deep South: it included criticism of slavery. One article reprinted the narrative of a writer who'd visited West Africa, from which many slaves had come. "I stood on Cape Montserado," the writer said. "Scenes of horror—of relentless cruelty" had taken place "along the whole border of this afflicted, this injured land." Surely "the Omnipotent" would end "the exile, sufferings, and degradation of the Africans," and allow them to be repatriated, as the American Colonization Society was beginning to do. This article edged up to or beyond the limits of permissible southern discourse. Authorities were increasingly anxious to suppress anything that might inspire a slave revolt. Even the Cherokees' own slaveholding elites might not have approved.

There seemed to be no particular reason to print the article on slavery except that it interested the editor, Elias Boudinot, one of the most fascinating characters in New Echota. When his paper started publication, he was around twenty-six—round-faced, clean-cut, and sometimes eloquent. He was not an experienced newsman, and his four-page newspaper had an initial circulation of just two hundred. Yet the structure of the nineteenth-century media gave the *Phoenix* an outsize influence. Over the years, Boudinot arranged to receive copies of about a hundred other papers by exchange, meaning that he was also mailing copies of the *Phoenix* to a hundred other newspapers. Editors read it. They said it "may very properly be regarded as *something new*," as the *Charleston Mercury* advised South Carolina readers, an assessment reprinted by the *United States Telegraph* in Washington. Many papers reprinted *Phoenix* articles, including religious journals that were the era's most widely read publications. Other papers replied to *Phoenix* editorials. In modern terms, it was as if a blog or social media feed caught the mainstream media's attention, causing its articles to go viral.

And so it was noteworthy when copies of that 1827 correspondence between John Ross and the federal commissioners made their way to the *Phoenix* printshop. On May 28, 1828, Boudinot gave over a substantial portion of the newspaper to publishing the letters. Though offered with little commentary, they read like an exposé. The commissioners came across as designing and arrogant, insisting on paying the "expenses" of native leaders they wanted to influence, and seemingly baffled by Indians who did not follow instructions. Ross seemed smooth and in control, insisting upon nothing more than the ordinary process of the law. The letters ended with the whole Cherokee government, under the new constitution, saying Cherokees "would never dispose of one foot more of land again." It was perfect Cherokee propaganda, distributed to newspaper after newspaper. Boudinot's services were worth what little the Cherokees were able to pay.

Boudinot lived with his wife and family a short walk from the newspaper office in New Echota. They occupied a wood-frame house with a "piazza," or columned porch, and a garden. The house included the era's closest approximation of running water, a well with a windlass built into the porch. Such a house suited Boudinot's status as a member of the Cherokee elite. He was a nephew of powerful Major Ridge, though not especially affluent. His wife, Harriett, struggled to maintain the growing household on the editor's salary of $400 a year. "Our water is so sweet & pure that I have almost substituted it for coffee & Tea," she wrote once, though a careful reading of the letter indicates she was really cutting back on coffee and tea because she couldn't afford it. It cost a lot, she noted, and Elias drank it constantly, as he worked days and nights, sometimes on the newspaper and sometimes translating religious texts for the missionary Samuel Worcester. Occasionally the strain on Elias showed up in the pages of his paper:

> The Editor of this paper regrets that, owing to indisposition, he is not able to render his present number as interesting as he would wish.

In another issue Boudinot expressed regret that the previous week's newspapers had all been delivered sodden after the mail carrier fell from his horse into a stream. And then there were days Boudinot apologized on page 2 for an error on page 1, having discovered the error only after the printer had run off the first page and the ink had dried. He was having trouble with the printer, a preoccupied and suspicious man. A Methodist, he disliked the Congregationalist missionary Samuel Worcester, and accused him of undue influence over Boudinot and the paper. Boudinot fired the printer and found a new one.

Whatever his struggles, the young editor was well positioned to translate Cherokees to the surrounding white world. He had seen some of it. When organizing the *Phoenix*, the editor-to-be supplemented the Cherokee government subsidy with a fund-raising tour, developing a speech he delivered in eastern cities. ("What is an Indian?" he asked a crowd in Philadelphia. "Is he not formed of the same materials as yourself?") He had in fact been traveling since his teenage years, and during his travels had acquired both a white man's name and a white wife.

He'd been called Buck Watie at birth, but like many Cherokees he changed his name as he grew older. In 1818, when Buck was sixteen, his family sent him to attend school in the North, and on the way he met an old man from New Jersey named Elias Boudinot, who'd been a leader of the Continental Congress during the Revolution. The old revolutionary was sympathetic to Indians, and had written a book investigating whether native peoples were "the descendants of Jacob and the long lost tribes of Israel"—the same theory that had long fascinated Indian sympathizers such as the eighteenth-century trader James Adair. There is no proof that Buck really believed he was an Israelite, but he was impressed enough to enroll in school a short time later using Boudinot's name.

The institution where he enrolled was the Foreign Mission School in Cornwall, Connecticut. It was a forerunner of the Fulbright scholarships and other American programs that would attract later generations of foreign students to study at American universities. The Foreign Mission School taught "Latin, Greek, Rhetoric, Navigation, Surveying, Astronomy and Theology" to young people from "heathen lands" as far away as Malaysia and Hawaii. Some came from "heathen lands" closer to home. The record of "public exercises" during school exams in 1820 included a "declamation in English" by "Elias Boudinot, Cherokee," and a "Dialogue" among Cherokee students on the possibility of "the removal of the tribe to the West." Naturally, a good part of Boudinot's education was simply walking around Cornwall and experiencing New England. Just as naturally, he met a girl. In 1825, after leaving the school because of illness, he wrote letters proposing marriage to the young woman, Harriett Gold.

Harriett Gold's family went through agony. It was "rash presumption & disobedience," a relative told her, "going among the heathen" for a "selfish" reason like marriage. She was burned in effigy by a crowd in the town commons, where Harriett's own brother lit the fire. The community was especially outraged because Boudinot was the second Indian student who had proposed to a woman from Cornwall; the first, a few years before, was John Ridge, the son of Major Ridge. The fury was revealing. The practice of interracial marriage between whites and Indians was more than two hundred years old—missionaries estimated that one-fourth of the entire Cherokee Nation had at least some white ancestry from interracial marriages that could be traced back six generations. Cherokees accepted these marriages to outsiders, which suited a society in which people were expected to marry outside their clan or nation, and white society also seemed to accept these marriages when they involved white men far out on the frontier. An Indian man's marriage to the youngest daughter of a white family in Cornwall was considered entirely different. The fury after Boudinot's proposal was so great that the Foreign Mission School soon closed.

Harriett married Elias anyway. By the time Elias went to work on the *Cherokee Phoenix*, good sense had prevailed among her family. Her parents even visited the young couple in New Echota. Elias Boudinot seems to have embraced his new family, though in letters to his in-laws he did not avoid reminding them who he was. He told Harriett's relatives that one of their children had "real Indian black eyes," and closed the letter:

> *I remain your Indian*
> *Brother,*
> *Elias Boudinot.*

Like his letters, the pages he composed for the *Cherokee Phoenix* sometimes called attention to the interactions of the white and Indian worlds.

AN IMITATION INDIAN—A person made his appearance in the city [of Boston] Thursday last, dressed in the costume of an Indian, and calling himself "Gen. William Ross," which is engraved on an apparently silver breast plate. He says his father is Daniel Ross, who is Chief of the Cherokee Indians, and that he is an authorized agent of the nation.

The *Phoenix* also spread information about the elections of actual Cherokee leaders, informing candidates that they must pay a fee in order to place "electioneering" letters and articles in the paper: Boudinot was charging for political advertising. But there were gaps in the political coverage, considering that 1828 was an election year to choose a president of the United States. One of the most savage campaigns in American history received little mention in the *Phoenix* until December 3:

Presidential Election.

The long contest is over, and we shall soon ascertain, who is to be the next President of the United States. From returns of the election received thus far, it is highly probable that Gen. Andrew Jackson will be Chief Magistrate of the Union.

It was an understandable oversight that the *Phoenix* covered the election so little. The campaign turned more on the personal qualities of the candidates than their contrasting views of Indian policy. And the *Phoenix* had more immediate issues to cover, like Georgia's latest efforts to gain control of Cherokee land. But if the *Phoenix* did not focus on the next president of the United States, the next presidential administration paid attention to the *Phoenix*. After Jackson took office, he received a letter from his attorney general, who happened to be a Georgian, outlining two strategic moves that would be sure to undermine the Cherokees' ability to resist removal. The first was to take away their sources of money. The second was to take away their printing press.

Eighteen

This Is a Straight and Good Talk

J ackson's inauguration in March 1829 is remembered less for what
he said than for what was done. After his speech at the East Portico
of the Capitol (it was a "serene and mild" day, witnesses reported,
with such "an immense concourse of spectators" at the base of the Capitol steps that most could not get close enough to hear the words of their
white-haired leader) the new president was mobbed. Margaret Bayard
Smith, that perceptive denizen of the capital, was in the crowd: "The
barrier that had separated the people from him was broken down and
they rushed up the steps all eager to shake hands with him. It was with
difficulty that he made his way through the Capitol and down the hill
to the gateway that opens on the avenue. Here for a moment he was
stopped. The living mass was impenetrable." Someone handed the new
president the reins to a horse, a passage was opened through the crowd,
and then "carriages, wagons and carts" pursued the rider to the Executive Mansion, the building that is today called the White House, along
with "country men, farmers, gentlemen, mounted and dismounted,
boys, women and children, black and white."

Though the ceremonial rooms could accommodate hundreds of
people, the house was so stuffed with well-wishers that china was

smashed, people climbed through windows to escape with their lives, and the new president was nearly crushed against a wall. He had to be wedged out of the house by a squad of men who formed around him. The near riot scandalized capital society but did Jackson no harm. In the long term the story of the irrepressible crowds would enshrine his inauguration as a triumph of the common man, and for the short term the general made a tactical retreat. He did not spend the first night of his presidency in the Executive Mansion. He slept at the new and luxurious National Hotel on Pennsylvania Avenue.

The National's proprietor was John Gadsby, whose prior hotel had served as Jackson's campaign headquarters in the winter of 1824–25. Back then Gadsby's was where Jackson met Lafayette at the stairs, and where Rachel worried about his health shortly before his defeat. Now the city was filled with celebrations of his victory, but at Gadsby's he was alone. Rachel was dead. She had fallen ill in December, and the shadow of this tragedy enveloped his triumph. While still at the Hermitage in January, he declined to attend an event in his honor, informing his would-be hosts in Kentucky that "the present season is sacred to sorrow." Days later he was compelled to answer a letter that had been written to Rachel shortly before her death. "It pleased God to take her from this world," Jackson informed Rachel's friend, "depriv[ing] me of my stay and solace whilst in it." His friends worried about him. Louisiana congressman Edward Livingston wrote from New Orleans to express confidence that Jackson would be able to focus on the presidency, though the phrasing of Livingston's letter suggested doubts. He urged Jackson to "abandon your just grief" in order to perform his duty.

Just before starting from Nashville to Washington, Jackson sent a sad letter to John Coffee: "I have this day got my dear Mrs. J Tomb, compleated, and am notified that the Steam Boat will be up tomorrow for me. . . . Whether I am ever to return or not, is for time to reveal," he said. "My mind is so disturbed . . . that I can scarcely write, in short my dear friend my heart is nearly broke." Yet the same letter showed that

Jackson was wrapping up his western affairs and preparing for a new season. He gave Coffee detailed instructions to pay off and collect debts for him, $100 here and $130 there. Having sent these instructions, Jackson hurried on to other business, hiring an overseer to run the Hermitage and drawing up an inventory of ninety-five slaves. Then he gathered his family (his nephew Andrew Jackson Donelson would serve as his private secretary, and Donelson's wife, Emily, would become the official hostess of the Executive Mansion) and went to the waiting steamboat—downriver to the Ohio, upriver to Pittsburgh, and overland to Washington. Now, as he rested at Gadsby's after the inauguration, his mind was turning to the challenges ahead.

Beyond the joyous crowds, as Jackson knew, the capital city was fractious. Secretary of State Clay and others in the Adams administration pretended to yield power cheerfully, though Margaret Bayard Smith was not fooled: "Every one of the public men who will retire . . . will return to private life with blasted hopes, injured health, injured or ruined fortunes, embittered tempers and probably a total inability to enjoy the remnant of their lives." The 1828 campaign had been the nastiest in decades. Jackson supporters had spent years hammering a single theme, which simultaneously smeared President Adams and turned Jackson's campaign into a cause. The 1824 election had been stolen through the "corrupt bargain" between Clay and Adams; the 1828 election was a fight to restore liberty and limited government. Adams supporters responded with everything they had. By the evening of his inauguration, Jackson the habitual newspaper reader would have had all the opportunities he could ever want to revisit the ghosts of his past. They were all in print, having been turned into campaign literature. In 1828 a publication called *Truth's Advocate and Monthly Anti-Jackson Expositor* reported on the execution of John Wood at Fort Strother in 1814. ("Shoot the damned rascal! Shoot the damned rascal!") Nor was that all. A special edition of the *Kentucky Reporter*, linked with Henry Clay, investigated the $20,000 bribe Jackson paid to secure a treaty from the Chickasaws. Unable to document the bribe, the author described his efforts to confront Jackson and his associates, pioneering a technique that would later become known as the ambush interview. The *Truth's Advocate and Monthly Anti-Jackson Expositor* also published an extended report of Rachel's disastrous first marriage and her too-early remarriage to Jackson. The writer warned that Jackson's election would result in "a degraded female placed at the head of the female society of the nation" and damage "the National character, the National interest, and the National morals." Jackson was so bitter about these attacks in what turned out to be his wife's final months that when he arrived in Washington, he refused to pay a courtesy call on the departing President Adams. The presidential transition did not include so much as a handshake.

The brutal campaign had finally and permanently split the old ruling Democratic-Republican Party, creating the opportunity for Jackson to begin shaping a new party of his own. To direct this effort, he had a new adviser: Martin Van Buren of New York, the former manager of one of Jackson's rivals. Jackson welcomed this northerner who, like himself, had risen from modest circumstances to become a senator. Bald, sideburned, double-chinned, courteous, and clever, Van Buren made himself indispensable to Jackson. In an 1827 letter to a Richmond newspaper publisher, he sketched out the political coalition that would form the heart of Jackson's new party. It was an updated version of the alliance that had borne Jefferson to power, "the planters of the South and the plain republicans of the North." The "plain republicans" were men like Henry Baldwin, the Pittsburgh industrialist with his iron and glass works and his devotion to Jackson; the planters were men like General Jackson's friends John Coffee and James Jackson. Van Buren traveled to court southern leaders, and made sure the party paid the necessary price for southern membership in the coalition: absolute quiet on the subject of slavery. The pro-Jackson alliance was so effective that there could be no question about the election results this time. The hero of New Orleans swept most of the nation, and Jackson made Van Buren his secretary of state.

There remained the question of what Jackson would do once in power. Letters he received overflowed with suggestions. Some solicited positions in government; one Caleb Atwater of Ohio wrote Jackson to say that the candidates for district judge in Ohio were unqualified, but that Caleb Atwater would do the job. Many of his supporters would indeed be rewarded with jobs, since Jackson proposed to fire long-serving elites and hire new employees. Jackson eventually justified this political patronage by proclaiming the principle of "rotation in office," meaning that many citizens deserved to take a turn on the federal payroll. Other constituents expected more than a paycheck. Religious figures had lately united behind a cause, reinforcing the sacredness of Sunday as a day of rest. "The curse of God will afflict a Sabbath-breaking nation," warned a Tennessean, who suggested that if Jackson would only stop Sunday mail delivery, he would more easily follow Rachel to heaven. Another letter quoted extensively from Lyman Beecher, a Boston preacher, who said Jackson would "distinguish himself as a patriot" by stopping Sunday mail. It apparently did not occur to Beecher that the hero of New Orleans might resent the implication that he was not already distinguished as a patriot. The new president would soon be falling out of step with clerics who claimed to represent a higher authority than Jackson, the Constitution, or the people. Before long some of the same clerics would be questioning Jackson's treatment of Indians.

The mailbag also included warnings from the South. In 1828, the last full year of the Adams administration, Congress had approved new taxes on imported goods, and South Carolina politicians so fiercely objected to this "Tariff of Abominations" that they began talking of their power to nullify federal law. Jackson received a letter of advice from a friend who had recently traveled through the coastal South. The friend suggested that the new president should cement southerners' loyalty to the union by making certain they saw something in return for their tax money—Jackson might commit, say, half a million dollars to public works on some "decent pretext," such as coastal defenses for South Carolina and Georgia.

.   .   .

Jackson at least had wide latitude to act. He was associated with no specific policy agenda. Even his inaugural address offered hints rather than
commitments, though it was a good speech for those near enough to hear
it. Standing behind a table draped in red cloth, Jackson promised to
remember the "limitations" of presidential power. This could be read as a
note of skepticism about Henry Clay's American System; whereas Clay
believed in a government that used its power to develop infrastructure
and promote economic growth, Jackson often saw development projects
as unconstitutional insider schemes. He promised "a strict and faithful
economy" in federal spending. He pledged to honor states' rights, trying
to conciliate the firebrands of the South. (An early draft of his speech
went further, pledging that "I . . . shall be the last to cry out treason"
against those who disagreed with him about the limits of federal power.)
His solicitude for the states may have sounded ominous to natives, who
were depending on federal protection from encroaching states, but Jackson offered kind words to the Indians too. "It will be my sincere and
constant desire," the new president said, "to observe toward the Indian
tribes . . . a just and liberal policy, and to give that humane and consider-
ate attention to their rights and their wants which is consistent with the
habits of our Government and the feelings of our people."

In this way he signaled respect for both the Indian map and the U.S.
map without saying how he would resolve the conflict between them. He
could have said; he already knew. Van Buren later recalled that Jackson had
a few objectives in mind "from the first moments of his elevation to power."

First, the removal of the Indians from the vicinity of the white
population and their settlement beyond the Mississippi.

This was the president's clearest goal, a signature domestic policy,
which he meant to pursue just as later presidents would become known

for a single overriding goal such as a tax cut or a health insurance plan. Jackson got to work on it promptly, and by late 1829 it would be the first major initiative he sent to Congress for action. Why was it Jackson's first big priority? In part, it was what he knew. He had strong opinions about banks and taxes and federal spending, which he would also act upon in time, but he had *experience* with Indians. Almost twelve years had passed since he believed he had accomplished the removal of the Cherokees with his treaty of 1817, which included incentives for their voluntary relocation. Cherokees spurned this offer, but Jackson was not a man inclined to quit. Even if he had wanted to put off a confrontation, the contending parties would not have allowed him to. The Cherokees' constitution of 1827 had announced they wouldn't surrender their land, and the Georgians escalated their pressure in December 1828. Georgia declared its state laws would soon extend over Indian territories within Georgia, effectively erasing the Indian map. The Georgia laws included measures that specifically targeted Indians, forbidding them from establishing their own governments, and adding: "No Indian, and no descendant of an Indian not understanding the English language shall be deemed a competent witness in any court." A white man could turn an Indian out of his house or even kill him, and no Indian witness could testify against him. Elias Boudinot, the editor of the *Cherokee Phoenix*, understood the purpose of such a law: "expulsion."

Georgia's act compelled the federal government to choose sides. Jackson chose. "The course pursued by Georgia is well calculated to involve her & the United States in great difficulty, unless the Indians can be got to remove west of the M," Jackson wrote his friend John Overton in June 1829. He was already facing a delicate situation with South Carolina, and did not need another fight with other southern states. Less than three weeks after his inauguration, he composed a letter to the Creeks who still possessed parts of Alabama, which was also applying state law to Indian land:

March 23rd. 1829

Friends & Brothers,

By permission of the Great Spirit above, and the voice of the people, I have been made a President of the United States, and now speak to you as your father and friend, and request you to listen.

Jackson informed the Creeks that "you and my white children are too near to each other to live in harmony and peace. . . . Beyond the great river Mississippi, where a part of your nation has gone, your father has provided a country large enough for all of you," Jackson said. "My white children in Alabama have extended their law over your country. If you remain in it, you must be subject to that law."

This is a straight and good talk. It is for your nation's good, and your father requests you to hear his counsel.

Andrew Jackson

Jackson, of course, was not ordering them to depart. He left them the freedom to choose, and merely set the conditions so that they would have only one choice.

The principal chief of the Cherokee Nation did not seem to understand at first what Jackson was doing, though he was in Washington at the time. When Jackson promised "a just and liberal policy" toward the Indians, it is likely that John Ross was in the crowd. He was staying at Williamson's Hotel, which faced Pennsylvania Avenue between the White House and the Capitol. Within a few years Williamson's would be rebuilt and rechristened the Willard, a seat of luxury and political intrigue for generations to follow. It was an ideal location, a little more than a mile from the inauguration, a straight walk down Pennsylvania toward the green copper Capitol dome. After the inauguration, Ross's walk back to his room would have led him on the same path as Jackson, meaning that he would have been walking among those masses ("boys, women and children, black and white") who trailed after their new president on his way to the Executive Mansion. Even if Ross did not continue all the way to the reception at the president's house, he surely knew of the chaos there, and might have heard it from Williamson's, two blocks away.

Ross, like Jackson, had arrived in Washington after a tragic end to the year. The Cherokee's family tragedy is difficult to detail, for he was never as personal in his letters. His only known comment on this disaster came in the final phrase of a short letter to Cherokee lawmakers on an unrelated subject.

> *I return herewith the resolutions of the Committee passed on this 28th inst. regulating the issuing of permits, which I am of opinion requires some alteration. Circumstances prevent me at present from stating the objections I have to approving it in its present shape; being compelled to return home immediately in consequence of the death of my infant child on this morning.*

This infant was the only one of Ross's six children with Quatie to die young. Whatever grief the child's death caused them went unrecorded, as did the cause; they buried the boy and went on with their lives, Quatie bearing another boy the following year. The chief's reticence may have reflected a stoical nature, or a stoical culture, or his feeling of responsibility as a leader. It may even have reflected the experience of a man who had grown up suspended between the white and Indian worlds, and had learned never to reveal too much of himself. Ross returned to work the day after the baby's death. He sent another letter to Cherokee lawmakers, offering the details on his veto of legislation from the day before, and making only an oblique mention of his dead child.

The matter Ross was addressing in that letter demonstrated the intensifying emotions of the conflict between Cherokees and white men. If Georgia was moving to disinherit the Indians, Cherokees were moving to reorder relations with whites. Cherokee lawmakers approved legislation forbidding white men from working inside the Cherokee Nation without a costly permit. In rejecting this plan, Ross softened the blow by telling lawmakers only that the legislation was badly drawn, though he likely understood that it was simply a bad idea. Every white person who lived or worked in the Cherokee Nation was a resource and a potential ally, a link to the white electorate on whom the Cherokees' fate depended.

But if Ross handled his own legislature deftly, his political instincts seemed to fail him once he reached Washington as part of the annual Cherokee delegation to the capital. His correspondence included no report of the inauguration, a revealing omission. His actions that winter suggested that he did not yet grasp the historic significance of the election. The Cherokees spent February trying to do business with officials from the outgoing Congress and administration, depressed and defeated lame ducks who would have no influence with the new powers in the capital. Ross had to start over again after the inauguration, beginning with the new president. "Respected Sir," he wrote Jackson on March 6—addressing the president as a fellow man, not as the Great White Father—"the present U.S. agent for the Cherokee Nation . . . does not . . . inspire . . . confidence." Ross complained of the agent's "apparent incompetency" and his unwarranted seizure of a hundred acres of Cherokee land. Ross's grievances went deeper than that: the agent had been seeking to infiltrate the Cherokee Nation with Cherokees from the western band. Some Cherokees who had been living beyond the Mississippi since 1808 had been recruited for a secret effort to persuade the main band of Cherokees to emigrate out of the east and join them. The effort produced another exposé in the *Cherokee Phoenix*, which somehow obtained the agent's correspondence about his secret mission. It was all published on March 11, including the Indian agent's embarrassing admission that despite all of his covert efforts "only a single Indian has yet enrolled" to move west. On April 6, after this well-timed scoop, Ross complained again to the president. But in the eight years that followed this complaint, as Jackson went through an unprecedented clearing out of the federal bureaucracy, he never got around to replacing the Cherokee agent.

It was only after raising these comparatively small complaints that Ross turned to the truly existential issue, the danger posed by Georgia. At Ross's request, the new secretary of war conferred with the president to determine whether the United States would protect the Cherokees. On April 18, 1829, the answer came back: No. The United States could "never" interfere with Georgia's legitimate exercise of its authority. Secretary of War John Eaton said it was the Cherokees' fault that Georgia was taking their land, because "the tribe established an independent government within the territory of the state." Cherokees must yield to Georgia's laws if they remained in Georgia, although the more "humane" alternative would be moving to the West, where "the soil shall be yours, while the trees grow or the streams run." This must have been the moment when John Ross fully understood the meaning of the election of 1828. Days later he acknowledged that his talks with federal officials had failed, and he left Washington for the season.

He didn't go straight home. He went northward first, up the East Coast. He intended to travel to New York and Albany, returning to the West by way of the new Erie Canal, but having remained in Washington "much longer than desired or anticipated," he didn't have time to see this latest wonder of the world. He made it no farther than Philadelphia, where he wrote a letter acknowledging that he had not achieved his objectives in Washington.

What will be the result of the unnatural course which Georgia has taken, or the ultimate fate of the Cherokee nation, I dare not attempt to predict—but . . . the nation is prepared passively, to meet the worse

of the consequences; than to surrender their homes, their all and to
emigrate.

It was a downbeat letter, yet it influenced future events. Just as
Jackson signaled his strategy in his letter from Gadsby's in 1825, John
Ross expressed his strategy in this May 6, 1829, letter from Philadelphia. "Passively" resisting oppression, Cherokees would neither rise in
arms nor "surrender." They would remain in place and demand that the
United States keep its obligations. In a later age, minority groups would
commit acts of civil disobedience to highlight rights they were denied.
John Ross contemplated civil *obedience,* following the law while high-
lighting rights he believed Indians already had.

Nineteen

The Blazing Light of
the Nineteenth Century

In the summer of 1829 a letter reached the offices of the *National Intelligencer* in Washington. A bundle of papers arrived with the letter. The writer proposed that his letter and the papers should be published under a pseudonym: "William Penn."

Gentlemen: I send for your paper two numbers of a series of Essays on the pending . . . controversy between the United States and the Indians, and hope you will insert them. . . . This is a subject which must be abundantly discussed in our country. . . . Some able members of Congress, to my certain knowledge, wish to have the matter discussed.

The *Intelligencer* had been linked with presidential administrations since the start of the century. No longer was it so: the paper was part of a capital elite that the new president did not like or trust. Jackson would steer business and information instead to the Jackson man who ran a rival Washington paper, the *United States Telegraph*, and when that editor proved insufficiently loyal, Jackson would import an editor from Kentucky to start yet another paper. This left the *National Intelligencer* free to speak, a paper that was still widely read and a clever choice for

Ross's ally to use. As an "inducement" to encourage the paper to print his essays, "Penn" promised this paper that was now part of Jackson's opposition that "I shall not agree with the present Executive of the United States . . . [who] has been greatly mistaken in his powers and his duty."

The *Intelligencer* printed this letter with an advisory: "The Essays shall be published."

It was common in the nineteenth century to write such articles pseudonymously, though the editors of the *Intelligencer* surely understood whom they were publishing. Word of his identity spread among the elites, many of whom knew his name and his work. He was a former magazine editor based in Boston, a sickly, hollow-cheeked New Englander known for the luminous intensity of both his feelings and his prose. "William Penn" was his avatar, to use the language of a later era, chosen because Penn, the founder of Pennsylvania, had set an example of recognizing Indian rights.

The writer's real name was Jeremiah Evarts. He had visited Cherokee country and now worked for an organization that supported missionaries there. It was called the American Board of Commissioners for Foreign Missions, and Evarts was the board's corresponding secretary. In modern terms he was the communications director, an influential voice in an organization that sent missionaries as far away as China and as near as New Echota. Samuel Worcester, the missionary in the Cherokee capital, was the American Board's man. He regularly wrote to Evarts and Evarts to him. Back when the missionary needed help obtaining a printing press for the *Cherokee Phoenix*, Evarts was the one who helped to have a press sent from Boston. Evarts was also an ally of John Ross. When Ross wrote his letter of May 6, 1829, outlining his strategy to "passively" resist removal, he sent it to Evarts. Ross was assuring him that Cherokees were not about to do anything foolish, that the growing religious movement could act in support of Indians without fear of embarrassment. Evarts acted.

Evarts, like Ross, was in Washington on the day of Jackson's inauguration, close enough to see that the new president kissed the Bible on which he took his oath of office, but not close enough to follow the new president's speech. "I could hear some words distinctly; but could not keep the connexion," he remembered later. It may have been just as well that Evarts did not hear the president's promise to pursue "a just and liberal policy" toward the tribes, because Evarts would not have believed it. He had been staying the past three weeks at Gadsby's and had met his fellow lodger, the president-elect. They talked about Indians. In a letter written afterward, Evarts said Jackson understood the "evil" of "a direct collision between the national and state authorities," but that Jackson was unwilling to do anything about it. "He is not now prepared to interpose, and defend the Cherokees from Georgia; and you may easily judge, whether it is probable he will be in more favorable circumstances hereafter to decide in favor of the weakest party."

"No relief can be hoped," Evarts decided, "except through the influence of the press. This may operate upon the members of Congress." Soon he was crafting his essays. He understood how to make an article spread from one newspaper to the rest of the media. Though the *Intelligencer* was a daily paper, he proposed to provide two essays each week, so that "they may be copied into semi-weekly papers, if their Editors see fit." He also understood his subject. In his first essay, printed on August 5, 1829, he quoted from a letter written by the secretary of war, the dismissive note telling John Ross that the government would not protect the Cherokees. In his following essays, William Penn shredded the substance of that letter.

Penn acknowledged that proponents of Indian removal believed they were performing "the greatest kindness," whether the Indians liked it or not. But "no subject, not even war, nor slavery, nor the nature of free institutions" would be so closely examined by the world. "If, in pursuance of a narrow and selfish policy, we should at this day, in a time of profound peace and great National prosperity, amidst all our professions of magnanimity and benevolence, and in the blazing light of the nineteenth century, drive away the remnants of the tribes, in such a

manner, and under such auspices, as to ensure their destruction . . .
then the sentence of an indignant world will be uttered in thunders,
which will roll and reverberate for ages after the present actors in human
affairs shall have passed away."

That was the first essay. Twenty-three more came after it.

Evarts was a man whose thinking wove together several of the great
strands of the early American intellect. He was a product of strict New
England religion, with a terror of idleness and an intense consciousness
of the sinfulness of man. But if mankind was marked by "narrow and
selfish" behavior, Evarts was also conscious of living in "the blazing
light of the nineteenth century," when advances in technology and communication sparked tremendous optimism. For many Americans, the
greatest innovation was America itself, a nation destined to play a special role in the world. For some, America's special role was offering a
beacon of liberty to a world ruled by kings. For others, including Evarts,
America's destiny was also to spread God's word to the "heathen lands"
around the globe, including the lands of Indians near home.

He was a Vermont farmer's son, and a product of Yale College in
New Haven, Connecticut. A Yale classmate said Evarts looked about
the same in college as he would twenty years later: "There sat Evarts, in
a plain rustic garb, with which fashion evidently had never intermed-
dled; his stature of middling height; his form remarkably slender; his
manners stiff; and his whole exterior having nothing to prepossess a
stranger in his behalf, except a countenance which bespoke as much
honesty as ever falls to the lot of man." Intense, focused and in time
deeply religious—he became a committed Christian during his senior
year—young Evarts was ferociously self-critical. He excoriated himself
for wasting time with "idle talking" or even "reading," and wrote once
in his journal: "In my leisure moments I think over the sins with which
my whole life has been filled. They appear dreadful." Evarts could be as
hard on others as he was on himself. Long before Evarts the writer

publicly challenged the president of the United States, Evarts the student found the courage to challenge the president of Yale. During a class discussion of the question "Is dancing a useful employment?" the young man was shocked to hear President Timothy Dwight say that dancing and balls were perfectly fine, if properly conducted. Evarts rose to say that dancing was a "temptation" and that a man of such prominence ought to know better than to endorse it.

If his intense focus on personal morals makes him seem like an ancestor of the modern religious right, the politics he espoused after leaving Yale also make Evarts seem like an ancestor of the modern pacifist left. From 1810 to 1821 he edited the *Panoplist*, a Boston religious journal. He wrote in its pages that America should commit to establishing schools and churches "in every part of the globe; the alleviation of human suffering of every kind . . . in a word, the entire subjugation of the world to Christ." He wrote antiwar articles. In 1811, when Britain and France were at war, he denounced generals who instilled in their soldiers "a stupid contempt of death." When the United States joined the global conflict by declaring war against Britain in 1812, Evarts did not allow patriotic sentiment to lead him away from his principles. Precisely as activists would do two centuries later during the war in Iraq, he attempted to crystallize opposition to the war by putting a price tag on the conflict. His newspaper calculated that the cost of weapons, ammunition, destroyed property, economic disruption, and ruined lives totaled $3.235 billion in 1813 alone. Once he became acquainted with Cherokee issues it was inevitable that he would attack those issues too, based on his own passionate morality.

Evarts gained his acquaintance with Cherokee issues because he traveled numerous times over the years from New England to the South. At first he went for his health, having been sickly all his life; doctors suggested that he seek restoration in the warm air of South Carolina and Georgia. After 1821 he was making the journeys for work too. That was when he became corresponding secretary of the American Board, the missionary organization. Evarts realized that he could support the board's work by prospecting for donations on his southern travels. "I was never in a place where so many people might give largely," he wrote once, strategizing about what kind of fund-raising letters might move their hearts. Of course, he knew the reason many in the South were able to "give largely," and he brooded over it. His hosts in Charleston once took him to see a slave auction, which he watched while taking notes with a pencil. Enslaved individuals and families were made to stand on a table, looking "exceedingly disconsolate, much as if they were led to execution." A carpenter and his wife were sold for $1,000 each, a "field woman" for $560. Many of the enslaved tried to recruit buyers whom they believed to be kind masters, for "they dread to be sold to a bad, or an unknown master," and if they failed to avoid this fate, they did not hide their despair. Such scenes reinforced Evarts's belief in gradual abolition, which he called the only way to avoid a slave revolt. "Black men will at last be free; and if they are not freed by kindness, under the direction of wisdom, they will gain their liberty by violence, at the instigation of revenge."

Slipping away from the commercial cities of the coast, Evarts traveled inland. He believed that long journeys on horseback would restore his health; one of his expense reports from those years recorded a journey of 768 miles, nearly all of it in the saddle. His journeys took him to the Cherokee Nation. He stayed for days at Brainerd, the best known of the Cherokee missions, admiring the sun setting through the open woods on the grounds. The American Board had purchased this twenty-five-acre compound from John McDonald, John Ross's grandfather, the old Scottish trader and master of intrigue. While it is not certain when Ross and Evarts first met, they were clearly collaborating from the mid-1820s onward, and both went to Washington lobbying for Cherokees. They worked together even though neither their principles nor their motivations precisely matched. Ross worried about the advancement of Cherokees; Evarts worried about the soul of the United

States. Evarts opposed slavery; Ross owned slaves. Evarts was deeply religious, and Ross only nominally so. And Evarts never defended traditional Cherokee religion or culture, instead promoting what he saw as moral progress and Christ. But in the summer of 1829, Evarts was exactly what Ross needed: a genuine ally who was willing to fight alongside him as an equal. Evarts was different from Henry Clay, who supported Indian rights but also thought Indians were doomed. While Clay thought Indians' "disappearance from the human family would be no great loss to the world," Evarts placed them on the same level as white men. His second "William Penn" essay, published on August 8, borrowed some of the phrasings of the Declaration of Independence. Thomas Jefferson had written "that all men are created equal, that they are endowed by their Creator with certain unalienable rights." Evarts wrote of truths he considered self-evident:

> The Cherokees are human beings, endowed by their Creator with the same natural rights as other men. They are in peaceable possession of a territory which they have always regarded as their own. This territory was in possession of their ancestors, through an unknown series of generations, and has come down to them with a title *absolutely unencumbered in every respect*. It is not pretended, that the Cherokees have ever alienated their country, or that the whites have ever been in possession of it. . . . We might as well ask the Chinese, what right *they* have to the territory which they occupy.

Here Evarts arrived at the strongest argument in favor of the Cherokees. They had a "natural right" to land where they had lived so long, and which they had improved by building farms and towns. Their claim of ownership was so strong that even the government of Georgia was not technically seeking to overturn it. Instead Georgia was proposing to extend state law over the Cherokee Nation while refusing to assimilate the Cherokee people. The people would be denied basic rights of citizenship—such as voting or testifying in court—which meant that they would be left with little choice but to depart. Evarts wrote that if Georgia's assertion of power over the Cherokees "is to be endured by an enlightened people in the nineteenth century, and if, in consequence of it, the Cherokees are to be delivered over, bound and manacled, if this is to be done in the face of day . . . hisses of shame and opprobrium will be heard in every part of the civilized world." Again and again Evarts emphasized that the world was watching. Certainly the nation was watching Evarts. Some forty other newspapers reprinted his essays. "The Letters of WILLIAM PENN," the *Intelligencer* commented, "have had a more general circulation in the public prints than any other series of Letters that have ever been published during our time." Evarts heard that even John Marshall, the chief justice of the United States, had read and approved of them. Probably Evarts did not anticipate that Marshall would someday rule on the Cherokees' case. But Evarts, who early in his career had been a frustrated lawyer, could not have failed to pause upon learning that his legal and political analysis had met with the approval of the nation's leading jurist. Perhaps Evarts even allowed himself a moment of quiet satisfaction before denouncing himself for the sin of wasting time. Jeremiah Evarts, forever seeking some great purpose that was worthy of his obligation to serve, had found his cause.

PART SIX

State of the Union

1829–1830

Twenty

They Have Been Led to Look Upon Us as Unjust

Arguments over Indian removal came in several forms. There was, for example, the straight racist argument, elegantly phrased by Lewis Cass of Michigan. "Every Indian," Cass explained in a magazine article, shared the identical upbringing and behaved in the same way. "Reckless of consequences, he is the child of impulse. Unrestrained by moral considerations, whatever his passions prompt he does." Indians had decreased in population not because of war, social convulsion, and European diseases but because they resisted civilization. They were "clinging with a death grasp" to their old ways. "To roam the forests at will, to pursue their game, to attack their enemies, to spend the rest of their lives in listless indolence . . . and to be ready at all times to die; these are the principal occupations of an Indian." They must be pushed away from civilized areas for their own good.

Cass was a veteran of the War of 1812. He was an unwilling participant in the war's first great disgrace, when his commander surrendered Detroit to a combined force of British troops and Tecumseh's Indians. He later fought in one of the war's great victories, the Battle of the Thames, in which Tecumseh was killed. Appointed in 1813 as governor of the Michigan Territory, Cass held the job for eighteen years. Once, he led an expedition into Indian country, present-day Minnesota, and discovered a lake that he thought was the source of the Mississippi River. Cass Lake is named for him today, though he turned out to be wrong. Cass's experience on the frontier made him an Indian expert. "We speak of them as they are; as we have found them after a long and intimate acquaintance," Cass wrote in his article urging removal. "Government is unknown among them. . . . They have no criminal code, no courts, no officers, no punishments." More pertinent than Cass's argument was the territory he represented. It was important for Jackson to have such a prominent northern supporter for what was being painted as a southern initiative. Jackson liked Cass, and would eventually give him oversight of federal Indian policy.

Against the straight racist argument was the straight moral argument, spread widely thanks to Jeremiah Evarts. After the *North American Review* published Cass's article in January 1830, the magazine published a rebuttal written by a student activist who became an acolyte of Evarts. The moral argument was having intriguing effects, influencing not just the people who heard it but also the people who made it. It was causing some to rethink another issue, slavery. Until the 1830s, as we have seen, the notion of immediately abolishing slavery was widely regarded as extremist, illegal, and impractical. The more socially acceptable alternative was gradually freeing slaves for transport to West Africa, but some activists opposing Indian removal now had to wonder. If it was wrong to solve white people's problems by removing Indians, was it any better to solve white people's problems by removing black people?

Between the straight racist case and the straight moral case lay several gradations, such as the moral argument for removal. Thomas Mc-Kenney, the Superintendent of Indian Affairs who had so many chiefs' portraits painted and hung on his walls, argued that Indians were being destroyed by their contact with their aggressive neighbors. "We believe, if the Indians do not emigrate . . . they must perish." Then there was the racist argument for Indians to remain, memorably expressed by Henry

Clay (Indians were "not an improvable breed" but the United States should uphold its obligations to them).

The time came late in 1829 for Andrew Jackson to make his own case to the public. He was expected in December to send Congress his message on the state of the union. In Jackson's time the annual message was not delivered in a speech but in a long and sober letter, dealing with everything from coffee tariffs to national defense. Jackson wrote an early draft himself, making it an unusually personal report on a president's political preoccupations. He proposed new rules for presidential elections (he wanted to prevent anyone from working the system as Henry Clay had in 1825). He defended the firing of public officials who were being replaced by Jackson supporters ("rotation in office" would limit corruption, and experienced officials weren't really needed for government jobs anyway). And then he turned to the subject of Indians. Here, Jackson and his aides struggled not over what to do, but how to express it.

The argument that Jackson wanted to make resembled Thomas McKenney's moral case for removal. In a letter to James Gadsden, one of his former army subordinates, Jackson professed to be a friend of Indians. He wanted them to move west to be "free from the mercenary influence of white men, and undisturbed by the local authority of the states." In the West the federal government could "exercise a parental control over their interests" and save them from extinction. There is no reason to doubt that Jackson believed he was acting in the natives' best interest. They were not an abstraction to him. He knew many of them intimately from treaty negotiations and war; he had defended the rights of the widows of Cherokee soldiers killed under his command. But he thought about Indian interests in a certain way. Just as General Jackson had analyzed national security in a way that matched his real estate interests, President Jackson defined his "parental" duty to natives in a way that matched his desire to clear land for white settlement.

His first attempt at selling his preferred solution began with a nod to Indian sympathizers:

The condition of the Indians within the limits of the U. States is of a
character to awaken our Sympathies, & enduce the inquiry if something
cannot be done to better their situation.

Having defined Indian welfare as his purpose, Jackson shifted focus.
The real problem was land, the two conflicting maps of the continent. It
was true, Jackson admitted, that the Indians could make a case: "These
unfortunate people, were once the uncontroled & indisputable owners of
this immense region of country," and they had gradually yielded "to the
solicitations of their white brethren" until they were now found only in
remote areas. "It is but Justice that a proper degree of sympathy should be
awakened in their behalf." But Georgia and Alabama had a far simpler
case: "The states of this Union are Sovereign." And so, "while a generous
feeling is entertained towards this race, it should not be at the sacrafice of
principle, and of the interests of others concerned."

What then is to be done? Let the plan of removal beyond the
Mississippi

Jackson's first draft ended in mid-sentence. He never finished. The
president may simply have been distracted, but it was a remarkable point
at which to stop. He seemed not quite ready to commit to paper an act
that would be remembered for ages. Smarter, more strategic, and further-
seeing than his opponents understood, Jackson paused. He may have
been straining to reconcile his chosen course with his understanding of
"Justice," that word he had characteristically capitalized just a few sentences earlier.

He left Indian removal for another day and another person. His secretary of war, John Eaton, tried to finish the passage but only came up
with bluster. Defending Indians would require the president to call out
the army against a state, "a power which should be placed in the hands of
no individual." Jackson discarded Eaton's draft, no doubt unwilling to
limit his own authority to call out troops against a state, which he was

soon to do against recalcitrant South Carolina. The president certainly *could* use his power to enforce federal law. He could have taken a stronger stand against Georgia. He needed reasons why he *would* not.

Returning to his first draft, Jackson rewrote and reordered it, making subtle but vital changes. No longer would he confess that the Indians had been the "uncontroled & indisputable owners of this immense region." Instead he would say that "our ancestors found them the uncontrolled *possessors* of these vast regions." The administration held that Indians had never really "owned" anything, having failed to develop and improve the land, which they merely passed through to hunt.

The final, polished document led off with Jackson's best argument for change: the federal policy he had inherited made no sense.

> It has long been the policy of Government to introduce among [the tribes] the arts of civilization, in the hope of gradually reclaiming them from a wandering life. This policy has, however, been coupled with another wholly incompatible with its success. Professing a desire to civilize and settle them, we have at the same time lost no opportunity to purchase their lands and thrust them farther into the wilderness. By this means they have not only been kept in a wandering state, but been led to look upon us as unjust and indifferent to their fate.

Even if Jackson's facts were wrong (Cherokees would not have said they were "in a wandering state"), he was making a frank confession. He said that white men had been too greedy for land. Of course, this confession led to a question: If it was damaging for Indians to be thrust "farther into the wilderness," why would Jackson advocate thrusting them even farther? Jackson had his reasons.

> A portion . . . of the Southern tribes, having mingled much with the whites and made some progress in the arts of civilized life, have lately attempted to erect an independent government within

the limits of Georgia and Alabama. These States, claiming to be the only sovereigns within their territories, extended their laws over the Indians, which induced the latter to call upon the United States for protection. Under these circumstances the question presented was whether the General Government had a right to sustain those people in their pretensions.

Here Jackson turned Ross's great achievement against him. Cherokees had governed themselves for centuries, dating back to a time well before the existence of Georgia. But when Ross and other Cherokee elites reformed and updated that government in accord with American republican principles, Jackson called it a new creation that Cherokees who "mingled much with the whites" had "lately attempted to erect." This was Jackson's political jujitsu. The Indians were no longer the inhabitants of the land from time immemorial; they were late-arriving interlopers on the long-standing powers of the states. John Ross was no longer a loyal chief who was insisting on his tribe's rights within "the great family of the Republic of the U. States," but instead a man seeking independence. Nevertheless, Jackson was willing to try to save the Cherokees by financing their journey west.

Surrounded by the whites with their arts of civilization, which by destroying the resources of the savage doom him to weakness and decay . . . [Indians are bound for extinction] if they remain within the limits of the States. . . . Humanity and national honor demand that every effort should be made to avert so great a calamity. . . . This emigration should be voluntary, for it would be as cruel as unjust to compel the aborigines to abandon the graves of their fathers and seek a home in a distant land. But they should be distinctly informed that if they remain within the limits of the States they must be subject to their laws. In return for their obedience as individuals they will without doubt be protected in the enjoyment of those possessions which they have improved by their industry.

Jackson did not mention that Georgia law would not allow Cherokees to vote or even to testify in court.

There was one more set of opinions to be heard before congressional debate began: the views of Indians. John Ross too wrote an annual message in 1829. Just as the president of the United States reported once a year on the state of the union, so the leader of the tiny republic within a republic reported once a year to Cherokee legislators. It was one more way the Cherokees imitated the United States. Ross's message in October 1829 insisted that the Cherokees still maintained sovereignty over their land, which could not be changed without their consent. But his tone was grim. "A crisis seems to be fast approaching when the final destiny of our nation must be sealed."

Twenty-one

The Expediency of Setting Fire

T he crisis was dramatized by gold discovered on Cherokee land. Interest in Georgia gold predated the existence of Georgia—it was rumors of gold that lured Hernando de Soto to explore the Cherokee country in 1540. It's hard to prove exactly when white men finally discovered gold in Georgia, although the first public announcement was a news article describing two discoveries in Habersham County in August 1829.

Habersham County was near the border of the Cherokee Nation, and prospectors soon ranged onto the Indian map. It was an early American gold rush, two decades before the discovery of gold in California, featuring "a most motley" group of men, according to one observer—"whites, Indians, halfbreeds and negroes, boys of fourteen and men of seventy . . . diggers, sawyers, shopkeepers, peddlers, thieves and gamblers." They came by the hundreds, and then by the thousands, populating a boomtown that would be called Dahlonega. Georgia's elites didn't think much of the rabble, described by the governor as "idle, profligate people" who had been "loosed from the restraints of the law." This seems unfair; at least the Indian prospectors had a right to be there, and none of the prospectors were idle. They were madly digging or sifting the earth, sleeping a few hours under the stars and returning to work again, knowing they could be evicted before they found anything.

Federal Indian agents understood that they had a duty to evict white intruders, but Georgians took offense, protesting that anything the federal government did interfered with state jurisdiction. In April 1830 the *Cherokee Phoenix* would report that the federal Indian agent had ordered many prospectors to leave the Cherokee country, and "almost all had departed, until it was ascertained that the agent had procured no warrants in Georgia, as it was supposed he would—they have new returned with redoubled force . . . encouraged by some of the leading men of the neighboring counties, by the lawyers especially, who will stand 'between them and all danger.'"

In later years the impression would arise that the greed for gold drove the Georgians to take Cherokee land. This was not quite accurate. Georgia's elites wanted the land even before the gold rush, and even afterward they wanted the land mainly because it was land. Over the course of 1830 the throng of miners sent $212,000 worth of gold to the U.S. Mint at Philadelphia. This was a fortune, even when divided among numerous prospectors, yet still a sideline compared with the value of the soil. Two hundred twelve thousand dollars in the gold rush was nothing compared with the millions that were made in the 1818 land rush in northern Alabama. There was an opportunity for a comparable bounty in the Cherokee country of north Georgia. The great prize, the primary prize, in the Cherokee Nation was not gold but real estate.

Land, like gold, caused men to be "loosed from the restraints of the law," leading to murderous incidents that John Ross struggled to contain. One such incident at the start of 1830 forced Ross to engage in some public relations damage control. On February 13, 1830, he sat down to write a letter while staying at Head of Coosa—the common name for the settlement at the headwaters of that river, where Ross had recently built a new home. Here he was near Major Ridge's white plantation house with its ferry, farm, and store, and also had a much shorter commute to New Echota. It was to New Echota that he was sending this letter, addressed to Elias Boudinot at the *Cherokee Phoenix.*

The previous autumn, the newspaper's publication had nearly been interrupted when Boudinot came to Ross and announced his resignation. Boudinot's family was growing, his work in two languages was overwhelming, and he could not go on producing nearly all the editorial material himself. Boudinot was irreplaceable on short notice, and Ross "could not for a moment think of seeing [the paper] stopped." Ross promised to find money to hire an assistant, even if it had to come from Ross's own pocket. Boudinot resumed his place in the printshop, buoyed by an extra $100 a year, and Ross quickly found it worth the investment. When he wrote his letter in February, he knew there was at least one sympathetic journalist to whom he could try to explain a tangled mess.

> *Sir*
>
> *With the view of preventing erroneous impressions from growing out of the various reports which will no doubt be circulated . . . I deem it my duty to make a true statement of facts.*

It is easy to imagine Ross pausing at this point and rubbing his forehead. Where to begin? The lawbreaking, the fires, the whiskey, the kidnapping, the body dumped by the side of the road . . . Probably it was best to start at the beginning.

> *It is generally known that there are divers intruders on Cherokee land . . . some of them being men of the most infamous character.*

This was a story of Cherokee efforts to evict white families living on Cherokee land. There was nothing new about the problem or its attempted solution. Burning out intruders was what John Ross had done when commanding the Cherokee Light Horse in 1820. But now the stakes were higher, the problem was worse, and something had gone grievously wrong. That was what John Ross was writing Elias Boudinot to explain. He described a recent effort to remove white settlers.

> *The General Council at its last session made it my duty to remove such of them as may be found amidst our citizens in possession of the improvements recently abandoned by the Cherokees, who have emigrated to the Arkansas.*

The intruders were occupying farms left behind by Cherokees who had decided to move west of the Mississippi. It was irresistible for a poor white family to take a chance on farming land already cleared by now-absent hands. Through much of 1829 the Cherokees had waited for the federal government to act against these intruders. The Indian agent did try to warn them off, but the new administration in Washington did not send troops to assist him. Late in 1829 Ross called attention to a decades-old treaty declaring that if any U.S. citizen should settle on Cherokee lands, "such person shall forfeit the protection of the United States, and the Cherokees may punish him or not, as they please." The Cherokee government decided to enforce this clause, and early in 1830 Ross ordered the deployment of a force of Cherokee horsemen like the one he had led years ago. He assigned the responsibility of command to his burly white-haired neighbor Major Ridge, who was apparently still willing to ride into harm's way as he approached the age of sixty. Ridge organized what must have been a substantial force, large enough to face down scores of white settlers. He enforced what discipline he could among his troops. "The men were prohibited from using ardent spirits whilst on duty," Ross stressed in his letter defending the expedition. Along a public road leading toward Alabama, Ridge's troopers rounded up no fewer than eighteen families, who were told to gather up their effects and leave the Cherokee Nation.

The company were fully persuaded that if the houses were not
destroyed, the intruders would not go away; they therefore determined
on the expediency of setting fire to them.

Possibly the smoke was visible in Carroll County, Georgia, the location of the nearest settlements on the whiteside.

Their mission seemingly accomplished, Major Ridge disbanded his men and sent them toward home in small groups, and this was when the mission began to go disastrously wrong. Andrew Jackson would never have made such a mistake. When Jackson received an order to disband his force in 1813 at Natchez, Mississippi, he disregarded his instructions and marched them together home to Middle Tennessee, partly to preserve them as a fighting unit under his command, and partly for their own protection. But Major Ridge may never have known this bit of Jackson lore, and in any case did not learn from it. As the small parties of Cherokees departed the field of their success, both security and discipline disappeared. Ross reported in his letter that four of Ridge's men "became intoxicated and remained" at a friend's house "where there was whiskey." They were in no condition to resist or even to flee when a party of twenty Georgians came across the border from the whiteside, seeking vengeance for the eviction of the settlers. The Georgians seized all four Cherokees and dragged them off toward custody in Carroll County. One of the prisoners, Chuwoyee,

who was unable to walk (being very drunk) was tied and put upon a
horse, but not being able to sit on, and falling off once or twice, he was
most barbarously beaten with guns &c. in the head, face, breast and
arms, and was then thrown across the pummel of a saddle on a horse,
and carried by the rider in that situation about one mile and then
thrown off.

Chuwoyee died the next morning, and was dumped on the road. Not until two days afterward was Ross able to send a wagon to pick up the corpse, and "he was decently buried at his own house by the side of the graves of his father and mother. The corpse was shockingly mangled."

> *If it is thus that the laws of Georgia are to be extended and*
> *executed over the Cherokees, it is very obvious that justice and*
> *humanity are not to be respected. . . . The Cherokees . . . will patiently*
> *wait for justice through the proper tribunal. Your ob't Serv't*
>
> *Jno Ross.*

Ross wrote several letters expressing his view of the tragedy, casting it as a sign of white perfidy, and in the months that followed, Elias Boudinot's *Cherokee Phoenix* adopted this view. But as Ross must have known, other people would interpret this as a tale of drunken Indians. And he also suspected that federal authorities would turn it into a story of Cherokees exercising extralegal authority. When news of the confrontation reached Washington, Ross's view did not prevail. Secretary of War John Eaton blamed the Cherokees for the violence, saying they should not have "arrogated to themselves" the right of "setting in judgment" on American citizens, and "driving them and their families from their houses." Eaton said he was instructing troops to march from Fort Mitchell, Alabama, to the Cherokee country to restore order, but in the weeks that followed, as federal troops began operating in Georgia, state authorities protested. Fully accommodating Georgia's insistence on states' rights, the army withdrew, eventually to be replaced by Georgia troops, who would begin enforcing the law in the Cherokee Nation in ways that served the state's interest.

What had really provoked these murderous events along the Alabama road? In the aftermath, the *Cherokee Phoenix* began to uncover evidence that the wave of intrusion may not have been just what it seemed. In April 1830, the *Phoenix* printed another exposé: "Some of the *officers of the United States* have been clandestinely encouraging intruders into the nation." When asked to explain what had possessed them to settle without authorization on Cherokee land, some of the white settlers explained that they had been acting on the highest authority. "A number of the intruders . . . have lately certified" that they had come to Cherokee land with the encouragement of a letter from "the President of the United States." Five white men signed a statement saying that they had heard federal Indian officials in the area read aloud from that letter back on September 29, 1829. As the men remembered the text, President Jackson promised that "any white person or persons was at liberty to settle any where in the Cherokee Nation on any place [from which Cherokees had] emigrated[,] that there was no danger in settling on any such land." President Jackson's representative went on to say that if white men would also "go and build at the Springs of Indians that had not emigrated that it would cause them to enrol themselves for the Arkansas."

The reputed letter by Andrew Jackson probably did not exist. Now that he was the personification of federal authority, Jackson would have been exceedingly unlikely to write a letter that explicitly instructed settlers to defy the law. It is more likely that Jackson appointed representatives who understood his long-standing opinions about intruders. Back in 1816, when ordering John Coffee to "run the line" to capture additional Indian territory in Alabama, Jackson had conspicuously failed to stop white settlers who took land without authorization. Instead he angrily defended them. In his mind he was simply standing up for impoverished Tennessee farmers. He was not violating the law, simply reinterpreting the law without regard for what it said. In the same way, he would have sympathized with the farmers and gold prospectors who moved into Cherokee country in 1829, and he would have known the intruders' strategic value. Any federal official familiar with Jackson's views would have understood what the chief executive in the distant capital wanted.

Twenty-two

Sway the Empire of Affection

D enied the right to defend their territory by force, Cherokees were reminded again that they depended on the power of the people. They must persuade the wider American public, as Jeremiah Evarts had tried to do with his much-reprinted essays of 1829. It was through Evarts that the campaign on behalf of the Cherokees now spread.

Evarts was composing his William Penn essays in Boston in 1829 when he had a visitor from out of town. He knew her through his friend Lyman Beecher, a Boston preacher. This was the same Lyman Beecher who had sent word before the presidential inauguration that Andrew Jackson would "distinguish himself as a patriot" if he would close the post offices on Sundays. Beecher and Evarts were allies on the matter of the Sunday mails. Their efforts on that issue were hopeless—limited Sunday mail service would continue until 1912—but their relationship proved productive for Evarts, because he came to meet Lyman Beecher's oldest daughter.

Catharine Beecher was twenty-nine years old in 1829, a woman notable for her self-confidence, independence, and sly wit. Neither wealthy nor married, she supported herself by running a school for girls in Hartford, Connecticut. Her pupils included her little sister Harriet, eleven years her junior and a precocious writer. Catharine was on her way to writing dozens of books on subjects ranging from housekeeping to child-rearing to education. When she met Jeremiah Evarts in Boston, he made a profound impression. Still thin and hollow-cheeked, sickly and unconcerned with his appearance, he was nevertheless filled with the passion of his beliefs. Inevitably the subject turned to Indians. As Beecher recalled many years later, Evarts warned of the "distressing and disastrous consequences" of removing the Cherokees, and then he made a suggestion. "He said that American women might save these poor, oppressed natives, and asked me to devise some method of securing such intervention. I was greatly excited," Beecher said, as she surely was. Jeremiah Evarts had just proposed the first mass political action by women in the history of the United States. Catharine Beecher agreed to take part.

What happened next was done in secrecy, using extraordinary measures to shield the identities of the women involved. Women were expected to play no direct part in politics. The accepted ways for women to express themselves were to quietly advise their husbands, or to participate in charitable organizations that promoted public virtue. They could not vote. The general broadening of voting rights for men was slowly provoking Americans to ask if women should also participate (within a few years young Abraham Lincoln, running for the Illinois legislature, would endorse voting rights for all taxpayers and veterans, "by no means excluding females"), but the discussion was not far advanced. Susan B. Anthony was nine years old in 1829. The historic Seneca Falls convention at which influential women would discuss and debate their rights would not come until 1848. Few women would be publicly credited with a major effect on mainstream political life before 1852, when Catharine Beecher's little sister Harriet, by then known as Harriet Beecher Stowe, published *Uncle Tom's Cabin,* her best-selling novel on the evils of slavery.

Yet in 1829 Catharine Beecher was one of a number of women Evarts urged to speak out. Beecher made herself heard, though she did not make herself known. So thoroughly did she keep her name from

being associated with her campaign that the inside details seem not to
have been disclosed until forty-five years later, when she finally published an account of them. But the results of the work by Beecher and
other women were visible almost immediately.

A photograph of Catharine Beecher in middle age shows a woman with
calm, curious eyes. There is a hint of mirth about the upward slant of
her eyebrows, and a hint of the Puritan in the white lace about her neck.
She has a shawl draped carelessly over her shoulders, giving her the
slightly rumpled look of the scholar. She is sitting on a wicker chair,
with a writing tablet balanced on her knee, pencil and paper poised at
the ready. It is plausible that she was sitting in a similar pose when she
began drafting an essay about the Cherokees.

> The present crisis in the affairs of the Indian nations . . . demands
> the immediate and interested attention of all who make any claims
> to . . . humanity.

She quoted from the Georgia laws that nullified the Cherokee government and prevented Indians from testifying. Describing such laws,
Beecher chose a word in common use in 1829, albeit in a different
context. "If these laws are permitted to take effect, the Indians are no
longer independent nations, but are slaves."

Never having spent time among the southern tribes, she was less
successful than Evarts in describing them in terms of equality ("Will
the naturalist, who laments the extinction of the mammoth race of the
forest," she asked in an unfortunate comparison, "allow this singular
and interesting species of the human race to cease from the earth?"), but
she seemed to relate to the Cherokees on a certain level. The Cherokees
were politically powerless, rather like women. Lacking the vote, they
had to rely on their voices. And much as John Ross of the Cherokees
had done, Beecher performed an act of political jujitsu. Ross used

George Washington's historic Indian policy to strengthen the Cherokee hold on land rather than weaken it. Beecher redefined women's political weakness as strength. She suggested that women's forced isolation from politics put them in a morally superior position.

> The females of this country . . . are protected from the blinding influence of party spirit, and the asperities of political violence. They have nothing to do with any struggle for power nor any right to dictate the decisions of those that rule over them.

But because women were free of "blinding influence" and "violence," they could "feel for the distressed." To a woman "it is given to administer the sweet charities of life, and to sway the empire of affection." This meant that women had a proper role to play in the Cherokee debate after all, because the Indians were distressed, and women had "duties" to help them. Women might in the end discover that they were "forbidden" from venturing into politics, but they should try the experiment. "It may be, that female petitioners can lawfully be heard, even by the highest rulers of our land." She referred to the biblical story of Queen Esther, who intervened to save the Jews from extermination. She added a postscript to the anonymous paper: "This communication was written and sent abroad solely by the female hand."

So it was: Beecher said years later that she recruited "judicious and influential" Hartford women to attend a meeting. She read her letter aloud, and the women agreed to act. "The circular was to be printed anonymously by a printer enjoined to secrecy, and all the ladies pledged themselves to similar secrecy. Then each lady gave the name of lady friends in some of the principal cities of the Northern, Middle and Western states; and it was remarkable how large a number was thus collected. Then a printed letter was sent to these ladies with a large number of the circulars, requesting each lady . . . to send them through the Post-Office to the most influential and benevolent ladies of her acquaintance." The Hartford women were starting a kind of chain letter, urging people across the country to organize public meetings on behalf of the Cherokees and, ultimately, to circulate petitions signed by thousands.

Why the secrecy? Partly it was custom—we have seen that Evarts too obscured his identity—but the measures taken by the Hartford women were far more elaborate than a pseudonym. When mailing copies of the circular, the Hartford women sent them from out of town so they would not bear a Hartford postmark. Nor did they simply take the bundle of letters to a single location where the postmaster might take note of the mass mailing; they used post offices in four different cities. It was as if they were anticipating a serious investigation to find the author. Some women may have felt they could not attach their names without compromising their husbands. (So closely were they identified with their husbands that many were not even referred to except by their husbands' names; when Catharine Beecher finally identified some of her collaborators, she called them, in the style of the age, "Mrs. Daniel Wadsworth, Mrs. Thomas Chester," and "Mrs. Sigourney," the last a prominent poet in Hartford. Catharine Beecher was not married, of course, but had her own reasons to keep her name hidden. She may have foreseen a backlash.

Or maybe it was just her style, because the secrecy was a kind of game, and Beecher had a playful view of the world. She was born in 1800, the oldest of thirteen children of a preacher who would struggle all his life to support so many. If Lyman Beecher was a stern figure of fire and brimstone, his first daughter was not. In her memoir, Catharine described spending her youth as an indifferent student: "It seemed as if I had a decided genius for nothing but play and merriment," she wrote. Sometimes, when her teacher tested the class by posing a series of predetermined questions to the students in order, Catharine's friends would covertly change places so the question that came to her would be the only one she could answer. Through such "contrivances" and "a few snatches" of reading, Catharine made it through school, though a teacher called her "the busiest of all creatures in doing nothing." She may not have been getting such a poor education. Rearranging her classmates to create the illusion that she had studied for a test, or figuring out the meaning of a book from reading a few "snatches," probably required more wit than simply doing her assignments. In 1829 she may well have delighted in the challenge of hiding her identity.

Experience had taught her to think for herself, even though it was not easy to get away with it. From an early age she battled her father on matters of religion. Lyman Beecher favored the Calvinist doctrine of original sin—that human beings were born in depravity rather than innocence. God had chosen in advance who would be saved and who would be consigned to eternal damnation; no one could change this predetermined fate. Though that would seem to remove the incentive for moral behavior, people were nevertheless urged to avoid sin and to hope for a moment of "conversion," an intense spiritual perception of God's grace that was taken as a sign of being one of God's elected. Lyman Beecher had his moment of grace as a young man, and later intensely pressured his daughter Catharine to have one too. Once while he was lecturing on her eternal fate she fell ill, apparently suffering a nervous collapse that left her unwell for days. In the early 1820s her fiancé died in a shipwreck, and Lyman Beecher said the young man was in hell, since his death had come before his conversion. Catharine refused to accept this as a certainty, instead agonizing over his fate.

She had never found another fiancé, which explained why she was supporting herself in her late twenties by running a school. Founding the Hartford Female Seminary, she became an innovator: finding that an arithmetic book did not seem well organized, she developed her own book. As the school grew—first filling a room above a Hartford store, then relocating to a church basement—Beecher visited leading citizens of Hartford and asked them to finance an entirely new school with a capacity for 150 girls. Men blanched, "but the more intelligent and influential women came to my aid, and soon all I sought was granted. This was my first experience of the moral power and good judgment of American women, which has been my chief reliance ever since." She was getting practice in politics: as the nation developed, no political question would become as universal as that of paying for school construction. Organizing women to push their husbands created a small-scale precedent for her campaign on behalf of Indians.

The circular written "by the female hand" created a response on a scale rarely seen before. The Hartford women hoped those who received the circular would forward it; an early clue that women were responding came when Catharine Beecher and her co-conspirators themselves began receiving letters in the mail. Women started recruiting husbands, sons, and brothers to the cause. One young man, spurred by his mother and sister, organized opposition at Andover, the seminary he attended. Newspapers reprinted the women's circular. Religious journals, with their outsize circulation, were so opposed to Indian removal that some printed the women's circular even though the editors were uncertain of its propriety. As Beecher recalled it, public meetings were held in every city to which the circular had been addressed, gatherings that were fed not only by the circular but also by the William Penn articles that were spreading from newspaper to newspaper. The meetings produced petitions to Congress. Although men usually signed them, women also affixed their names, however hesitantly. A letter from eighteen women in Farmington, Maine, began with an extended apology for writing at all, referring to "that delicacy of feeling and the Duty of deportment which should ever characterize the female Sex, [which] might forbid the profanity of offending ourselves upon the notice of the Legislative Council of the Nation, on any ordinary occasion."

People naturally began wondering who wrote the original Ladies' Circular. Some even posed the question to Catharine Beecher, who attempted to answer without actually lying. "I was asked one day by an outsider," she recalled, "and I replied that it was attributed by many to [her co-conspirator] Mrs. Sigourney, but it was not at all in her style, and much more like a gentleman I mentioned." She topped off this dissembling statement by saying of the circular that "I had never read anything that interested me so much." The game must have been energizing, but also stressful. Some people disapproved of the circular. One religious newspaper, the *Christian Watchman*, said Congress should be able to see the Indian question "righteously decided" without the intervention of women. Since the circular mentioned the biblical Queen Esther, so did the editors of the *Watchman*—adding the detail that Esther spoke up to save the Jewish people not through her own acts but by appealing to her husband.

Catharine Beecher wrote that there were "consequences" for the added "excitement" of her life: "I suddenly found myself utterly prostrated, and unable to perform any school duty without extreme pain and such confusion of thought as seemed like approaching insanity." The first American woman to mastermind a significant campaign of political activism was already under great stress, trying to raise an endowment for her school. Now she took a leave of absence, fleeing to the homes of friends to rest. She finally resigned, and the school went into decline.

The women's campaign had memorable effects on the nation and on Beecher. Her brush with "approaching insanity" apparently left her with a narrower view of women's roles, and the next time she made a prominent statement about politics, her role was entirely reversed. In the late 1830s, she engaged in a famous debate with a political activist, Angelina Grimké, a Quaker from South Carolina who felt that women should organize against slavery. "We affirm, that every *slaveholder* is a *man-stealer*," Grimké declared. Beecher agreed that slavery was an evil, yet she believed that Grimké was overstepping her bounds, and said so in dueling essays with the Quaker activist. Amazingly, given her secret experience, Beecher wrote that "petitions to congress, in reference to the official duties of legislators, seem, IN ALL CASES, to fall entirely without the sphere of female duty." Abolitionists were "irritating," and female abolitionists especially so. Although Grimké wanted northern women to organize local antislavery groups as they once organized against

Indian removal, Beecher saw this as counterproductive meddling in the affairs of the South. She had come to view political activism as a distraction from women's true calling in education, just as her own past political activism had taken her away from her seminary for girls. And this time Beecher signed her name to the essay. She became known to history not as a pioneering women's activist, but as the foil of a pioneering women's activist.

But the Ladies' Circular of 1829 had gone out into the world. Wilson Lumpkin, a representative from Georgia in the House of Representatives, would remember Congress being flooded with "thousands of petitions, signed by more than a million of men, women and children." This was an overstatement—the scores of yellowed petitions that remain today in the National Archives bear thousands of signatures, not a million—but Lumpkin's guess does suggest how large the petitions must have loomed in his mind.

Thomas Hart Benton cheerfully spoke about the women's campaign on the Senate floor. Benton, the former military aide whose 1813 quarrel with Andrew Jackson ended with a bullet in Jackson's shoulder, had since reconciled with his chief and was a powerful pro-Jackson senator from Missouri. He was amused by the petitions. He meant "no disrespect" to benevolent women, he said. They were better than "unbenevolent males." Benton would have been less amused had he looked carefully at the addresses from which the petitions had come. The New England women had appealed to women in "the Northern, Middle and Western states," but apparently not the South. The petitions that arrived in the capital came from Massachusetts, Maine, Vermont, Connecticut, New York, New Jersey, Pennsylvania, Ohio, and Indiana—but no southern state or slave state. Indian removal was rapidly becoming a template for another, greater conflict between North and South. Its victims would eventually include Senator Benton, a great Unionist who was thrown out of office by his badly divided slave state.

Indian removal was beginning to influence the thinking of people in "the Northern, Middle and Western states" in ways that neither Benton nor Catharine Beecher could have anticipated. Beecher helped to energize a network of respectable, religious citizens. These new opponents of Indian removal had commonly *supported* what might be termed African removal, the movement to gradually free slaves and send them to a colony overseas. After 1830 some activists concluded that if Indian removal was wrong, so was African removal. The old antislavery movement had recognized the rights of slave owners, cast them as victims of history, and promised that unfettered black people would not be left in their midst. Now a new movement declared that slaves should be immediately emancipated and allowed to live free in the United States. Activists cast slave owners as evil and challenged white Americans to rethink their views about race.

One of the new activists was William Lloyd Garrison, a Boston writer and fierce critic of slavery. As late as 1829 he favored African colonization, but by 1831 he had completely repudiated the idea. Between those two moments Garrison witnessed the debate over Indians. Imprisoned in April 1830 for libeling a slave trader, he sat in his cell reading accounts of the Indian removal debate in Congress. He emerged from jail declaring that forcing Indians to move would bathe America's name in "eternal infamy." His influential antislavery publications, first the *Genius of Universal Emancipation* and then the *Liberator,* reprinted articles from the *Cherokee Phoenix* alongside news about slavery. In Garrison's mind, the moral issues raised were the same.

PART SEVEN

Checks and Balances

1830–1832

Twenty-three

Legislative

A spring day in Washington: the House of Representatives came to order on Monday, May 17, 1830. The lawmakers' agenda was as diverse as the country that elected them. Records of that day indicate that they began by voting down a proposal to repeal the tax on salt. Next the House resumed debate on a measure that had consumed its time for much of the year.

The chairman recognized Representative Wilson Lumpkin of Georgia—a member of Congress for three years now, a lawyer and a rising political star. He was forty-seven, trim and impressive, with his dark hair piled thick atop his head something like the curving crest on the head of a cassowary bird. But as he stood at his desk in the cavernous chamber, Lumpkin showed no inclination to strut. "My life has never been free from care and responsibility," he said, but he had never felt "more deeply impressed with a sense of that responsibility, to God and his country," than "at the present moment."

Lumpkin said this burdensome feeling did not arise from his concern for the welfare of the constituents who elected him. No matter what Congress did about the Indians, Georgia and other states could "take care of themselves." He was motivated by his concern for the Cherokees and other tribes. "To those remnant tribes of Indians whose good we seek, the subject before you is of vital importance. It is a measure of life and death. Pass the bill on your table, and you save them. Reject it, and you leave them to perish."

The bill on the table would be known as the Indian Removal Act. The legislation drawn up by Jackson's allies in Congress provided the president the power to offer land west of the Mississippi to "such tribes or nations of Indians as may choose to exchange the lands where they now reside." They would voluntarily trade their lands to the east for lands to the west, and half a million dollars was committed to paying any costs of the transaction. For Representative Lumpkin, the bill was the culmination of his service in Congress; he had arrived in 1827 with something like this in mind. Nothing had changed his convictions about the wisdom of his course, though he was well aware of the tremendous opposition. Lumpkin was the same lawmaker who later claimed "more than a million" people had signed petitions against removal, whom he dismissed as "Northern fanatics, male and female." But if he did not accept their arguments, he clearly had taken care to read them, for the speech he delivered on May 17 was tailored to blunt the moral force of the opposition.

Lumpkin's speech did not deliberately denigrate Indians as a race. He agreed that some could be "brought" to civilization, and "entirely reclaimed from their native savage habits." But sadly, Cherokees were undermining their own reclamation by remaining in Georgia: "They will every day be brought into closer contact and conflict with the white population," and this would "diminish the spirit of benevolence" that white men felt toward the Indians, causing white citizens to withhold aid from "these unfortunate people." Cherokees must surrender their land to avoid irritating "philanthropic" Georgians who merely wanted to help them. Congressman Lumpkin said that he favored Indian interests, and that he assessed those interests more realistically than the Indians' pious supporters among the missionaries and the women.

Probably not everyone in the House chamber was able to hear Lumpkin's words, because the acoustics were no better in 1830 than they had been during the presidential voting in 1825. The reverberations persisted while the country outside the walls perceptibly changed. A nation that had been enthralled in 1825 by the opening of the Erie Canal was turning its attention to railroads. By May 1830 service was opening on the first dozen miles of the Baltimore and Ohio line. Around the same time the first railroad was chartered west of the Appalachians—a line beginning in Tuscumbia, Alabama, on Tennessee Valley land Andrew Jackson had obtained from Indians during his frantic period of "running the line" a decade and a half before. Within a few years this first western railroad expanded parallel to the Tennessee River, offering a way to bypass the shallows and rapids at Muscle Shoals. Of 12.8 million Americans counted in the 1830 census, several million lived in the Appalachians and westward. Many were shifting farther west than they had been. In 1830 Thomas Lincoln, having once moved his family from Kentucky to Indiana, moved again to Illinois, bringing along twenty-one-year-old Abraham. Jefferson Davis of Mississippi had recently graduated from the military academy at West Point and now was posted to a frontier fort guarding against Indians in what is now Wisconsin.

The earliest cohorts of western leadership had by necessity consisted mainly of men transplanted from the East—William Blount, William Henry Harrison, Henry Clay, Lewis Cass, and Andrew Jackson. Now the region was producing homegrown leaders; as Wilson Lumpkin delivered his speech on May 17, the man in the chair overseeing the debate was Representative Charles Wickliffe, born in Kentucky. Lands once seen as empty, save for Indians, were becoming solidly settled. Their growing populations attracted the interest of additional newcomers. In 1830 Lyman Beecher's Boston church burned, prompting jokes that the fire-and-brimstone preacher had experienced a touch of hell, but also causing him to think of casting off from New England. By 1832 he would be running a seminary in Cincinnati, Ohio. He wanted to win the West for Protestants over Catholicism. He brought along Catharine Beecher, who started another girls' school.

The South, too, was growing, and growing restive. Second

Lieutenant Robert E. Lee, who like Jefferson Davis had recently graduated from West Point, was posted to Georgia. Lee was an engineer,
instructed to help build a coastal fort at Savannah—just the sort of visible expenditure of federal tax revenue that President Jackson's allies
hoped would cement the southern states' allegiance to the union. It
wasn't enough. South Carolina politicians went on promoting their
doctrine of nullification, and it gradually became known that their supporters included South Carolina's John C. Calhoun, President Jackson's
own vice president. Facing a challenge both to the federal government
and to his personal authority, Jackson avoided a direct confrontation
until April 1830. At a dinner in honor of Thomas Jefferson's birthday,
the president was called upon to give a toast. He declared, "Our Federal
union—it must be preserved." Calhoun was forced to reply with a toast
of his own: "The Union—next to our liberty, most dear."

Americans continued to identify in complicated ways with Indians.
No one personified this impulse more spectacularly than Edwin Forrest,
one of the greatest actors of his generation, who resolved that he would
like to play an Indian. Twenty-four years old, acclaimed for his role as
Shakespeare's Othello, Forrest had ambitions to promote the growth of
American literature, and offered a prize for an original play on the
aboriginal Americans. The result was *Metamora*, whose title character
was loosely based on an actual seventeenth-century chief defeated in war
and killed by white men. In December 1829, at New York City's Park
Theater, Forrest appeared onstage as Metamora. "White men, beware!"
he howled at the audience as he died. "The wrath of the wronged Indian
shall fall upon you like a cataract that dashes the uprooted oak down the
mighty chasms." The standing-room-only crowd swooned. *Metamora*
was a monumental hit. Traveling repertory companies were soon making plans to perform it on stages across the nation, even in Congressman
Wilson Lumpkin's home state of Georgia.

Five southern Indian nations still possessed significant lands east of
the Mississippi: the Choctaws and Chickasaws near the great river, the
Creeks and Cherokees farther east, and the Seminoles in Florida. All

were formally at peace with their white neighbors, though newspapers reported ominous events. One such event began on February 1, 1830, when a man in the Creek Nation attempted to flag down a passing stagecoach. The stage was carrying passengers and mail through Creek country, roughly the same route General Lafayette had taken years before. Believing the Creek man was drunk, the driver maneuvered past while a passenger leaned out to insult the Indian.

The Creek man, named Tuskina, wanted to complain that the U.S. mail contractor was failing to pay tolls to the Creek Nation as promised. When the stage did not stop, Tuskina took a shortcut across a curve and emerged in front of the stage a second time, now clutching his only weapon, a common folding pocketknife. The alarmed driver and passengers stopped the stage for an hour and a half until the man calmed down. That should have been the end of the incident, except that when the stage finally passed out of the Creek Nation into white Alabama, the passengers spread exaggerated stories of an Indian attack. The community flew to arms. Two troops of cavalry, along with a troop of volunteers, were sent into Creek territory in search of Tuskina. Authorities also made an effort to isolate the Creek Nation, ordering every white man not married to an Indian to depart Creek areas within fifteen days.

Even some white Alabamans were startled by the overreaction, which "has thrown the whole country into commotion," wrote the editor of the *Mobile Register*, "drawn out the troops of the government, and occasioned a parade and show of authority that, as the times are, would hardly be exceeded were the dissolution of the union to be attempted." The editor was "mortified" that "a single Indian, in a whiskey frolic, should be able to stir up the government to such an exhibition of its power." A British traveler visiting the Creek Nation was equally dismayed to see "severe measures" against the entire nation "on account of the delinquency of one individual." The anxiety of Alabama authorities was revealing. It was as if white settlers *expected* an Indian assault, for they knew they had been courting trouble for years. Men and women who were building the American interior, who were proud of that work and believed it to be their national destiny, still understood there was another side of the story. When a Georgia legislative committee reported in 1827 on the state's right to take possession of Indian land, the lawmakers openly acknowledged the ambiguity of their argument. "It may be contended, with much plausibility, that there is, in these claims, more of *force,* than of *justice,*" said the Georgians, but the claims "have been recognized and admitted by the whole civilized world," and "under such circumstances, *force* becomes *right.*"

The Alabama soldiers never caught up with Tuskina, but troops riding through Creek villages created the danger of far more tragic confrontations. Concerned Creek leaders held a solemn conference (they were "handsomely dressed," the British traveler observed; their "scarlet turbans, their blue dress covered with beads, and their long spurs, gave them an imposing appearance, when their accoutrements were not too nearly inspected") but the Creeks did not respond with force. Tuskina turned himself in, and when he was put on trial May 7, 1830, the evidence began to show his crime was considerably less dramatic than first described. The judge fined Tuskina for obstructing the mail and set him free. Postal service continued as before. The newspapers did not report if the Creek Nation ever received its unpaid tolls.

Throughout the passionate debate in Washington in the spring of 1830, members of a divided House surprisingly agreed on one thing: it was detrimental to Indians to live in the South. Not only did Lumpkin of Georgia say it, so did Henry R. Storrs of New York, though perhaps not for reasons that Lumpkin would have approved. The northern lawmaker said he could "cheerfully" support a bill to move the Indians, if the "real object" was to offer refuge to those who wanted to leave "of their own free choice." Indeed, approval of such a bill would be automatic: "No philanthropic man can look at the condition to which these unfortunate people have become reduced . . . without fervently wishing

ABOVE: Outside Florence, Alabama, stand the ruins of Forks of Cypress— a plantation house on former Cherokee land obtained by Andrew Jackson. It was built after 1818 by one of the general's close friends. It is a supreme example of the layered history visible in the territory we call Jacksonland.

LEFT: Andrew Jackson posed for this portrait in 1819, after his victories at Horseshoe Bend and New Orleans, as well as his capture of vast Indian lands through a series of treaty negotiations. The painting by Rembrandt Peale is notable for its realism, showing Jackson's lined face, slightly pained expression, and emaciated body.

John Ross was one of many Indian leaders whose portraits
were painted when visiting Washington for treaty negotiations
and other business. Commissioned and collected by a federal
Indian official, the paintings reflect the outward transformation
of native elites—a transformation encouraged by the federal
government, though not purely for altruistic reasons.

ABOVE: Ross lived for many years in a two-story log home in what is still called Rossville, near the Georgia-Tennessee line.

LEFT: Jackson lived in a two-story log cabin until 1819, when he was earning substantial profits from cotton grown on land he had obtained from the Cherokees. He began upgrading his living quarters at the Hermitage outside Nashville.

Before he invented the telegraph, Samuel F. B. Morse was a painter who in 1822 depicted the House of Representatives in session. The Marquis de Lafayette spoke here in 1824; in 1830 it was the scene of a close vote on the Indian Removal Act.

Cherokee legislators met in a more modest wooden council house, which has been reconstructed at the site of the former Cherokee capital at New Echota.

Major Ridge, a
Cherokee friend of
Andrew Jackson and a
vital ally of John Ross
at the beginning.

Henry Clay, Jackson's
rival, who opposed
Indian removal even
though he said the
extinction of Indians
would be "no great loss
to the world."

TOP: John Ross's signature on an 1834 note
requesting a meeting with President Jackson.

BOTTOM: Andrew Jackson's postscript on an
1838 letter demanding "Why is it that the
Scamp Ross is not banished from the notice
of the administration [?]"

TOP: Catharine Beecher, a Connecticut teacher who became author of the "Ladies' Circular," which opposed Indian removal: "It may be that female petitioners can lawfully be heard, even by the highest rulers of our land."

RIGHT: Cherokees were cleared from their farms at the head of the Coosa River, which included the home of Major Ridge and also one of the homes of John Ross. The settlement was renamed Rome, Georgia, and remains today a prosperous manufacturing center. The stores and restaurants on the main street include the Old Havana Cigar Co., established in 2003 and decorated with a wooden Indian.

LEFT: The Cherokee settlement called Ross's Landing grew into the city of Chattanooga, Tennessee. In the late nineteenth century, the Walnut Street Bridge was built near the site of Ross's Landing to connect the city's downtown to the north side of the Tennessee River.

BELOW: This cluster of signs suggests the layering of cultures in the modern-day city of Cherokee, North Carolina. The street signs are in both English and Cherokee. Paul's Family Restaurant offers "Indian tacos," while a local Catholic church offers a weekly service in Spanish, reflecting yet another migration to this part of North America.

that they were already removed far beyond the reach of the oppression—and, I was about to say, the example of the white man." But Storrs said that helping Indians was never the purpose of the Indian bill. It was "chiefly intended" to clear Indians from southern real estate. Most northern lawmakers opposed the bill, representing as they did states that had produced the missionaries to the Indians, the women's petitions, and the public meetings in support of the tribes. Storrs also represented a state where white settlement, warfare, and migration to Canada had already devastated the Indian populace, meaning lawmakers could oppose Indian removal without threatening their constituents' interests. But there was something heartfelt about Storrs: "I am sick—heart-sick of seeing them at our door as I enter this hall, where they have been standing during the whole of this session, supplicating us to stay our hand. There is one plain path of honor. . . . Retrace your steps. Acknowledge your treaties. Confess your obligations. Redeem your faith. Execute your laws. Let the President revise his opinions. It is never too late to be just."

Could Jackson have pursued a different course? Jackson was right that something must be done. The clash between the white map and the Indian map was eating away at the old Indian policy. Washington's policy had been a wise and careful stalling tactic, putting off bloodshed until the day when a basic problem of the nation's founding might resolve itself. It was one of several compromises that the Founders had used to manage the contradictions attending the nation's birth. Now a new generation was testing the compromises.

From a distance of centuries, it is possible to imagine several alternatives to Indian removal. The simplest was the only one seriously discussed at the time: uphold the old policies a little longer. ("Retrace your steps. Acknowledge your treaties. Confess your obligations. Redeem your faith. Execute your laws. Let the President revise his opinions.") This could not have been a policy of inaction or of moderation. Sustaining the Cherokees against the ceaseless pressure of Georgia would have required Jackson to use persuasion, threats, and federal troops. He would have had to run the risk of civil conflict with Georgia, much as he was soon to do with the nullifiers of South Carolina. Even supporters of the Indians had to acknowledge the possibility of war. If properly protected, the Cherokees might have prospered. Or they might have become isolated and mired in poverty, as later generations of Indians did on western reservations.

There was also Thomas Jefferson's alternative, his long-ago wish that Indians would "incorporate with us as citizens of the United States." We have seen that in the mid-1820s John Ross suggested that Cherokees someday might obtain "admission as [U.S.] citizens." Some treaties actually did award citizenship to limited numbers of Cherokees, but this was not tried on a large scale. Nor would it have been easy to impose the more radical alternative that Ross also envisioned: that the Cherokee Nation could become "a Territorial or State government," combining the Indian map with the U.S. map. There was precedent for creating new states out of older ones, as had happened with Kentucky, Mississippi, Alabama, and Tennessee. Had southern power brokers seen their interest a certain way, they might have approved this move, which would have confounded their northern critics by adding a slave state to the national political balance. But the move would have demanded a level of respect for Indians that simply did not exist, and it probably would have destroyed the Cherokees as an Indian nation. A new territory would certainly have to be open to white settlers, who would arrive in such numbers that they could win elections.

Finally, the Cherokee heartland in Georgia could have been incorporated into the state as one of its counties. Call it Cherokee County, with the county seat at New Echota, where the nation might for a time continue running its affairs. But the Cherokees could never have consented to such an arrangement unless the state provided Indians with equal protection under the law. Eventually, Georgia demonstrated the terms under which it was willing to create such a county, because the state actually did so. From 1829 onward the state asserted that the

borders of several counties had expanded to include Cherokee land, and
in 1831 the state created a vast new entity that really was called Cherokee County. Cherokees were allowed no voice in governing the county,
which eventually had no Cherokees in it.

Georgia's Wilson Lumpkin already knew the course he wanted to follow, though he faced a host of critics in May 1830. He cast their vigor
and energy as a sign of weakness. "We have been inundated with memo-
rials, pamphlets, and speeches made at society and town meetings. But,
sir, let it be remembered that weak minorities always made the most
noise. Contented majorities, conscious of their strength, are never found
praying for a redress of grievances." It was that silent majority for whom
Lumpkin said he spoke.

In the Senate, Jackson supporters demonstrated their strength. A
handful of lawmakers took up the Indians' cause ("Georgia will yield,"
said Theodore Frelinghuysen of New Jersey, so long as the federal government held firm, because the state would not want "the guilt" of
bringing on "the horrors of civil war"), but they were easily outvoted.
The South had half the seats in the Senate, and could count on the support of loyal Jackson men from the North. The calculus was different in
the House, where seats were apportioned to each state according to
population, and the North enjoyed greater strength. Those who spoke
against the bill included Edward Everett of Massachusetts. In November 1863 Everett would be the featured speaker at the dedication of a
cemetery at Gettysburg, the orator who delivered the long speech before
Lincoln's very short one; in 1830 Everett was a young congressman. He
calculated that the Indian Removal Act was far more expensive than its
sponsors claimed. Moving tens of thousands of Indians would cost
many times more than the half million dollars advertised.

A few southerners opposed the measure too. David Crockett, that
rebellious veteran of Jackson's army in the early phase of the Creek War,
was now a Tennessee congressman. He was a Jackson-style politician, a

frontier leader who had risen from humble beginnings, and had been elected as a Jackson man in 1826. But Jackson had a complex relationship with many politicians of his home state, some of whom chafed under the force of his will. Crockett was persuaded that the Indian bill was a "wicked, unjust measure," and opposed it even though party discipline demanded his support on a measure so closely associated with the president: "Several of my colleagues got around me, and told me how well they loved me, and that I was ruining myself." Crockett walked into the cavernous House chamber on May 19. "I have been told I will be prostrated," he declared, but he would "bear the consolation of conscience." The bill was "oppression with a vengeance," and Crockett said he must vote against the measure even if every other lawmaker from Tennessee chose to support it.

Jackson's opponents had yet to form a coherent party, but the man who would be that party's natural leader had just returned to the news. Indian removal brought back Henry Clay, out of office now but still closely watched by an attentive public. His friend Margaret Bayard Smith observed that Clay "has an elasticity and buoyancy of spirit, that no pressure of external circumstances can confine or keep down." Invited to give a speech to the Colonization Society of Kentucky about sending freed slaves to Africa, Clay inserted a passage about Indians: "We are enjoined by every duty of religion, humanity and magnanimity to treat them with kindness and justice, and to recall them, if we can, from their savage to a better condition." The speech was printed for wider distribution. Wilson Lumpkin of Georgia was still irked by it five months later when delivering his May 17 speech in the House chamber. He offered Clay a backhanded compliment. "The distinguished orator of the West" had spoken of the Indians with "his usual zeal and ingenuity," delivering an address so "pious" that Lumpkin might have mistaken Clay for a "preacher" had he not known Clay's true "character." Lumpkin complained that the opposition to Indian removal was purely partisan. "Where do you find one solitary opponent of President Jackson

in favor of the measure on your table? I do not know one. Sir, I have
tried to prevent party considerations from operating on this question;
but our opponents are an organized band; they go in a solid column."

Late in May it began to seem that the bill might not survive. The
vote in the cavernous House chamber was sure to be extremely close.
For Jackson the timing was bad. Congress had just passed a highway
bill, a seemingly unrelated measure, but in Congress anything could be
related. Jackson wanted to veto the highway measure, but many of his
allies favored it. If he rejected the road bill, his friends might be so
offended that they would turn against him on the uncomfortable vote
he was demanding on the Indian bill. The situation called for a maneu-
ver as ruthless as any Jackson had executed as a general. When it was all
over, the writer for *Niles' Weekly Register* looked back in amazement.

> We . . . hope yet to have a full account of what happened in the
> three or four last days of the session.

Just as General Jackson had once seized land from his allies after
the Battle of Horseshoe Bend, President Jackson conducted an operation on his allies in Congress.

The highway bill was known as the Maysville Road Bill, after the
new federal highway it would finance beginning in Maysville, in Henry
Clay's Kentucky. Jackson didn't favor it. He said it wasn't an interstate
road. It was to be built entirely within one state, which Jackson considered inappropriate for a federal project even though it was to be connected to a larger interstate road network over time. But the president
did not veto the bill at first. He left it on his desk, waiting the full ten
business days the Constitution allowed before acting. This gave House
leaders time to push the Indian debate toward its close. On May 17, as
Congressman Lumpkin of Georgia delivered his speech for removal,
the ten-day clock was already running. The fight grew desperate as
time began to expire; many members of Jackson's new party were

wavering under pressure from constituents who protested removal. Party leaders made the vote an issue of loyalty, according to *Niles' Weekly Register*:

> Those who were friends of the administration were privately and publicly entreated to support the bill, and others were scolded; indeed Mr. Lewis, of Alabama, in our hearing, went so far as to proclaim in the house, with extraordinary heat, those of the party to be "traitors" who should not uphold this leading measure of the executive.

When the roll was called on May 26, David Crockett turned aside the appeal for loyalty as he said he would, and voted no. But just enough Jackson men stayed firm. The Indian Removal Act passed with 102 votes in favor and 97 against.

Only after the bill had safely cleared the House did President Jackson send a message that he had vetoed the Maysville Road Bill. It arrived on May 27, the last day he was permitted. He said an overactive federal government would undermine liberty and drive up taxes. But by setting back the popular roadbuilding program, he betrayed allies who had just loyally supported him.

> After the passage of the Indian bill, and the reception of the president's veto on the Maysville road bill, there was often much confusion in the house, with a general bitterness of expression, used by many of the members towards their fellows, that every reflecting man must regret.

The *Niles' Weekly Register* writer was "entirely confident, that, had the veto appeared half an hour previous to the final vote on the Indian bill, *it would have been rejected by a much larger majority than that by which it was carried,* being only five votes." Now it was too late. Some lawmakers grasped for ways to undo their own vote on the Indian bill, asking if the text had been sent to the president. Maybe the clerks had not yet finished making the final copy of the legislation, a ritual known as enrolling it. There might be some way to prevent Jackson from receiving the bill, which could not become law without his signature. But Jackson had timed his strike well enough to make this desperate measure impossible. A messenger had already carried the Indian bill down Pennsylvania Avenue to the Executive Mansion. Jackson signed it.

Twenty-four

Judicial

A short walk from the public square in New Echota, a path led across a stream and through the trees. At the end of the path was a clearing, and in the clearing stood a wood frame house with upper and lower porches overlooking the yard. Inside, a massive brick fireplace and oven dominated one of the rooms, a feature less in keeping with north Georgia's temperate climate than with New England, from which the residents of the house had come. It was the home built by Ann Worcester and her husband, Samuel, who was a missionary to the Cherokee Nation.

Samuel Worcester was in his early thirties. Life among the Cherokees seemed to agree with him; even years later, when it was possible for him to pose for a photograph, he still had a youthful face, with full lips and earnest eyes and thick hair that, combed back from his forehead, looped forward again over his temples. He had been sent to this posting by the American Board of Commissioners for Foreign Missions, the same organization whose corresponding secretary, or communications director, was Jeremiah Evarts. It was Evarts who wrote John Ross back in 1825 to announce Worcester's appointment, saying the missionary was "laborious, highly intelligent, Judicious, sincerely devoted to the interests of your nation." Samuel Worcester became the American Board's man in New Echota. He was also one of the Cherokees' links to the white world, who upheld the promise that he would be devoted to their interests. He was the missionary who, through the American Board, helped obtain a press for the *Cherokee Phoenix*. He was also the one suspected by some whites of having too much influence over the newspaper, an accusation he denied. It was true that he worked with the editor, Elias Boudinot, but not on the newspaper; he employed Boudinot on the side, to translate religious texts into Cherokee. "We are now publishing a small Hymn Book, about 50 pages," Boudinot reported in a letter in January 1829. "It is the first Cherokee book ever published." The Worcesters and Boudinots also saw each other socially, sometimes dining at each other's homes. The two couples had much in common—their relative youth, their New England ties, and their vital roles in the daily life of a most unusual village.

Their lives began to change on March 13, 1831, when horsemen rode into New Echota and followed the path to the Worcester house. They were members of the Georgia Guard, charged with imposing state authority over Cherokee land. The guardsmen arrested Samuel Worcester. They said he was violating a Georgia law decreeing that no white person should live on Cherokee land without a permit from the state.

Brought before a state judge some miles away in Gwinnett County, Georgia, Worcester defended himself. He was conducting missionary work by permission of the federal government, which had sole authority over Indian affairs. He was also a U.S. official, having served for years as the postmaster at New Echota. Perhaps in 1861 the Georgia authorities would be ready to imprison a federal official, but not in 1831. Worcester was released, and returned to his home and his family at the end of the path.

He was still there weeks later when the riders returned to his door. This time they were bearing a letter. George Gilmer, the governor of Georgia, had written Worcester and other missionaries to accuse them of "criminal" conduct. Worcester's defenses had been stripped away: President Jackson had fired him as postmaster and affirmed that the missionaries were not acting as agents of the federal government. Gilmer warned one of Worcester's fellow missionaries that they must leave soon or face the "punishment which will certainly follow your further residence."

The riders went back down the path and away, under orders to delay arresting Worcester until he had an opportunity to depart. He thought about it, and declined the opportunity. His wife was ill, and could not easily move. He also believed in his work. He wrote the governor on June 10, saying, "I cheerfully acknowledge" disagreeing with the president's removal policy, but this brought him no "consciousness of guilt." He was guilty only of "that freedom in the expression of opinion, against which, under the Constitution of our Country, there is no law." He added, "My own view of duty is that I ought to remain, and pursue my labors for the spiritual welfare of the Cherokee people, until I am forcibly removed." So the Georgia Guard rode down the path again and arrested him on July 15, 1831. Worcester and other missionaries were held for several days, then allowed to post bail and released until trial in September. His release offered Worcester another opportunity to slip away, avoiding a four-year prison sentence, but again he declined to leave. Instead he wrote an account of his arrest for the *Cherokee Phoenix*, including a backhanded compliment to his jail guards ("only two or three individuals offered us any insult"), and prepared to face his trial.

It was gradually becoming apparent that the Georgians were on the verge of a strategic mistake. While Samuel Worcester was no longer a federal official, he was still a pastor, whose imprisonment would certainly cause an outcry. More to the point, he was a citizen of the United States, with a right to sue the Georgians in federal court if treated improperly.

Ever since the passage of the Indian Removal Act, John Ross had been trying to bring the defense of his nation's rights before the federal courts. He was acting on the advice of supporters in Congress, New Jersey's Theodore Frelinghuysen and the great Massachusetts senator Daniel Webster among others. As opponents of Jackson, both senators had a political motive to keep the Cherokee case going. But the law-makers also had reason to believe that a court challenge would receive a sympathetic hearing. In May of 1830, Senator Frelinghuysen had received a letter:

> *Dear Sir*
> *. . . I received your speech on the removal of the Indians which I have read with equal interest and attention. The subject has always appeared to me to affect deeply the honor, the faith and the character of our country. The cause of these oppressed people has been most ably though unsuccessfully sustained . . .*
>
> *J. Marshall.*

John Marshall was the chief justice of the United States. He made it clear that he would listen if a proper case reached him.

Going to court would cost thousands of dollars, and before Worcester's arrest President Jackson guaranteed that Ross would have trouble paying. It was in June 1830, soon after the passage of the Indian Removal Act, that Attorney General John Macpherson Berrien sent his letter urging the president to deny the Cherokees two great sources of strength, their printing press and their money. In a country that valued the freedom of the press it would take time to silence the *Phoenix*, but the Cherokees' funding was easily cut off. The Cherokee government's income derived principally from real estate. Past treaties ceding land to the federal government included an annuity to the Cherokee Nation: the United States was in effect making annual mortgage payments. Attorney General Berrien proposed that the United States should simply stop paying and defund the Cherokee resistance. Of course, default would be illegal, so the attorney general proposed a clever ruse, which Jackson accepted. Rather than outright refusing to pay the money, the administration would instead "insist upon its distribution among the Indians at large," spreading a few cents to each individual Cherokee so that the money conveyed no sustenance to their government. Cherokees adamantly refused to accept, and no payments were made for years. Ross would spend those years scrambling to pay lawyers, arranging loans from individual Cherokees, and raising money from sympathizers in northern cities. Sometimes when a bank draft arrived in the mail from New York or Boston, Ross sent it directly to his underpaid defense team. He nevertheless did engage Georgia lawyers to represent the Cherokees in state courts, and went looking for lawyers of great repute to work at the national level.

There was a moment when Ross believed that Senator Daniel Webster would join the defense team—Godlike Daniel, as his admirers called him, a public speaker so brilliant that it was later said that he could win a court case against the devil—but Webster was a busy man, not known for serving low-paying clients. Instead the lead role went to William Wirt of Baltimore. Wirt may have been the best possible choice, and if his name echoed less through the ages than Webster's, he was hardly less prominent at the time. He had served as attorney general under Presidents Monroe and Adams. He knew all the players in Washington. He was also a distinctive American character, author of a famous biography of the Revolutionary orator Patrick Henry, which Wirt apparently improved by inventing phrases that Henry never said, such as "Give me liberty or give me death." The book at least marked Wirt as a great wordsmith. Most important, Wirt had the stature and self-confidence to take the case even though he knew it would make an enemy of the president. Jackson wrote in the summer of 1830 that the lawyer's course was "truly wicked" and would "lead to the distruction of the poor ignorant Indians."

I have used all the persuasive means in my power; I have exonerated the national character from all imputation, and now leave the poor

*deluded creeks & cherokees to their fate, and their annihilation, which
their wicked advisers has induced.*

It was a private letter, but Wirt and the Cherokees did not need to see it
to know they were on their own.

The common way to reach the Supreme Court would be to contest a
case before the Georgia judiciary, and then appeal an unfavorable result
to the high court. But there was reason to think the Georgians would
never allow a proper test case to be concluded. Wirt decided on a more
direct route. The Constitution said the Supreme Court had original
jurisdiction over cases involving foreign nations. Could the Cherokees
qualify as a foreign nation? If they could, the court was the first and
only place to hear their plea. Wirt wrote in the fall of 1830 that he "personally had strong doubts" that this would work, but as with his writing
of Patrick Henry he plunged ahead, compiling a list of complaints against
Georgia. He said state authorities ordered Cherokees to stop prospecting at gold mines, and indicted the members of the Cherokee court.
Federal troops who should have ordered the Georgians to desist instead
advised John Ross in writing that they would assist in enforcing state
law. A Cherokee known as George Tassel, accused of killing another
Cherokee, was arrested and convicted under Georgia law, and when he
appealed to the federal courts, Georgia made the case moot by having
Tassel hanged.

Wirt mailed a copy of his complaint to John Ross in New Echota,
who decided he would personally serve the papers on the governor of
Georgia. Ross found a companion for the journey, a white man named
George Lavender, who ran a store for Major Ridge; possibly the company of a white man would make it easier for the Cherokee chief to be
taken as white and left unmolested. It took nearly a week in early winter
to reach the capital of Milledgeville, a town of a few thousand dominated by its state capitol building, with its churchlike windows and
crenellated roofline. Ross and Lavender rode into town on the day after

Christmas and had the governor served with papers in the morning. If Governor Gilmer greeted Ross at all when the Cherokee delivered the papers, Ross did not record what was said. The Cherokee chief rode on with his companion to Augusta and served identical papers to the state attorney general, finishing the work in time to mail a report to William Wirt on New Year's Day, 1831. "Mr. Lavender and myself are threatened with the Penitentiary for what we had done," Ross reported. "We have some strong friends here and I shall treat those threats with silent contempt." Someone gave the Cherokee chief shelter along the way, maybe friends from his trading days, or friends of his Georgia lawyers, or maybe even one of the wealthy slave-owning families whom Jeremiah Evarts had cultivated for contributions.

In the end it was the Georgians who treated the Cherokee suit with "silent contempt," refusing to accept the Supreme Court's jurisdiction and refusing to send a lawyer to argue the case. So it was that Wirt's side alone appeared before the Supreme Court in March 1831, in the case known as *Cherokee Nation v. Georgia.* Justice Marshall presided over the chamber, backlit by a window behind him that looked out over the Capitol grounds. Squinting, perhaps, to see more than the silhouettes of the justices in front of him, Wirt argued his case. In a brief filed in advance, he had said Georgia's laws were "repugnant to the constitution, laws, and treaties of the United States." Wirt clearly felt the weight of the power arrayed against him. "If we could have perceived any other course of moral or professional conduct that remained for us . . . we should not have troubled your honours with this motion." But Wirt knew he had to do his "duty" and "leave the issue to Providence." He was in reality leaving the issue to Marshall, the man silhouetted at the window, who also had a duty to perform.

Marshall rejected the Cherokees' lawsuit. He ruled against them even though he openly expressed sympathy for the Cherokee cause. He could not bring himself to accept the case that Wirt presented. Writing for the majority of the court, the chief justice refuted the idea that the Cherokees constituted a foreign nation. Their treaties with the United

States made them a "domestic dependent nation," rather like a state government. In later years, scholars suggested that Marshall felt that he could not push the issue too far; at the time of his ruling, hostile lawmakers in Congress were circulating ominous legislation that would take away some of the court's authority. To avoid damage to his own institution, Marshall required a case so strong that his ruling would be indisputable. This case wasn't it.

But if he disappointed the Cherokees, Marshall had not betrayed them. Examining Marshall's ruling from his home in the Cherokee Nation, John Ross perceived what the chief justice did not say. He had never ruled against the substance of the Cherokees' complaints, only against their legal standing. "The denial of the injunction has no bearing whatever upon the true merits of our cause," Ross insisted, and the ruling was "conclusively adverse to the pretended claims of the President." To make certain his people did not lose faith, Ross spent three weeks in April and May riding back and forth across the Cherokee Nation, speaking with any voter who wanted to see him. The "tattlers and intriguers" would claim there was "no hope left," Ross told his people, but "you have . . . met oppression & injustice with fortitude & forbearance and I trust you will persevere in this prudent course; as it will not fail in due time to lead you to a safe deliverance."

When considering why, in later years, his people stayed at Ross's side through every defeat and disaster, seemingly willing to follow him even to their own doom, it is worth recalling this three-week journey by the principal chief. Accompanied by Cherokee leader George Lowrey and solid, strong Major Ridge, he saw his people at home—poor farmers and their families in modest cabins, living from harvest to harvest, the adults often illiterate, the children possibly learning to read in one language or the other. Ross paid attention to them. People remembered. Ross remembered too: he understood how devoted the people were to their homes, and knew that if he wanted their support, he must never forfeit their rights. He came to feel, as Jackson did, that the people spoke through him.

. . .

The months in which John Ross was urging his people to wait for deliverance were the same months in which Samuel Worcester was being
urged to leave New Echota, then being arrested for the second time,
and then scheduled for trial. If Worcester were convicted, his case might
be the one that would propel the Cherokees back into the Supreme
Court. Ross's legal team knew this almost for a certainty, because they
had been advised of it by Chief Justice Marshall, who now played a role
in obtaining a second chance for the Cherokees' cause.

Marshall was the man whom later generations would credit for
establishing the court as a powerful branch of government. He did so in
part simply because of his longevity. In his early twenties, during the
Revolution, he had been a junior officer in George Washington's army.
In 1801, when Marshall was not quite forty-six, the defeated and
departing President John Adams appointed him to the court; thirty
years later Adams and nearly all the Revolutionary leaders were gone,
but Marshall was where they had left him. The precedents he set—such
as *Marbury v. Madison,* the 1803 case establishing the court's authority
to decide whether legislation was unconstitutional—would be maintained for decades by the very chief justice who set them. The Constitution did not explicitly grant or deny the court such power; most of its
powers had been left to be determined by Congress. The very architec-
ture of early Washington, DC, implied a court that was not quite the
equal of the legislature or the executive; there was not a separate court
building, leaving the justices for most of Marshall's tenure tucked in their
chamber on the ground floor of the Capitol, literally underneath the
Senate. But by establishing his court as the arbiter of the meaning of the
Constitution, Marshall sometimes pruned the other branches.

Shown in portraits with strong features and a confident expression,
the silver-haired chief justice remained formidable deep into his seventies, a political as well as a judicial figure. During the summer of 1831

he exchanged letters with William Wirt, telling the Cherokees' lawyer exactly what to do: identify an individual with proper standing whose rights were denied before a Georgia state court. The decision by the state court could be appealed to Marshall's Supreme Court, which had the right to hear such appeals. This would create the basis for Marshall to draft a ruling that blocked Georgia from extending its laws over the Cherokees.

In many modern-day courtrooms it would be considered unusual, if not unethical, for a judge to give private strategic advice to a plaintiff with whom he sympathized. But concepts of ethics were different in 1831 (and even in later days, the Supreme Court would largely exempt itself from conflict-of-interest rules that applied to other courts). Marshall, part of Washington's elite for as long as there had been a Washington, was comfortable showing his cards to another member of that elite in order to orchestrate the outcome he believed to be right. Wirt did not miss the significance of Marshall's advice. He wrote to John Ross, advising his client to attempt the "experiment" of Marshall's strategy. Ross, though struggling to pay the legal team's bills (he was sending money whenever it came in, as little as $100 at a time), authorized the effort. The "experiment" turned out to be Samuel Worcester.

On September 16, 1831, Worcester was one of eleven missionaries who appeared as required for their state trial in Lawrenceville, Georgia, on charges of living without a state permit on Indian lands—or "unsettled areas," as the Georgians called them. All eleven were convicted. All received sentences of four years "at hard labor" at the prison in the state capital. Governor Gilmer, apparently understanding the potential for disaster, persuaded nine of the eleven to accept clemency and leave the state. Two missionaries declined—a man named Elizur Butler, and Samuel Worcester. They were put to work making cabinets at the state prison at Milledgeville. Worcester did not complain much about conditions, however, and even found time to obtain northern newspapers and read them. Once, he read a newspaper stating that the two missionaries were being forced to assemble "lottery wheels," the machines that Georgia was using for a lottery to parcel out Cherokee land to lucky white citizens. Worcester, with characteristic irony, wrote a letter to the editor to say it wasn't true; the lottery wheels were being built at the prison, but the warden "studiously avoided calling on us to assist in that work," since it might offend their feelings.

John Ross knew he had a case, and wrote to his lawyer Wirt about it in early October. The records of the trial were already on their way to Wirt, Ross assured him. Ross worried only that the state of Georgia would find some way to make the case moot.

> Should the legislature of Georgia repeal the law under which the missionaries have been committed and liberate them . . . what effect will it have upon these cases? Will the S Court proceed to decide upon the question of the Constitutionality of the Law of Georgia exercising jurisdiction or not? Please to inform me.

Georgia, it turned out, was not yet willing to go to the extreme of repealing its law. William Wirt appealed to the high court in a case that came to be known as *Worcester v. Georgia,* and John Marshall with other justices heard the arguments on the Capitol's ground floor on February 20, 1832.

There wasn't much drama in the court; the defendant's table was empty. Georgia again refused to send a representative. The drama came later, in Marshall's written ruling. The chief justice posed as a reluctant participant, who had no choice but to address the case because it so clearly fell under his court's jurisdiction. "This duty, however unpleasant, cannot be avoided," Marshall wrote, overlooking his own role in making certain that the duty came his way.

Marshall reviewed the entire history of relations between the Indians and the settlers who had come from Europe. He had lived through a substantial part of that history, and had given it much thought. He began with a reference to "the right of discovery," the initial basis of

European claims in North America, essentially that colonial powers gained authority over land by exploring it.

America, separated from Europe by a wide ocean, was inhabited by a distinct People, divided into separate nations, independent of each other and of the rest of the world, having institutions of their own, and governing themselves by their own laws. It is difficult to comprehend the proposition, that the inhabitants of either quarter of the globe could have rightful original claims of dominion over the inhabitants of the other, or over the lands they occupied; or that the discovery of either by the other should give the discoverer, rights in the country discovered, which annulled the pre-existing rights of its ancient possessors.

Marshall did not believe that the Europeans could become the owners of land simply by sending "adventurers" to go "sailing along the coast, and occasionally landing on it." Nor did he accept that "nature" granted the Europeans the right to take the land simply because they believed they had a more sophisticated economy or civilization. It was true that the settlers and their descendants had gained control of much of the land through "power, war, conquest," and that the United States now possessed rights that were "conceded by the world." But there was no evidence that the Cherokee Nation had surrendered its remaining rights to its remaining land. Congress had approved a series of treaties with Indians, dating back as far as 1778, which again and again affirmed Indian nations in the possession of their land—and from this point on, Marshall could almost have been reciting his history from memory, for he was old enough to recall it. Here and there, the Indian treaties contained ambiguous phrases that might be interpreted to mean that the United States now owned all the land, and that the Indians were only to be "allotted" some of it, but Marshall did not believe the Indian leaders of past generations "who could not write, and most probably could not read," would ever have understood such subtle interpretations, and could hardly have been said to have agreed to them. Indian nations were "distinct, independent political communities, retaining their original natural rights, as the undisputed possessors of the soil, from time immemorial." They still possessed rights, even if they had placed themselves under the protection of the United States. "Protection," Marshall wrote acidly, "does not imply the destruction of the protected." Georgia could not interfere in their affairs; Congress alone had, in the words of the Constitution, "the powers of war and peace; of making treaties, and of regulating commerce . . . with the Indian tribes." The state law under which Samuel Worcester was imprisoned was "consequently void, and the judgment a nullity . . . repugnant to the constitution, laws, and treaties, of the United States."

Marshall resolved the dissonance between the Indian map and the map of the United States. It is better said that he destroyed it. There really was no conflict. The states controlled those parts of the continent that had been gained through legitimate purchases, treaties, or war. Indian nations controlled the territories that remained. The federal government was supreme over both states and the Indian "domestic dependent nations," which was exactly the role Marshall wanted for the federal government; he was an old Federalist, who believed in the value of a strong central authority. He was interpreting the law in a way that fit his own politics, but he was also relying on what the law, treaties, and facts demonstrated. Of all the era's arguments over Indian removal, Marshall's ruling was the clearest and best summary of what he called "the actual state of things." The pressures that Georgia, and by extension the president, brought to bear on the Cherokee Nation were simply fraudulent pretensions. Would "these powerful considerations" produce the freedom of Samuel Worcester? Marshall answered simply: "We think they will."

Twenty-five

Executive

When word of Marshall's ruling reached the Cherokee Nation, people held feasts and dances. Elijah Hicks, a Cherokee politician, wrote that "every Indian knows now that he stands upon a solid foundation," although Cherokees also knew "that immediate relief does not follow as a consequence" of the court's decision. John Ross allowed himself a moment of celebration, the first that had been warranted in years. "Our adversaries are generally down in the mouth," he wrote in a letter.

There are great rejoicings throughout the nation on the decision of the supreme court upon the Cherokee case. Traitors and internal enemies are seeking places where to hide their heads.

But there was also something discordant about the letter. Traitors? Internal enemies? Ross did not seem like a man triumphantly enjoying a feast.

The principal chief of the Cherokee Nation had reason to doubt that he could keep all of his people behind him. Some in the elite wondered how long they could continue on Ross's course. Despite the ruling, Worcester was still hammering cabinets at the prison at Milledgeville. The Georgia Guard continued enforcing state laws in the Cherokee Nation. Cherokee legislators were no longer meeting in New Echota, fearing arrest for defying Georgia's abolition of their government; they had to meet across the Tennessee line. "Georgia," reported the *Cherokee Phoenix*, "has commenced her survey of the Cherokee country notwithstanding the decision of the supreme court. Our country is now overrun with surveyors, laying off the land into small sections of about two hundred acres. The gold region is to be laid off into lots of forty acres. . . . Five hundred and fifty men employed in surveying, marking trees, or otherwise." The *Phoenix* cited a federal law forbidding surveys of Indian land, punishable by a $1,000 fine and a prison term of up to twelve months. Federal authorities did nothing to enforce it. The surveyed lots were to be apportioned among white citizens through a random drawing, using the "lottery wheels" being built at the Milledgeville prison.

And then word came from Washington that Justice Marshall's ruling might not have been as conclusive as Marshall believed it should be.

At the time of the ruling, the annual Cherokee delegation was in Washington, and received an invitation to meet with Supreme Court justice John McLean. He was a member of the court majority that had just ruled in the Cherokees' favor. He had even gone so far as to write an opinion concurring with Marshall's ruling. The Cherokees may have thought that they would be greeting an ally. But McLean was a new justice on the Supreme Court, having recently been appointed by President Andrew Jackson, who could not have been pleased with his appointee's action. Now it fell to Justice McLean to be the one to deliver a message from the administration.

The delegates reported back to Ross, who later summarized what he had learned: "It was [McLean's] firm belief that we are not to realize what we expected from the decision of the court. It was however the duty of the court to have done what they did, but the executive would not sustain them." Jackson's appointee to the court was saying that Jackson would refuse to enforce the law. McLean then moved to close off the Cherokees' next avenue of hope: it was an election year, yet even if

Jackson were to lose his job it would make no difference. "Allowing there should be a change in the administration of the govt. he explained the impossibility of enforcing the decision unless Georgia voluntarily submitted." Another avenue was closed: "Were the missionaries released, it would not amount to a withdrawal of the laws of the states from our Territory." Finally, McLean offered some advice to the Cherokee Nation: "to unburden itself by a removal."

The Supreme Court had moved elegantly but not ruthlessly. It could not operate with the speed of one of Andrew Jackson's armies; nor could it, like Jackson, disregard the law when convenient, since its sole weapon was the law. Marshall had to follow legal procedure. The Judiciary Act called for the court to send the Georgians notice of their error and give the Georgia courts an opportunity to comply. Only after the Georgia courts failed would Marshall be in a position to push for federal measures against them. It was considered inevitable that the Georgia courts would fail to comply, but the Supreme Court did not stand in readiness for this to happen, adjourning for the year on March 17. The court would not sit again until January 1833, so it would be many months before it could even attempt to add more pressure.

Henry Clay worried about where the country was heading. He wrote that if Georgia resisted the ruling, "and the President refuses to enforce it, there is a virtual dissolution of the Union." But President Jackson seemed unconcerned. He took no steps, formal or informal, to encourage Georgia's compliance. Unlike with neighboring South Carolina—where during the same period he was using appeals, persuasion, threats, and finally legislation that allowed him to raise an army—Georgia's judicial nullifiers had his support.

Many years later, a political enemy of Jackson's claimed the president had said, "Justice Marshall has made his decision; now let him enforce it." Historians have questioned this statement, which did not appear in print until decades later, but similar statements were attributed to the president in real time. Two days after the ruling a New York newspaper reported Jackson's saying that the Supreme Court had no

more right to order him around than he had the right to order the
Supreme Court. The same day a Philadelphia newspaper said Jackson
was telling people in private conversation that he "would not aid in carrying that judgment into effect." Yet another correspondent reported
that Jackson "sportively said in private conversation" that if called upon
to enforce the ruling "he will call on those who have brought about the
decision to enforce it." He wrote his friend John Coffee:

> *The decision of the Supreme Court has fell still born, and they find*
> *that it cannot coerce Georgia to yield to its mandate.*

The word "it" referred to the court's decision; "they find that it cannot coerce Georgia . . ." The ruling, simply a piece of paper, was indeed
ineffective if no one acted on it. Some of Jackson's statements might be
dismissed as angry bravado, except that he apparently made a similar
statement directly to an influential Cherokee. Shortly after the ruling
the president met with Major Ridge's son John Ridge, and spoke so
forcefully that Jackson himself believed he had sent Ridge away in
"despair." Jackson had not misread the young Cherokee diplomat, whose
loss of faith in the Cherokee cause would soon have fatal effects.

Some historians have offered a limited defense of President Jackson:
he technically could not be said to have defied the court, since the
moment had not yet arrived when it was imperative for him to act. But
while awaiting those formalities, Jackson was negligent at best. He could
have said, as later generations of political leaders would say of Supreme
Court rulings, that he disagreed but would respect the decision. He
could have signaled to the Georgians that they must obey federal law,
just as South Carolina must. He could have openly recognized the
implications of Justice Marshall's ruling, which spread far beyond the
imprisonment of Worcester and Butler. If the law used to imprison
the missionaries was unconstitutional, then *all* Georgia laws relating to
the Cherokees were unconstitutional. Jackson should have taken the
cue that he must block the Georgians' survey of Cherokee land, and

enforce existing federal law. He did nothing, and a justice close to Jackson informed the Cherokees that the very opposite of Jackson's duty would be done.

The significance of Jackson's course becomes clearer when compared with that of another chief executive in a comparable situation. In 1957, one of Jackson's successors also faced pressure to enforce a controversial Supreme Court decision that involved the rights of a racial minority in a southern state. In this case the racial minority was African Americans. The court ruling, made three years earlier, was *Brown v. Board of Education*, which outlawed racial segregation in public education. States with segregated schools were instructed to devise ways to comply. School authorities in Little Rock, Arkansas, made plans to allow nine black students into Little Rock Central High School in the fall of 1957, only to face the defiance of Arkansas governor Orval Faubus, who ordered the National Guard to block the integration. President Dwight D. Eisenhower viewed it as his duty to enforce the ruling, and he ordered the 101st Airborne Division of the U.S. Army to protect the nine black students. To avoid the possibility of combat between state and federal forces, Eisenhower also used his authority to federalize the Arkansas National Guard, taking it out of the governor's hands. The school was desegregated, the Supreme Court vindicated, and despite intense debate the country at large sustained the president. Had Eisenhower done otherwise, catastrophe would have loomed.

Jackson did seem to understand, after his reelection was assured in 1832, that he was about to create a monster. The Georgia courts were not acting to free Worcester and Butler. In early 1833 Marshall would rule against Georgia again, and then Federal marshals or federal troops would be called upon to liberate the missionaries. If Jackson refused to enforce the ruling at that desperate moment, he would devastate the authority of the court as well as the authority of federal law. Worse, Jackson himself might look weak—backing down before the Georgians on an Indian question, just as John Quincy Adams had done before him. Yet if Jackson decided after all that he would enforce the law, he risked a crisis with Georgia at the same time as the nullification crisis with South Carolina.

Jackson's administration began working to make the problem go away. He had a new secretary of war by late 1832—Lewis Cass, the former Michigan governor who had so publicly made the case for Indian removal—and Cass appealed to Georgia to simply free the missionaries. "Other important considerations," meaning the confrontation with South Carolina, made this necessary, Cass said. His letters were addressed to Georgia's new governor, Wilson Lumpkin, the same politician who as a member of Congress had led the fight for the Indian Removal Act. Lumpkin agreed with Cass's appeal. In fact, he had already cleared the ground to resolve the issue. That fall in Milledgeville the governor had dined with the wives of Worcester and Butler, assuring them he held no ill will toward their husbands. More dramatically, on December 22, he had signed a repeal of the law under which Worcester and Butler had been convicted. This would allow the missionaries to accept a pardon without, as the law had required, swearing an oath of allegiance to Georgia. The missionaries themselves had come to believe that "considerations of a public nature" made it necessary that they stop pursuing their Supreme Court case. Governor Lumpkin freed the missionaries on January 14, 1833, avoiding a final ruling by the Supreme Court.

The powerful dynamic of sectional politics was now beginning to work against the Indian cause. Previously, sectional politics had worked in their favor, drawing New England missionaries, northern women, congressmen, and others more easily to their side. Now the northerners were staring into the abyss. They began to see Indian removal as a conflict that could wreck national institutions, even leading to civil war. Theodore Frelinghuysen of New Jersey, who had spoken eloquently against the Indian Removal Act, advised the Cherokees that it was time to negotiate a generous treaty with the United States and move west. One of the Cherokees' own lawyers, Elisha Chester, appeared in the

Cherokee Nation and infuriated John Ross by revealing that he had switched sides, becoming a government agent seeking a treaty of removal. The worst defection was that of the American Board of Commissioners for Foreign Missions. This group, more than any other, had helped the Cherokees make their case to the nation—sending them Samuel Worcester, obtaining a printing press, and of course providing the passionate support of Jeremiah Evarts. Evarts was dead now; his fragile constitution had finally failed him in 1831, at the age of fifty. Late in 1832 the board's governing committee sadly sent advice to John Ross that it was in the "best good" of the Cherokees to sign a removal treaty.

Americans were passing through a series of crises in these decades before the Civil War, and though none could foresee when the calamity would come, many saw the risk of it. ("While the Union lasts," Daniel Webster declared while debating a South Carolinian in the Senate in 1830, "we have high, exciting, gratifying prospects spread out before us and our children. Beyond that I seek not to penetrate the veil. God grant that in my day, at least, that curtain may not rise! God grant that on my vision never may be opened what lies behind.") The fear of disunion was driving several decades' worth of sectional compromises. In 1820, a dispute over slavery in western territories had been resolved with the Missouri Compromise. Later the Compromise of 1850 would put off the crisis again. In 1833 the sectional crisis focused not directly on slavery but on economic power, as the slave states of South Carolina and Georgia resisted anything they regarded as interference with their interests. It was widely understood what was at stake if Jackson failed to find a resolution, and even his opponents fell behind his leadership as the elements of his policy fell together. South Carolina was to be isolated and stared down—and also offered a compromise, in the form of revised tariffs crafted by none other than Henry Clay, now back in the Senate. Georgia must give in on the matter of the missionaries, but would suffer no harm to its long-term goal of removing the Indians. The Cherokees would be sacrificed for the larger interest of the nation.

"We consider ourselves as a part of the great family of the Republic of the U. States," Ross had written back in 1816, "and we are ready at any time to sacrifice our lives, our property & every thing sacred to us, in its cause." Ross probably had not anticipated the manner in which the great republic would take his offer.

PART EIGHT

Democracy in
America

1833-1835

Twenty-six

The Purest Love of Formalities

A sign of the dawning age came on June 6, 1833, when Andrew Jackson became the first president to board a train. Beginning a triumphal tour of eastern cities, he rode between Ellicott City, Maryland, and Baltimore. It was the initial stretch of the Baltimore and Ohio Railroad, which was projected to run westward across Maryland to the Potomac, and then over the Appalachians.

Beyond those mountains the westering nation was taking shape. Chicago was founded in 1833. That same year Stephen A. Douglas of Vermont, age twenty, moved to Illinois and found temporary work as a schoolteacher, while Abraham Lincoln was appointed the postmaster of tiny New Salem, Illinois. Lincoln's politics should have disqualified him. He was trying to win a seat in the state legislature as a member of Henry Clay's opposition party, who were soon to become known as the Whigs. Years later Lincoln explained that his posting in such a tiny town was "too insignificant, to make [my] politics an objection," though it seems just as likely that he gained the appointment thanks to the support of his personal friends and admirers, who included politically active Jackson Democrats.

Jackson was beginning his second term, which he may have won despite his Indian policy rather than because of it. The policy had certainly been criticized during the campaign, as Jackson's adviser Martin

Van Buren knew personally. Nominated in 1832 to serve as Jackson's vice president, Van Buren was traveling through upstate New York when he stopped for a night at the home of a female relative, who apparently was part of the women's movement against Indian removal. "After I had retired to my room," Van Buren recalled,

> she entered it, and after a kind introduction and welcome soon proceeded to a spirited denunciation of our proceedings (for she associated me with the President) towards the Cherokees in general and the Missionaries in particular, with the utmost severity. . . . Well aware of the tenacious grasp with which her opinions, in matters of conscience, were held . . . I made but little answer to her charges, and, on leaving the room, she said, yet holding the door in her hand, "Uncle! I must say to you that it is my earnest wish that you may lose the election, as I believe that such a result ought to follow such acts!"

Voters interested in Indian removal certainly had a choice. Jackson's strongest opponent was his old enemy Senator Henry Clay, whose gradually coalescing opposition party would eventually include many of the same politicians who had worked against Indian removal—Daniel Webster, Edward Everett, Theodore Frelinghuysen. A strong third party emerged, nominating none other than the Cherokees' lawyer William Wirt. But Indian removal was not the predominant issue. Henry Clay made sure of that when he brought a different issue forward, committing yet another of his too-clever political acts that led to unexpected consequences.

Clay sensed a political advantage when the president, always suspicious of banks, objected to the very existence of the Bank of the United States. It was the era's nearest equivalent of a central bank, and a vital part of Clay's American System. Like the modern-day Federal Reserve, the bank influenced interest rates and the availability of credit, and was considered essential to the growing economy. In 1832 Clay pushed through legislation giving an early renewal to the bank charter. So overwhelming was the bank's support that even many of Jackson's allies voted in favor of it, and Clay was certain that Jackson would be forced to sign the bill in an election year. Jackson vetoed it. It was the beginning of Jackson's fight to destroy the bank, which put the entire economy at risk but was far less damaging to Jackson's reelection than expected. Because the bank served wealthy and well-connected businessmen (and even politicians such as Clay who received bank loans), attacking the bank fit Jackson's ideology. Democrats said they were fighting big-government elites, and campaigned with organization and enthusiasm never seen before. Men raised giant hickory poles for Old Hickory. One observer said a pro-Jackson parade in New York was "nearly a mile long." The president himself sidestepped the traditional ban on campaigning, taking an unprecedented fall tour from the Hermitage to Washington, which, of course, was not campaigning, merely a president attending barbecues and parades as he traveled through a series of contested states just before an election. When the ballots were counted, Jackson easily won.

The ideology of Jackson's party seeped into business as well as politics. By the early 1830s even millionaires stood up for the rights of the common man. In New York, Cornelius Vanderbilt—the ferry and stagecoach operator who had once driven the Marquis de Lafayette in a carriage across New Jersey—opened a "People's Line" with steamboat service northward from New York City, running up the broad Hudson River between the mountains to Albany for the incredibly low rate of one dollar. It was service within the means of ordinary citizens, and upscale passengers were dismayed to see the enthusiastic rabble with whom they never before had been forced to share a steamer deck. Vanderbilt advertised in a pro-Jackson newspaper using Jacksonian rhetoric, saying the Albany service was battling the "aristocratic monopoly" that ran a competing line. Left unmentioned was Vanderbilt's own record as an aristocratic monopolist, who did everything possible to destroy his competitors on other ferry and stage routes. He was driving down prices on the Albany route to punish the rival company for competing with him elsewhere. When his rival surrendered, offering an extortion payment of $100,000, Vanderbilt shut down the People's Line to Albany, allowing the "aristocratic monopoly" to restore high prices and leaving the common man to shift for himself.

Possibly at some point one of Vanderbilt's many steamers carried the French writer Alexis de Tocqueville, who was traveling around the United States in the early 1830s, making observations he would later publish as *Democracy in America*. Tocqueville marveled at a country that seemed to be founded on the principle of social equality. "Birth, condition, or profession" no longer raised one man above another; "hardly anything but money remains to create strongly marked differences between them." So powerful was the ethos of equality that a man falling behind in the race would scramble to catch up with his neighbors, while a man edging ahead of his neighbors might be tripped up by them. "They call for equality in freedom; and if they cannot obtain that, they still call for equality in slavery. They will endure poverty, servitude, barbarism; but they will not endure aristocracy." Tocqueville was not entirely complimentary about this trait. Universal education was equal in its mediocrity: "I do not think that there is any other country in the world where, as a proportion of the population, the ignorant are so few and the learned still fewer." He also took notice of black people and Indians, to whom equality did not apply.

The Frenchman said that Americans—by which he meant white Americans—were notable for their "singular mildness," yet inflicted "cruel punishments" on enslaved people, who were not perceived as equals. It was precisely because black people were not seen as equals that citizens could tolerate slavery as "an evil which does not affect them." While Tocqueville was in the United States in 1831, authorities in Virginia suppressed a slave uprising and executed more than fifty alleged perpetrators, including the leader, Nat Turner. Afterward Virginia legislators debated a proposal to gradually abolish slavery, but decided instead to entrench it.

And then there was the United States' Indian policy, which Tocqueville compared with that of the Spanish who began the conquest of the New World. The ruthless Spaniards "loosed their dogs on the Indians as though the natives were ferocious beasts," yet Indians eventually intermarried with the colonizers and became a large portion of Hispanic society. "By contrast," Tocqueville wrote,

> the conduct of the Americans of the United States toward the Indians exhibits the purest love of formalities and legalities. Provided the Indians remain in the savage state, the Americans do not interfere in their affairs and treat them as independent peoples. They will not occupy Indian land until it has been duly acquired by contract. And if by chance an Indian nation can no longer live within its territory, the Americans offer a fraternal hand and lead the natives off to die somewhere other than in the land of their fathers. The Spaniards, despite acts of unparalleled monstrousness that left them indelibly covered with shame, were unable to exterminate the Indian race or even prevent the Indians from sharing their rights. The Americans of the United States achieved both results with marvelous ease, quietly, legally, philanthropically, without bloodshed, without violating a single one of the great principles of morality in the eyes of the world. To destroy human beings with greater respect for the laws of humanity would be impossible.

In saying that removal proceeded "without bloodshed," Tocqueville was not entirely correct. Occasional gunfire erupted on the frontier. In 1832 a group of Indians had crossed the Mississippi into Illinois, attempting to reoccupy land they had lost through a disputed treaty many years before. Indian fighters battled militia forces and killed white settlers. Their best-known chief was Black Hawk, and the fight to repel this Indian incursion came to be known as the Black Hawk War. Abraham Lincoln volunteered for service in a militia company whose men, in the democratic style of the age, elected him captain. His company saw no combat and he later said he shed no blood except from "mosquitoes." Other white units battled and defeated the Indian band. Black Hawk surrendered and was escorted into captivity by a pair of young U.S. Army officers, Robert Anderson of Kentucky and Jefferson Davis of Mississippi.

Black Hawk was sent to Washington, where he received a scolding from President Jackson, and onward to prison at Fort Monroe on the coast of Virginia. Federal authorities soon approved his release, but ordered him to tour eastern cities so he would go home knowing the size and power of the United States. He was driven in a carriage through the prosperous city of Baltimore. In that city on June 6, 1833, he sat through a performance called *Jim Crow*, featuring a popular white actor in blackface. A more incredible experience awaited Black Hawk when the play was over. President Jackson was in the audience, having just taken his historic train ride into town that day, and on the way out of the theater the Indian leader chatted with his acquaintance the Great Father of the nation. "You will see," Jackson told Black Hawk of his eastern tour, "that our young men are as numerous, as the leaves in the woods. What can you do against us?" Black Hawk replied, "I ought not to have taken up the tomahawk. But my people have suffered a great deal." The Sauk chief was becoming an object of public fascination, drawing crowds nearly as large as those attracted to the president. Finally the masses became so disruptive that Black Hawk had to be taken out of the center city and put up for the night at Fort McHenry.

The white settlement of former Indian lands continued at an incredible rate. In 1810, the future states of Mississippi and Alabama had a non-Indian population of 16,000. By 1830 the two states had a combined population of 450,000. Between 1830 and 1840 the populace would more than double again, to 965,000. Georgia was enjoying its own steady growth; prominent citizens were planning a new city at the head of the Coosa River, as soon as the land could be cleared of its current occupants, including Major Ridge and John Ross.

Other Georgia cities were growing in wealth and in cultural refinement. A theater in Augusta hosted a traveling company performing *Metamora*, the smash-hit play from New York about an Indian chief killed by white men. The Augusta stage echoed with the chief's final words ("From the east to the west, in the north and in the south shall the cry of vengeance burst, till the lands you have stolen groan under your feet no more!"). *Metamora* was just beginning its decades-long run as one of the most popular performances on stages across the country, but its premiere in Georgia was not received nearly as well as it had been elsewhere. "Long before the climax was reached," an observer reported, the crowd began to show "evident dissatisfaction." The actor playing Metamora was the target of "loud yells and a perfect storm of hisses from the excited audience, who seemed [ready] in their fury to tear everything to pieces. Order was with difficulty restored, and the performance continued until the curtain fell upon the dying chief amid unqualified evidences of disapprobation." No one attended the play the following night.

Twenty-seven

I Have the Right to Address You

At last the endgame approached, though none could say how near the end might be. Once the missionaries Worcester and Butler withdrew their Supreme Court case at the start of 1833, it was clear that the Cherokees had been blocked at every level and before every branch of government. Even when they won, they lost. Other Indians were doing no better. The Choctaws had been the first to agree to depart under the Indian Removal Act, signing the Treaty of Dancing Rabbit Creek in 1830. The U.S. negotiators included Jackson's friend John Coffee. The Chickasaws too would be crossing the Mississippi, and if the Creeks or Seminoles would not leave, the army was ready to use force.

One thing changed for the Cherokees beginning in 1833. President Jackson demonstrated a more generous attitude. He was still determined to obtain Cherokee land, but wanted the conflict settled. So did Van Buren, now the heir apparent to the presidency, who still had his niece's invective ringing in his ears (he would remember her tongue-lashing vividly enough to include it in his memoirs more than twenty years later). Years of resistance had finally forced Jackson to take the Cherokees seriously, and the administration now offered a treaty with far more liberal terms than in past negotiations. In 1816, as we have seen, Jackson paid tens of thousands of dollars for more than a million acres of Cherokee land; in 1817 he took additional land for no money at all. In 1830, an enraged president declared that Cherokees were holding out for money, and that the "speculating tribe" hoped to "make fortunes out of the United States"; Jackson vowed to leave them to suffer "anihilation." Now Jackson decided that money could solve the problem. The president offered $2.5 million for the remaining Cherokee real estate, or $3 million if the Cherokees would assume the cost of transportation to the west. Comparing Jackson's 1833 offer with his previous ones allows us to estimate the market value of the nationwide political support that Cherokees had generated in the meantime: instead of a few cents per acre at most, Jackson was offering something close to 50 cents. But Ross, as an occasional speculator in land and reader of newspapers, would have known that the market value of Cherokee land was greater than that. In any case he was bound by his nation's policy never to sell. He made another of his clever counterproposals, which Jackson must have found infuriating: instead of relocating Indians, the United States should spend its money *relocating white settlers* who had won Georgia's lottery for Cherokee land. Having delivered this rapier thrust, which was not accepted, Ross began packing for the journey home to the Cherokee Nation and another season of struggle.

Ross believed his resistance reflected his nation's will. Just as Jackson always believed that the majority of the people supported him, Ross had reason to believe that the overwhelming majority of *his* people supported *him*. Yet as he traveled toward home in 1833 he also knew that Cherokee unity was cracking under pressure. Crucial members of the Cherokee elite believed Ross was deluded, that he had no realistic path to victory, that he was leading his people toward doom.

During all of Ross's adult life there had been Cherokees who sensed that the land of their fathers could no longer be the land for them. He was still a teenager when the 1808 treaty had opened the way for the first large band of Cherokees to relocate to the Arkansas country. Ross himself seemed to be flirting with the idea of living among the western Cherokees when he started his boat journey to visit them at the end of 1812. We have seen that other Cherokees migrated over the years, such as the Cherokee woman at Melton's Bluff, who left her white husband as well as the eastern land after Jackson obtained the area in 1816. Sequoyah, the inventor of the Cherokee syllabary, took his writing system westward when he moved in the 1820s. By 1833 several thousand lived in the Arkansas country. They had been established for so long west of the Mississippi that they even had time to be removed; a few years earlier, white settlers had elbowed them out of what was now called the Arkansas Territory, pushing them into land even farther west, which was once again promised to them forever.

Now some of the principal chief's most significant allies were asking if life beyond the Mississippi might rescue the rest of their nation. When Supreme Court justice John McLean told Cherokees in 1832 that the ruling he had just approved was useless to them, those absorbing this shock included the son of Major Ridge. John Ridge had heard the same depressing news in an audience with the president himself; he was the one who left the Executive Mansion in "despair." It may have been no coincidence that Ridge returned home and aired his own doubts. In early 1833, Ridge composed a letter to his chief. "The usual scenes which our afflicted people experience are dreadfully increased," he reported. Cherokees "are robbed & whipped by the whites almost every day." The subtext was that Ross's stubborn course left Cherokees exposed to suffering. Ridge hoped Ross would find some way to relieve his people.

> You very well know that other Gentlemen with myself had despaired of the existence of our dear nation upon its present Location . . . it may be, that the discussion of this project may be disagreeable to you. But Sir, I have the right to address you . . . [Once it is admitted] that we

can't be a nation here, I hope we shall attempt to establish it somewhere else! Where, the wisdom of the nation must try to find.

Losing John Ridge was a blow. He was one of the Cherokee faces to the outside world, handsome and eloquent in English, with his Cornwall education and his white wife. Ross had relied on the younger man not only to join delegations to Washington but to travel up and down the Eastern Seaboard raising money for the Cherokee cause. Ridge was also dangerous because he had the ear of his powerful father, Major Ridge.

Nor was Ridge the only defection. Elias Boudinot too could no longer bear to follow his chief. The newspaperman told Ross in 1832 that he intended to resign, and unlike his previous effort to quit, in 1829, there would be no talking him out of it. He wanted to allow debate in the pages of the *Cherokee Phoenix* about whether to stay or go; Ross was not ready for this. They were acting out the dilemma that constantly afflicted embattled minorities: whether to allow disagreement that outsiders might perceive as weakness or insist on the appearance of unity. The editor felt he was being muzzled. "Were I to continue as editor," Boudinot told Ross, "I do not know whether I could, at the same time, satisfy my own views, and the views of the authorities of the nation." Aside from editorial policy, Boudinot felt like a failure. He had influenced the national debate to an extent many a modern-day journalist would envy, with his stories reprinted, debated, and commented upon across the United States, but he felt it had been pointless. "The public is as fully apprised as we can ever expect it to be, of our *grievances*. It knows our troubles, and yet never was it more silent than at present. It is engrossed in other local and sectional interests."

Boudinot had always taken a relatively dark view of his people's condition, and his work as a newsman had not brightened it. Although he traveled the cities of the East promoting Cherokee advances in civilization, he described those advances modestly. He did not proclaim, as others would, that the Cherokees were living through a golden age.

And he was painfully aware that so long as the Cherokees persisted in their eastern domain they would be surrounded by the corrupting influences of white men's intimidation and alcohol. In 1826, while giving a fund-raising speech in Philadelphia, Boudinot said of the Cherokees that it was easy to see "the evil effects of their intercourse with their immediate white neighbors . . . and it is evident from this intercourse proceed those demoralizing practices which in order to surmount, peculiar and unremitting efforts are necessary." Boudinot was reaching the same conclusion as Henry R. Storrs, the New York congressman who during the 1830 debate over Indian removal had "fervently" wished that the Indians "were already removed far beyond the reach of the oppression—and, I was about to say, the example of the white man." After quitting the *Phoenix*, Boudinot only grew more grim. He would eventually declare that his beloved nation was "almost a dreary waste." His people faced "moral degradation," yet it seemed that Ross worried only about money, about material things, about land.

The great mass of Cherokees, the "dreary waste," remained strongly behind John Ross. All the available evidence said so. True, it was no longer possible to test Ross's support through an election; Cherokee legislators should have faced a vote of the people in 1832, but it was understood that the Georgia Guard would disrupt any balloting. Cherokee lawmakers by necessity extended Ross's term along with their own. There are few detailed accounts of the views of ordinary Cherokees in 1832; there probably were conflicting currents among the suffering people, making it hard to say what would have happened if Ross had faced the pressures of a campaign. But when, a little later, white men engineered votes of Cherokees at mass meetings, hoping to prove that the people had turned against Ross, Cherokees instead supported their chief almost unanimously. Men such as Boudinot admitted that they were a small minority in their nation, which they could explain only by saying that Ross was deluding the masses. Even Cherokee traditionalists seemed to have fallen in line behind the English-speaking modernizer whose leadership they once doubted. In the winter of

1832–33, according to one account, people attending events in support of their chief "donned feathered headdresses, strapped turtle shells filled with pebbles onto their legs and ankles, beat drums, whooped, yelled, and danced all night in the manner of the ancients."

Ross also maintained solid majorities in the legislature, but as men like Ridge and Boudinot hardened in their opposition, political parties began to form. The men who favored negotiating for removal were called the Treaty Party. Those against were the National Party, or simply the Ross Party. This was one more way that the tiny republic in the Cherokee Nation mirrored the larger republic that surrounded it. Each was spawning a two-party system under the pressure of change. In spirit, the members of the Treaty Party were a little like Henry Clay's emerging party, soon to be known as the Whigs: moralistic and too closely associated with the elites for their own good, but absolutely convinced that their nation's chief executive was bent on ruin. The Ross Party, in spirit, was a little like Jackson and the Democrats—tough, politically innovative, determined to win. If Jackson fought stubbornly for principle in his economically perilous war to kill the Bank of the United States, so did Ross in his life-and-death struggle over land. If Jackson was a member of the frontier elite whose story captured the imagination of ordinary people, Ross was a member of the frontier elite whose struggle reflected the spirit of *his* people. In the years to come each man was forever defending, and forever defended by, the common man.

Twenty-eight

We Are Yet Your Friends

Ross's critics were right, though. He did not have a way forward, could not find a way around the Georgians or Jackson. He tried one more time at the start of 1834, beginning yet another long journey from the Cherokee Nation to Washington.

Ross had been joining delegations to Washington for most of his adult life. There had not been a notably successful visit since 1816, when the group including Ross blocked Jackson's effort to "run the line" and capture two million acres. But whatever else happened, Cherokee delegates typically had a chance to meet with the president, which Ross planned to do when he arrived. He checked into Brown's on Pennsylvania Avenue, a hotel also known as the Indian Queen. Here, on the morning of February 3, the Indian chief applied his most elaborate cursive to the page.

> *The undersigned Principal Chief of the Cherokee Nation, inbehalf of himself and the Cherokee delegation, present their respects to the President of the United States and beg leave to inform him that they are desirous to have an interview with him, for the purpose of having a free and full conversation . . .*
>
> *Jno. Ross.*

Word came back that Jackson would see them at noon on February 5. The Executive Mansion was near enough for Ross to walk there on the appointed day, about ten blocks up Pennsylvania Avenue through the unfinished city, with the green-domed Capitol at his back.

The "free and full conversation" with the president could not have been entirely cordial. Jackson was unhealthy and distracted—in a letter that day to his son in Tennessee, the sixty-six-year-old president scribbled that he was "quite unwell, with pain in my left breast & shoulder," the places he had been shot in the duel in 1806 and the gunfight in 1813; he went on to complain that Andrew Jr. was failing to keep him informed about the Hermitage cotton crop. Amid such personal annoyances the Cherokees arrived in his office. The men who had spurned his offer of $2.5 million in 1833 were back again. If the conversation followed the same lines as the letters the participants sent each other in the days that followed, then the Cherokees spent the meeting searching for any solution that would satisfy Jackson short of removal. Jackson said that only removal would do. The Cherokees appealed for protection from Georgia's oppression. Jackson replied that he was powerless, and bade the Cherokee delegation a polite good-bye.

Ross returned to the Indian Queen. In keeping with custom, additional negotiations would take place in writing, slowly, over a period of weeks. Left with time to think, he realized that he had been dealing with Andrew Jackson for two decades now. Twenty years earlier, he had received the summons to rejoin the Cherokee Regiment for the march toward Horseshoe Bend. Some of the years since then had been times of steady gains for Ross and for his people. But since Ross's election as principal chief in 1828, the props had been steadily knocked out from under his world.

Another prop was being knocked out that winter. Ross's brother Andrew joined a small group of Cherokees who created an opposition delegation to Washington. They arrived in the capital with a letter of introduction from the governor of Tennessee, who said they would "be of great use in accomplishing the objects of the government." The opposition delegation were not credible enough to pose as leaders of the Cherokee Nation, and Jackson did not negotiate a treaty with them. But the president now knew that the fault lines in the Cherokee Nation ran very near Ross's feet, and Ross, gathering intelligence about the rival delegation at the Indian Queen, knew that Jackson knew.

Outside the windows of the Indian Queen, the traffic on Pennsylvania Avenue would have given Ross no sign of the political turmoil in the capital. President Jackson was still driving to destroy the Bank of the United States, while Senator Henry Clay and his emerging Whig Party were determined to save it. Arguing that the bank's excessive power was a danger to a free republic, Jackson began withdrawing the federal government's deposits in 1833, overriding the objections of virtually all his advisers. The law did not permit him to withdraw the deposits unless the bank was unsafe, which nobody believed; his act was so far beyond the law that his treasury secretary resigned rather than give the order. Senator Henry Clay orchestrated an investigation, and when Jackson refused to produce a document as demanded, the Senate voted for the only time in history to censure the president. The Bank of the United States also retaliated. From its headquarters in Philadelphia, a stone-columned building modeled on the Parthenon, bank president Nicholas Biddle began calling in business loans, so swiftly contracting the credit available to the economy that it triggered financial chaos. Some contraction was necessary to protect the bank as it lost such a large portion of its deposits, but Biddle went beyond what the emergency required. He was hoping that the risk of calamity would prompt businessmen to pressure Jackson to relent. But when businessmen complained to Jackson, the president simply told them to complain to Biddle.

If Ross took notice of the crisis, he did not write down his thoughts. He was preoccupied. March 28, the day the Senate took its historic vote on censure, was the day Ross wrote a new proposal to the president.

This latest letter showed just how desperate the chief's position had become, although it began on a personal note.

> *Twenty years have now elapsed since we participated with you in the*
> *toils and dangers of war, and obtained a victory over the unfortunate*
> *and deluded red foe at [Tohopeka], on the memorable 27th March 1814,*
> *that portentous day was shrouded by a cloud of darkness, besprinkled*
> *with the awful streaks of blood and death. It is in the hour of such times*
> *that the heart of man can be truly tested and correctly judged. We were*
> *then your friends—and the conduct of man is an index to his*
> *disposition. Now in these days of profound peace, why should the gallant*
> *soldiers which in time of war walked hand in hand thro' blood and*
> *carnage, be not still friends? We answer, that we are yet your friends.*

It was only one of the extraordinary paragraphs in the most extraordinary letter he ever wrote. There is something jarring about Ross's choice of words, and so carefully did he deploy language that the choice could hardly have been accidental. "The unfortunate and deluded red foe," he said, referring to red men as if he were not an Indian himself, as if he regarded himself as something rather different. It is hard not to believe that John Ross was subtly leaning away from his Indian ancestry, and leaning toward his Scottish forebears—leaning, in other words, toward the side of his ancestry that he shared in common with Andrew Jackson. Ross was straining to make a connection with a ruthless and prejudiced man, who would do anything to smite his enemies but would also do anything to aid his friends. The principal chief of the Cherokee Nation was seeking one more time to pass as white.

Ross made this emotional appeal in support of a new proposal. He went far beyond anything the Cherokee legislature had authorized him to do; he would face sharp criticism for it when he returned home. All he wanted was the protection of federal law, which should already have been assured him by treaties and by the courts. For this he was now willing to pay an extraordinary price.

Will you agree to enter into an arrangement on the basis of the
Cherokees becoming prospectively citizens of the United States;
provided the Nation will cede to the United States a portion of its
territory for the use of Georgia? And will you agree to have the laws
and treaties executed and enforced for the effectual protection of the
nation on the remainder of its Territory for a definite period?

Georgia would be offered a slice of land—while Ross looked forward "prospectively" to a day when Cherokees would become citizens, abandoning their final shreds of national independence. His delegation regarded this as the ultimate concession.

It is plausible that Ross did not really mean it. He may have intended only to buy time to reach the end of Jackson's administration, leaving the "prospective" plan for eventual citizenship to be pushed into the future and finally discarded. Or Ross may well have meant it, understanding that it was time for a step that had been on his mind at least since the mid-1820s. Ross faced a choice between the perpetuation of the Cherokee Nation as a political entity and the preservation of at least some Cherokee land—and he decided that the land was more important.

The principal chief's true intentions would never be known, because Jackson did not test them. Although the letter was addressed to Jackson, there is no record that he answered it personally. Instead a disapproving note came from an aide, and the president maintained his course. A partial solution would not satisfy the Georgians, and according to Jackson it was the Georgians alone with whom Ross must come to terms. Georgia, not Jackson, was destroying the Cherokee Nation; the president was merely standing aside to let it happen. So it was with the national economy—the Bank of the United States, not Jackson, was wrecking it. So it had been twenty years earlier when his soldiers were preparing to execute John Wood. "Between [the] law & its offender," he had written then, "the commanding General ought not to be expected to interpose."

Twenty-nine

Should They Be Satisfied with the Character of That Country

On December 28, 1835, a federal Indian agent went for a walk in central Florida. The agent's name was Wiley Thompson, and his walk took him outside Fort King, the army stockade near which he worked. Thompson strolled with an army lieutenant who had earlier joined him for lunch. They were walking through a lightly populated area, with fields that were brown in this chilly month but verdant in season. Thompson had a plantation in this wide and fertile country, which was connected to the outside world by a narrow trail. It pointed southward toward Tampa Bay, and northward toward the old Spanish fortress at St. Augustine. A branch of the trail also led to Jacksonville, the town named in honor of the man who once had conquered Florida.

Wiley Thompson was in his fifties, a former congressman and a Jackson man. He had seen service in one of the forces fighting the war against the Creeks in 1813–14, and afterward was named a major general in the Georgia militia. As a congressman from Georgia, he had been in the House in May 1830 to cast his vote in favor of the Indian Removal Act. Thompson closely followed the struggles of the Cherokees of his state, and in 1833 wrote a letter expressing his "deep regret" at the "sudden and unaccountable" resistance of John Ross to Jackson's $2.5 million offer for a "speedy adjustment." Shortly afterward Thompson left Congress, and President Jackson appointed him to oversee Indian affairs in Florida for $1,500 a year. Thompson was supposed to work himself out of a job, ushering the Seminoles out of Florida and closing down the federal Indian agency. But two and a half years later the plan to close the agency had been delayed, and the Seminoles were still in place.

In the 1820s the Seminoles had been pushed away from the coastal areas and into about four million acres of the interior of the peninsula. In 1832 they were asked to give up the remainder. James Gadsden, a former officer in Jackson's army, summoned Seminole headmen to Payne's Landing, in central Florida, and caused their marks to appear on a treaty of removal. Gadsden was the diplomat who years later would negotiate a famous purchase of land from Mexico that completed the American Southwest. In this case he bought central Florida for about 2 cents an acre. And the terms grew even better through their interpretation. The treaty seemed to say the Seminoles were not actually obliged to give up their land unless their representatives visited and approved of their proposed new territory in the West—the natives would move "should they be satisfied with the character of that country"—but the United States took the view that the Seminoles must depart whether they liked it or not.

Thompson was having trouble enforcing the treaty. Some of the fifteen Seminole leaders involved, all of them apparently illiterate, began denying that they had ever put their marks on such a document. Whether they marked it or not, the chiefs were having trouble persuading their people to follow it. Seminoles were an exceedingly complex people. Their numbers included descendants of generations of migrants, survivors, and refugees—Creeks and others who fled to Florida to escape Indian warfare or marauding white settlers, or who lost their land through treaties. (The Creeks who retreated to Florida after the Battle of Horseshoe Bend were following a century-old pattern of migration.) There was another kind of refugee too: escaped slaves lived among the Seminoles, some of them accorded free status and others enslaved by Indians. In either case their social status was different than in white society. Some intermarried with the Seminoles and even held positions of influence. Many opposed the treaty, knowing that if they ever came out of central Florida, they would probably end up in a slave market. Preparations for migration stalled. Gunfire and Seminole raids had been reported before Agent Thompson and his companion took their walk on December 28.

The two men were being watched. A small band of Seminoles had been waiting for an opportunity to settle some business with Thompson. Their leader was known to white men as Powell, and among Seminoles as Osceola. He was a Jackson man of a different sort: his parents were Creek Red Sticks, who had battled against Jackson's army and other white forces in the Creek War of 1813–14 before escaping to Florida when Osceola was a boy. Now, having grown up among the Seminole populace, he was a prominent warrior.

Even from a distance, Osceola had no trouble recognizing Thompson, for they had had intimate dealings for some time. The young man had come to Thompson's attention for his speeches on the injustice of removal. Wiley Thompson found Osceola so frustrating that he took the extreme step of having the Seminole clapped in irons. This was considered an even greater humiliation in native culture than it would have been in white culture. Thompson would not free the younger man until he agreed to sign the disputed removal treaty, which Osceola did—only to renege as soon as he was released. He said that Seminoles who agreed to move west should be killed, and then actually killed a leader whose X mark was on the treaty. Now he waited for his moment to confront Thompson—and when the agent and his companion were too far from Fort King to hope for help, the Seminoles fell upon them. It was said Thompson's scalp was cut into pieces so that each man could take away a souvenir.

The assassination of Jackson's man in Florida was part of a two-pronged attack. A second, much larger party of Seminoles were watching the southerly trail approaching Fort King, for they knew that soldiers were marching from Tampa Bay to reinforce the tiny garrison in the fort. One hundred eight soldiers appeared on the trail before them, bundled up against the chill of the day; the Seminoles opened fire from behind pine trees and palmettos, and their opening volley killed or wounded up to half the unprepared troops. The commander, Major Francis Dade, was among the dead. Surviving soldiers managed to blast away with a cannon they had dragged up the trail; its covering fire briefly drove off the attackers and bought the soldiers time to make a breast-work out of fallen trees. They fought until they ran out of ammunition. The attackers killed all but three wounded men, who slipped away.

What became known as the Second Seminole War was fully under way. There was no glory in it. It was fought under horrifying condi-tions, amid palmetto scrub or knee-deep in swamps. The bands of Seminoles were near starvation at the start of the war and suffered even more as they eluded white troops. White soldiers flailed about in swamps while their commanders flailed about for a winning strategy. In its various stages the war would last seven years, nearly as long as the United States' formal combat involvement in Vietnam. The number of U.S. military deaths in the Second Seminole War was 1,535. As a per-centage of the national population, this was considerably greater than the number of military deaths in the United States' twenty-first-century war in Iraq. Most of the army's deaths were from disease. Seminole deaths and white civilian deaths, though not fully counted, were con-siderable. No heroes emerged from the war except Osceola, who mur-dered a federal agent in cold blood as part of what a later generation might have labeled a coordinated terror attack—and yet before the end of the conflict, the government would treat Osceola so dishonorably that it triggered another wave of revulsion at Indian removal.

The seemingly endless conflict would relate in more than one way to the Cherokees and John Ross. For one thing, Ross was eventually lured into playing a small but embarrassing part in it. In a larger sense, the rebellion of the Seminoles illustrated the road Ross had chosen not to take. If Ross was performing an experiment in the limits of peaceful resistance, the Seminoles were performing a simultaneous experiment in guerrilla warfare. And Ross would always have to keep in mind that many senior Seminole leaders had not chosen to start this conflict. It had been driven by junior leaders such as Osceola, who felt their elders had given away too much. Ross knew he could keep most of his people united behind a peaceful policy so long as he was firmly resisting the government. But if he ever thought of giving in, he had to wonder if some Cherokee Osceola might rise up in protest and force the nation toward war.

PART NINE

Tears

1835–1838

Thirty

Five Millions of Dollars

F irst they took his house. It happened in early 1835, while Ross was in Washington for more failed negotiations (the Senate raised the offer to $5 million; Ross had seemed ready to accept whatever the Senate would pay, but then backed away; he was by then demanding $20 million). While the principal chief was away in the capital, the white family that claimed Ross's home through the Georgia lottery took possession. The Georgia Guard tried to send word to Ross in Washington that his house was gone, but the message missed him. He had no idea as he made the long journey home. He arrived at Head of Coosa late at night to discover his family missing and a different family in their place. The new owner, irked to be awakened, barked that he had no idea where the Indian's wife and children might have gone. Softening a little, and noting the lateness of the hour, the man offered Ross a room for the night, and in the morning charged Ross a fee for the care of his horse. Ross tracked down his family and moved them to Cherokee land in Tennessee, where they took up residence in a two-room cabin.

After taking his home, they took Ross's voice. In August 1835 the *Cherokee Phoenix* printing press was still located at New Echota, though publication had been suspended due to the difficulty in finding a competent staff. Ross sent a wagon to bring the press to Tennessee, but the Georgia Guard reached New Echota first. They seized the press, finally following the advice of Jackson's onetime attorney general, John Macpherson Berrien, who had said that this instrument of Cherokee power should be removed. Generations later, archaeologists would find no sign of the *Phoenix* except about fifteen hundred pieces of old metal type on the ground.

After his voice, they took Ross's freedom. On the night of November 7, 1835, he was in his Tennessee cabin with a visitor. They heard dogs barking outside, and then a hoarse voice: "Ross, Ross!" Armed men crowded into the house. "We have business with you, sir," said one of the rifle-toting men. "You are to consider yourself a prisoner."

Ross's guest at the time of the intrusion was a well-known writer and playwright, John Howard Payne. He was in the Cherokee Nation gathering material for a literary magazine, and was about to obtain more material than expected. According to the account Payne wrote soon afterward, Ross remained calm. "Well, gentlemen, I shall not resist," Ross told the gunmen. "Why am I a prisoner? By whose order am I taken?"

"You'll know that soon enough," one of his captors replied.

The gunmen were members of the Georgia Guard, so zealous in protecting the sovereignty of Georgia that they had invaded Tennessee. The men loaded Ross, his visitor, and their papers onto horses and rode south into Georgia. "A wild storm arose," Payne recalled, and "rain poured in torrents. The movements of our escort were exceedingly capricious; sometimes whooping and galloping and singing obscene songs, and sometimes for a season walking in sullen silence." Payne claimed to have heard one of his guards humming "Home, Sweet Home," a popular tune of the era. Payne was delighted. He was the author of that song. By dawn the dripping party had reached its destination, a windowless cabin where Ross and Payne were instructed to remain with the door always open and guards nearby. The gunmen would later accuse Ross and his guest of a conspiracy "to raise an insurrection among the negroes, who are to join the Indians against the whites."

Payne wrote a description of the Cherokee leader at the time of his detention. Ross was "of middle size—rather under than over;—his age about five & forty: he is mild, intelligent & entirely unaffected." Georgians had previously warned Payne not to waste time with this "sordid" and "silent" man, but Payne found Ross "different in every respect from what he had been represented to be." Ross feared for a time that they might be lynched, but their captors became less strident as the days passed. Possibly their improving attitude was a reaction to the uproar spreading in the world outside the cabin. Tennesseans regarded the raid as a violation of their state sovereignty. A Tennessee newspaper dubbed the raiders a "mob extraordinary," while the governor of Tennessee wrote his counterpart in Georgia demanding that he disavow the raid or else Tennessee might raise a paramilitary force of its own. Georgia's governor danced away from the controversy, saying he knew nothing of the arrest except "common street rumor." Ross and Payne were both released by late November.

Having monitored the chatter of his guards, Ross concluded that his detention was not directed by the state. The Georgia Guard seemed to have acted at the urging of a federal Indian agent—the Superintendent of Cherokee Emigration, a representative of President Jackson. Ross's suspicion proved to be correct. The agent, Major Benjamin F. Currey, a native of Nashville and an associate of the president, had been taking progressively more extreme measures. It was Currey who persuaded the Georgia Guard to seize the printing press, and who persuaded a friendly guard unit to stage the cross-border raid. He was hoping that an illegal detention would separate Ross from his people, even though his eventual release was inevitable. It was a bonus to have John Howard Payne swept up in the dragnet. In a letter to a newspaper, Currey declared that Payne was a member "of the whig party, and rumor makes him an abolitionist," who was conspiring with hostile newspapers to publish articles for "political effect."

.   .   .

The most revealing part of Ross's capture was the chain of events leading up to it. The raid on his house went forward only after Major Currey tried for years to bypass the chief using less drastic measures.

When first assigned to the Cherokee country in 1831, Major Currey
and other Jackson men assumed they were battling corrupt tribal elites.
Their attitude resembled that of Americans in later generations who
tried to control nations such as Iraq. They were so convinced of the
righteousness of their values and their commonsense policies that it was
hard to imagine that any native could honestly disagree. If the natives
opposed U.S. policy, it could only mean that they were deluded or
intimidated by corrupt leaders. Jackson's men, infused with the democratic spirit of the era, were so certain that the common people of the
Cherokee Nation must be on their side against John Ross that they
repeatedly tried to appeal to the Cherokee masses through democratic
means. In this way they created a lengthy record of what many Cherokees actually believed.

White authorities' starting assumption about the Cherokees was
put on paper around the time of Major Currey's arrival in 1831. In that
year a Georgia official investigated the Cherokee leadership and concluded that Ross and his allies were not Indian enough. The official's
report found that "the native Indian has but little part" in ruling the
Cherokee Nation, which was controlled "exclusively by those who are so
remotely related to the Indian, as gives them but slender claims to be
classed among that people." Half-breeds and mixed-bloods could not
possibly represent the will of the more numerous full-blooded Indians.
It was to break the grip of these mixed-bloods that Currey and other
white officials attempted to apply the corrective tonic of democracy.

They arranged a series of public votes on the issue of Cherokee
annuities. Jackson was still refusing to pay the Cherokee government
for past sales of land rights, vowing instead that the money must be

distributed to individuals. In 1834 Jackson's men called for a plebiscite to resolve the stalemate at a poorly attended meeting at Red Clay, Tennessee. Though Jackson's men refused to allow Ross to observe the balloting, Ross won the vote, with 388 in favor of paying the Cherokee government, and only one single Cherokee voting to pay individuals. Concluding that this must have been a Ross-orchestrated fraud, the administration still held back the money and tried democracy again. There was another vote at a much larger meeting of Cherokees in the summer of 1835. This mass meeting was addressed by the Reverend John F. Schermerhorn, a representative of Jackson's administration who had taken on Indian removal as a holy cause. Schermerhorn, regarding Ross as the "devil," wanted to become the instrument of Cherokee salvation. He had a pulpit constructed from which to deliver his speech. Ross, too, addressed the crowd, and when it came time to vote, Ross won, 2,225–114, capturing 95 percent of the vote.

In October 1835 Reverend Schermerhorn and Major Currey tried yet again at a meeting of the Cherokee legislature. They wanted the lawmakers to endorse a proposed removal treaty that had been worked out by a renegade delegation of the Treaty Party. The legislators rejected the treaty. Ross not only won again, he even managed to unite his party and the opposition, at least on the surface. It was agreed that Cherokees from both parties would be included in the delegation to be sent to Washington that winter—John Ridge and Elias Boudinot would be there alongside Ross, seeking to find some agreement with the government together. This was the final outrage for Major Currey. "The strange results of this council, and the increased insolence of the Indians," he wrote, must be a result of Ross's vile influence as well as that of Payne the writer. Casting off democracy, Currey summoned a friendly unit of the Georgia Guard, and the November arrest went ahead.

It is hard to say what role Ross's days out of circulation in November played in the disaster that followed soon after. He could not keep his coalition together. John Ridge remained a member of the delegation assigned to travel to Washington, but made it clear that he was hoping to persuade his chief to sign a removal treaty. Elias Boudinot dropped out of the delegation entirely. By December Ross was leaving the Cherokee Nation, heading for the capital while leaving Boudinot and dissenting members of the Treaty Party behind. As soon as Ross was gone, Reverend Schermerhorn proposed a national council for a treaty negotiation to begin in the Cherokee Nation on December 19. He declared that any Indians who failed to attend this national council would be presumed to accept whatever was done. To give the meeting what legitimacy he could, Schermerhorn said the negotiation should take place in New Echota, the Cherokee capital, from which the government had been forced to relocate long ago.

The leaders of the Treaty Party began gathering in New Echota in the week before Christmas. They found the village, which had never been large, partly empty and decrepit. The council house and courthouse had not served their appointed functions in years. The printshop was empty except for some scattered Cherokee type. The Worcesters were long gone from their house down the path, although Elias and Harriett Boudinot still had their home in the lonely village, where they were expecting another child. Buildings were in disrepair. As discussions began in the council house, the roof caught fire, forcing a temporary evacuation. But for ten days before and after Christmas the village came to life.

There was relatively little negotiation required. The Treaty Party already had a template, the provisional treaty Cherokee legislators had just rejected. They had a price range as well, the offer of $5 million John Ross had rejected at the start of the year. What remained was for the Treaty Party and the federal negotiators to agree on details and persuade the world that their act represented the will of the Cherokee people. This would not be easy. Public attendance at the conference was disappointingly small. At most, a few hundred Cherokees attended.

The one time a vote was held, only eighty-two men were counted, seventy-five for the motion and seven against. But if they did not have numbers or the sanction of Cherokee law, they did have a giant among them—a leader, a diplomat, the uncle of Elias Boudinot, the father of John Ridge, the onetime political sponsor of John Ross. He was the friend of Andrew Jackson, known in Washington for his wealth and cultivation, whose portrait hung for years in the Indian office: a man substantial enough to make a dubious treaty seem real.

The Treaty Party had Major Ridge.

Why did he proceed? There is one account of a speech Major Ridge is said to have given to the group at New Echota. "The Georgians have shown a grasping spirit lately," he is recorded as saying, "but I can do them justice in my heart. They think the Great Father, the President, is bound by the compact of 1802 to purchase this country for them, and they justify their conduct by the end in view. They are willing to buy these lands. . . . We can never forget [our] homes, I know, but an unbending, iron necessity tells us we must leave them . . . any forcible effort to keep them will cost us our lands, our lives, and the lives of our children." It was an eloquent speech, though it is uncertain Ridge ever said it. It only appeared in print fifty years later, and even then was recorded by a sympathetic white Georgian who was unlikely to be familiar with the original Cherokee. Better evidence of Ridge's thoughts is contained in the letters of his son and nephew, who probably reflected some of Ridge's views. John Ridge recorded the sufferings of the Cherokee people and the unrealistic stubbornness of Chief John Ross. Elias Boudinot argued for the right of an elite group like the Treaty Party to make a decision for the people at large. Never pretending to command a majority in this age of majority rule, Boudinot knew that he must explain. "If one hundred persons are ignorant of their true situation," he wrote, "we can see strong reasons to justify the action of a minority of fifty persons—to do what the majority would do if they understood their condition." The minority must save the people from "destruction" and from "moral degradation."

Major Ridge's personal economic calculation was significantly different from that of the common people on whose behalf he acted. Removal would cost him his land, but Ridge would find new land in the West. He would be paid for his handsome house and other improvements that he was leaving behind. And he would be able to take along his most valuable property, his highly portable workforce of slaves. Poorer people could not see the move the same way. They had less portable property and would be paid much less for their improvements. But the decision for Ridge could not have been merely financial, for observers twice recorded him saying he expected to be killed for signing the treaty. By way of explanation it can only be said that Ridge was a leader. He had led the way in overturning the ancient law of revenge. He had led the way in the civilization program. Now he would lead his people west.

Ridge and the others negotiated a treaty under excellent terms, so long as they were not viewed too closely. The treaty called for the Cherokees to be paid the unprecedented sum of "five millions of dollars." There was to be a school fund, investments in "safe and most productive public stocks," and much more. Only a careful reading showed how these benefits were minimized. The money for the school fund and the investments were to be *subtracted from* the "five millions of dollars." The compensation for houses and fences and other improvements on the land were *also* to be subtracted from the "five millions of dollars," meaning that in reality, the Cherokees would receive much less than $5 million for the acreage itself. Debts the Cherokees supposedly owed would be deducted from any payments they received. The United States would pay for the support of Cherokees who were near starvation after the upheaval of recent years, but this money would be taken out of their future annuity payments—meaning the Cherokees were being relieved from their years of pain and suffering not with federal funds but with their own money. Whatever was left of the "five millions" would be divided equally among individual Cherokees, a democratic touch that would probably benefit many poor families, though it would also scatter the legacy of the land sale and keep the Cherokee government cash-poor. Dividing a federal payment among individuals was precisely the idea that 95 percent of Cherokee voters had rejected the previous summer.

There could be no submitting such a treaty to the Cherokee legislature, which would reject it. But on December 29, at the home of Elias Boudinot, Major Ridge signed the Treaty of New Echota. So did Boudinot and a number of other prominent men, including John Ross's brother Andrew. Reverend Schermerhorn and Major Currey signed it too, and Currey rushed it to Washington. He arrived in mid-January to find that John Ross had begun his own negotiations with Jackson's administration, but as soon as the administration learned of the Treaty of New Echota, it broke off talks with Ross. It had no more use for him. The game was over. Jackson sent the treaty for ratification by the Senate, which after bitter debate held a vote in the spring of 1836. A two-thirds majority was required. Henry Clay's anti-Jackson forces had the votes to block the treaty, if they were united. They were not. The treaty prevailed by a single vote. The majority ruled.

Thirty-one

The War Department Does Not Understand These People

S oon after the Senate ratified the Treaty of New Echota, President Jackson sent the army to the Cherokee Nation. More precisely, he sent a single army general, John E. Wool. There weren't troops available to send along with Wool, since much of the army was tied down by the Seminole war in Florida, and some of the rest was battling an Indian insurgency as the Creeks were driven out of Alabama. Brigadier General Wool was instructed to proceed to East Tennessee, recruit a thousand volunteers, and plant them in Cherokee country. Wool's recruits marched from the Tennessee River down to New Echota, repairing roads and handing out rations to people left hungry by the Georgians' depredations—trying to win hearts and minds while also showing their strength.

General Wool was a veteran of the War of 1812, in his early fifties, with the last of his hair elaborately combed forward to obscure his baldness; yet he was nearer the beginning of his career than the end of it. He would serve with distinction for decades after his duty in the Cherokee Nation, leading troops in combat in Mexico and even serving, in his late seventies, in the Civil War. First, however, he would spend a year in Cherokee country as the conduit between Jackson and

John Ross—outmaneuvered by one, rebuked by the other, and increasingly doubtful of the course each pursued.

Senate ratification had started a clock ticking. The treaty allowed two years from ratification for all Cherokees to be gone—two years exactly after May 23, 1836. Wool was to make sure nothing slowed preparations for the migration. In the early days he met with Major Ridge and other members of the treaty faction, who convinced him that the only real obstacle to removal was John Ross. Wool was so certain of this that his troops briefly arrested the principal chief and several other leaders on the morning of August 3, 1836, Ross's second detention in less than a year. Like the Georgians, Wool had to let Ross go. Later, when Wool had seen more of the Cherokee country for himself, he began to sense the true nature of his mission. "The War Department does not understand these people, and no man can understand them until he goes among them," Wool declared in a letter to the War Department.

> For three weeks after my arrival at Athens [Tennessee], from the daily reports made to me, I was induced to believe that a large proportion of the nation was prepared to submit to the treaty and remove west at the proper time; a few days at the mouth of Valley river convinced me I was mistaken. A few white men and some few half-breeds only could be found to advocate a submission to the treaty. This is not fiction but truth.

A "large majority" of the Cherokee Nation not only opposed the treaty but did not believe it would ever be enforced. "What course," Wool asked his superiors, "under such circumstances, would you pursue?" Wool foresaw disaster. Cherokees would make no preparations to move. They would also remain "the prey of the white men" who were inventing "debts" that the Cherokees supposedly owed. When the deadline arrived, chaos or war would ensue.

Wool met the Cherokees' principal chief, and did not find him helpful. Ross informed the general that he planned to hold a mass meeting in September 1836 to discuss the treaty with his people. He asked if Wool had the authority to prevent a meeting; Wool, not wanting to repeat his initial heavy-handed tactics, said that he did not.

> *I advised [Ross], however, to be careful . . . any discussion [of opposing the treaty] would find no favor with the President, who was determined to have the treaty executed. He merely replied that he thought the President would be convinced that he had been in error, and that he would finally yield, and be willing to do justice to the Cherokees. I answered . . . that the President I knew was determined to have the treaty executed.*

The meeting must be used only to explain the treaty and to plan for obedience to it. Ross nodded mildly and went away without having made any promises.

On the appointed day Ross arrived at Red Clay, Tennessee, where his government had held its meetings for several years. It was a clearing in the woods, in a wide green valley, with an abundant source of cool water from a limestone spring. Contemporary visitors were charmed by the sight of Cherokee mass meetings there. When large crowds gathered, the woods and clearings around the council house became a temporary city, with "huts for the accommodation of strangers," and a kind of main street lined with "huts, booths and stores." Around these structures and through the woods flowed "an unceasing current of . . . men, women, youths, and children, moving about in every direction, and in the greatest order; and all, except the younger ones, preserving a grave and thoughtful demeanor." People might linger for days, waiting on the meeting to begin, their many cooking fires visible throughout the neatly cleared woods as they ate corn and freshly killed beef. When the time came for government business, horns would echo through the woods. People congregated around the council house, a roof mounted on poles, open except for a railing on all sides so that thousands outside could listen.

General Wool, whose troops camped near the meeting ground, estimated before the meeting started that the crowd already numbered three thousand. Eventually attendance grew to between four and five thousand; yet Wool found them "peaceful," operating with "order and decorum." Once the meeting came to order, the Cherokees calculated the approximate number of voters who were attending, "upwards of twenty-one hundred male adults." This was out of a total Cherokee population of about 16,500, of whom about half were male, and 3,992 were males over the age of eighteen. "Upwards of twenty-one hundred" male adults, if the count was accurate, would be a clear majority of the entire voting population, who had come over terrible roads during a time of severe economic deprivation. This great crowd fell silent as their principal chief stood up to speak in the council house.

A description survives of Ross around that time. Forty-seven years old, he was still trim. His once-dark hair was now "streaked with gray," remembered this observer, and "his complexion was a little florid. He had a dark, brown, brilliant eye." Something about his charisma succeeded in crossing the language barrier; at assemblies like this he spoke in English and was translated sentence by sentence into Cherokee, his words repeated far out into the crowd. He was addressing the sort of meeting at which Cherokees for centuries had been called forth to hear or to ratify the decisions of their leaders. But it was also a meeting in the emerging democratic tradition, the kind of gathering at which politicians raised their voices to be heard across the crowd, knowing that within that crowd lay the power to decide. This Cherokee meeting was a massive endorsement of Ross. On the last day of the session, Cherokee leaders endorsed a letter declaring that the treaty was "a fraud upon the government of the United States and an act of oppression on the Cherokee people." Ross was one of thirty-three leaders who signed the letter, a roll call of resistance. Here were men of the elite who had stayed with Ross, like George Lowrey, the assistant principal chief. Here were men who went by their English names like James Spears, and by their Cherokee names like Choo-noo-luh-hno-kee. Here, as on the list of casualties at Horseshoe Bend, were names that fit the attributes or personalities of the bearers: Bean Stick, the Bark, Bushyhead, Money Crier. It was even signed by White Path, the traditionalist who had once led a quiet revolt against Ross and the modernists; now they were on the same side.

The Cherokees gave their letter to General Wool, with its declaration that they relied on the "good faith" and "magnanimity" of "the President and the Congress." Wool forwarded the letter to the president in Washington. The president read it and sent it right back to Wool in New Echota. He declared the letter was "disrespectful" to the president and the Senate. A War Department functionary instructed Wool to "immediately return it" to the signers, and tell them the treaty would be enforced "without modification." Not only that,

you will deliver a copy of this communication to Mr. Ross, and will thereafter cease to hold any communication with him, either orally or in writing, in regard to the treaty.

The president also criticized his general for allowing the mass meeting to continue after it became clear it was being used to strengthen opposition to the treaty.

Wool continued to regard Ross as a dangerous obstructionist, but he was also contemplating the potential horror of prodding an entire nation to move at gunpoint: "The people are opposed to the treaty, and are unwilling to leave this country for the Arkansas. The amount of force [required] in this country will entirely depend on the course which John Ross and his party will pursue." Wool repeatedly voiced sympathy for ordinary Cherokees, and even protested a plan for some law-abiding Creeks in Cherokee territory to be "dragged like so many beasts to the emigration camp." The administration began to seem unnerved by the general's reports; whose side was the army on? Secretary of War Cass wrote the general with a warning about disloyalty. "If any officer of the army should countenance resistance or opposition to the treaty, you will arrest him." Wool never did "countenance resistance"—he thought Cherokees should move west for their own good—but continued warning of the risk of disaster. He predicted that when the May 1838 deadline arrived, it would be hard to avoid "the shedding of human blood. . . . It is sufficient to say that the rights of this people have been too often disregarded, too often trampled upon, too often violated without a cause or justification, with impunity, not to have sunk deep into their hearts."

It is remarkable, given such statements, that General Wool lasted in his assignment as long as he did. He was an effective organizer, hard to replace when the greater part of the army was bogged down fighting Indians elsewhere. But he increasingly came into conflict with the white men who surrounded the Cherokees. Alabamans were upset when he interfered with white men selling alcohol in Cherokee country; North Carolinians said he insulted their sovereignty. When a white man in Alabama seized a Cherokee's property "improvement," meaning cleared fields or buildings, General Wool took it back. State authorities complained to Washington, and General Wool was instructed to relinquish command to a subordinate officer as of July 1, 1837. Supposedly he was recalled from command at his "own request," although General Wool spoiled this fiction by writing that he was not actually requesting a recall at the time. Returning to the capital, he entered a lengthy defense of his conduct, in which he sounded a bit like John Marshall, insisting that the Cherokee treaties trumped the power of the states. A military court of inquiry, composed of sympathetic officers, cleared Wool of any wrongdoing. He had been ordered to enforce a fictional treaty. It had not been easy to square his orders with reality, but he had followed them.

Thirty-two

Perchance, You May Have Heard
That the Cherokees Are in Trouble

B y then Andrew Jackson had left Washington for the final time. He had staggered to the end of his second term in miserable health—correspondence from his final year includes a note from a functionary saying that the president could not even be shown a letter because of his "severe illness." In his farewell message on March 4, 1837, the president declared that "advanced age and a broken frame warn me to retire from public life." But he had triumphed over all. The national debt had been retired. The power of the Bank of the United States was broken, and the bank itself would soon be liquidated. Not only that, the Indians were gone, or so Jackson said in his message. Indian removal, his first major legislative proposal, was the first concrete achievement he listed in his farewell letter: "The States which had so long been retarded in their improvement by the Indian tribes residing in the midst of them are at length relieved from the evil." Now, he told his fellow citizens, "if you are true to yourselves nothing can impede your march to the highest point of national prosperity."

The union under Jackson had been preserved, and was on the verge of expanding. For much of his life Jackson had believed the Mexican state of Texas should belong to the United States, and by the time he left office it nearly did. In early 1836 Texas revolutionaries were slaughtered at the Alamo, among them that wayward former member of Jackson's army, David Crockett, but afterward Jackson's protégé Sam Houston rescued the cause of Texas independence. Houston, the talented if erratic hero of Horseshoe Bend, had arrived in Texas after a shooting-star political career in Tennessee. He led a small army to victory at the Battle of San Jacinto, and his infant Republic of Texas promptly asked to be annexed by the union. Jackson declined. The time was not yet right. But Jackson could confidently leave such matters to his successor, since Jackson had chosen the successor: Martin Van Buren, Jackson's vice president and the winner of the 1836 election. His victory underlined the strength of the political party Jackson had founded, the first party in American history with sufficient organization and popular identity to last for generations.

Leaving Van Buren in charge in Washington, Jackson took the roads and rivers homeward, stopping now and then to rest or to greet cheering crowds. The people loved him; even his enemies applauded his service. Jackson was said to be so overcome with sentimental emotions that he expressed regret over his estrangement from Henry Clay. He cried when a crowd greeted his carriage in Tennessee. Reaching Nashville, he once again walked the grounds of the Hermitage, when he was well enough to walk. From a rear porch the old man, now seventy, could oversee enslaved workers tending the fields near the mansion. Guests approaching the Hermitage saw the white-columned front porch between two rows of trees in the yard, and walked into a high foyer wallpapered with an Italianate scene of balconies and trees. Next they would be shown into a sitting room to meet the sticklike, white-haired master of the house, whose mood was returning to normal. His sentimental feelings toward his political enemies soon passed. He read his many regular newspapers and raged at the news, scrawling notes in a shaky hand to politicians, cabinet members, even Van Buren himself. He remained a political force of nature, a volcano at the Hermitage, occasionally erupting.

The downsides of Jackson's brand of presidential leadership would all be left to Van Buren. The new president had been in office just two months when a financial panic struck New York. The causes were complex, but seemed to grow in part out of Jackson's dislike of banks. Distrusting paper money, which in that era was issued by banks, Jackson in 1836 had declared that buyers of federal land must pay for their real estate only in gold or silver. Instantly he undermined public confidence in paper currency and created a shortage of gold, which contributed to a credit crisis. In responding to the crisis, Van Buren was hamstrung by Jackson's small-government philosophy: the government had neither the duty nor the authority to help those in need. A catastrophic depression stained Van Buren's entire presidency. Then there were the Indians. Only in Jackson's farewell address were they all removed. The truth could be found in another document from that year, the first annual report to Congress by President Van Buren's secretary of war, who was forced to offer explanations and excuses for the soaring expense and frustration of the Seminole campaign.

The war in Florida continued as Jackson left office, though his 8,249-word farewell letter did not mention it. It was as inconclusive as counterinsurgency campaigns usually were. Osceola and other leaders carefully planned their attacks and slipped away. A succession of army commanders tried different ways to trap them.

Van Buren must have thought that he would begin his administration by putting the sad and brutal conflict to an end. Soon after he took office, several Seminole leaders agreed to negotiations with the army and signed a truce, which included an agreement to give up their land and move west. However, the agreement called for them to go west with the escaped slaves who lived among them and fought on their side. White Floridians were outraged, feeling that if they could not recapture slaves, they would rather continue the war. Osceola did not accept the deal either. Fighters under Osceola and another leader descended on Tampa Bay in mid-1837 and turned out hundreds of Seminoles being held in a detention camp awaiting transportation to the West.

In October the army commander, General Thomas Jesup, hit upon a way to strike back. The general agreed to send officers to meet Osceola for peace talks. Osceola, with a group of followers, arrived under a white flag—and then, by prearrangement, 250 soldiers surrounded him and took him prisoner. Memorable in his outfit of blue and red, Osceola was paraded through celebrating crowds in St. Augustine, and shipped up the coast to a prison cell in Fort Moultrie, on Charleston Harbor in South Carolina. One of his last sights before being led into the fort may have been a man-made island in the harbor, fifty thousand tons of granite and cut stone, the recently built foundation for Fort Sumter.

General Jesup went on to use this kind of treachery several more times to capture Seminoles. But his triumph turned to ashes for Van Buren's administration. Osceola had been captured dishonorably, in what everyone understood to be a violation of the laws of war, and having been captured this way, he died at Fort Moultrie on the last day of January 1838. He had been suffering from malaria. The stories of his exploits, followed by the manner of his capture, turned him from a murderer into a martyr in the eyes of many whites. A popular painter, George Catlin, had visited Osceola in prison to make what became a famous portrait, the classic Indian hero with his feathered headdress and shells around his neck and a soulful look on his youthful face. Osceola was celebrated across the nation as neither a savage nor a terrorist but a defender of his homeland. In the years to follow, a later historian noted, there would be "twenty towns, three counties, two townships, one borough, two lakes, two mountains, a state park, and a national forest bearing his name." Some of these places were named not in later generations but shortly after the Seminole's death. Osceola County, Michigan, received its name in 1843. Though the army captured Osceola and disease killed him, democracy kept his name alive.

This embarrassment for Van Buren and his administration was only beginning to unfold in the fall of 1837 when John Ross arrived in Washington. There was a brief hope that the new president might be more flexible toward the Cherokees than the old one, and might even

extend the 1838 deadline for Cherokee removal. This did not happen;
Van Buren had been elected by roughly the same political coalition that
had elected Jackson, and the southern wing of that coalition had the
same interests. But there was a new secretary of war, Joel R. Poinsett,
who was nothing if not creative; his previous assignments had included
a term as the U.S. envoy to Mexico, where he had attempted audaciously
to induce the Mexicans to sell Texas. Now Poinsett, overseeing the blood-
soaked catastrophe that was federal Indian policy in 1837, discovered a
peaceful if irritating Indian sitting in his office at the War Department.
Poinsett proposed to put the Indian to use: Would Ross be willing to
appeal to the Seminoles to stop their senseless war?

Ross pondered this. He had been told that if he aided the government, it would be regarded as a service the government would repay. He
also wanted the Seminole war to end; stories of savages fighting in the
Florida forests contributed to prejudice against all Indians. He agreed
to write a letter, a "talk," to Seminole leaders. Dipping his pen in ink in
Washington, on October 18, 1837, Ross undertook to persuade Seminoles whom he did not know to make peace with a government he did
not trust. This called for considerable art in letter-writing. If in 1834
Ross had subtly obscured his Indian roots in an effort to slip past the
defenses of Andrew Jackson, in 1837 he put all his weight on those
roots.

*I am of the aboriginal race of redman of this great Island—and so
are you.*

"We are strangers," Ross went on, "yet, the time was, when our
ancestors once smoked the pipe of peace together—therefore, I ask you
to listen to my talk." Ross did not go along with a War Department suggestion that he tell the Seminoles they must agree to removal as a condition of peace. He would not be used to that extent. Instead he tried to
use the letter for his own purposes, suggesting that the Seminoles should
try to negotiate a new and better treaty as the Cherokees wanted to do.

Perchance, you may have heard that the Cherokees are also in trouble about their own lands—this is true—but I have spoken to my people, and they have listened. . . . That, the laws & treaties for the security and protection of our rights were the only weapons with which we must defend [our lands]. That, if it has been our misfortune to suffer wrongs from the hands of our white brethren we should not despair of having justice still extended to us by the U. States.

Ross had been writing letters seeking justice for more than twenty years now, at least since his 1816 letter declaring Cherokees part of the "great family of the Republic of the U. States." He may have believed in the ideals and the justice of the great republic even more than some of the men who governed it. His letter was sent onward in the hands of four Cherokees, who carried the paper to an army fort in Florida. This letter was used to lure within the fort's walls a delegation of Seminoles, including their leader Micanopy, who came under a white flag to hear it read, after which the army's General Jesup had the visiting Seminoles arrested. They were sent off to prison at St. Augustine.

Distraught, the four Cherokees followed the prisoners until they found an opportunity to express their regret and to insist that they had nothing to do with the white man's treachery. The Seminoles believed them.

Thirty-three

The Thunder Often
Sounding in the Distance

S ome Cherokees did not wait until the May 1838 deadline to take
their leave of their homeland. Major Ridge joined a party that
departed more than a year early. Four hundred sixty-six people,
half of them children, converged on Ross's Landing for their departure.
A few inevitably got drunk among the liquor shops of the riverside settlement, but finally tumbled with the rest of the party into a dozen
flatboats that had been gathered for them on the Tennessee River. They
cast off from the Cherokee Nation on March 3, 1837.

The water was low, and they made slow progress, sometimes only a
few miles a day. At Decatur, Alabama, they could travel no farther; Muscle Shoals loomed ahead, its water too low for navigation. The emigrants
hoisted their belongings through the town of Decatur and were taken to
a set of iron rails. They heard a clattering in the dark. A steam locomotive
arrived, pulling a string of open freight cars: the first railroad to be chartered west of the Appalachians had now completed a set of tracks that ran
parallel to Muscle Shoals, and the Cherokees now climbed into the freight
cars to continue their migration. Hands on the sides of the freight cars,
watching the countryside blurring past in the dark, they rode across the
landscape south of the river. The rocking cars bypassed Jackson's former

plantation at Melton's Bluff before creaking to a halt at the bottom of Muscle Shoals, at Tuscumbia, near the square mile of land Jackson had bought at auction in 1818 and across the river from Florence, where his onetime real estate partners James Jackson and John Coffee still lived. Here the emigrants descended the bluffs to the Tennessee, its waters smoother now. They transferred back to boats, for their route was the same one taken back in 1812 by young John Ross in his keelboat—down the Tennessee to the Ohio, then southward down the Mississippi, then westward up the Arkansas. Major Ridge's party reached its destination by the end of March. It had taken less than a month and resulted in no reported deaths.

There were also parties traveling by land to the Arkansas country, and their experience was a better indication of what future emigrants would face. On October 13, 1837, 365 emigrants loaded their wagons to begin the land route, which like the water route led well to the northwest before angling back southwestward. Slowed by terrible roads, over which the elderly and children had to walk—for even those who had seats in wagons climbed down to lighten the load on steep slopes—it took them two weeks to travel the first two hundred miles or so to Nashville, where they stopped to wash clothes, repair wagons, and shoe horses. Some took advantage of this pause to visit the Hermitage. They stood before the house, with its two-story white columns, and paid a call on white-haired General Jackson. No doubt Jackson treated his guests with courtesy and respect now that they were doing what he expected of them.

The War Department had hired a "conductor" to guide the Cherokees, one B. B. Cannon, who kept a terse daily journal. In the early weeks he remarked on the worsening condition of his charges ("the Indians appear fatigued this evening—road extremely rough"), but not until after leaving Nashville did he record the first death.

> *Nov. 1st 1837*
>
> *Marched at 8 O'C A.M. buried Ducks child, passed through Hopkinsville Ken . . . issued corn & fodder, Flour and bacon. 19 miles today.*

By November 8, Cannon was describing stragglers who could not continue "without endangering the lives of their children." As the party crossed the Ohio River, southern Illinois, and the Mississippi, the reports of mortality became frequent.

Nov 29th 1837

Remained in camp. Sickness still increasing. Buried Corn Tassle's child today.

. . .

Dec. 4th 1837

Marched at 9 O'C A.M. Buried George Killion, and left Mr. Wells to bury a waggoner (black boy) who died this morning. Scarcely room in the waggons for the sick.

. . .

Dec. 8th 1837

Buried Nancy Big Bear's grandchild. Marched at 9 O'C A.M. . . . Several drunk.

On December 15 Cannon's record of bacon distributed, miles marched, and bodies buried was punctuated by news from a woman who had walked or ridden hundreds of miles in recent weeks:

Joseph Starr's wife had a child last night.

On December 17 they buried two people as it snowed. The entry for December 25 recorded a march of fifteen and a half miles and made no mention of the holiday. On December 28 a child born the day before was buried. The survivors reached their destination in time for the New Year, having been two and a half months on the road.

These were journeys of people who had agreed to move, chosen the timing for their departure, and prepared for it. Behind them in the eastern Cherokee Nation were thousands who had not agreed, had not prepared, and would not have a choice of time. For these thousands the journey would be harder, physically and spiritually, should they finally be forced out on May 23, 1838. And they would be forced, according to a handbill circulating in the Cherokee Nation. "We will not attempt to describe the evils that may fall upon you, if you are still obstinate, and refuse," read the warning authored by federal commissioners and copied on a printing press at Athens, Tennessee. John Ross "may have deceived himself," but must no longer deceive his people. Reality was about to arrive on the point of a bayonet.

Ross faced a choice in the spring of 1838. He could see his people sacrificed in a futile defense of their rights. Or he could admit defeat and attend to their survival.

Ross refused to do either. He decided that if his people were to be removed, they must at least get a better deal.

The last census of the eastern Cherokees before their emigration was conducted in 1835. It showed a people who, after being severely diminished by centuries of war and disease, were beginning to grow in numbers again. The total population of 16,542 was very small but very young, with a median age around eighteen. In other words there were at least as many minors as adults, as was also the case in the wider United States. A little less than one-third of the entire population was able to read in English or Cherokee. The Cherokee Nation had a relatively diverse rural economy—2,809 farmers growing corn and wheat, 339 mechanics, 3,129 spinners, and 2,484 weavers. There were 24 mills as well as the inexplicably precise number of 66.5 ferryboats. Nobody was listed as a "hunter" or a "warrior," the activities that advocates of removal described as the sole occupations of the Indian. The census drew elaborate racial distinctions: about three-quarters of the nation were counted as "Fullbloods," and the remainder were "Halfbloods" with one Cherokee parent, "Quarterbloods" with a Cherokee grandparent, or else people like John Ross who had less than one-quarter Cherokee ancestry. A few were "Mixed Spanish" or "Mixed Negro." There were 1,592 slaves.

To evict them all, President Van Buren assigned the army's ablest officer, Major General Winfield Scott. It was Scott who now assumed the command that had once been held by General Wool, overseeing all military matters in the Cherokee country. Scott was a hero of the War of 1812, a recent veteran of the Second Seminole War, and the author of an army manual on infantry tactics. He was a superb bureaucratic infighter who managed to keep his job even though he was a Whig with ambitions to succeed the Democratic presidents he served. An oversize man with a love of fine food, Scott also had an oversize ego, often vindicated by his ability.

General Scott received his orders in Washington at the start of April, less than seven weeks before the deadline. He heard that John Ross was in the capital and left his card at the Cherokee chief's lodgings. As Ross recalled, they met later and "had a long talk."

Scott . . . says his object is avoid the shedding of blood if possible, and should it so happen that one drop of Cherokee blood be spilt that he will weep!

Scott nevertheless had his orders, and went southward to the Cherokee Nation prepared to use force if necessary to move Cherokees on May 23. The War Department assured him that he would receive a regiment of infantry, a regiment of artillery, and six companies of dragoons or mounted soldiers from the regular army. Most of these soldiers would arrive late or not at all; the insurgencies in Alabama and Florida had stretched the army to the limit. Even cadets at the military academy at West Point were being ordered that spring to prepare to be thrown immediately into active duty. Instead of regular troops, Scott would rely mainly on about three thousand volunteers raised by the affected states, especially the Georgians, whom he did not trust. He was convinced that every Georgia volunteer left home vowing "never to return without having killed at least one Indian," and feared the

Georgians might commit abuses that would trigger war. He issued orders that any soldier seen committing "acts of harshness" was to be immediately arrested, and decided to supervise the Georgians personally. He at least had help overseeing such men from a small staff of regular army officers—phlegmatic veterans such as his aide-de-camp, Lieutenant Robert Anderson. In 1861, Anderson would become famous as the Union commander who defended Fort Sumter on the opening day of the Civil War, but in 1838 he was known as an Indian fighter; he was one of the men who had taken Black Hawk into custody a few years before.

Arriving at Athens, Tennessee, fifteen days before the deadline, Scott wrote out an address to the Cherokees and had copies run off on the local printing press. His message was a mixture of bluster and grace. The general said his "powerful army" was large enough "to render resistance and escape alike hopeless." Dismissing his private misgivings about this force, Scott assured Cherokees that the soldiers were "your friends. . . . The desire of every one of us is to execute our painful duty in mercy. We are commanded by the President to act toward you in that spirit, and such is also the wish of the whole people of America."

In surrounding white communities there was an atmosphere of anticipation. A North Carolina newspaper noted that "a company of volunteers marched through Morganton on Thursday . . . toward the Cherokee service, in fine spirits and to the cheers of their friends." North Carolina also announced its plan to begin selling former Cherokee land. Among Cherokees there was anticipation of a different kind. John Ross's brother Lewis, monitoring developments at the federal Indian agency near General Scott's headquarters, sent a letter to Washington. "Dear Brother. . . . Nothing but destruction stares us in the face. What is to be our fate *god only knows.*" The only people who seemed entirely unaffected by the crisis were ordinary Cherokees, who were supposed to be the focus of it. Early that spring, the federal Indian agent had made an observation so disturbing that the agent forwarded his discovery to Washington. He had seen Cherokees serenely planting their corn crops, as if expecting to be present for the harvest in the fall.

Unrolling maps on a table, peering into the mountains, General Scott reviewed the infrastructure for removal that was already in place. The previous commander, General Wool's successor, had established twenty-three military posts throughout the Cherokee Nation, most including stockades. From these posts, when Scott gave the order, troops would range out to round up local Cherokees until the stockades were filled. The troops would then send their prisoners under guard to one of three embarkation points, and afterward repeat the operation, refilling the stockades. To man these posts, the army had enrolled so many volunteer soldiers that Scott was tempted to send some home. In particular there were too many Georgia horsemen, who moved too quickly to control and were no good for standing guard duty.

General Scott was writing a report to his superiors in Washington about his final plans when an officer asked to see him. The officer had come across some intelligence: a piece of paper. Scott read the paper and then, stunned, resumed his report to Washington: "Whilst writing the foregoing, a letter has been brought to me," Scott reported. It was a letter that was circulating among wildly excited Cherokees. "The letter is substantially credited by almost every body here but myself." It came from Washington—from the Cherokee delegation that included John Ross. It said Ross and the government were on the verge of delaying the emigration for two years.

If the letter was accurate, then Scott's address, the volunteers, and the stockades were all for nothing. If the letter was false, and the emigration must proceed, then Scott's job would be infinitely harder, because no Cherokees would voluntarily leave if they believed their principal chief might have found a way for them to stay.

Scott had to treat this news as a rumor. He had no official word either way. He finished his own report with a request for the War Department to clarify the situation. It was May 18. It would take up to two weeks for his letter to reach the capital. The deadline for emigration was five days away.

It may have been the corn planting that finally moved federal authorities to begin talking seriously with John Ross. There was something unnerving about Cherokees plowing the same fields that they had plowed for years. White men had said long ago that Indians "in a wandering state" could not really claim land simply because they passed through it while hunting. The way to claim land was to improve it—to build a house, to put up fencing, to work a farm. To become the owner of land in this way was a natural right of man. Indians failed to exercise this right, it was said—except that the Cherokees had done it for decades now, long enough that the one-half of the Cherokee Nation who were under eighteen could not remember any other way. Now in the spring of 1838 the farmers of the Cherokee Nation proved their ownership of the land one more time. White men who missed the philosophical depth of this act of peaceful defiance thought they instead detected madness. Calamity loomed.

Until news of the corn planting arrived, Ross had spent a frustrating winter in Washington. Federal authorities seemed to have lost interest in him. Then, early in April, a War Department official named Samuel Cooper met with President Van Buren; they apparently discussed the Cherokee corn crop. Soon afterward Cooper went to meet with John Ross. Ross reported afterward that Cooper brought up the corn planting, and said the Cherokees

> were evidently deluded—that if I and the Delegation would write a
> letter home advising the people that they were compelled to move under
> the Treaty by [May 23] and that they must prepare to do so—that a
> proposition from us for a new arrangement would then [be] received
> and considered.

Ross declined this offer. He knew by now that his people must move. He wanted to improve the terms under which they agreed to do so. But he would not tell his people to move and *then* seek an agreement. He needed an agreement first.

> *I replied that I had never deluded the Cherokees on any subject . . . and that the US agents had themselves enlightened them on this subject in my absence and in their own way. That so far as the Cherokees were planting corn and were not preparing for a removal, it was not a new fact nor was it to be wondered at, for their opposition to a removal was too generally known to be contradicted.*

The War Department official, Ross said, was then "silenced and asked me to call again on tomorrow."

It was a bad time for the Van Buren administration to risk a humanitarian disaster in Cherokee country. The president had difficulties enough. The financial Panic of 1837 still loomed over the nation, despite brief and illusory signs of recovery. By 1841 one study would estimate that the depression had forced the closure of thirty-three thousand businesses. Van Buren's administration was becoming less popular, and political protest against Indian removal was growing again. More petitions were flooding Congress. Once again, religious groups led the way—this time Quakers, who had a presence in Pennsylvania, a vital state in the Democrats' coalition. Indian removal was becoming the sort of morass in which even politicians who approved of the policy goal could score points by attacking its botched execution. Van Buren had no need of chaos, or violence, in the Cherokee Nation on May 23.

Ross was in better spirits as the talks intensified. His friend John Howard Payne was in town—Payne, the famous songwriter who'd been arrested with Ross and was now becoming obsessed with writing Cherokee propaganda for the press. The two men spent some leisure time together. On April 10 Ross received a note from a younger woman in town, and he immediately wrote back to "Miss E M," as he addressed her.

*My friend Mr. Payne and myself will do ourselves the honor of calling
this evening for you & Sister, to attend Mr. Catlin's lecture.*

Mr. Catlin: that was George Catlin, the painter who had made a
portrait of Osceola during the Seminole leader's last days. Catlin was
displaying many paintings in a traveling exhibition—"Catlin's Indian
Gallery," as it was called in an advertisement in the *National Intelligencer.* His lecture, which the paintings illustrated, was so detailed that
it required "two successive evenings" for Catlin to report on his visits
with "38 different tribes" speaking "38 different languages," and to talk
of "their Villages, Dances, Religious Ceremonies &c . . . and also many
splendid specimens of Costume, Weapons, &c." The two sisters, John
Howard Payne, and the principal chief of the Cherokee Nation paid 90
cents each to watch the show.

Refreshed by this entertainment, Ross composed a letter to President Van Buren: "The interests of your people cannot be dearer to you,
than those of mine are to me." He said he could help Van Buren achieve
removal peacefully if the president would improve the treaty terms. To
a War Department official he bluntly said he would do nothing to help
the government unless it helped him.

*You can expel us by force, we grant; but you cannot make us call it
fairness.*

Poinsett, the secretary of war, said later that Ross would never leave
Washington unless he got a new deal. Perhaps Poinsett felt coerced by
people whom the government was more accustomed to coerce: "The
presence in this city of the chiefs and head-men, who alone possess the
necessary influence to induce their people to yield a ready submission to
the wishes of the Government, and their positive refusal to return to
the nation, rendered it unavoidable to treat with them here." A possible
agreement took shape. The Treaty of New Echota would technically
not be voided; doing so would meet political resistance, and a new treaty

would require the approval of two-thirds of the Senate. But some added terms could be negotiated and slipped through Congress by attaching them to unrelated legislation. Ross, calculating the value of Cherokee real estate, said that "five millions of dollars" must be increased to $13 million. And the Cherokees would voluntarily migrate if given an additional two years to set their affairs in order. (It was when this deal began to seem plausible that the Cherokee delegation sent its letter back home, confounding General Scott.) The final deal was less generous, though Ross got some of what he wanted. Thirteen million dollars was more than the government would pay, but the amount could be increased to more than $6 million. More important, money would be paid to the Cherokee government instead of being spread among individuals. Van Buren rejected the extra two years for emigration, but Ross would be allowed to organize the emigration at government expense, taking it out of the hands of the army and gaining control over the conditions under which the journey was made.

Ross had achieved all he could. He had made the transaction with the United States somewhat less unfair. He had preserved his people as a people. Now he would lead them to a new country. Poinsett had done what no other U.S. official seemed able to do: reach an agreement with John Ross. The secretary of war could feel relieved at gaining a partial reprieve for the conscience of his nation. However much they may have been coerced, the Cherokees would at last go on their own; the history of the United States need not forever be stained by the specter of soldiers rousting thousands of unarmed civilians from their homes at bayonet point. Poinsett wrote a letter to General Scott confirming the sudden change in plans, and dropped his letter in the mail for its two-week transit to the Cherokee Nation.

The date on his letter was May 23.

"No communication has reached me from Washington," wrote General Scott on May 22. He had his orders, and had received no others; he would proceed. On his own authority, he might have put off the emigration until the news from Washington was clarified, but Scott believed the security situation demanded action. He constantly worried that if the Cherokees did not leave quickly enough, white settlers would attack them.

Scott departed his headquarters, leaving instructions for any mail to be forwarded. On the twenty-third he arrived at New Echota, intending to keep an eye on the Georgians. On the twenty-fifth he watched as two new regiments of Georgia infantry were organized; these foot soldiers would require less maintenance and be easier to control than the horsemen. The reinforcements were still en route to their stations when the roundups began on May 26, 1838.

The soldiers cleared out one farm at a time, one valley at a time. Approaching a house, the troops would surround it so that no one would escape, then order out the occupants with no more than they could carry. One Cherokee house contained Rebecca Neugin, who was about three years old at the time, one of nine children of a Cherokee family. Decades later she gave the family story of how they were led into captivity. "When the soldier came to our house my father wanted to fight," she said,

> but my mother told him that the soldiers would kill him if he did and we surrendered without a fight. They drove us out of our house to join other prisoners in a stockade. After they took us away, my mother begged them to let her go back and get some bedding. So they let her go back and she brought what bedding and cooking utensils she could carry and had to leave behind all of our household possessions.

On May 30 a Cherokee student wrote a letter to a friend in the North; her letter was published in newspapers, its author described only as a "young Cherokee girl." She was staying at a missionary school near Red Clay, Tennessee. She heard drums beating "as we were going from school to dinner," and briefly feared the school was to be invaded, but the soldiers were leaving the mission alone for the moment. "Two hundred or more" men marched past "with their bright gems glittering in the sunshine and beating their drums, and playing fiddles and fifes, which seemed to the people who were very sad, as if they meant to mock at them." Many people "expected speedy extermination. . . . The whites just take the Indians without waiting or warning. They then lock up the doors every where, and leave all their things to be valued according to their own notions." One day she saw "a considerable number" of Cherokees passing. "They had run away from the soldiers. They had nothing with them but the clothes they wore on their backs. . . . The crop looks very flourishing indeed, and the wheat has begun to head, and our garden looks very nice; but every body seems very much plagued, and there has been a considerable number of deaths in the neighborhood."

Though some Cherokees fled, there was no organized resistance. On May 29 a white engineer was encamped "in a pretty section of the country" near New Echota, where his crew was surveying a future road: "Many of our friends are troubling themselves about our danger from the Indians. We never think of the subject . . . the Cherokees are a peaceable, inoffensive people." General Scott believed the troops also were peaceable, although there was no way to minimize the shocking moment when the soldiers came over a fence or through a door. Long afterward, an ethnographer who lived among the Cherokees listened to some of their stories: "Families at dinner were startled by the sudden gleam of bayonets in the doorway and rose up to be driven with blows and oaths along the weary miles of trail that led to the stockade. Men were seized in their fields or going along the road, women were taken from their wheels and children from their play." Sometimes civilians followed the detachments of soldiers, waiting to plunder the homes left vacant, or even digging up graves, "to rob them of the silver pendants and other valuables deposited with the dead."

A captain in the First Artillery Regiment, L. B. Webster, ranged out in June to round up eight hundred Cherokees in far western North Carolina. Escorting them toward one of the main emigration camps near Calhoun, Tennessee, Webster's company picked up about a hundred additional Cherokees on the way. The Cherokees greatly out-numbered his troops but made no move to resist. "I experienced no dif-ficulty in getting them along," he wrote home to his wife, "other than what arose from fatigue, and . . . the roads over the mountains, which are the worst I ever saw. We were eight days making the journey (80 miles) and it was pitiful to behold the women & children, who suffered exceedingly—as they were all obliged to walk, with the exception of the sick."

There were varied descriptions of the detention camps in which the Cherokees were held. People who did not have to live in them remem-bered them more fondly than people who did. Long afterward General Scott recalled the camp where Captain Webster brought his prisoners as "happily chosen," a "well shaded" area that was twelve miles by four and bounded by a river—a place where sullen, protesting Cherokees at first refused even the food they were offered, but finally accepted gener-ous sustenance. Scott was at least correct when he suggested that the Cherokees were spread over a considerable distance. A doctor who treated them did not describe them as penned in like cattle, but instead "scattered and dispersed" in "family camps" that fell within a "general encampment." Yet in a letter written at the time of his military opera-tions, General Scott confessed that the Cherokees suffered from the loss of their cooking utensils, clothes, and other goods "consequent upon the hurry of capture and removal." Evan Jones, a missionary who lived among the Cherokees, described them as "prisoners" who had instantly been hurled from "comfortable circumstances" into "abject poverty." Captain Webster, the Tennessee volunteer, was overcome with feelings of foreboding as his company guarded the prisoners. He wrote a letter to his wife to say there were "seven or eight thousand" Chero-kees in various camps around his company, "and they are the most quiet people you ever saw." The only consistent sound was that of preachers, white and Cherokee, who went among prisoners and soldiers alike try-ing to save souls. Captain Webster was not consoled. "Among these sublime mountains and in the dark forests with the thunder often sounding in the distance," the talk of God only made him wonder what would "fall upon my guilty head as one of the instruments of oppression."

So efficient was General Scott's operation that thousands of Cherokees had been rounded up into the emigration camps before he finally received the letter from Secretary of War Poinsett in Washington making it clear that none of this had really been necessary, and that John Ross would arrive soon to take charge of a voluntary emigration.

In two follow-up letters, Poinsett advised the general of his concern that "sickness may result from the Indians being collected in great numbers at the depots." The longer the Cherokees stayed at their collection points, the greater the risk of disease. Perhaps, Poinsett suggested, it would be better to "consult the dictates of humanity as well as prudence," and gather the Cherokees only a short time before their actual journey west. It was sage advice, had it arrived in time for Scott to follow it. The camps were death traps. If there were "seven or eight thousand" Cherokees spread around Calhoun, Tennessee, that was in 1838 the equivalent of a bustling large town. Any settlement of that size would have grown over the course of years, allowing development of a corresponding infrastructure to deliver food, shelter, basic sanitation, and clean water. The Cherokee camps had been populated in weeks. Neither the sites nor the people were prepared.

But the people were already in the camps, and General Scott had concluded that there could be no going back. The Georgia land lottery winners believed that they had possession of their plots of land as of May 24. To send large numbers of Cherokees home, or even to stop collecting them from the countryside, would expose them to murderous encounters with the new owners of their houses and fields. In Alabama many Cherokee properties had already been taken over by white squatters, "and the *squatters*," Scott said, "are as likely to annoy, to dispossess, and make war upon the Indians, as if each squatter and occupant were the hereditary owner of the ground, and the poor Indians the intruders or invaders." If sending home the Cherokees was not an option, neither was sending them forward. Two parties of emigrants were shipped westward in early June, but it was becoming impossible to move large parties in the height of summer. Severe drought had struck. Even great streams like the Tennessee were not navigable in places, and the land route would be desperately short of drinking water. Scott decided to put off the migration until the fall. "Not only the comfort, but the safety of the Indians . . . has forced this decision upon me."

Rather than send them back to their homes to die, or send them out on the road to die, the Cherokees were left in their camps to die. J. W. Lide, one of the doctors contracted to care for the emigrants, reported

a high grade of Diarrhea, hazardous Dysentery, and urgent Remittent Fever prevailing to a great and deplorably fatal extent. Measles and Whooping Cough appeared epidemically among the Cherokees about the first of June which Diseases more generally much aggravated by the Circumstances connected with the assemblage.

It was all a "natural result" of collecting "men, women and children of all ages and conditions, changing suddenly, and very materially all their habits of life, especially in reference to Regimin, Exercise, &c., with exposure to the intense heat that has prevailed in this country." Doctors moved among the Cherokees attempting to treat them but encountered constant frustration. The doctors often did not speak their patients' language, and could not persuade suspicious natives to take prescribed medicines. Given the level of medical science in 1838, some Cherokees may have been making rational decisions. The lack of records makes it impossible to estimate the number of fatalities in the camps, but the claims made at the time were devastating. One missionary with the Cherokees (Elizur Butler, the same man who, with Samuel Worcester, went to a Georgia prison in 1831 for ministering to the Cherokees without a license) wrote home that he had heard claims that "two thousand" people had died in the camps. If this claim was even half true, it meant that more people perished in the camps than would die on the road during the migration to follow.

Winfield Scott and some Cherokees (including Major Ridge, following these events from his new home in the West) knew who was to blame for the catastrophe. "The loss was the fault of the Cherokees," said Scott, "for having faith in the ability of John Ross to save them." Ross and his people, they said, should have recognized sooner that they must depart. Nobody died in Major Ridge's party, which had moved at a good time and in good order. It was undeniably true that Ross bargained until the very last day. He had used his people as a bargaining chip. Had he told them to prepare for emigration, he would have lost his leverage. Instead he forced the government to deal with him.

But to blame Ross for not capitulating sooner presumes too much. This argument presumes that the people would have followed his directions no matter what those directions were. It suggests that ordinary people among the Cherokees could not think for themselves, even on a subject that directly affected their homes, their families, and every other aspect of their lives. They *had* thought for themselves, and truly, deeply did not want to surrender their homes. Ross had some power to shape events, but had to govern his actions by what public opinion could bear. If he had abruptly announced in 1835 or 1837 or even at the start of 1838 that he favored removal, it is not clear how many people would have followed him. Major Ridge, with all his power and prestige, had persuaded only a small minority. Even after Ross agreed to lead the emigration, a significant fraction of Cherokees defied the decision to move west, and faded into the North Carolina mountains. The principal chief's political situation demanded that he fight to the end, proving to his people that absolutely everything possible had been done in their defense. That was the only way he could have the credibility to rescue them from the true cause of their trouble: the government that was compelling fifteen thousand people to move against their will.

Even after his agreement with Poinsett was struck, Ross remained in Washington for several weeks, until he was certain that the government was producing what it promised.

1838 June 25

Paid to John Ross, by requisition of the Treasury . . . arrears of annuities, per act 12th June, 1838

25,000.00.

He also insisted that the Treasury pay his delegation's travel expenses, $7,000 for two seasons in Washington. His bags weighed down with cash, the chief took a route home through North Carolina. This allowed him to retrieve his seventeen-year-old daughter, Jane, from the Moravian school she was attending in the town of Salem. Jane, too, would now be going west. Father and daughter took a stagecoach on one of the arduous routes over the Appalachians—Salem was near Cherokee country, but the mountains required a detour more than a hundred miles to the northwest, a painful four-day ordeal to Abingdon, Virginia, and several more days to come back south again. Along the way John and Jane Ross encountered other passengers who climbed in and out of the stagecoach, sharing bits of what Ross called "thrilling news" about "the unhappy condition of the Cherokees." (He doubtless meant "thrilling" in an old sense of the word—piercing or penetrating.) It is not clear if the travelers knew the identity of the brown-eyed, gray-haired father to whom they passed on their information and rumors.

Arriving in the Cherokee Nation, Ross began working to ensure that the Cherokees accepted emigration. Cherokee leaders held a council in late July, at which Ross did not quite admit he had made an agreement with Secretary Poinsett; he said talks were going well until Poinsett "suddenly terminated" the discussions and dictated terms. But he also explained how the terms were better than before, and said that Winfield Scott was a man they could deal with.

Scott was such a man. He was a man of the army, determined to protect his reputation and his service, but could see the Cherokee point of view. When he learned of his superiors' arrangement with Ross, he wrote a barbed letter to Washington. "I shall not stop here to complain that . . . the whole subject has been contemptuously taken out of my hands," he wrote as part a 106-word sentence that listed all of the complaints he said he was not making. But the same letter said he would be "extremely delighted if something more could be done to soothe the feelings of the Cherokees, and to compensate them in money, at least, in part discharge of that great debt of justice due from the United States." Scott negotiated a contract with Ross, under which designated Cherokees would arrange the emigration and the United States would pay the expenses. Ross said moving the Cherokees westward would cost $65.88 per person, probably something well in excess of $700,000. Scott found this excessive, but being "extremely unwilling to delay the emigration," he accepted.

There was a different general who could not accept the accommodation with John Ross. It was the man who commanded Ross at Horseshoe Bend in 1814, who had been outmaneuvered by Ross for a time in 1816, and who could not spare soldiers to help Ross defend Cherokee land against intruders in 1820. It was the man who had been elected president in 1828, the same year that Ross was made principal chief, and who like Ross had made innovative use of political tools in a dawning democratic age. It was the man who had met Ross in the Executive Mansion, who had offered him $2.5 million for Cherokee land in 1833 only to see him spurn it, who believed that Ross agreed to $5 million in 1835 only to see him reject that, and who had finally gone around Ross by signing a treaty with his opposition. It was the man who sent word in 1836 that the U.S. government would have no more communication with Ross, "either orally or in writing," about the terms of Cherokee removal. Now it emerged that Ross *had* been able to communicate about removal, had increased the payout, had restored his government's revenue, and had regained some control of the situation.

At the time, the master of the Hermitage was the most well-connected and influential convalescent senior citizen in America. "I am still in the land of the living," he began a chatty letter to Francis P. Blair, the publisher of the main Democratic paper in Washington. Friends sent him inside information on the Missouri election ("Benton is safe beyond a doubt"), offered him political advice ("It is *indispensable* for us to have a new candidate for the Vice Presidency"), and appealed for help ("It has been the wish of my youngest son James . . . to be placed at West Point"). So it was natural that an appeal came to Jackson on August 23, 1838, from a federal official unhappy about John Ross. It was the superintendent of Cherokee removal, who was in effect being replaced by the Cherokee chief. The superintendent wrote a friend in Nashville, who personally carried his complaint to the Hermitage. The volcano erupted. Jackson sent a message to President Van Buren's attorney general, writing in a hand so shaky as to be almost indecipherable.

private

My dear Sir,

Col. Walker has just shewn me several communications from Genl Smith removing agent for the Cherokees, & others. . . .

The contract with Ross must be arrested or you may rely on upon it, the expence and other evils will shake the popularity of the administration to its centre.

What madness & folly to have had any thing to do with Ross, when the Agent was proceeding well with the removal and on principles of economy that would have saved at least 100 percent from what the contract of Ross will cost.

Ross would consume so much money that the administration would be forced to ask Congress for more, creating "a fine chance" for the Whigs to attack.

> *I have only time to add as the mail waits, that the contract with Ross must be arrested.*

And the more he repeated this, the more he sensed a partisan conspiracy.

> *The time & circumstances under which Genl Scott made this contract shews, that he is [no] economist, or is, Subrosa, in league with Clay & Co, to bring disgrace on the administration—the evil is done—it behooves Mr VanBuren to act with energy to throw it off his shoulders.*
>
> *I enclose a letter under cover to you, unsealed, which you may read, seal, & deliver it to him, that you may aid him with your views in getting out of real difficulty.*
>
>

yr friend in haste,
Andrew Jackson

> *P.S. I am so feeble I can scarcely wield the pen—but friendship dictates it, & the subject excites me. Why is it that the Scamp Ross is not banished from the notice of the administration*

He continued writing until he had reached the extreme lower-right-hand corner of the page, without even leaving room for punctuation at the end.

One reason Jackson was still considered powerful, of course, was that he had installed his own adviser as president. But the responsibility was Van Buren's now. He did not act on Jackson's advice. The administration left Ross in charge of the emigration despite swirling concerns about the cost.

Ross was, to be sure, questioned about whether it would really cost

$65.88 per person to move the Cherokees. He thought about this, and replied that instead of lowering the price, he would raise it. He had left out an allowance for soap on the trail; with soap, the total cost should be $66.24. After the removal, which proved slower and more expensive than anyone had anticipated, Ross raised the price again to $103.25 per person, based on actual expenses—more than $1.2 million in all. His critics were outraged that Ross assigned the contract to his own brother Lewis, leading to suspicions that the family was profiteering. It does seem very likely that John Ross's brother took a profit from the contract, just as white contractors would have done; it is plausible some of the benefits found their way to the principal chief. Ross, like Andrew Jackson, had a way of making political decisions that matched his interests or those of his family and friends. But John Ross took no actual salary for his work on the removal. And in his billing practices, it would be hard to claim that Ross bargained any harder than the U.S. authorities who had bargained so long and so ruthlessly with him. After the removal, the federal government tried for years to avoid paying the full sum the Cherokees demanded. John Ross, studying his figures, tweaked the price upward yet again, this time to $1.357 million, which was finally paid in full in the 1840s. Fifty-seven years after the emigration, in 1895, one more federal audit found that Ross's billing was reasonable, given the horrible conditions and slow travel on the roads. Removal was "accomplished with a much less expense to the United States than if it had been involuntary," with armed guards herding civilians.

Some of Ross's last days in the eastern Cherokee country were spent on the banks of the Tennessee River. He arrived on the evening of Saturday, November 10, to find many campfires burning on the south bank. It was the quiet campsite of one of the last Cherokee parties to leave for the west—1,613 people in this detachment, their goods and supplies loaded in ninety-one wagons, most of the people on foot and footsore, the horses off somewhere in the dark. The detachment had come here to cross the river at a place called Blythe's Ferry. Peering across the dark water, Ross saw lights on the far bank, and learned that a dozen wagons had already been shipped across the river that day, from the Cherokee Nation to the whiteside. Actually, both sides were the whiteside now. The Indian map, in this part of the country, was no more. Ross paid his respects to the conductor of the group, found a place to sleep amid the campfires, and woke to a scene that he later described with a note of pride to Winfield Scott:

> At dawn of day the Emigrants were in readiness and Commenced crossing the river—four boats were put in requisition and continued running until dusk, two of them were manned by Cherokees themselves. At the close of the day about sixty one waggons of the detachment with the people were safely lodged across the river. The business of crossing was again resumed early this morning, and before twelve Oclock eighteen waggons, carriages &c with all the people were over. . . . In this performance of this duty it is admitted by all who were present, and I assure you there were not few, including travelers, that nothing but good management, perseverance and energy could have accomplished it so satisfactorily.

The Cherokee Nation had been divided into thirteen groups, each of them somewhat more or less than a thousand. Eleven groups were on the road ahead of this detachment, which was the last to travel by road; one final detachment was a small group of those especially sick or unfit, and Ross would travel with them in December, leaving late enough in the season that the water route should be open. The groups had been moving out one by one since September, ready or not: a detachment encamped near Fort Payne, in Alabama, was reported to be in no condition to travel ("at least Two third are in a destitute condition and in want of shoes Clothing and Blankets"), but the soldiers at Fort Payne told them they would be issued no more rations if they remained in place after October first. Another party made it on the road even though it was being harassed by debt collectors, with "horses taken from our Teams for the payment of unjust & just Demands."

None could know what lay ahead, that the summer drought would be followed by a severe winter, that people "in want of shoes Clothing and Blankets" would be held up for weeks in southern Illinois while half a dozen detachments waited for a chance to cross the frozen Mississippi River. ("The Ice on the Mississippi says to the foremost stand still, and each Detachment to the other hold on.") Though the journey had been projected to take 80 days, different parties would require 100 or even 150 days. To be sure, the number of deaths on the road was probably less than that in the camps, and also less than would be experienced on arrival in the Arkansas country. Had the deaths on the road been the only deaths, the Trail of Tears would have been a markedly less devastating event. A contemporary federal report put the figure of deaths actually in transit around 600, while one Cherokee list recorded 324. But the road was bad enough. Throughout the broader era of removal, a modern study has estimated that the Cherokee population may have been reduced by as many as eight thousand from what it otherwise would have been.

But at this moment at Blythe's Ferry in November, Ross could not foresee what lay ahead. He knew only that the parties were on the way. From Blythe's Ferry he was able to gather news of the detachments spread out ahead on the road. A man who'd been sent to communicate with one of the forward parties had reached it at Reynoldsburg, Tennessee, and then had seen several of the detachments on his way back; all were reported to be moving in good order, "excepting sickness." Lewis Ross was astride the road in Nashville, resupplying the parties as they passed. The chief's brother had assistance there from one Thomas N. Clark, who was regularly writing updates to the principal chief. In mid-November Clark reported that he was headed west out of Nashville, hoping to catch up with some of the detachments and if possible speed them along. Clark was an admirer of John Ross, and knew the affection with which he was regarded by his people. Just before heading west he sent a letter to the Cherokee chief, saying his job would be easier if John Ross was by his side.

> *I wish I could have your influence for a few days in order that I might move these people—farewell.*

Epilogue

lmost two centuries after the events of this book, I took a long
drive through the Deep South. In southeastern Alabama I
walked the battlefield at Horseshoe Bend. The great bend of
the Tallapoosa followed about the same course as it did in 1814. Rain fell
in the channel that Cherokee attackers swam and paddled across to
strike the Creek defenses from behind. White stakes were lined up across
the neck of the peninsula to show the location of the Creek defenders'
fortified wall, and a blue-wheeled cannon rested atop the hill from which
Jackson blasted that wall. In the rain I had the battlefield almost to
myself, sharing it with two rangers in the office and some deer in a field.

Of the many square miles around the battlefield the most striking
thing was the emptiness—little towns half vacant or entirely so, separated by modest homes and churches and great stretches of forest. A
large portion of eastern Alabama is woodland now, and some is designated the Talladega National Forest, beyond the reach of real estate
development and held by the nation. It is said that nineteenth-century
settlers once deforested the region, but some of their descendants moved
on, depopulating many rural counties after 1920. Today, in the miles
between thriving cities such as Montgomery and Auburn, enough land
has returned to nature that should the ghosts of the Creeks return, they
might recognize it. There would be room for them now.

By late the next afternoon I was well to the northeast, standing on the Walnut Street Bridge in Chattanooga, Tennessee. It is a pedestrian bridge across the Tennessee River, a blue steel span dating from the late nineteenth century, flying out from the high ground on the south side. A historic marker on the pedestrian walkway said Ross's Landing once occupied the south bank nearby. Nothing remained of the old ferry, warehouse, and taverns; everything about the scene had changed but a nearby stone bluff, and even the bluff seemed to have grown, topped off by the modernistic gray stone walls of the Hunter Museum of American Art.

Walking off the bridge into central Chattanooga, I found my car and pointed it westward, driving down the Tennessee River valley toward Alabama. The river weaved so much it was impossible for the road to stay on one side of it; Interstate 24 slashed across Nickajack Lake where the channel was dammed by the Tennessee Valley Authority during the Great Depression. The names on the road signs were heavy with history—Huntsville, Scottsboro, Lookout Mountain.

On the north side of the river, on Route 72 in Jackson County, Alabama, I saw a billboard lettered in black and white:

FIRST JACKSON BANK

The face of Andrew Jackson glowered out at the cars and the fields.

A few miles later he appeared again on the sign at the First Jackson Bank headquarters, so I pulled over to study his unruly hair and thin face. The picture was based on his image from the twenty-dollar bill, although on the bank sign he seemed a bit tougher, his glare a bit colder. It was hard to say what a man who so distrusted banks would have thought about being the logo for one. The bank was a redbrick building fronted by four white columns, evoking a plantation house. The particular house that came to mind was the home of James Vann, a famously wealthy Cherokee planter from the early years of the nineteenth century.

The road led back across to the south side of the river on the long bridge and causeway at Decatur, which was home to plants operated by GM and 3M. The route was crossing into country claimed by Cherokees until Jackson obtained it for white settlement through his treaty of 1816. Sometimes rails ran alongside the highway, the route of the first railroad chartered west of the Appalachians, whose early passengers included Cherokee emigrants being shipped west. High cornfields stretched as far as I could see in the last of the sun. Somewhere out of sight to my right was Muscle Shoals, its waters deep and placid now ever since the river was dammed to turn the shoals into a lake. Beyond the shoals I crossed the river yet again to the north bank, on a bridge that flew between the river bluffs. It was dark by the time I parked and walked up the main street of Florence, which was guarded by the statue of a Confederate soldier on the plaza in front of the courthouse. I had dinner at the bar of an upscale restaurant, fell into conversation with the young man and woman at the next two stools, and in the morning heard the blare of brass instruments in town. The University of North Alabama marching band was practicing for the upcoming football season. So many small American cities have hollowed out over time, their reason for existence long gone; Florence lived.

Five town lots that Andrew Jackson once owned were now the location of a parking lot and a public housing complex. Outside town the ruins of his friend James Jackson's mansion were still visible on a farm. The house burned down in the twentieth century, leaving only the brick columns that surrounded all four sides. When I first saw the columns at the top of a slope, they took my breath away. They seemed like some remnant of ancient Rome. On the day I visited, a white horse was grazing beside them. A member of the owner's family happened by and allowed me to wade through the high grass and stand amid the ruins.

While in Florence I encountered one of the joys of writing about the South: even when researching centuries-old events you find people to interview. Milly Wright, a local historian, had spent much time gathering historic Florence real estate records and maps and generously made copies available. We met at her home, which dated from the 1820s and was the house of another friend of Andrew Jackson. Occasionally, she said, African Americans from Chicago or elsewhere arrived at her door, wanting to see where their white ancestor had lived. It was also from Ms. Wright that I learned of a stone wall in Florence, built by a local man in honor of his Indian ancestor who was removed in the 1830s and apparently made her way back.

Signs of Indians were everywhere in this land that had been cleared of them. Back in Georgia I'd stopped at New Echota, now a historic site with buildings that are reconstructed or moved from elsewhere. Many residents of the region believe old cabins on their property date from Cherokee times, and at least some of the homes are authentic. In Rossville, Georgia, I'd found the two-story log house where John Ross was living in 1820. The house is in excellent shape, though the caretaker said it was a short distance from its original location, having been moved up the street in recent decades to make room for a store and a coin laundry. One last, little Indian removal.

The place for which Jackson opened the way was a world of its own. There was no denying his achievement. It was Jacksonland, the Deep South, vital then and now to American life and the American identity. It was opened for development by his armies, acts, treaties, or laws. Jacksonland is not only Florence and Jackson County, Alabama; it is the famous Muscle Shoals recording studio and the manufacturing centers of the Tennessee Valley, as well as the steel mills of Birmingham and the Sun studio in Memphis. It is the Civil War battlefields of Chickamauga and Missionary Ridge. It is Jackson and Oxford, Mississippi, as well as the elegant and prosperous city of Rome, Georgia, where Major Ridge's old home is now preserved as a museum, and where a downtown cigar bar is presided over by a wooden Indian. The South of William Faulkner, George Wallace, Robert Johnson, and Rosa Parks could not exist until Andrew Jackson cleared the way for it. Orlando, Florida, and Walt Disney World: that too is Jacksonland.

An 1861 map showed the Black Belt, the name that was given to a great crescent of settlement where slaves and the plantations they worked were heavily concentrated. A substantial part of the Black Belt was Jacksonland. That map had a powerful influence when completed at the start of the Civil War. It illustrated what opponents of slavery wanted to destroy. A famous painting of Lincoln signing the Emancipation Proclamation showed him in a crowded office that was cluttered with documents, among them the map of the Black Belt. Lincoln's 1863 proclamation did not apply to loyal slave states or to Union-controlled areas, only to rebel-held zones, which in large measure meant Jacksonland. In the generations after the final emancipation in 1865, millions of former slaves and their descendants migrated to the North, yet twenty-first-century maps still show an identifiable Black Belt—the descendants of enslaved farm workers, of freedmen and freedwomen, of soldiers, sharecroppers, steelworkers, railroad workers, writers, pastors, washerwomen. Other twenty-first-century maps, showing migration and settlement patterns, make it just as easy to spot signs of the great migration from northern Britain that, sweeping through the Appalachians and beyond, also populated Jacksonland—the descendants of slave owners, soldiers, sharecroppers, steelworkers, railroad workers, writers, pastors, and washerwomen.

Though Jackson died in 1845, his political influence persisted for another generation. His Democratic Party, that coalition of "plain republicans" of the North and planters of the South, won four of the six presidential elections after he left office. After the annexation of Texas in 1845 a protégé of Jackson's, President James Polk, went to war with Mexico over the international boundary, confirming a greater Texas and also conquering California. Another protégé of Jackson's, James Gadsden, completed the continental United States with the Gadsden Purchase. Jackson appointed yet another of his protégés, Roger Taney, to be chief justice of the Supreme Court when John Marshall died in 1835. Taney served for decades, and issued the Dred Scott decision of 1857, declaring that black people had no rights that white people must respect. Only in 1860 did Jackson's direct influence begin to ebb. His party

fractured on sectional lines—the "planters of the South" breaking ranks
with the "plain republicans of the North"—and opened the way for the
election of Republican Abraham Lincoln. Yet there was something striking about Lincoln, which was visible in that famous painting of the signing of the Emancipation Proclamation. The artist faithfully reproduced
the portrait that Lincoln had chosen to hang over his office fireplace. It
was a portrait of Andrew Jackson. The great unionist of the 1830s was
shown watching over the most momentous act of his successor.

Jackson persists, as Jacksonland persists. And within Jacksonland,
something else persists: Indians.

It is true that most natives headed west of the Mississippi during
the era of the Trail of Tears—most of them. A glance at a modern census map makes it clear that Native Americans and their descendants
have also remained in some of their ancestral homes throughout the
Deep South. Though the Creeks were removed, small numbers remained
or returned, and eventually gained federal recognition and small reservations. Some of the reservations are in southeastern Alabama, by the
Florida border, land that Andrew Jackson insisted the Creeks must cede
in 1814. Tiny Chickasaw and Choctaw populations remain in Mississippi. In Florida, the Second Seminole War ended with most natives
killed or removed—yet federal authorities, tiring of the conflict,
declared an end to the fighting in 1842 while some Seminoles were still
at large. They withdrew into South Florida and the Everglades. Though
they later clashed with landowners in yet another war, and their numbers dwindled to as little as a hundred, the Seminole population later
increased. They now possess several federally recognized zones around
Lake Okeechobee and the Everglades. They have granted permission
for Osceola to serve as the mascot of Florida State University.

Nor did all the Cherokees end up in the West.

John Ross moved to the West, of course. He departed with the final
group of Cherokees in December 1838. They took the water route, and

it was apparently on a riverboat that Ross's wife, Quatie, died in early 1839. She was buried after the boat tied up at Little Rock, Arkansas. Ross continued on to the Cherokees' western territory, where he was confirmed in his continued leadership of the Cherokee Nation.

Soon afterward the Treaty Party was decapitated: Major Ridge, John Ridge, and Elias Boudinot were all murdered in their homes.

The killers were never identified. No evidence linked John Ross to the crime, though it is reasonable to suppose that some part of the Cherokee leadership endorsed the coordinated assassination, just as Cherokee leaders endorsed killing Doublehead for selling land many years before. Ross, not yet fifty at the time of the killings, remained the leader of his nation through another generation—all the way until the Civil War, when many Cherokees fought for the Confederacy, though Ross tried to remain on the side of the Union, and many Cherokees also fought and died on the Union side. Ross lived long enough to see the Union prevail. In 1865, Ross was in Washington for the second inauguration of President Lincoln, which he described in an exultant letter home to Mary Ross, his second wife: "The clouds vanished and the rain ceased to fall—behold, the effulgent rays of the noonday sun shown out upon the great multitude that assembled, around the magnificent Capitol of the Nation." Ross died in 1866, just as his nation was completing a peace treaty with the United States. The treaty, in the customary manner, required Cherokees to cede some of the land that had previously been granted to them forever.

Land assigned to Cherokees and many other nations was known as the Indian Territory. In the early twentieth century a movement arose for Indian Territory to seek the status of a state—the future that Ross seemed to have envisioned for his nation as early as 1825. Residents, both Indian and white, participated in drawing up a proposed constitution for the state of Sequoyah. President Theodore Roosevelt's administration rejected the idea, instead incorporating Indian Territory with non-Indian areas to form the state of Oklahoma.

That was the story of the Cherokee Nation in the West, but there was also a continuing story of Cherokees in the East. Some simply would not be removed from their ancient homeland. During the early phases of the removal in 1838 it had been clear that a few Cherokees would stay; a number of Cherokees in North Carolina had embraced provisions in old treaties that allowed them to claim U.S. citizenship. To these few in 1838 were added fugitives from the forces of Winfield Scott. The Smoky Mountains and the surrounding terrain in far western North Carolina were the least accessible areas of all the Cherokee country, and there some Cherokees hid after eluding the soldiers.

The fugitives included a man known as Tsali, or Charlie. He was so determined to stay at home in the North Carolina mountains that he petitioned to take advantage of a treaty provision allowing him to become a U.S. citizen, as some other North Carolina Cherokees had done. Tsali was bitterly disappointed that soldiers rounded up his family anyway. He slipped away, only to be captured again. Conflicting stories describe his motives for what he did next, but according to an account by his wife, Tsali declared "he had been treated so bad by the whites [that] life had lost all its endearments." Tsali and his male relatives killed two soldiers and escaped. John Ross could do nothing except try to avoid collective punishment; when informed by Major Robert Anderson of the killings, Ross emphasized that it was "one of those unfortunate individual occurrences" for which only the perpetrators, not the whole Cherokee Nation, should be punished. It may have been to avoid such punishment that North Carolina Cherokees assisted in hunting down Tsali and his relatives. For some, this collaboration created an opportunity. The soldiers had never been eager to chase Indians through the rough landscape of the Smokies. The nearest army commander promised that the roundup of Cherokees would end once Tsali was captured, and so it was that Cherokees themselves put Tsali on trial for the murders, chained him to a tree, and had him shot by a three-man firing squad. He was sacrificed. Many Cherokees were permitted to stay in North Carolina. They slowly came out of hiding and established towns and farms, often living on land that was held for their use by white relations or by a sympathetic white trader, William H. Thomas, who in time was adopted by the Cherokee band and even named their chief.

Eventually the eastern Cherokees received a formal reservation, which I visited in 2014. A portion of the land was in Cherokee County, North Carolina. The federal Indian agency had offices in the town of Cherokee, on Tsali Boulevard. Homes on reservation land spread out in valleys outside town. Far from hiding in the mountains, local merchants advertised their shops as "Indian owned." The main street was lined with stores selling moccasins and tom-toms. A statue of a bare-chested Indian at least twenty feet high announced the Indian Ink Tattoo Studio. Cherokee was a tourist town, accessible from the resort communities of Asheville, North Carolina, and Gatlinburg, Tennessee. The biggest draw for tourists was an enormous Harrah's casino. On a gaming floor the scale of a basketball arena, patrons worked rows of slot machines, while others drank at a bar that had electronic poker machines built into the surface. It was possible without leaving the grounds to dine in an upscale Italian restaurant, join a high-stakes poker game, or spend the night in a high-rise hotel. The labor demands of the casino and hotel were likely responsible for some of Cherokee's diversity: the Our Lady of Guadalupe Catholic Church in town advertised a mass in Spanish. Next to the church, an Indian-owned restaurant advertised Indian tacos—flat circles of fry bread piled high with hamburger, beans, lettuce, and tomatoes.

To become an enrolled member of the Eastern Band of Cherokee Indians, it was necessary to demonstrate ancestry from an official roll taken in 1924. The Eastern Band claimed fifteen thousand members—which is to say its population had recovered to nearly the size it was before the bulk of the eastern Cherokees were removed in 1838. According to the 2010 census, fewer than ten thousand actually lived on reservation land near Cherokee, but they were part of a substantial Indian population scattered throughout the South—several hundred thousand people, on and off reservations. The eastern Cherokees are regulated under the authority of Congress, which recognizes their sovereign right to choose their leaders, use land, run schools, and issue casino licenses. They are not required to pay state taxes. They are also U.S. citizens, a status that was gradually conferred on Indians through a series of laws over several generations. By participating in tribal life while also participating fully in the wider civic life of the United States, the eastern Cherokees live by roughly the same principles that John Ross proposed more than once in the 1820s and 1830s. He was more than a century ahead of his time.

On the first day of summer, on the advice of a friend, I drove westward out of Cherokee, past the Arrowhead Motel and a billboard promoting a local woman who was a contestant for Miss Indian World. The roads led deeper into the mountains, so near the westernmost point of North Carolina that the stations on the car radio were out of Tennessee. Reaching Robbinsville, I parked the car and joined a group of people taking a commemorative walk along a bit of the Trail of Tears. It was a seven-mile hike down a steep and winding U.S. Forest Service road. Local people said the dirt and gravel road ran roughly parallel to an old trail into Tennessee, which the army used in 1838 to haul Cherokee detainees over the mountain. About twenty participants in this annual event were walking in the opposite direction that the emigrants traveled—instead of going over the mountain and away, they walked back down the mountain and returned to town. Their destination was the Junaluska Museum, named for a Cherokee who fought in Andrew Jackson's army at Horseshoe Bend. Removed in 1838, Junaluska escaped from Oklahoma, returned to his home mountains, and is buried by the museum in Robbinsville.

Participants welcomed me to join them. It was a perfect morning, cool in the shade of the woods. For a time I walked alongside Sheree Peters, who described her ancestry as both Cherokee and Irish. She speculated that an Irish-Cherokee marriage may have made it possible for her Cherokee ancestors to remain in North Carolina after 1838. Also in our knot of walkers was Adam Wachacha, a member of the governing council of the Eastern Band. Wachacha said he had recently completed thirteen years in the U.S. Army. He was posted for a time at South Carolina's Fort Jackson, the name of which he found irksome. At Fort Hood, Texas, he was attached to a unit whose regimental history included fighting Indian wars. He sometimes commented on the irony when talking with other natives in the unit. Serving in an army that flew Black Hawk and Apache helicopters, Wachacha was deployed to South Korea, where he was stationed at Camp Red Cloud. He found the army's profuse use of Indian names to be less offensive than the name of Fort Jackson, and wasn't enthused about the general movement to have Indian names effaced. "A little too much political correctness," he said.

It was common to encounter veterans among the eastern Cherokees. At the Museum of the Cherokee Indian I sat with another man, Jerry Wolf, whose weathered face appeared on posters for the museum. He could often be found working at the museum's front desk, though he was nearly ninety years old when I met him. Wolf told me that he was in the navy on D-day in 1944. He vividly remembered serving as part of a crew that brought a landing craft full of army Rangers to the beaches at Normandy. He also recalled something of his family history. Born in 1924, he said he had grown up knowing stories about his family in the Civil War, but not about the period of Indian removal. He said his parents did not like to talk about that era—they were "edgy" about it, fearing that the government "could still come and gather us up." Wolf did not know how his family persisted after 1838, only that they had.

One Cherokee I met knew a portion of his family's removal story. He was Freeman Owle, a local public speaker who had often told it. The heart of his story was that his family was sent westward, but that one woman and her child broke away and returned; that child was Freeman Owle's ancestor. There was no way to prove this family lore except that Freeman Owle was here by the eastern Cherokee reservation, sitting with me on a rock near the entrance to the Great Smoky Mountains National Park.

Freeman Owle told his story without bitterness. "Andrew Jackson is dead," he said. "Junaluska is dead." He said he would rather "accept today as today," and that, while it was vital to remember those who died on the Trail of Tears, it was also necessary to focus on those who survived.

"We don't expect our land back," he added. "We are an invisible minority. That's what we are. But we don't expect anything other than the truth to be told."

I asked if Indian removal was, for him, less a story of removal than a story of persistence.

He answered that it was. "We are," he said, "still here."

SOURCES AND ACKNOWLEDGMENTS

Writing this book required me to join a centuries-old argument. Martin Van Buren was right: he predicted that while other controversies that "agitated the public mind in their day" would fade, the emotions aroused by Indian removal would probably "endure . . . as long as the government itself." Each generation of Americans has interpreted Indian removal differently—arguing at different times that it was inevitable, tragic, genocidal, better left unexamined, or, in the words of an early Jackson biographer, "wise and humane."

Division and Reunion, a popular history of the United States published in 1893, declared that white men "very naturally" would not tolerate red men setting up a government in their midst. The book all but excused subverting the law to remove them. The author was Woodrow Wilson, and his history was still in print after he was elected president in 1912. A Georgia school textbook in 1913 said slave owners "were as religious, moral, high-minded a race of men who ever lived," and described the removal of Creeks and Cherokees as an obvious practical response to the problem that their land was needed for white settlement. But there were always dissenting opinions, and gradually the acts Wilson called "natural" became controversial. Historians in the 1930s highlighted the cruelties of Indian removal, while those who admired

Jackson found it necessary to emphasize other parts of his career. In 1945 Arthur Schlesinger won a Pulitzer Prize for *The Age of Jackson,* which made a case for Jackson as a hero of democracy, and mentioned Indian removal in a single passing phrase.

In later years, Howard Zinn's best-selling *A People's History of the United States* went to the opposite extreme, taking a wild swing at Jackson, while the ethnographer Ronald Takaki labeled him "the Metaphysician of Indian-Hating," playing off a phrase penned by Herman Melville. Even the visitor center at the Hermitage, Jackson's home in Tennessee, began playing a documentary on Jackson's life that acknowledged many Indians viewed him as "the devil." In 2009, Congress passed and President Barack Obama quietly signed a formal apology for the Trail of Tears. But Congress also specified that Native Americans could not use the apology to reclaim land, and the historical pendulum was already swinging back. Recent Jackson biographers, such as Jon Meacham and H. W. Brands, candidly described the human cost of Jackson's policy while keeping it in the perspective of his broader career. Sean Wilentz, in *The Rise of American Democracy*, observed that while Jackson was a "paternalist," telling Indians what was best for them, that was not the same as genocide.

One especially intriguing treatment of America's engagement with native nations is a project that was never finished. Starting in 1888, Theodore Roosevelt devoted some of his phenomenal energy to writing *The Winning of the West,* which chronicled western settlement from colonial times onward. In his role as a historian, Roosevelt documented brutal violence: settlers and Indians disregarded the rules of war, and even noncombatants were "harried without ruth." As an ardent nationalist, however, Roosevelt insisted that this ruthlessness was redeemed by the result. The spread of civilization was a noble task, America had its destiny to fulfill, and critics of the ugly methods were overlooking the "race-importance" of the work. Roosevelt's four volumes continued the story up to the start of the nineteenth century. He never finished two additional books in which he intended to bring forward the story into the 1830s. The later volumes necessarily would have covered many of the events of *Jacksonland*.

I came to think of *Jacksonland* as a modern substitute for one of Roosevelt's missing volumes. While discarding his theories of "race-importance," I found something valuable in his insistence upon the cold reality of events. Facts should be pursued "without ruth." And that included facts about John Ross, who like Jackson has been portrayed differently at different times. *The Cherokees* by Grace Steele Woodward makes him a beloved hero, while *Trail of Tears* by John Ehle paints a stubborn egotist "determined to defeat removal and extol himself." Some writers do not even describe Ross as an Indian; *Toward the Setting Sun* by Brian Hicks styles him "the first white man to champion the voiceless Native American cause." It took me time to recognize that the complexity of Ross's story is the point of it. His mixed culture and ancestry, not to mention his membership in the great tribe of politicians, make him a modern figure, and cast a different light on our past.

That this book was ever finished is a credit to my family. Carolee and our daughters put up with countless evenings and weekends spent researching and writing. It was especially challenging because Ana joined our family while the book was being written. Her older sister, Ava, asked to assist with the book, and occasionally took dictation. In several instances, when nobody was looking, she typed the word "Fart" in the manuscript. I may have caught them all.

Ann Godoff of the Penguin Press supported this project from the morning I proposed it over breakfast in 2012 and has kept faith with it ever since. It is impossible to imagine a wiser publisher or a more thoughtful editor. Nor can I imagine a more supportive agent than Gail Ross.

Many friends read chapters and offered constructive comments. I treasured the insights of Charla Bear and Andrew Exum. Joe DeMarie brought a screenwriter's eye to the story. Anne Kornblut of the *Washington Post* and Nishant Dahiya of NPR critiqued chapters in their spare time, even though their day job is also editing. NPR colleagues such as Tracy Wahl and Selena Simmons-Duffin also offered insights. I am especially grateful for the assistance of several subject matter experts. All, including Dr. Duane King of the Gilcrease Museum in Oklahoma and Dr. Susan Abram of Western Carolina University, offered invaluable advice. Kathryn Holland Braund of Auburn University critiqued portions of the manuscript. Florence, Alabama, historian Milly Wright not only read several chapters but conducted her own research to offer corrections. Barbara Duncan of the Museum of the Cherokee Indian, upon being sent several chapters, immediately asked to review all of it. Any errors, of course, are mine.

Many people supported this book in other ways. The death of my father, Roland, while this book was being written gave occasion to recall that he and my mother, Judith, bought the books that began my love affair with history. Renee Montagne and David Greene covered for me when I was away from NPR and writing. Ellen McDonnell and other executives at NPR graciously permitted me to take time off. Tom Gjelten and Martha Raddatz have sponsored and advised me for many years, thinking of me even when I didn't realize they were. Madhulika Sikka created conditions for my work to thrive; Michele Norris inspired me to think more deeply about race and diversity. Steve Coll, David Ignatius, and Lawrence Wright affected my work simply because they wrote such good books, and because they let me ask them questions about writing. Mary Louise Kelly quit NPR to write thrillers, and knowing a thriller writer made me aspire to tug a reader into my story as strongly as I was drawn into the world of her novels.

A vital source of material was the Library of Congress. It is a magical place, where one may walk into a room and be presented with actual yellowed copies of the *Cherokee Phoenix*, or a book that has been out of print for more than a hundred years. One of the treasures of that library is its librarians. The staff was particularly helpful in guiding me through the correspondence of Jackson, including many original letters—such as a tender letter to Jackson's wife in 1814, or the page from 1825 on which he accuses Henry Clay of receiving "thirty pieces of silver." Items not available at the Library of Congress were often available nearby at the National Archives.

The University of Tennessee is in the midst of publishing Jackson's papers in book form; the volumes published so far probably shortened this project by years. The current editor, Daniel Feller, and his staff were infinitely patient and helpful when I made queries about papers not reproduced in the volumes. Feller also critiqued the resulting book. I will be forever grateful to Gary E. Moulton, a man I never met, who wrote a rigorous biography of Ross and edited Ross's papers into an accessible two-volume set; original papers are collected at the Gilcrease Museum at the University of Tulsa. Another thick pair of volumes, known as the *Payne-Butrick Papers*, put many priceless source writings about Cherokees within convenient reach. Further documents were at the Museum of the Cherokee Indian, where Nelda Reid opened the archives on an off day so that I might study them. Images of John Coffee's papers were accessible through the Florence-Lauderdale Public Library, an extraordinary local institution in Florence, Alabama. Ove Jensen, formerly of the National Park Service at Horseshoe Bend, is one of several people who directed me to documents that otherwise would have taken much more time to find. Marsha Mullin and other staff members at the Hermitage were greatly helpful, as were the keepers of the John Ross home in Georgia.

Several books to which I referred, such as James Parton's 1860 biography of Jackson, I found in the crowded aisles of Parnassus Books in Yarmouth Port, Massachusetts. Used books I have bought from independent sellers all my life are worth many times more than I paid.

For a researcher, the greatest discoveries still lurk beyond the electronic cloud, but the Hathi Trust is helping the cloud to catch up. The trust has reproduced countless nineteenth-century newspapers and documents with great fidelity, such as the *Truth's Advocate and Monthly Anti-Jackson Expositor* of 1828. The American State Papers, maintained online by the Library of Congress, offer an incredible trove of documents on almost anything in the early nineteenth century that came to the attention of Congress. The library also has access to a fantastic collection of old newspapers in searchable form. Oklahoma State University shaved much time from this project by putting many Indian treaties in searchable form.

This book has been a joy to write, even though it tells a difficult story. It is about my country, which makes it a love story. Of the many ways to show one's love, one of the best is to tell the truth.

NOTES

Prologue: The Indian Map and the White Man's Map

1 **a wooden flatboat** Ross to Return J. Meigs, December 15, 1812, Moulton, *Papers of Chief John Ross*, vol. 1, p. 15.

2 **calico, gingham, buttons, beaver traps, and shotguns** Moulton, *John Ross, Cherokee Chief*, p. 9.

2 **He grew so frustrated . . . trading for a keelboat** Ross to Meigs, December 15, 1812, Moulton, *Papers of Chief John Ross*, vol. 1, p. 16.

2 **black-haired, brown-eyed, slight but handsome** Other sources have said he had blue eyes, but John H. Underwood, who knew him, said otherwise, according to Wilkins, *Cherokee Tragedy*, p. 199. A full-color lithograph of his portrait also shows brown eyes, and is reproduced in McKenney and Hall, *Indian Tribes of North America*.

2 **a Cherokee interpreter, an older Cherokee man named Kalsatee** Moulton, *John Ross, Cherokee Chief*, p. 9.

2 **Kooweskoowe** There are various spellings; this is the one Ross used in letters, such as his letter to the Seminoles, October 18, 1837, Moulton, *Papers of Chief John Ross*, vol. 1, p. 526.

2 **"we was haled by a party of white men"** Ross to Meigs, Dec. 31, 1812, ibid., pp. 16–17.

3 **"I told them we had no news . . . mounted their horses & galloped off"** Ibid.

4 **"we concluded it was good policy to let Kalsatee out of the boat"** Ibid.

4 **"a disagreeable walk of about thirty miles"** Ibid.

4 **"convinced . . . being an Indian boat"** Ibid.

5 **twenty-five hundred white frontiersmen** Parton, *Life of Andrew Jackson*, vol. 1, p. 365.

5 **burned by Potawatomi warriors** The garrison, told to evacuate due to trouble providing supplies, was attacked and forced to surrender in the summer of 1812, after which the fort was torched. Quaife, "Fort Dearborn Massacre," pp. 561–73. Also Quaife and Forsyth, "Story of James Corbin, A Soldier of Fort Dearborn," pp. 219–28.

6 **in 1816 temporarily blocked one of Jackson's great land acquisitions** As will be discussed in chap. 8.

6 **"shall forever hereafter remain unalterably the same"** Cherokee constitution, reprinted in *Cherokee Phoenix*, February 21, 1828, p. 1.

7 **"We consider ourselves as a part of the great family . . . in its cause"** Ross to George Graham, March 4, 1816, Moulton, *Papers of Chief John Ross*, vol. 1, pp. 24–25.

8 **"The object of the Govt . . . into markett this land & have it populated"** Jackson to Coffee, February 13, 1816, Owsley et al., *Papers of Andrew Jackson*, vol. 4, p. 12.

9 **forty-five thousand acres sold in the Tennessee River valley** According to federal land records referenced in chap. 8.

Part One: Horseshoe, 1814
Chapter One: Every Thing Is to Be Feared

13 **an open-sided tent, or marquee** Jackson is described during the campaign as using a "markee" in Crockett, *Narrative*, p. 90.

13 **"Respectfully your Most Obedient Servant"** For example, his angry letters to military contractors on March 22 and 23, 1814, Andrew Jackson Papers, 1775–1874, reel 9.

13 **"Sir," and signed his first and last name** For example, Jackson to John Coffee, February 17, 1814, and Jackson to Rachel, April 1, 1814, Owsley et al., *Papers of Andrew Jackson*, vol. 3, pp. 32, 54.

13 **nor even check the spelling of his name** Librarians at the University of Tennessee, a prime repository of Jackson papers, have been unable to establish with certainty which spelling was correct. Jackson's spelling does not match that of the surviving court record.

13 **"John Woods . . ."** All text of the March 14, 1814, letter as recorded in his letter book, kept by an aide, Andrew Jackson Papers, 1775–1874, reel 9.

14 **the narrow target inside Jackson's bulky overcoat** Parton, *Life of Andrew Jackson*, vol. 1, p. 300.

14 **The lead ball was still in his body** Ibid., pp. 394–95.

14 **"lived on any thing we could get . . . dry cowhide"** Transcript of the autobiography of Ebenezer Hearn, Alabama Department of Archives and History. Hearn, born in 1794, wrote a summary of his life that was discovered in 1906, after his death, and transcribed.

14 **draping his body over a sapling** Parton, *Life of Andrew Jackson*, vol. 1, p. 548.

15 **Some of its borders had not even been surveyed** Not until after the war, for example, did Jackson's friend John Coffee survey the Georgia–Alabama line.

16 **until recently had been away on business in the Cherokee Nation** As evidenced by Ross to Return J. Meigs, March 2, 1814, Moulton, *Papers of Chief John Ross*, vol. 1, pp. 19–20.

16 **a warrior could refuse to go to war if he did not want to** King, *Memoirs of Lt. Henry Timberlake*, p. 36.

16 **"dark blue or brown . . . at the election of the wearer"** Parton, *Life of Andrew Jackson*, vol. 1, p. 367.

16 **"a tall delicately framed youth . . . these formed his equipment"** Ellen Call Long to her son Richard Call Long, August 16, 1853. The writer describes her memories of Richard Keith Call, "your grandfather." Call and Brevard Family Papers, box 5, folder 19, item 1. Digitally posted by Florida Library and Information Services: http://www.floridamemory.com/items/show/180858?id=1.

17 Jackson had prevented a mass of troops from marching away Parton, *Life of Andrew Jackson*, vol. 1, p. 471.

17 Later he wrote the Tennesseans a letter Ibid., pp. 473–74.

17 "very clamorous and I fear will not do much good" John Coffee to his wife, Mary, January 8, 1814, reproduced in Sioussat, ed., "Letters of General John Coffee to His Wife," p. 280.

17 "it was not to be expected . . . so unhappily prevailed" Eaton and Reid, *Life of Andrew Jackson*, p. 151.

17 Wood ignored an officer's order to pick up some bones Account of his fellow soldiers, Robert Ferguson, February 14, 1828, printed in *Truth's Advocate* and *Monthly Anti-Jackson Expositor*, April 1828, p. 123.

17 "a fit occasion . . . mutinous spirit" Ibid.

18 The execution was scheduled for noon George A. Brock, eyewitness account printed in *Truth's Advocate and Monthly Anti-Jackson Expositor*, April 1828, p. 125.

18 appointing an assistant topographical engineer His aide-de-camp John Reid signed the note "by order of the commanding general," March 14, 1814, Andrew Jackson Papers, 1775–1874, reel 9.

18 bury the man "with the honors of war" Jackson aide-de-camp Robert Scarey, March 14, 1814, ibid.

18 A copy of the letter soon made it to Nashville Appearing in the *Nashville Clarion*, April 5, 1814, and *Nashville Whig*, April 6, 1814. Owsley et al., *Papers of Andrew Jackson*, vol. 3, p. 49n.

18 "sacrifice, essential . . . the happiest effects" Eaton and Reid, *Life of Andrew Jackson*, p. 152.

19 "Shoot the damned rascal!" Creek War veteran Thomas Couch, in *Truth's Advocate and Monthly Anti-Jackson Expositor*, April 1828, reports that Jackson said this "several times," pp. 122–23. In the same publication, George A. Brock repeats the same allegation, p. 124, while another witness approximates the same quote.

19 "by the Eternal God" As quoted in ibid., p. 123.

19 There had been an earlier altercation The earlier altercation unfolded in December or early January, according to Parton, *Life of Andrew Jackson*, vol. 1, p. 505, but Wood did not join the unit until afterward, according to his friend and comrade George A. Brock, writing in *Truth's Advocate and Monthly Anti-Jackson Expositor*, April 1828, p. 125.

19 "make it easy . . . shoot him if he does not" Surviving fragment of court-martial record, March 11, 1814, Andrew Jackson Papers, Chicago History Museum.

20 "He could have the opportunity of enlisting . . . opposed it violently" Wood's comrade was George A. Brock, who said he spoke with both Wood and Jackson in an effort to save his friend. He told his story years later to an anti-Jackson publication, but his story rings true because it seems to explain Jackson's acts more than it damns them. *Truth's Advocate and Monthly Anti-Jackson Expositor*, April 1828, p. 124.

20 Jackson's staff ordered a court-martial for another soldier His adjutant general ordered the man confined to camp until trial. Statement by aide-de-camp Robert Scarey, March 14, 1814, Andrew Jackson Papers, 1775–1874, reel 9.

20 Eight days later he ordered yet another court-martial Order by the adjutant general to court-martial several men, recorded by Jackson aide Robert Scarey, March 22 and 23, 1814, ibid.

20 **sixty-two of a hundred men from a single company** The names of men who deserted from this company and others are in the report of the Committee on Military Affairs, February 11, 1823, *Proceedings of a Court Martial Ordered for the Trial of Certain Tennessee Militiamen,* pp. 132–34.

20 **"I have no doubts but you hear a great deal of stuff about Tyranny"** John Coffee to his wife, Mary, January 3, 1814, transcribed in Sioussat, "Letters of General John Coffee to His Wife," p. 279.

20 **"The snarling *curs* may grin"** Jackson to Coffee, February 17, 1814, Owsley et al., *Papers of Andrew Jackson,* vol. 1, pp. 32–33.

21 **"on an elevated piece of ground"** . . . **"the performance of divine service"** . . . **one step forward** Letter "From Our Correspondent," *Nashville Whig,* April 6, 1814.

21 **They shot Private Wood on schedule** Ibid.

21 **Wood's farewell was composed in rhyme** Statement of George A. Brock, in *Truth's Advocate and Monthly Anti-Jackson Expositor,* April 1828, p. 126.

Chapter Two: Urge On All Those Cherokees

22 **the courier found . . . John Ross** Ross to Return J. Meigs, March 2, 1814, Moulton, *Papers of Chief John Ross,* vol. 1, pp. 19–20.

22 **Second Lieutenant John Ross, an adjutant, or assistant to a senior officer** Moulton, *John Ross, Cherokee Chief,* p. 11.

23 **"I have this moment received by Express"** All text of this letter from Ross to Meigs, March 2, 1814, Moulton, *Papers of Chief John Ross,* vol. 1, pp. 19–20.

23 **his trading firm had signed a contract to supply the Cherokee Regiment** The firm was called Meigs and Ross, and consisted of Ross and the son of the federal Indian agent. Moulton, *John Ross: Cherokee Chief,* p. 8.

24 **Colonel Gideon Morgan** Wilkins, *Cherokee Tragedy,* p. 67.

24 **Jackson had promised that the Cherokees would receive the same pay and benefits** Jackson recalled this promise in a letter to George Graham on July 9, 1817, Owsley et al., *Papers of Andrew Jackson,* vol. 4, pp. 125–26.

24 **George Guess . . Old Brains, Whiteman Killer** Names from transcript of Cherokee Muster Roll, Horseshoe Bend National Military Park.

24 **Tahseekeyarkey** Shoe Boots's Cherokee name as spelled in Anderson et al., *Payne-Butrick Papers,* vol. 2, p. 106.

24 **after the high European-style boats** Ibid.

24 **"chicken heart"** As quoted in ibid., p. 107.

24 **Tobacco Juice . . . a unit of "spies," or scouts . . . General Jackson's bodyguard** According to transcript of Cherokee Muster Roll, Horseshoe Bend National Military Park.

24 **hint of a brogue** Parton, *Life of Jackson,* vol. 1, p. 4

25 **buckskin hunting jacket** Duncan, *Cherokee Clothing in the 1700's,* chap. 12. Also Wilkins, *Cherokee Tragedy,* p. 60.

25 **John Ross . . . spied wearing a Middle Eastern–style turban** Woodward, *The Cherokees,* p. 157.

25 **Cherokee women . . . commonly wore modest full-length dresses** Duncan, *Cherokee Clothing in the 1700's,* chap. 12.

26 **"honorable to the national character . . . sound policy"** Washington, Third Annual Message, October 25, 1791, Prucha, *Documents of United States Indian Policy,* p. 16.

26 **Ridge . . . promoted the idea that Cherokees should raise a force** Wilkins, *Cherokee Tragedy*, p. 60.

26 **white men would categorize all Indians as either with them or against them** Ibid., p. 63.

26 **"They are real horsemen"** Ibid, p. 60.

27 **"What could have occasioned you"** Jackson to Pope, Branham, March 22, 1814, Andrew Jackson Papers, 1775–1874, reel 9.

27 **eight days' rations** Jackson to Major Baster, March 23, 1814, Andrew Jackson Papers, 1775–1874, reel 19.

Chapter Three: Stamping His Foot for War

29 **Middle Tennessee formed a salient** This is illustrated by U.S. Census Bureau, "Following the Frontier Line, 1790 to 1890," September 6, 2012.

30 **in September 1811, associates of Robert Fulton completed a steamboat** Philip, *Robert Fulton*, pp. 270–71.

30 **butcher knives, cotton hoes, coffee, "Segars," chocolate** Account Book, Jackson's Nashville Store, 1795, Owsley et al., *Papers of Andrew Jackson*, vol. 1, appendix 4, p. 455.

30 **farmers often paid Jackson with cotton** Parton, *Life of Andrew Jackson*, vol. 1, p. 245.

30 **"nine pounds of nails for each person in the state"** There were 7,270,825 pounds of nails produced, 810,000 people. Coxe, *Statement of the Arts and Manufactures of the United States*, p. xxxi.

30 **"the most considerable of our manufactures . . . family looms"** Ibid., p. xxviii.

31 **more than three and a half gallons for every man . . . "moralizing" and "salubrious"** Author's calculation, based on population of 7.2 million. Ibid., pp. xl–xlii.

31 **mix a little gin with the water he was drinking** Parton, *Life of Andrew Jackson*, vol. 1, p. 548.

31 **Jackson sent a bottle of wine** Ibid., p. 300.

31 **"ardent spirits have been banished from among us"** *Niles' Weekly Register*, November 28, 1829, vol. 37, p. 213.

31 **Jefferson urged state governors to crack down** Jefferson to governors, December 31, 1808, Prucha, *Documents of United States Indian Policy*, pp. 24–25.

32 **"almost entirely inhabited . . . duplicity and overreaching"** Levasseur, *Lafayette in America*, vol. 2, p. 81.

32 **"is generally well-clothed, healthy . . . depraved wretches on earth"** Harrison writing in 1801, quoted in Adams, *Formative Years*, vol. 2, p. 673.

32 **treaties in 1804, 1805, and 1809** Ibid., pp. 674–76.

32 **"it was easier to begin a war than to end one"** His statement is reported in Stiggins, *Creek Indian History*, p. 86.

33 **"ascend to the top of a mountain"** Ibid., p. 86.

33 **"about one hundred slave men . . . clear blue eyes"** All quotes from Miss Austill are from Austill, "Memories of Journeying through Creek Country," pages unnumbered.

34 **Red Sticks, apparently because of the red war clubs held by their prophets** Braund, "Red Sticks," in Braund, ed., *Tohopeka*, p. 86.

34 **"fanatical riots of shaving their heads"** Stiggins, *Creek Indian History*, p. 103.

34 **"civil war . . . the Superior force of the rebels"** Ross to Meigs, July 30, 1813. Moulton, *Papers of Chief John Ross*, vol. 1, p. 19.

34 **Some . . . were traveling to Spanish-controlled Florida** One such journey is described in Stiggins, *Creek Indian History,* p. 85.

34 **"One morning . . . mother, sister and myself"** Miss Austill's quotes are from Austill, "Memories of Journeying through Creek Country," pages unnumbered.

36 **Considerably modifying his instructions, Jackson kept his unit together** Parton, *Life of Andrew Jackson,* vol. 1, pp. 377–83.

36 **he was in bed with a lead ball in his shoulder** Parton finds him dismissing his injury as a brief "indisposition," though he had difficulty moving for many weeks after the shooting. Ibid., p. 423.

36 **he had to be helped onto his horse at the appointed time** Ibid., p. 425.

37 **"with his arm in a sling looking pale and emaciated"** Ellen Call Long to her son Richard Call Long, August 16, 1853. The writer describes her memories of Richard Keith Call, "your grandfather." Ellen Call Long, Call and Brevard Family Papers, box 5, folder 19, item 1. Digitally posted by Florida Library and Information Services: http://www.floridamemory.com/items/show/180858?id=1.

Chapter Four: It Was Dark Before We Finished Killing Them

38 **"taking revenge for the blood of the innocent"** Ross to Return J. Meigs, March 2, 1814, Moulton, *Papers of Chief John Ross,* vol. 1, pp. 19–20.

38 **The commander did not believe slaves in nearby fields** Parton, *Life of Andrew Jackson,* vol. 1, p. 413.

38 **726 men** Stiggins, *Creek Indian History,* p. 108.

38 **could even hear the white men talking** Ibid., pp. 109–10.

39 **Weatherford's brother-in-law** Historian George Stiggins is so identified in ibid., p. 17.

39 **Weatherford who persuaded a Red Stick council** Ibid., p. 106.

39 **under orders to race across the surrounding fields** Ibid., pp. 110–11.

39 **spiritual leader . . . 202 Creeks were killed** Ibid., pp. 113–14.

39 **"Indians, negroes, white men, women and children . . . permit me to describe"** Parton, *Life of Andrew Jackson,* vol. 1, p. 418.

39 **"horrid butcheries" with a "spirit of revenge"** Ibid., p. 423.

39 **"she and our little children would be left . . . war could bring it right again"** Crockett, *Narrative,* pp. 72–74.

40 **mounted volunteers** Ibid., p. 74.

40 **"I burnt three towns but never saw an Indian"** John to Mary Coffee, October 24, 1813, Sioussat, "Letters of General John Coffee to His Wife," p. 275.

40 **hungry troops . . . "burned the town to ashes"** Crockett, *Narrative,* p. 84.

40 **retreated into a single house. . . "burned it up with the forty-six warriors in it"** Ibid., p. 88.

40 **"a small skirmish with the Indians"** John to Mary Coffee, November 4, 1813, Sioussat, "Letters of General John Coffee to His Wife," p. 276.

40 **"It was, somehow or other, found out"** Crockett, *Narrative,* pp. 89–90.

41 **"When I reflect"** Jackson to Rachel, November 4, 1813, cited in Remini, *Andrew Jackson and the Course of American Empire,* p. 193.

41 **"I send on a little Indian boy for Andrew . . . All his family is destroyed"** Brands, *Andrew Jackson,* p. 198.

41 **the Cherokee Regiment ... first engagement in the fall of 1813** Ross was present according to Moulton, *John Ross, Cherokee Chief,* p. 11.

42 **"Nature furnishes ... artfully arranged"** Jackson to Governor Blount, reprinted in newspaper *The War,* vol. 2, no. 46, May 5, 1814.

42 **two rows of heavy logs, placed about four feet apart ... packed clay** Dickens, *Archaeological Investigations at Horseshoe Bend,* diagrams and maps, pp. 44–45.

42 **hill, just 125 yards from the nearest portion of the wall** Ibid.

43 **"gun parts and ammunition ... ceramics and glass"** Ibid., p. 198.

43 **"destitute condition of a people whose homes had been recently burned"** Ibid.

44 **Three Cherokees, led by a man known as the Whale** The story is recounted in "Restoration of a Rifle to a Cherokee Warrior," *Harrisburg Democratic Union,* September 6, 1843, p. 1.

44 **the party is known to have included Major Ridge** Wilkins, *Cherokee Tragedy,* p. 76.

44 **"when I found those engaged in the interior of the bend"** Jackson to Rachel, March 28, 1814, Owsley et al., *Papers of Andrew Jackson,* vol. 3, p. 54.

44 **Houston compelled a comrade** Parton, *Life of Andrew Jackson,* vol. 1, p. 518.

44 **their second line of defense, a tangle of felled trees** This line of defense is identified on the battlefield today.

44 **set fire to the underbrush** Parton, *Life of Andrew Jackson,* vol. 1, p. 519.

45 **"unfortunate and deluded red foe ... tested and correctly judged"** Ross to Jackson, March 28, 1834, Moulton, *Papers of Chief John Ross,* vol. 1, pp. 282–84.

45 **"It was dark before we finished"** Jackson to Rachel, March 28, 1814, Owsley et al., *Papers of Andrew Jackson,* vol. 3, p. 54.

45 **"buried in their watry grave"** Ibid.

45 **"River of blood," "very perceptably bloody" "10 O'clock at night"** Lt. Alexander McCulloch to Frances L. McCulloch, April 1, 1814, transcript of letter in Horseshoe Bend National Military Park files.

46 **"Capt. Jno. Speirs Severely ... The Seed slightly"** Undated, about April 1814, Moulton, *Papers of Chief John Ross,* vol. 1, pp. 20–21.

46 **26 killed, and up to 107 wounded, depending on the count** Coffee said 106 wounded, John to Mary Coffee, April 1, 1814, Sioussat, "Letters of General John Coffee to His Wife," p. 283; Jackson said 107 wounded, Jackson letter from *National Intelligencer,* April 25, 1814, reprinted in "Jackson's Victory," in the newspaper *The War,* May 5, 1814.

46 **"Having now nearly compleated our business"** John to Mary Coffee, April 1, 1814, Sioussat, "Letters of General John Coffee to His Wife," p. 283.

47 **"many of the Tennessee soldiers"** Ball and Halbert, *Creek War of 1813 and 1814,* pp. 276–77.

47 **"when the Horse Shoe village was set on fire ... killed an Indian"** Ibid., p. 277.

47 **"would have become an Indian some day"** Ibid.

47 **"I did believe ... fell in Battle"** Jackson to George Graham, July 9, 1817, Owsley et al., *Papers of Andrew Jackson,* vol. 3, p. 125.

48 **Three hundred eleven heads of families took the offer** McLoughlin, "Experiment in Cherokee Citizenship, 1817–1829," p. 4.

48 **"cut to pieces ... appropriate punishment"** Jackson letter from *National Intelligencer,* April 25, 1814, reprinted in "Jackson's Victory," in the newspaper *The War,* May 5, 1814.

48 **Jackson ... let Weatherford go free** Brands, *Andrew Jackson,* p. 222.

49 "I made this war" Drake, *Biography and History of the Indians of North America*, p. 69.

49 "Brothers . . . friends will sign the treaty" Jackson to Big Warrior, August 10, 1814, Owsley et al., *Papers of Andrew Jackson*, vol. 3, pp. 109–10.

50 friends in Nashville, who appealed to a bank for $50,000 Andrew Jackson to James Jackson, August 28, 1814, Moser et al., *Papers of Andrew Jackson*, reel 4.

Part Two: Origins, 1767–1814
Chapter Five: Send a Few Late Newspapers by the Bearer

53 "whiteside" Ross to Jackson, June 19, 1820, Moulton, *Papers of Chief John Ross*, vol. 1, p. 41.

54 Born October 3, 1790, he spent his early years Moulton, *John Ross, Cherokee Chief*, p. 5.

54 She let him change into traditional Indian dress Ibid., p. 6.

54 Kooweskoowe There are other spellings, such as Guwisguwi; Kooweskoowe is how Ross spelled it in a letter on October 18, 1837. Moulton, *Papers of Chief John Ross*, vol. 1, p. 526.

54 Cherokee Bird Clan Anderson et al., *Payne-Butrick Papers*, vols. 4–6, p. 454.

54 Ghigooie Moulton, *John Ross, Cherokee Chief*, p. 2.

54 a quarter-million people, a migration that played an enormous role Fischer, *Albion's Seed*, p. 606.

54 Enrolled as a British soldier Moulton, *John Ross, Cherokee Chief*, p. 4.

55 Andrew Jackson himself took a secret oath The written and signed oath is transcribed in Remini, "Andrew Jackson Takes an Oath of Allegiance to Spain," p. 9.

55 he went on the Spanish payroll Moulton, *John Ross, Cherokee Chief*, pp. 4–5.

55 Of their nine children, John Ross was the third Ibid., p. 5.

56 the most recent newspapers available on the frontier Ibid., p. 6.

56 "send a few late newspapers by the bearer" Ross to Meigs, July 30, 1813, Moulton, *Papers of Chief John Ross*, vol. 1, p. 19.

56 boots and a jacket . . . broad-brimmed, flat-crowned planter's hat Woodward, *The Cherokees*, p. 157.

57 purchasing remote tracts in hopes Moulton, *John Ross, Cherokee Chief*, pp. 21–22, 202.

57 "My grandfather, father and Auntie were bought by John Ross" Miles, *Ties That Bind*, p. 85.

57 Ross wasn't a true Indian, they charged The state of Georgia study investigated Ross's ancestry in 1831 and made this allegation. Moulton, *John Ross, Cherokee Chief*, pp. 46–47.

58 Ross himself was granted 640 acres The treaty of 1819 ceded substantial land to the federal government, but allowed some Cherokee residents to keep their home plots, and also recognized properties claimed by various leading Cherokees, including "John Ross, six hundred and forty acres, to be laid off so as to include the Big Island in Tennessee river, being the first below Tellico." Charles J. Kappler, ed., "Treaty with the Cherokees, 1819," in Kappler, *Indian Affairs: Laws and Treaties*, vol. 2, *Treaties, 1778–1883*, p. 178.

Chapter Six: I Am Fond of Hearing That There Is a Peace

59 had been driven by some calamity into the mountains Woodward, *The Cherokees*, pp. 18–19.

60 **"persons, customs, &c. are not singular"** Adair, *History of the American Indians,* p. 11.

61 **population . . . may have been cut in half** Ibid., p. 232.

61 **In 1711 the colonists of Charles Towne supplied guns to the Cherokees** Woodward, *The Cherokees,* p. 57.

61 **"The Cherokees are of a middle stature"** King, *Memoirs of Lt. Henry Timberlake,* p. 24.

62 **town house for public meetings** Woodward, *The Cherokees,* pp. 43–46.

62 **"mixed aristocracy and democracy . . . ancient bards did in Britain"** King, *Memoirs of Lt. Henry Timberlake,* p. 36.

62 **The chief encountered four strange men of an unknown tribe** The story is reported in the *Cherokee Phoenix,* November 26, 1828, pp. 3–4.

63 **"Their alliance with the French seems equal"** King, *Memoirs of Lt. Henry Timberlake,* p. 37.

63 **only other Indians could defeat them. He urged Virginia** Ellis, *His Excellency,* p. 25.

64 **"We shall push our trading houses"** Jefferson to William Henry Harrison, February 27, 1803, Prucha, *Documents of United States Indian Policy,* p. 22.

64 **"the wisdom of exchanging what they can spare"** Thomas Jefferson's message on Indian trade, January 18, 1803, ibid., p. 21.

64 **"incorporate with us as citizens of the United States"** Jefferson to William Henry Harrison, February 27, 1803, ibid., p. 22.

64 **"conjure men"** Author interview with Freeman Owle, Cherokee, NC, June 21, 2014.

65 **he joined a church in 1829** Moulton, *John Ross, Cherokee Chief,* p. 7

65 **Charles Hicks was providing Ross with tutorials on tribal history** Ibid., p. 31.

65 **"warwomen . . . as famous in war, as powerful in the council"** King, *Memoirs of Lt. Henry Timberlake.* p. 36.

66 **"I am fond of hearing that there is a Peace"** *Gazette of the United States,* July 25, 1789, p. 1.

66 **"beloved woman"** Mooney, *Myths of the Cherokee,* p. 204.

66 **program altered the status of some women, and certainly the elites** Scholars debate how widely these cultural changes spread beyond the elites. Perdue, *Cherokee Women,* p. 10.

66 **customs of inheritance . . . seemed problematic** McLoughlin, *Cherokee Renascence in the New Republic,* pp. 294–95.

66 **"white or striped homespun"** Duncan, *Cherokee Clothing in the 1700's,* chap. 12.

66 **"I can only say that their domestic cloths are preferred by us"** Ibid.

67 **"The Good Woman," who according to a modern scholar were men** Names from transcript of Cherokee Muster Roll, Horseshoe Bend National Military Park. The modern scholar is Dr. Susan Abram, author of a forthcoming book on the Creek War. Sue Abram, in correspondence, December 1, 2014.

Chapter Seven: Every Thing That Was Dear to Me

68 **Many were poor, proud, and seeking to make a slightly better living** They sought "material betterment," and in some cases "famine and starvation" were among their motivations for leaving. Fischer, *Albion's Seed,* p. 611.

68 **"hoosiers," or rough backwoodsmen** This definition may surprise those who know "Hoosier" as a name for people from Indiana. David Hackett Fischer reports that "hoosier," like "cracker" and "redneck," was a widely used term for the "backcountry underclass," and that it originated in northern Britain, from where the backwoodsmen's ancestors came. *Albion's Seed*, pp. 756–58. Today "hoosier" is still sometimes used in St. Louis as a term for a low-class or disreputable person, but Indiana people took ownership of the word, turning it into a term of pride so long ago that very few in the state today can explain the word's meaning or origin.

68 **"The features and shape of head of General Jackson"** Parton, *Life of Andrew Jackson*, vol. 1, pp. 47–48.

69 **"tough, vehement, good-hearted race . . . natural element of some of them"** Ibid., p. 33.

69 **"I was born for a storm, and calm does not suit me"** Meacham, *American Lion*, p. ix.

69 **she essentially became the housekeeper** Parton, *Life of Andrew Jackson*, vol. 1, p. 58.

70 **declared that he was a prisoner of war** Eaton and Reid, *Life of Andrew Jackson*, pp. 16–17.

70 **"The sword point reached my head . . . durable as the scull"** Jackson to Amos Kendall, undated, Owsley et al., *Papers of Andrew Jackson*, vol. 1, p. 9.

70 **"the struggle for our liberties, in which I lost every thing that was dear to me"** Remini, *Andrew Jackson and the Course of American Empire*, vol. 1, p. 173.

70 **smashing their glasses and the furniture of the tavern** Parton, *Life of Andrew Jackon*, vol. 1, p. 108.

70 **"Andrew Jackson Esquire" took possession of "a Negro Woman named Nancy"** Washington County Court, November 17, 1788, Remini, *Andrew Jackson and the Course of American Empire*, vol. 1, p. 15.

70 **"When a man's feelings and charector are injured"** To Waightstill Avery, August 12, 1788, ibid., p. 12.

71 **both men firing in the air** Ibid., p. 39.

71 **he lived with Rachel in a two-story log house** The house, later cut down to a single floor, remains today on the Hermitage grounds behind the mansion the Jacksons built after 1819.

71 **dry goods store and riverside boatyard . . . tavern and a racetrack** Remini, *Andrew Jackson and the Course of American Empire*, vol. 1, p. 132.

72 **Jackson let the other man shoot first** A detailed account of the duel is in Parton, *Life of Andrew Jackson*, vol. 1, pp. 289–306.

72 **together with Rachel for years before she completed her divorce** Remini, *Andrew Jackson and the Course of American Empire*, vol. 1, pp. 61–66.

72 **husband and wife from 1790 or 1791 onward** Though Andrew maintained that he married Rachel in 1791, not realizing her divorce was incomplete, biographer Robert Remini finds evidence that they were together from 1790 onward, and finds no proof they married at that time. Ibid., pp. 63–67.

72 **They had to be remarried in 1794 to clear up doubts** A bond affirming the legitimacy of the second marriage is in Owsley et al., *Papers of Andrew Jackson*, vol. 1, p. 428.

72 **Jackson's slave trading** Remini, *Andrew Jackson and the Course of American Empire*, reports Jackson trading and transporting slaves between Nashville and Natchez, vol. 1, pp. 50, 133. Parton, *Life of Andrew Jackson*, recounts one of Jackson's quarrels, which broke out on the Natchez Trace while Jackson was "deputed to take a number of negroes to the lower country for sale," vol. 1, pp. 354.

73 **to support his personal land speculation** Remini, *Andrew Jackson and the Course of American Empire*, vol. 1, p. 51.

73 **the two men talked for days and Jackson sold boats** Parton, *Life of Andrew Jackson*, vol. 1, pp. 316–17.

Part Three: Old Hickory, 1815–1818
Chapter Eight: Address Their Fears and Indulge Their Avarice

77 **291 redcoats killed** All Battle of New Orleans numbers according to the U.S. Army Center for Military History.

78 **"some pretext or color of fraud about you"** Coffee to Jackson, December 27, 1815, Jackson, Andrew Jackson Papers, 1775–1874, reel 20.

78 **"It is evidence of wanton wickedness . . . such a man"** Jackson to Coffee, February 2, 1816, Owsley et al., *Papers of Andrew Jackson*, vol. 4, p. 7.

79 **Each . . . blamed the other"** Coffee to Jackson, December 27, 1815, Jackson, Andrew Jackson Papers, 1775–1874, reel 20.

79 **"receiver of Publick money"** Jackson to Coffee, February 2, 1816, Owsley et al., *Papers of Andrew Jackson*, vol. 4, p. 7.

79 **"We have succeeded . . . establishment for your old age"** Arthur Peronneau Hayne to Jackson, August 5, 1817, Owsley et al., *Papers of Andrew Jackson*, vol. 4, pp. 130–31.

80 **shallows known as Muscle Shoals, forty miles that were perilous** Today submerged beneath a reservoir, the nineteenth-century shoals are so described in Dupre, "Ambivalent Capitalists on the Cotton Frontier."

81 **"The water being high made a terrible roaring . . . . in danger of striking"** From Donelson's journal, reprinted "entire" in Ramsey, *Annals of Tennessee to the Eighteenth Century*, p. 200.

81 **"ever kind of rapine & murder on our women & children"** Jackson to John Coffee, February 13, 1816, Owsley et al., *Papers of Andrew Jackson*, vol. 4, p. 11.

81 **Tennessee militiamen moved south and burned the village** Haywood, *Civil and Political History of the State of Tennessee*, pp. 231–33.

81 **Local lore held that Melton was a river pirate** This story is related in Royall, *Letters from Alabama*, p. 59.

82 **In 1783 a North Carolina land company** Moore, *History of Alabama*, p. 103; Chappell, "Some Patterns of Land Speculation in the Old Southwest," p. 463.

82 **A second effort to capture land around Muscle Shoals** A map of the Tennessee Company's target real estate can be found in Treat, *National Land System, 1785–1820*, p. 348.

82 **From 1789 onward Jackson traveled this road to and from Natchez** The important Spanish-controlled city on the Mississippi River above New Orleans. Remini, *Andrew Jackson and the Course of American Empire*, p. 55.

83 **"three thousand dollars in valuable merchandise"** Charles J. Kappler, ed., "Treaty with the Cherokee, October 25, 1805," in *Indian Affairs: Laws and Treaties*, vol. 2, *Treaties, 1778–1883*, pp. 82–83.

83 **Doublehead...was renting that land to farmers** Wilkins, *Cherokee Tragedy*, pp. 35–36.

83 **murdered him in 1807** Ibid., pp. 36–38.

83 **Jackson was involved in a deal for eighty-five thousand acres that fell apart** Remini, *Andrew Jackson and the Course of American Empire*, vol. 1, pp. 129–30.

84 **"Do you progress with the line"** Jackson to Coffee, February 13, 1816, Owsley et al., *Papers of Andrew Jackson*, vol. 4, p. 11.

84 **"25 mounted gunmen as a guard . . . in the Creek country"** Jackson to Coffee, February 13, 1816, ibid. Also Coffee, journal entry, February 16, 1816, Dyas Collection—John Coffee Papers.

85 **"immediate punishment"** Jackson to George Colbert, February 13, 1816, Owsley et al., *Papers of Andrew Jackson*, vol. 4, p. 11.

85 **"I would be glad to be informed"** Coffee to Jackson, December 27, 1815, Andrew Jackson Papers, 1775–1874, reel 20.

Chapter Nine: Men of Cultivated Understandings

86 **"the Burnt Buildings . . . red morocko pocket Book"** William Riley of Washington County, MD, scrawled language for an ad in the *National Intelligencer* on December 23, 1814. Gales and Seaton Papers.

87 **signed his name instead of making a mark** One such letter is that of the Cherokee delegation to George Graham of the War Department on March 4, 1816; Ross signed his name, while the document shows the Cherokee leaders George Lowrey, John Walker, the Ridge, and Cheucunsenee made a mark. Moulton, *Papers of Chief John Ross*, vol. 1, pp. 24–25.

87 **"These Indians are men of cultivated understandings"** From *National Intelligencer*, reprinted in *Niles' Weekly Register*, March 2, 1816, vol. 10, p. 16.

88 **"Brother . . . we hope you will no longer delay"** Ross to William H. Crawford, March 12, 1816, Moulton, *Papers of Chief John Ross*, vol. 1, p. 27.

88 **"During the late war"** Ibid.

88 **"Beginning at a point where Vann's old Store"** Cherokee delegation to George Graham, ibid., p. 24.

88 **Crawford and President James Madison approved a treaty** Wilkins, *Cherokee Tragedy*, pp. 91–92.

88 **home with silver-plated rifles** Apparently of the three rifles, one was intended for the Whale, who first swam the Tallapoosa, but the rifle never reached him. He was awarded a replica, decades later, that included "a plate-likeness of General Jackson." "Restoration of a Rifle to a Cherokee Warrior," *Harrisburg Democratic Union*, September 6, 1843, p. 1.

89 **"The idea of resisting the authority of the government"** Crawford to Jackson, July 1, 1816, Owsley et al., *Papers of Andrew Jackson*, vol. 4, pp. 48–49.

89 **"Tennesseeans . . . are recorded as the worst sort of robbers"** Jackson to Crawford, June 16, 1816, ibid., p. 45.

89 **"the risk of being murdered at every wigwam . . . value of the land"** "Remonstrance Against the Treaty," undated among papers from 1816, American State Papers, *Indian Affairs, 1815–1827*, pp. 89–91.

90 **"extra service of the most unpleasant nature"** Jackson to Crawford, November 12, 1816, ibid., p. 117.

90 **a warning that their nation might be destroyed** Wilkins, *Cherokee Tragedy*, pp. 93–94.

90 **"some small presents to the fifteen chiefs that attended here"** Jackson to Coffee, September 19, 1816, Owsley et al., *Papers of Andrew Jackson*, vol. 4, p. 63.

90 **George Guess of Sequoyah** His signature is on "Treaty with the Cherokee, September 14, 1816," Kappler, ed., *Indian Affairs: Laws and Treaties*, p. 133.

90 **The Cherokees succeeded in retaining** Wilkins, *Cherokee Tragedy*, p. 94.

Chapter Ten: Let Me See You as I Pass

92 **"I know of no situation combining so many advantages"** Jackson to Crawford, November 12, 1816, American State Papers, *Indian Affairs, 1815–1927*, p. 117.

93 **"I am so deeply impressed"** Jackson to Monroe, November 12, 1816. Owsley et al., *Papers of Andrew Jackson*, vol. 4, pp. 73–74.

93 **Coffee would be an excellent choice** Ibid.

93 **"I wrote to Genl Parker"** Jackson to Coffee, December 26, 1816, ibid., p. 77.

94 **"white with cotton and alive with negroes"** Royall, *Letters from Alabama*.

94 **southern planters generally needed to sell cotton for 10–15 cents a pound** Glaeser, "A Nation of Gamblers," NBER Working Paper 18825, p. 13.

95 **Cotton reached 32 cents . . . 35 cents** All price figures from Cole, *Wholesale Commodity Prices in the United States, 1700–1861*, chart, republished by Centers for International Price Research.

95 **Tennessee Valley soil could produce far more pounds of cotton per acre** From 800 to 1,000 pounds per acre, compared with 300 pounds in the North Carolina uplands. Glaeser, "Nation of Gamblers," p. 13.

95 **sixty field hands could probably have picked six hundred acres** Alan Olmstead and Paul Rhode note a variety of estimates that had been made over generations for how many acres an enslaved field hand could pick in a season—such as 12 acres, 14 acres, 42.5 acres, or even more—but cast doubt on them, and observe that ratios above 10 acres per person were considered exceptional on plantations in the early nineteenth century. My calculation of Jackson's operations therefore aims low, assuming 10 acres per field hand and no more. Olmstead and Rhode, "Slave Productivity in Cotton Production," pp. 4–20.

95 **exceeded $35,000, which in 1817 was an income for a prince** This estimate makes the following assumptions:

> 300 acres under cotton cultivation
>
> 600 pounds of cotton per acre
>
> 30 cents, gross sale price per pound of cotton
>
> 10 cents, cost per pound of cotton production
>
> 20 cents, profit per pound of cotton
>
> 300 acres x 600 pounds x 20 cents = $36,000

The calculation conservative estimates for all the numbers. There may have been up to 600 acres under cultivation; Glaeser in "Nation of Gamblers" notes that Alabama soil was said to produce 800 pounds per acre; and prices that year reached 35 cents per pound.

95 **"If I have not that sum in the Bank"** Andrew Jackson to James Jackson, August 28, 1814, Moser et al., *Papers of Andrew Jackson: A Microfilm Supplement*, reel 4.

95 **in 1819 . . . Andrew and Rachel Jackson gave up living in their two-story log house** So says the Hermitage staff; also Parton, *Life of Andrew Jackson*, vol. 1, p. 307.

95 **The old log house was cut down to a single floor and converted into slave quarters** Parton, author of *Life of Andrew Jackson*, apparently saw it in the 1850s, and it can still be seen there.

95 **"Let me see you as I pass"** Jackson to Coffee, September 28, 1817, Owsley et al., *Papers of Andrew Jackson*, vol. 4, p. 138.

96 **dividing the property into city blocks for a new town** Jackson to James Monroe, November 15, 1818, ibid., p. 246. Lots for Marathon had been auctioned in October, according to Rohrbough, *Land Office Business*, p. 123.

96 **"will become one of the largest towns"** Jackson to Coffee, August 12, 1817, Owsley et al., *Papers of Andrew Jackson*, vol. 4, p. 132.

96 **"I am yet confined at this loathsome place"** John Coffee to his wife, Mary, January 3, 1814, transcribed in Sioussat, "Letters of General John Coffee to His Wife," p. 279.

97 **Food was so scarce that prices soared** Rohrbough, *Land Office Business*, p. 121.

97 **"many gentlemen from the Eastern States"** Ibid.

97 **a log cabin in Huntsville** Ibid., pp. 122–23.

97 **close to a million acres** In 1817 the office sold 5,610 acres; in 1818 it would be 973,361.54 acres. Ibid., p. 123.

97 **Buyers formed coalitions . . . their efforts collapsed** An account of this pattern can be found in Chappell, "Some Patterns of Land Speculation in the Old Southwest," pp. 471–72.

97 **And then $78** Coffee to Jackson, February 12, 1818, notes prices of $50, $70, and $78. Andrew Jackson Papers, 1775–1874, reel 24. Also Chappell, "Some Patterns of Land Speculation in the Old Southwest," p. 472.

97 **"The prices have surpassed any ever known in the U.S. heretofore"** Coffee to Jackson, February 12, 1818, Andrew Jackson Papers, 1775–1874, reel 24.

97 **he had failed to forward some $80,000** Numerous documents, including the receiver's admission that he had come up short and a chart of his purchases, are in American State Papers, House of Representatives, 17th Cong., 1st Sess., *Public Lands*, vol. 3, pp. 485–93.

97 **federal patents for more than fifteen thousand acres** According to author's review of the Bureau of Land Management General Land Office Records database.

98 **James Jackson's name would eventually appear** Ibid.

98 **"to purchase or enter lands in the Alabama Territory"** Article of Agreement, March 2, 1818, Owsley et al., *Papers of Andrew Jackson*, vol. 1.

98 **John Donelson, Andrew Jackson's brother-in-law . . . Philadelphia investors** The investors are listed in ibid.

98 **6,700 acres was bought for the partnership, and possibly much more** An examination of federal land records for this book found two or more of the partners' names to be together on land purchases amounting to 6,700 acres. It is possible that other purchases, bearing only a single partner's name, were for the partnership.

99 **"This section I bought at two dollars"** Jackson to Isaac Shelby, November 24, 1818, Owsley et al., *Papers of Andrew Jackson*, vol. 4, p. 250.

99 **sometimes lived there for a month at a time** Jackson to Richard Keith Call, November 27, 1822, ibid., vol. 5, p. 225.

99 **"I am determined to push that farm for a livelihood"** Jackson to John Coffee, ibid., pp. 157–58.

99 **he advertised a $50 reward** *Nashville Whig*, April 24, 1822. James, *Andrew Jackson*, p. 29, quotes a May 1 advertisement from the *Nashville Whig*, and assumes the slave must have been from Melton's Bluff; but Jackson had long since surrendered the bluff for the creation of the town of Marathon. The April 24 advertisement calls it the plantation "near the Big Spring, in Franklin County."

99 **In 1823 he personally led the effort** Ibid., p. 31.

99 **At least one of those tracts became Jackson's third plantation** Jackson's papers include a bill for "sundries" for "the farm of A. J. Hutchings," January 27, 1823, Owsley et al., *Papers of Andrew Jackson*, vol. 5, pp. 245–56.

99 **twenty-two hundred acres were purchased under the name of William Donelson** According to author's review of the Bureau of Land Management General Land Office Records database.

100 **it paid $85,000 for the land** Garrett, *History of Florence, Alabama*, p. 4.

100 **quickly resold it (in half-acre town lots) for $229,000** *History of Florence* has a list of buyers whose purchases total this amount, pp. 4–7. A March 1818 document, "List of Purchasers of Lots in the Town of Florence," reflects a similar tally as reconstructed by company officials after the 1827 fire that destroyed Cypress Land Company documents. The List of Purchasers, from the record of an 1840s lawsuit, was copied by Florence historian Milly Wright, who graciously supplied it to the author.

100 **taking the title of a Florence man's home** "Fulton to Jackson & others," in Lauderdale County Deed Records, February 21, 1829, book 4, pp. 304–5, states that William Fulton owed Jackson and others $400 for his purchase of "Florence Stock" as well as other debts, and so would surrender the 7½ acres "whereon the said William Fulton now lives." Signatories included "Andrew Jackson, by his attorney in fact John Coffee."

101 **he advanced $20,000 to buy a strip of land . . . . "doceur"** The transaction is described in the journal kept by federal negotiators, in the entry for October 17, 1818. Jackson, Shelby, et al. *"Secret" Journal on Negotiations of the Chickasaw Treaty, 1818.*

101 **repaid James Jackson's $20,000** Farrell, *"James Jackson, Thomas Kirkman and the Chickasaw Treaty of 1818,"* p. 2.

102 **"correct" his reports** James Monroe to Jackson, July 19, 1818, Owsley et al., *Papers of Andrew Jackson*, vol. 4, p. 227.

103 **their offered report included a veiled reference to it** The Senate report, February 24, 1819, reprinted in the *National Intelligencer*, says that Jackson's motive "seems to have been to involve the nation in a war without her consent, and for reasons of his own, unconnected with his military functions."

103 **"hypocritical lying puppy"** Jackson to Coffee, April 3, 1819, Owsley et al., *Papers of Andrew Jackson*, vol. 4, pp. 279–80.

103 **John Donelson . . . carrying a letter of introduction from Andrew Jackson** According to an affidavit by Thomas Childress, January 12, 1820, ibid., p. 351.

103 **"Pensacola speculation"** John McCrea to Jackson, April 15, 1819, ibid., p. 285.

103 **"friendly motives"** Affidavit by Thomas Childress, January 12, 1820, ibid., p. 351.

104 **A pamphlet during the 1828 campaign** This was a special edition of the *Kentucky Reporter*, a newspaper linked to Henry Clay. A barely readable copy of the pamphlet is in Dyas Collection—John Coffee Papers.

104 **On December 14, 1827... fire consumed the building** Garrett, *History of Florence*, p. 4.

Part Four: Young Prince, 1820–1828
Chapter Eleven: This Unexpected Weapon of Defence

107 **The house said alot about Ross** Ross may have built it after 1816, though local tradition dates it earlier. DeWeese et al., "Dating of the Chief John Ross House," *Southeastern Archaeology*, Winter 2012, p. 221.

108 **"I have been induced to accept of the command of the Cherokee Light horse"** All text of this letter comes from Ross to Andrew Jackson, June 19, 1820, Moulton, *Papers of Chief John Ross*, vol. 1, pp. 40–41.

108 **"I have no troops within three hundred miles of the cherokee nation"** Jackson to Return J. Meigs, February 28, 1820, Owsley et al., *Papers of Andrew Jackson*, vol. 4, p. 358.

109 **"talk big"** Ibid.

109 **intruders had ignored a January first deadline to depart** Correspondence to and from the office of Secretary of War John C. Calhoun shows an Indian agent being told on October 11, 1819, that he must order white intruders to "remove by the 1st January next, and that, after that time, no indulgence will be given them." On January 29, 1820, the deadline past, the agent is merely told to urge the intruders to leave, although "force must be used" at some undetermined time if they have not. Meriwether et al., *Papers of John C. Calhoun*, vol. 4, pp. 369–70, 616.

109 **"shrubing" work was "indispensible"** Jackson to John C. Calhoun, May 17, 1820, Owsley et al., *Papers of Andrew Jackson*, vol. 4, p. 369.

110 **"will give us the whole country in less than two years"** Jackson to John Coffee, July 13, 1817, ibid., p. 126.

110 **"except those prepared for agricultural persuits, civil life, & a government of laws"** Ibid., pp. 126–27.

111 **imposed over the protest of dozens** Sixty-seven leaders, according to Moulton, *John Ross, Cherokee Chief*, p. 19.

111 **"the interposition of your Fatherly hand"** Ross to James Monroe, March 5, 1819, Moulton, *Papers of Chief John Ross*, vol. 1, pp. 34–35.

112 **"the conduct of the malitious and lawless class"** Ross to William H. Crawford, March 12, 1816, ibid., p. 27.

112 **a little army of about seventy** Richard Keith call to Jackson, July 8, 1820, Owsley et al., *Papers of Andrew Jackson*, vol. 4, p. 373.

113 **Jackson believed it was a mistake** He expressed this view to George Graham, July 22, 1817, ibid., p. 128.

Chapter Twelve: Ominous of Other Events

115 **"in direct lines to the South seas"** Colonial charter quoted in Harden, *Life of George M. Troup*, p. 1.

115 **"These parts are little known"** Gabriel, *Elias Boudinot, Cherokee, and His America*, 1799 map reproduced on unnumbered page.

115 **A map made by a Virginian** The story of the map is told in Cohen, *Mapping the West*, pp. 58–59.

116 **"The government is determined to exert all its energy"** Jefferson's letter was reprinted in *Niles' Weekly Register,* January 23, 1830, p. 357.

116 **"extinguish the Indian title . . . peaceably obtained, on reasonable terms"** Articles of Agreement and Cession, April 24, 1802, American State Papers, 7th Cong-, 1st Sess., Doc. 69, pp. 113–14.

116 **"The same treaty ought to have extinguished"** Harden, *Life of George M. Troup,* p. 198.

117 **"insisting" on an "immediate fulfillment"** Letter reprinted in ibid., p. 218.

117 **"insult" . . . "defiance"** Adams diary entry, February 12, 1824, *Memoirs of John Quincy Adams,* vol. 6, p. 255.

117 **"His Excellency, Governor and Commander"** For example, in a document reprinted in Troup, *Governor's Message,* p. 73.

117 **"The President spoke of the compact"** Adams diary entry, March 29, 1824, *Memoirs of John Quincy Adams,* vol. 6, p. 272.

118 **"manners and deportment . . . like ourselves," "purfled scarf"** Ibid., p. 373.

118 **"They are now . . . about fifteen thousand"** Ibid., p. 272.

118 **"write their own State papers"** Ibid., p. 373.

118 **"general expressions of kindness"** Ibid.

119 **"The great difficulty arises from the progress of the Cherokees"** Ibid., pp. 272–73.

119 **"I suspected this bursting forth of Georgia"** Adams diary entry, February 12, 1824, ibid., p. 256.

Chapter Thirteen: The Taverns Were Unknown to Us

120 **take over part of Florida** John Ross et al. to secretary of war, early 1824, cited in Harden, *Life of George M. Troup,* p. 202.

120 **"enter into a treaty with the United States"** Ibid., pp. 202–3.

120 **"the day would arrive . . . *prejudice* will be removed"** Ross et al. to "His Excellency John Q. Adams," March 12, 1825, reproduced in Troup, *Governor's Message,* pp. 127–28.

122 **A full-color portrait shows Major Ridge** McKenney and Hall, *History of the Indian Tribes,* vol. 2, p. 76.

122 **"He who slays the enemy in the path"** Ibid., p. 77.

122 **his father loaded the family onto canoes and fled** Ibid., p. 78.

122 **"I shall make you dreadful"** Ibid., p. 79; Wilkins, *Cherokee Tragedy,* pp. 11–12.

122 **Ridge killed a white man with a spear** Wilkins, *Cherokee Tragedy,* p. 15.

123 **"I came along the top of the mountain"** McKenney and Hall, *History of the Indian Tribes,* vol. 2, p. 77.

123 **a pistal, a tomahawk, and a spade** Wilkins, *Cherokee Tragedy,* pp. 37–38.

123 **Sehoya or Susanna, may have spurred him** Wilkins, *Cherokee Tragedy,* p. 28.

123 **1,141 peach trees . . . thirty slaves** Ibid., pp. 181–83.

124 **a ferry, a toll road, and a popular trading post** Ibid., p. 183.

124 **tribute totaling $25,000** Major Ridge received $10,000; his son, John Ridge, $15,000. Ibid., p. 171.

124 **Pathkiller . . . [and Charles Hicks] had died** Anderson et al., *Payne-Butrick Papers,* vol. 2, pp. 143–44.

124 Charles Hicks . . . had been tutoring Ross on Cherokee history Moulton calls him
     Ross's "mentor," in *John Ross: Cherokee Chief*, p. 33. Upon Hicks's death he left Ross
     papers on Cherokee history, which were still in his possession years later. Anderson
     et al., *Payne-Butrick Papers*, Introduction to Vols. 1–3, p. xvi.

125 a hundred one-acre lots Cherokee legislative resolution, November 12, 1825, quoted
     in Woodward, *The Cherokees*, p. 151. David Gomez, manager of the New Echota
     historic site, adds that some buyers purchased multiple acres, giving New Echota
     more the feel of a rural village; interview, September 2014.

125 "would be called respectable in Litchfield County" Benjamin Gold to Gold and
     Vaill, October 29, 1829, reproduced in Gaul, *To Marry an Indian*, p. 166.

125 two floors, one for each branch of the legislature, with simple wooden benches The
     original structure is long since gone, but a replica stands at the New Echota historic
     site.

125 "From my earliest Boyhood . . . firmly confirmed" Ross to Andrew Johnson, June
     28, 1866, Moulton, *Papers of Chief John Ross*, vol. 2, p. 678.

126 "We, the representatives of the people of the CHEROKEE NATION" *Cherokee
     Phoenix*, February 21, 1828, p. 1.

126 In 1810, one Christian mission Conversion figures from McLoughlin, *Cherokee
     Renascence*, chart p. 382.

127 scholar reported that they did not want to expose tribal divisions Ibid., pp. 391–93.

127 1821, when some local chiefs allegedly conspired Ibid., pp. 269–70.

127 "Article I, Sec. 1" *Cherokee Phoenix*, February 21, 1828, p. 1.

128 "every expense" John Cocke to John Ross and Major Ridge, October 1827, reprinted
     in *Cherokee Phoenix*, May 28, 1828.

128 despised the federal practice of calling special meetings Ross to Monroe, March 5,
     1819, Moulton, *Papers of Chief John Ross*, vol. 1, pp. 34–35.

128 "We are correctly informed" John Cocke to John Ross and Major Ridge, October
     1827, reprinted in *Cherokee Phoenix*, May 28, 1828.

129 "We are sorry to discover" Ross and Ridge to Cocke et al., October 11, 1827,
     reprinted in *Cherokee Phoenix*, May 28, 1828.

129 "It is true there is no palace" John Cocke to John Ross and Major Ridge, October
     1827, ibid.

129 "We do not understand the idea" Ross and Ridge to Cocke et al., ibid.

129 "As to the four taverns spoken of we assure you that they were unknown to us" Ibid.

130 "In giving you this definitive reply" Ross and other Cherokee legislators to Cocke et
     al., ibid.

Interlude: Hero's Progress, 1824–1825
Chapter Fourteen: Liberty, Equality, and True Social Order

133 "walking and talking and coughing" Smith, *First Forty Years of Washington Society*,
     p. 146.

134 "At an early hour the galleries" *Argus of Western America*, January 5, 1825, p. 1.

134 women had been granted a rare dispensation *National Intelligencer*, December 11,
     1824, p. 3.

134 "A great number of additional seats" *Argus of Western America*, January 5, 1825.

134 contested vote, 90–69 *National Intelligencer*, December 11, 1824, p. 3.

135 **"General La Fayette entered the House"** *Argus of Western America*, January 5, 1825, p. 1.

135 **"Few of the members who compose this body"** Clay speech reprinted in *Argus of Western America*, January 5, 1825.

136 **Jackson was in Washington that December** He arrived on December 7. Jackson to William Berkeley Lewis, December 8, 1824, Owsley et al., *Papers of Andrew Jackson*, vol. 5, p. 453.

136 **"the forests felled"** *Argus of Western America*, January 5, 1825, p. 1.

136 **estimated at fifty thousand** Unknown, *Life of Lafayette*, p. 127.

137 **an article on Lafayette appeared in** *Tuscumbian*, September 8, 1824, p. 3.

137 **"the Oriental languages"... "Rhetoric and Eloquence"... "the useful arts"** Levasseur, *Lafayette in America*, vol. 1, pp. 40–41.

137 **"immense and splendid cut-glass chandelier"** Unknown, *Life of Lafayette*, p. 151.

137 **Vanderbilt boats... Northeast Corridor** Stiles, *Commodore*, p. 70.

137 **"three hundred weavers... one hundred and fifty butchers"** Unknown, *Life of Lafayette*, p. 154.

137 **"the thunder of a cannon a thousand times repeated"** Levasseur, *Lafayette in America*, vol. 1, p. 107.

138 **"houses, trees and animals"** Ibid., p. 96.

138 **"without resting one day"** Jackson to William Berkeley Lewis, December 8, 1824, Owsley et al., *Papers of Andrew Jackson*, vol. 5, p. 453.

138 **"My dear husband was unwell nearly the whole of our journey"** Rachel Jackson to Elizabeth Kingsley, December 23, 1824, ibid., p. 456.

138 **"is in better health than when we came"** Ibid.

139 **a Pawnee chief, in full headdress, observing the proceedings** The House historian describes the chief as Pawnee. Office of the Historian and Clerk of the House, "Old Hall of the House of Representatives," *History, Art & Archives, United States House of Representatives*, history.house.gov.

139 **"continued devotion to liberty"** Levasseur, *Lafayette in America*, vol. 2, p. 15.

139 **"your consistency of character"** *Argus of Western America*, January 5, 1825, p. 1.

139 **"very evidently affected"** Ibid.

140 **"Well may I stand firm and erect"** Ibid.

140 **$50 REWARD** Ibid.

141 **A proposal for a tax... was defeated, 33–30** Ibid.

142 **between "rash" abolitionists and those who found slavery a "blessing"** Clay, *Speech of the Hon. Henry Clay Before the American Colonization Society*, January 20, 1827.

Chapter Fifteen: Clay Is Politically Damd

143 **"paralyzed all the electoral ardour"** Levasseur, *Lafayette in America*, vol. 2, p. 23.

143 **"been able to restrict... ambitious and designing"** Ibid.

144 **secretary of state preparing to sleep with the common passengers** Ibid., pp. 161–62.

144 **"I had never thought the probability of my election sufficient"** Adams diary entry, December 15, 1824, *Memoirs of John Quincy Adams*, vol. 6, p. 443.

144 **"Pennsylvania Hospital for Sick and Insane Persons"** Adams diary entry, October 4, 1824, ibid., p. 423.

144 **the experience had not reformed him in any way** Levasseur, *Lafayette in America*, vol. 1, p. 154.

145 "vice and guilty lives . . . and scorn" Adams diary entry, October. 4 1824, *Memoirs of John Quincy Adams*, vol. 6, p. 423.

145 "the emotion of revolutionary feeling was aroused in them both" Rachel Jackson to Elizabeth Kingsley, December 23, 1824, Owsley et al., *Papers of Andrew Jackson*, vol. 5, p. 456.

145 "He wears a wig" Ibid.

146 "nothing but shew" Jackson to Coffee, January 23, 1825, ibid., vol. 6, p. 18.

146 "when I have . . . become a little acquainted" Jackson to William Berkeley Lewis, December 9, 1824, ibid., vol. 5, p. 453.

146 ended an alcohol-lubricated dinner by dancing Heidler and Heidler, *Henry Clay: The Essential American*, p. 45.

147 "Whatever he is, is all his own" Smith to Mrs. Boyd, 1829, Smith, *First Forty Years of Washington Society*, p. 285.

147 opponents who said they were not authorized by the Constitution Clay's accomplishment is summarized in Schlesinger, *Age of Jackson*, pp. 11–12.

148 "Wonderful energy . . . within the pale of the Constitution" Clay, *Speeches of Henry Clay*, p. 155.

148 "did not lose a word" Smith, *First Forty Years in Washington Society*, p. 145.

148 Jackson was growing so famous he was mobbed in the streets Remini describes such scenes in *Andrew Jackson and the Course of American Empire, 1767–1821*, vol. 1, pp. 374–75.

148 "pure . . . principle of insubordination" Clay, *Speeches of Henry Clay*, p. 161.

148 "dictatorial spirit," and "utterly irreconcilable" Ibid., p. 148.

148 "came and sat a few minutes" Smith, *First Forty Years in Washington Society*, p. 146.

149 "Clay is politically damd . . . I wish him to scorch him" Jackson to William Berkeley Lewis, January 30, 1819, Owsley et al., *Papers of Andrew Jackson*, vol. 3, pp. 268–69.

149 "personal vengeance, even to cutting off the ears of some of the members" *National Intelligencer*, March 2, 1819, p. 2.

149 Jackson mastered his rage. He met Clay for dinner One such dinner in November 1823 is described in Heidler and Heidler, *Henry Clay: The Essential American*, p. 164; another came in February 1824, and is described in *Memoirs of John Quincy Adams*, vol. 6, p. 258.

150 "If Louisiana has not voted for Mr Clay he is not in the house" Jackson to William Berkeley Lewis, December 9, 1824, Owsley et al., *Papers of Andrew Jackson*, vol. 5, p. 453.

150 "I should never have aspired to the responsibility" To John Overton, December 19, 1824, ibid., p. 455.

150 his supporters reached out to Clay Clay to Francis Preston Blair, January 8, 1825, does not name names but describes their arguments, Hopkins et al., *Papers of Henry Clay*, vol. 4, p. 9.

150 One was Sam Houston Parton, *Life of Andrew Jackson*, vol. 3, pp. 57–58. Also John Sloane to Clay, May 9, 1844, in Hopkins et al., *Papers of Henry Clay*, vol. 10, p. 58.

151 Buchanan . . . took a similar message directly to Clay Ibid., pp. 56–57.

151 "some confidential conversation upon public affairs" Adams diary entry, January 1, 1825, *Memoirs of John Quincy Adams*, vol. 6, p. 457.

151 "choice of evils" Clay to Francis Preston Blair, January 8, 1825, Hopkins et al., *Papers of Henry Clay*, vol. 4, p. 9.

151 "In the election of Mr Adams" Ibid., p. 10.

151 **"Too much of a Soldier to be a civilian"** Meigs to Clay, September 3, 1822, ibid., vol. 3, p. 282.

151 **Latin was taught in many schools . . . set up for Indians** Such as the Foreign Mission School in Cornwall, Connecticut. Starr, *History of Cornwall,* p. 141.

151 **introduced to Greek and Roman writers while serving as an apprentice** Peterson, *Great Triumvirate,* p. 9.

152 *"Veni, vidi, vici"* Clay, *Speeches of Henry Clay,* p. 148.

152 **"gross" . . . "preference would be for me"** Adams diary entry, January 9, 1825, *Memoirs of John Quincy Adams,* vol. 6, p. 464.

152 **fifty to a hundred a day** Rachel Jackson to Elizabeth Kingsley, December 23, 1824, Owsley et al., *Papers of Andrew Jackson,* vol. 5, p. 456.

153 **"I have been interrupted twenty times"** Jackson to William Berkeley Lewis, January 29, 1825, ibid., vol. 6, p. 22.

153 **"2 Extra Dinners in Private Parlour"** Account for "Genl Jackson & Lady," January 1825, ibid., p. 16.

153 **"wager wine"** Ibid.

153 **He'd arrived in Washington with $2,300** Jackson to John Coffee, January 23, 1825, and February 19, 1825, ibid., p. 35.

153 **"We are all well . . . my advise was nothing"** Rachel Jackson to Mary Purnell Donelson, January 27, 1825, ibid., pp. 20–21.

153 **Jackson slipped on his way up Gadsby's stairs** Parton, *Life of Jackson,* vol. 3, p. 63.

153 **"Let me rise or fall"** Jackson to John Overton, December 19, 1824, Owsley et al., *Papers of Andrew Jackson,* vol. 5, p. 455.

154 **Jackson gained 42 percent** Figures here calculated from Jenkins and Sala, "Spatial Theory of Voting and the Presidential Election of 1824," Table, 1, p. 1160.

155 **"With regard to the Presidency"** Jackson to Chandler Price, January 9, 1825, Owsley et al., *Papers of Andrew Jackson,* vol. 6, p. 11.

155 **"should this unholy coalition prevail"** Letter reprinted in *National Intelligencer,* February 4, 1825.

155 **have turned upon me . . . think imp[lies] guilt"** Clay to Francis Preston Blair, January 29, 1825, Hopkins et al., *Papers of Henry Clay,* vol. 4, p. 46.

156 **"open and sincere"** Levasseur, *Lafayette in America,* vol. 2, p. 24.

156 **"determined opposition"** Adams diary entry, February 11, 1825, *Memoirs of John Quincy Adams,* pp. 506–7.

156 **Clay hesitated, sensing the danger, but accepted** Heidler and Heidler, *Henry Clay: The Essential American,* p. 184.

156 **"such a bare faced corruption . . . his end will be the same"** Jackson to Lewis, February 14, 1825, Owsley et al., *Papers of Andrew Jackson,* vol. 6, p. 29.

Chapter Sixteen: We Wish to Know Whether You Could Protect Us

157 **"The walls are entirely covered"** Trollope cited in Wilkins, *Cherokee Tragedy,* pp. 173–74.

157 **"noble and warlike . . . simplicity"** Ibid.

157 **"Our heads have become white"** Wilkins, *Cherokee Tragedy,* p. 163.

158 **"Our hearts have been with you always"** Ibid.

158 **commissions totaling $25,000** Ibid.

158 **"Friends and Brothers ... limits of Georgia"** McKenney to John Ross et al., March 12, 1825, reproduced in Troup, *Governor's Message*, p. 121.

158 **"It would seem from the enquiry ... unchangeable"** Ross et al. to McKenney, March 12, 1825, ibid.

159 **"essentially inferior" "I fear there is too much foundation"** Adams diary entry, December 21, 1825, *Memoirs of John Quincy Adams*, vol. 7, p. 89.

159 **"small, solitary inn"** Levasseur, *Lafayette in America*, vol. 2, pp. 30–31.

159 **"The coolness of the night"** Ibid., p. 45.

159 **"balls, displays of artificial fire-works, and entertainments"** Ibid., p. 48.

159 **the great man was saluted with cannon fire from Fort Moultrie** Ibid., p. 56.

159 **Army engineers were finally planning a new fortress** A National Park Service paper says it was proposed in 1805 and construction began in December 1828. Ferguson, "An Overview of the Events at Fort Sumter, 1829–1991," p. 5.

159 **pervasive emotion: "fear"** Levasseur, *Lafayette in America*, vol. 2, p. 52.

160 **Denmark Vesey was plotting a slave insurrection.** An account of the plot is found in Robertson, *Denmark Vesey*.

160 **One measure decreed that when ships docked** Freehling, *Road to Disunion*, vol. 1, p. 254.

160 **"insubordination" was "paramount" to "all laws" and "all constitutions"** Reid, *Origins of the American Civil War*, p. 53.

160 **"scaffolding, scaffolding, Sir—it will come away when the building is finished"** Peterson, *Great Triumvirate*, p. 257.

160 **sleeping in the only house that had a roof** Levasseur, *Lafayette in America*, vol. 2, p. 39.

161 **They sold their stake in South Carolina for $5,000** Moulton, *John Ross, Cherokee Chief*, pp. 15–16.

161 **unlimited funds from the treasury** Harden, *Life of George M. Troup*, p. 298.

161 **family Bible recorded their flight** Ibid., p. 2.

162 **"to stand to your arms" ... "fanatics"** Troup, May 23, 1825, *Governor's Message*, pp. 7–8.

162 **Horses pulled them on a kind of parade float** Levasseur, *Lafayette in America*, vol. 2, p. 58.

162 **"La Fayette mania ... the *nations jest*"** Wood, *Mary Telfair to Mary Few*, pp. 51, 54.

162 **"a civilized speck lost in the yet immense domain"** Levasseur, *Lafayette in America*, vol. 2, p. 70.

162 **Once the party had to cross a stream** Ibid., p. 79.

163 **"[Hamley's] countenance became somber"** Ibid., vol. 2, p. 73.

164 **the president ... concluded that the men acted as agents for Georgia** Adams diary entry, December 20, 1825, *Memoirs of John Quincy Adams*, vol. 7, p. 87.

164 **a bribe of $2,000 ... "Nobody shall know it"** Letter is copied in Anderson et al., *Payne-Butrick Papers*, vol. 2, pp. 195–96.

164 **offered $10,000 and five square miles** Troup, May 23, 1825, *Governor's Message*, pp. 7–8.

165 **"We are happy to inform you that the 'long agony is over'"** Ibid., pp. 71–72.

165 **instructions on how to send $2,000 that Troup had promised** Ibid., p. 74.

165 **"If [critics of the treaty] should attempt"** Ibid., p. 87.

165 **Contact with white men was destroying the Creeks** Levasseur, *Lafayette in America*, vol. 2, p. 75.

165 **He might have burned to death** An account of the killing is in Wilkins, *Cherokee Tragedy*, p. 165.

166 **"infinitely rather"** Adams diary entry, December 21, 1825, *Memoirs of John Quincy Adams*, vol. 7, p. 89.

166 **"commit suicide"** Ibid., p. 106.

166 **"the most momentous message I have ever sent to Congress"** Adams diary entry, *Memoirs of John Quincy Adams*, vol. 7, p. 221.

167 **the first white settler in Tennessee** Levasseur, *Lafayette in America*, vol. 2, p. 512. Also *Niles' Weekly Register*, May 28, 1825.

167 **"having in view the same object"** Henry Baldwin to Jackson, April 11, 1825, Owsley et al., *Papers of Andrew Jackson*, vol. 6, p. 58.

167 **"I believe myself worthy of them"** Levasseur, *Lafayette in America*, vol. 2, p. 157.

Part Five: Inaugurations, 1828–1829
Chapter Seventeen: We Are Politically Your Friends and Brethren

171 **and increasingly afterward became its own self-confident creation** Among those identifying 1828 as a year of division is David Reynolds, in *Waking Giant*, p. 238.

172 **$1,500 toward establishing the newspaper and a National Academy** Wilkins, *Cherokee Tragedy*, p. 187.

172 **he paid the bills from his own pocket** Ross described giving the paper's editor funds in a letter on November 4, 1829, Moulton, *Papers of Chief John Ross*, vol. 1, p. 176.

173 **thirteen colonies supported 37 newspapers . . . 1828 there were 802** All figures from the U.S. Post Office Department, as recorded by Simmonds, "Statistics of Newspapers in Various Countries," pp. 120–22.

173 **cheap "penny papers" . . . would vastly expand newspaper circulation** Reynolds, *Waking Giant*, pp. 240–41.

173 **Henry Clay once loaned an editor $1,500** The editor was Amos Kendall, who later went over to Andrew Jackson. Cole, *A Jackson Man*, p. 89.

173 **a year and a half's worth of issues** According to Marsha Mullin, chief curator, the Hermitage. A receipt for 17 subscription payments is in Moulton, *Papers of Andrew Jackson*, May 1825, vol. 6, pp. 66–67.

174 **first black-owned and black-operated newspaper** Bacon, "The History of *Freedom's Journal*," p. 1.

174 **Samuel Worcester . . . obtaining the necessary equipment** Bass, *Cherokee Messenger*, pp. 78–79. Also Malone, "The Cherokee Phoenix: Supreme Expression of Cherokee Nationalism," p. 165.

174 **"Murder . . . not heard of the circumstances"** *Cherokee Phoenix*, March 26, 1828, p. 3.

174 **leaving the suspect "unmolested"** Ibid., April 3, 1828, p. 2.

174 **He was acquitted** Ibid., June 11, 1828, p. 2.

174 **"Subscribers who can only read the Cherokee language"** Ibid., April 10, 1828.

174 **population conservatively estimated at thirteen thousand . . . 46,700 hogs** Ibid., May 14, 1828, p. 3.

175 **"shall lay violent hands . . . to her consent"** Ibid., p. 1.

175 **"Resolved by the National Committee"** Ibid., April 24, 1828, p. 1.

175 "I stood on Cape Montserado . . . degradation of the Africans" Ibid., March 6, 1828, p. 3.

176 receive copies of about a hundred other papers Perdue, ed., *Cherokee Editor: The Writings of Elias Boudinot*, p. 16.

176 "may very properly be regarded as *something new*" *United States Telegraph*, March 17, 1828.

176 religious journals that were the era's most widely read publications Hershberger, "Mobilizing Women, Anticipating Abolition," p. 18.

176 a well with a windlass built into the porch Harriett Gold to Herman and Flora Gold Vaill, January 7, 1831, Gaul, *To Marry an Indian*, p. 172.

177 "Our water is so sweet & pure" Ibid.

177 "The Editor of this paper regrets" *Cherokee Phoenix*, April 8, 1829, p. 2.

177 the printer . . . A Methodist Elias and Harriett Boudinot to Herman and Flora Gold Vaill, January 23, 1829, Gaul, *To Marry an Indian*, p. 161.

177 "What is an Indian?" Boudinot's 1826 speech is quoted in Gabriel, *Elias Boudinot*, p. 3.

178 "long lost tribes of Israel" Boudinot, *Star in the West*, p. iii.

178 "Latin, Greek . . . removal of the tribe to the West" Starr, *History of Cornwall*, p. 141.

178 "rash presumption & disobedience" Gaul, *To Marry an Indian*, p. 91.

178 Harriett's own brother lit the fire Ibid., p. 1.

179 one-fourth of the entire Cherokee Nation had at least some white ancestry Kilpatrick and Kilpatrick, *New Echota Letters*, pp. 84–85.

179 "I remain your Indian Brother" Elias and Harriett Boudinot to Herman and Flora Gold Vaill, January 23, 1829, Gaul, *To Marry an Indian*, p. 161.

179 "AN IMITATION INDIAN" *Cherokee Phoenix*, July 2, 1828, p. 3.

180 "electioneering" letters Ibid., July 23, 1828, p. 2.

180 "Presidential Election" Ibid., December 3, 1828, p. 2.

180 The first was to take away . . . printing press John Macpherson Berrien to Jackson, June 25, 1830, Owsley et al., *Papers of Andrew Jackson*, vol. 8, p. 392.

Chapter Eighteen: This Is a Straight and Good Talk

181 "serene and mild" . . . "an immense concourse of spectators" *Niles' Weekly Register*, vol. 36, 1829, p. 28.

181 "The barrier that had separated the people" Smith, *First Forty Years of Washington Society*, p. 294.

181 "carriages, wagons and carts" . . . "women and children, black and white" Ibid.

182 had to be wedged out of the house Meacham *American Lion*, p. 62.

182 "the present season is sacred to sorrow" Jackson to Francis P. Blair et al., January 1, 1829, Owsley et al., *Papers of Andrew Jackson*, vol. 7, pp. 3–4.

182 "It pleased God to take her from this world" Jackson to Katherine Duane Morgan, January 3, 1829, ibid., p. 5.

182 "abandon your just grief" Edward Livingston to Jackson, January 3, 1829, ibid., p. 6.

182 "I have this day got my dear Mrs. J Tomb" Jackson to Coffee, January 17, 1829, ibid., pp. 12–13.

183   inventory of ninety-five slaves Ibid., pp. 8–10.
183   "Every one of the public men" Smith, *First Forty Years of Washington Society,* p. 259.
183   "Shoot the damned rascal!" *Truth's Advocate and Monthly Anti-Jackson Expositor,* April 1828, pp. 121–27.
183   A special edition of the *Kentucky Reporter* A tattered copy of it is found in *Dyas Collection—John Coffee Papers.*
184   "a degraded female . . . National morals" *Truth's Advocate and Monthly Anti-Jackson Expositor,* January 1828, p. 4.
184   "the planters of the South" Howe, *What Hath God Wrought,* pp. 279–80.
185   one Caleb Atwater of Ohio Atwater to Jackson, Owsley et al., *Papers of Andrew Jackson,* vol. 7, pp. 44–45.
185   "The curse of God will afflict a Sabbath-breaking nation" Charles Coffin to Jackson, January 21, 1829, ibid., pp. 16–17.
185   "distinguish himself as a patriot" From Ezra Stiles Ely to Jackson, transcribing a note from Beecher, ibid., p. 21.
185   "decent pretext" H. M. Breckenridge to Jackson, February 4, 1829, ibid., pp. 29–30.
186   "I . . . shall be the last to cry out treason" Draft of inaugural address, undated, ibid., p. 76.
186   "First, the removal of the Indians" Van Buren, *Autobiography,* p. 275.
187   "No Indian, and no descendant" *Cherokee Phoenix,* December 3, 1828, p. 3.
187   "expulsion" Ibid., p. 2.
187   "The course pursued by Georgia" Jackson to Overton, June 8, 1829, Owsley et al., *Papers of Andrew Jackson,* vol. 7, pp. 270–71.
188   "Friends & Brothers . . . hear his counsel" Jackson to the Creek Indians, March 23, 1829, ibid., pp. 112–13.
189   "I return herewith the resolutions" Ross to the National Committee, October 29, 1828, Moulton, *Papers of Chief John Ross,* vol. 1, p. 145.
189   only an oblique mention of his dead child He referred only to "the sudden manner in which I was called home," Ross to Lewis Ross, October 30, 1828, ibid.
190   "the present U.S. agent . . . does not . . . inspire . . . confidence" Ross to Jackson, March 6, 1829, ibid., p. 157.
191   "the tribe established an independent government" John Eaton to Ross, April 18, 1829, ibid., pp. 162–63.
191   "the soil shall be yours, while the trees grow or the streams run" Jackson quoted in ibid.
191   "much longer than desired or anticipated" Ross to Jeremiah Evarts, May 6, 1829, ibid., p. 164.
191   "What will be the result" Ibid.

Chapter Nineteen: The Blazing Light of the Nineteenth Century

193   "Gentlemen: I send for your paper" *National Intelligencer,* August 1, 1829.
194   "I shall not agree with the present Executive" Ibid.
194   Evarts was the one who helped to have a press sent from Boston Bass, *Cherokee Messenger,* pp. 78–79.
195   "I could hear some words distinctly; but could not keep the connexion" Evarts to Henry Hill, March 5, 1829, cited in Oliphant, *Through the South and West with Jeremiah Evarts in 1826,* p. 50.

195 **"a direct collision between the national and state authorities"** Evarts quoted in ibid., p. 49.

195 **"No relief can be hoped"** Evarts, March 10, 1829, quoted in ibid., p. 53.

195 **"they may be copied into semi-weekly papers, if their Editors see fit"** *National Intelligencer*, August 1, 1829. Tracy, *Memoir of the Life of Jeremiah Evarts, Esq.*, p. 33.

195 **"the greatest kindness . . . shall have passed away"** *National Intelligencer*, August 5, 1829.

196 **"There sat Evarts, in a plain rustic garb"** Tracy, *Memoir of the Life of Jeremiah Evarts, Esq.*, p. 11.

196 **"In my leisure moments"** Ibid., p. 33.

197 **dancing was a "temptation"** Ibid., p. 13.

197 **From 1810 to 1821 he edited the *Panoplist*** Ibid., p. 55.

197 **"the entire subjugation of the world to Christ"** Ibid., p. 64.

197 **"a stupid contempt of death"** Ibid., p. 77.

197 **$3.235 billion** Ibid.

198 **"I was never in a place where so many people might give largely"** Ibid., p. 117.

198 **"exceedingly disconsolate, much as if they were led to execution"** Journal extract, from ibid., p. 114.

198 **"Black men will at last be free"** Ibid., p. 84.

198 **a journey of 768 miles** Oliphant, *Through the South and West with Jeremiah Evarts in 1826*, p. 117.

198 **He stayed for days at Brainerd . . . admiring the sun setting** Evarts journal reproduced in Tracy, *Memoir of the Life of Jeremiah Evarts, Esq.*, pp. 120–21.

198 **twenty-five-acre compound . . . John McDonald** Moulton, *John Ross, Cherokee Chief*, p. 7.

199 **"disappearance from the human family would be no great loss to the world"** Clay's remark described in Adams diary entry, December 21, 1825, *Memoirs of John Quincy Adams*, vol. 7, pp. 89–90.

199 **"The Cherokees are human beings"** *National Intelligencer*, August 8, 1829.

200 **Some forty other newspapers reprinted his essays** Portnoy, *Their Right to Speak*, p. 26.

200 **"The Letters of WILLIAM PENN"** *National Intelligencer*, October 14, 1829, quoted in ibid., p. 27.

200 **even John Marshall . . . read and approved of them** Oliphant, *Through the South and West with Jeremiah Evarts in 1826*, p. 55.

Part Six: State of the Union, 1829–1830
Chapter Twenty: They Have Been Led to Look Upon Us as Unjust

203 **"Every Indian . . . principal occupations of an Indian"** Cass, "Removal of the Indians," p. 75.

204 **"We speak of them as they are"** Ibid., p. 74.

204 **the magazine published a rebuttal** Portnoy, *Their Right to Speak*, p. 26.

204 **"We believe, if the Indians do not emigrate . . . they must perish"** Banner, *How the Indians Lost Their Land*, p. 209.

205 **"not an improvable breed"** Adams diary entry, December 21, 1825, *Memoirs of John Quincy Adams*, vol. 7, p. 90.

205 "free from the mercenary influence...control over their interests" Jackson to James Gadsden, October 12, 1829, Owsley et al., *Papers of Andrew Jackson*, vol. 7, pp. 491–92.

206 "the condition of the Indians within the limits" Ibid., pp. 609–10.

206 "a power which should be placed in the hands of no individual" Eaton draft of first annual message, ibid., p. 623.

207 "our ancestors found them the uncontrolled *possessors* of these vast regions" Jackson's first annual message as delivered, December 8, 1829, *Journal of the Senate*, 21st Cong., 1st Sess., p. 6.

209 "A crisis seems to be fast approaching" Ross, Annual Message, Moulton, *Papers of Chief John Ross*, vol. 1, p. 172.

Chapter Twenty-one: The Expediency of Setting Fire

210 it was rumors of gold that lured Hernando de Soto Williams, *Georgia Gold Rush*, p. 8.

210 the first public announcement was a news article Ibid., p. 24.

210 "whites, Indians, halfbreeds" Ibid., p. 26.

210 boomtown that would be called Dahlonega Ibid., p. 25.

210 "idle, profligate people...loosed from the restraints of the law" Governor George Gilmer, cited in ibid., p. 26.

211 "almost all had departed" *Cherokee Phoenix*, April 7, 1830, p. 2.

211 Over the course of 1830...$212,000 worth of gold to the U.S. Mint Williams, *Georgia Gold Rush*, p. 28.

212 "could not for a moment think of seeing [the paper] stopped" Ross to National Committee and National Council, November 4, 1829, Moulton, *Papers of Chief John Ross*, vol. 1, p. 176.

212 from Ross's own pocket Ibid.

212 "With the view of preventing erroneous impressions" All text of letter from Ross to Boudinot, February 13, 1830, ibid., pp. 184–87.

213 The Indian agent did try to warn them off *Cherokee Phoenix*, March 11, 1829, p. 3, and December 30, 1829, p. 2.

213 "such person shall forfeit the protection of the United States" Ross, Annual Message, Moulton, *Papers of Chief John Ross*, vol. 1, p. 172.

215 "arrogated to themselves...from their houses" *Cherokee Phoenix*, April 7, 1830, p. 2.

215 "Some of the *officers of the United States*...enrol themselves for the Arkansas" From statement by settlers, March 19, 1830, reprinted in ibid.

Chapter Twenty-two: Sway the Empire of Affection

218 "distressing and disastrous consequences...I was greatly excited" Beecher, *Educational Reminiscences and Suggestions*, p. 62.

218 charitable organizations that promoted public virtue Hershberger, "Mobilizing Women, Anticipating Abolition," pp. 18–19.

218 "by no means excluding females" Lincoln to the editor of the *Sangamo Journal*, June 13, 1836, *Speeches and Writings, 1832–1858*, p. 5.

219 "The present crisis" This and the following Beecher quotes from Ladies' Circular as printed in "Circular Addressed to Benevolent Ladies of the United States," *Connecticut Courant*, December 29, 1829, p. 1.

220 "The circular was to be printed" Beecher, *Educational Reminiscences and Suggestions*, p. 63.

221 "It seemed as if I had a decided genius" Ibid., p. 13.

221 "the busiest of all creatures in doing nothing" Ibid., p. 26.

222 Catharine refused to accept this as a certainty White, *The Beecher Sisters*, p. 6.

222 she developed her own book Beecher, *Educational Reminiscences and Suggestions*, pp. 28–29.

222 "but the more intelligent and influential women came to my aid . . . ever since" Ibid., p. 33.

223 Women started recruiting husbands, sons, and brothers Portnoy, *Their Right to Speak*, p. 26.

223 One young man . . . organized opposition at Andover Hershberger, "Mobilizing Women, Anticipating Abolition," p. 40.

223 Newspapers reprinted the women's circular For example, *Connecticut Courant*, December 29, 1829, p. 1.

223 editors were uncertain of its propriety Hershberger, "Mobilizing Women, Anticipating Abolition," p. 18.

223 public meetings were held in every city Beecher, *Educational Reminiscences and Suggestions*, p. 64.

223 that delicacy of feeling Petition from Farmington, Maine, February 22, 1830. National Archives, Box HR 21A-G-7.1 to HR 21A-G-8.2.

223 "I was asked one day by an outsider" Ibid.

224 "I suddenly found myself utterly prostrated" Ibid., p. 65.

224 "We affirm, that every *slaveholder* is a *man-stealer*" Grimké, *Letters to Catharine E. Beecher*, p. 4.

224 "petitions to congress" Beecher, *Essay on Slavery and Abolitionism*, p. 104.

225 "thousands of petitions, signed by more than a million" Lumpkin, *Removal of the Cherokees from Georgia*, p. 47.

225 thousands of signatures Petitions to Committee on Indian Affairs, 1830–31, National Archives, Box HR 21A-G-8.2, Box HR 21A-G-8.2 (cont'd), Box HR 21A-G-7.1 to HR 21A-G-8.2, Box HR 21A-G-9.1. In studying them the author was following the example of Alisse Portnoy, author of *Their Right to Speak*.

225 "no disrespect . . . unbenevolent males" Hershberger, "Mobilizing Women, Anticipating Abolition," p. 29.

226 Massachusetts, Maine, Vermont Petitions to Committee on Indian Affairs, as above.

226 activists concluded that if Indian removal was wrong Hershberger, "Mobilizing Women, Anticipating Abolition," pp. 35–37.

226 "eternal infamy" Ibid., p. 36.

226 reprinted articles from the *Cherokee Phoenix* Ibid., p. 36.

Part Seven: Checks and Balances, 1830–1832
Chapter Twenty-three: Legislative

229 "My life has never been free from care and responsibility" All of Lumpkin's speech from Lumpkin, *Removal of the Cherokees from Georgia*, pp. 57–74.

230 **"such tribes or nations of Indians as may choose to exchange the lands"** American State Papers, Senate Bill 102, 21st Cong., p. 1.

230 **he had arrived in 1827 with something like this in mind** Lumpkin, *Removal of the Cherokees from Georgia*, p. 42.

231 **first dozen miles** *Niles' Weekly Register*, May 22, 1830, p. 232.

231 **what is now Wisconsin** It was Fort Winnebago. Monroe and McIntosh, eds., *Papers of Jefferson Davis*, pp. 129–67.

231 **In 1830 Lyman Beecher's Boston church burned** Hayward, *Lyman Beecher*, p. 47.

232 **Second Lieutenant Robert E. Lee** Thomas, *Robert E. Lee*, p. 57.

232 **"White men, beware . . . mighty chasms"** Lepore, *In the Name of War*, p. 202.

233 **on February 1, 1830, when a man in the Creek Nation** *Niles' Weekly Register*, June 5, 1830, vol. 38, p. 270.

233 **roughly the same route General Lafayette had taken** Both were likely on or near the federal road described in Benton, *Very Worst Road*.

233 **Believing the Creek man was drunk** Details of the incident as reported by the *Mobile Register* and reprinted in *Niles' Weekly Register*, June 5, 1830, vol. 38, p. 270; also Stuart, *Three Years in North America*, p. 166.

233 **Two troops of cavalry, along with a troop of volunteers** Stuart, *Three Years in North America*, p. 168.

233 **"has thrown the whole country into commotion"** *Mobile Register*, reprinted in *Niles' Weekly Register*, June 5, 1830, vol. 38, p. 270.

233 **"on account of the delinquency of one individual"** Stuart, *Three Years in North America*, p. 168.

234 **"It may be contended, with much plausibility"** Ibid., p. 174.

234 **"handsomely dressed . . . not too nearly inspected"** Ibid., p. 168.

234 **"cheerfully . . . the example of the white man"** American State Papers, Register of Debates, 21st Cong., 1st Sess., May 15, 1830, p. 993.

236 **"incorporate with us as citizens of the United States"** Jefferson to William Henry Harrison, February 27, 1803. Prucha, *Documents of United States Indian Policy*, p. 22.

237 **"Georgia will yield . . . the horrors of civil war"** Speech printed in Evarts, *Speeches on the Passage of the Bill for the Removal of the Indians*, p. 29.

237 **Moving tens of thousands of Indians would cost many times more** Speech printed in ibid., pp. 290–94.

238 **"Several of my colleagues got around me"** Crockett, *Narrative*, pp. 205–6.

238 **"I have been told I will be prostrated"** Evarts, *Speeches on the Passage of the Bill for the Removal of the Indians*, p. 253.

238 **"has an elasticity and buoyancy of spirit"** Margaret Bayard Smith to Mrs. Boyd, Spring 1829, Smith, *First Forty Years of Washington Society*, pp. 285–86.

238 **"We are enjoined by every duty"** Clay, *Address Delivered to the Colonization Society of Kentucky*, p. 4.

238 **"The distinguished orator of the West"** Lumpkin, *Removal of the Cherokees from Georgia*, p. 73.

238 **"Where do you find one solitary opponent"** Ibid., p. 74.

239 **"We . . . hope yet to have a full account"** *Niles' Weekly Register*, June 5, 1830, vol. 38, p. 268.

240 **"Those who were friends of the administration"** Ibid.

240 **102 votes in favor and 97 against** American State Papers, *Journal of the House of Representatives 1829–30*, May 26, 1830, p. 730.

240 **"After the passage of the Indian bill"** *Niles' Weekly Register*, June 5, 1830, vol. 38, p. 268.

Chapter Twenty-four: Judicial

242 **"laborious, highly intelligent, Judicious"** Evarts to Ross, September 17, 1825, Moulton, *Papers of Chief John Ross*, vol. 1, p. 107.

243 **"It is the first Cherokee book ever published"** Elias Boudinot to Herman and Flora Gold Vaill, January 23, 1829, collected in Gaul, *To Marry an Indian*, pp. 161–62.

243 **Their lives began to change on March 13, 1831** White, "Memorial of Rev. Samuel Austin Worcester," p. 281.

243 **He was also a U.S. official . . . postmaster at New Echota** Berutti, "Cherokee Cases," p. 303.

243 **accuse them of "criminal" conduct** So Gilmer said to Rev. John Thompson, May 16, 1831. Kilpatrick and Kilpatrick, *New Echota Letters*, p. 106.

244 **"punishment which will certainly follow your further residence"** Ibid.

244 **His wife was ill** Ibid., p. 107.

244 **"I cheerfully acknowledge" . . . no "consciousness of guilt"** Worcester to Gilmer, June 10, 1831, reprinted in *Cherokee Phoenix*, ibid., p. 109.

244 **"that freedom in the expression of opinion . . . until I am forcibly removed"** Ibid., p. 111.

244 **So the Georgia Guard . . . arrested him on July 15, 1831** Worcester to *Cherokee Phoenix*, July 25, 1831, ibid., p. 101. Also, Marshall et al., *Worcester v. Georgia*, p. 4.

244 **"only two or three individuals offered us any insult"** Worcester to *Cherokee Phoenix*, July 25, 1831, Kilpatrick and Kilpatrick *New Echota Letters*, p. 101.

244 **Theodore Frelinghuysen and . . . Daniel Webster** Wirt to Judge Carr, June 21, 1830, as reproduced in Kennedy, *Memoirs of the Life of William Wirt*, vol. 2, p. 254.

245 **"I received your speech on the removal of the Indians"** Marshall to Frelinghuysen, May 27, 1830, Johnson et al., *Papers of John Marshall*, vol. 11, p. 374.

246 **"insist upon its distribution among the Indians at large"** Berrien to Jackson, June 25, 1830, Owsley et al., *Papers of Andrew Jackson*, vol. 8, p. 392.

246 **spreading a few cents to each individual Cherokee** John Howard Payne believed the payment to each Cherokee would be "less than half a dollar" per year. Anderson et al., *Payne-Butrick Papers*, vol. 2, p. 159.

246 **Ross sent it directly to his underpaid defense team** One example is in Ross to Wirt, May 10, 1831, *Papers of Chief John Ross*, vol. 1, p. 220.

246 **"Give me liberty or give me death"** A persuasive argument that Wirt invented this and other phrases and attributed them to Henry without evidence is contained in Raphael, *Founding Myths*, pp. 145–56.

246 **"I have used all the persuasive means in my power"** Jackson to William B. Lewis, August 25, 1830, Owsley et al., *Papers of Andrew Jackson*, vol. 8, p. 501.

247 **"personally had strong doubts"** Wirt to Ross, September 22, 1830. A summary is in Moulton, *Papers of Chief John Ross*, vol. 1, p. 199.

247 **Georgia made the case moot by having Tassel hanged** Berutti, "Cherokee Cases," p. 299.

248 **"Mr. Lavender and myself are threatened"** Ross to Wirt, January 1, 1831, Moulton, *Papers of Chief John Ross*, vol. 1, pp. 209–10.

248 **repugnant to the constitution . . . leave the issue to Providence**" Peters, ed., *The Case of the Cherokee Nation against the State of Georgia*, p. 66.

249 **Marshall felt that he could not push the issue too far** Berutti, "Cherokee Cases," p. 300.

249 **"The denial of the injunction . . . claims of the President"** Ross to the Cherokees, April 14, 1831, Moulton, *Papers of Chief John Ross*, vol. 1, p. 217.

249 **"tattlers and intriguers"** Ibid.

249 **Accompanied by Cherokee leader George Lowrey and . . . Major Ridge** Wilkins, *Cherokee Tragedy*, pp. 217–18.

251 **"experiment" of Marshall's strategy** Wirt to Ross, July 18, 1831. A summary of the letter is contained in Moulton, *Papers of Chief John Ross*, pp. 221–22.

251 **four years "at hard labor"** Marshall et al., *Worcester v. Georgia*, p. 6.

251 **making cabinets at the state prison at Milledgeville** Miles, "After John Marshall's Decision," p. 526.

252 **"studiously avoided calling on us to assist in that work"** Worcester to *Cherokee Phoenix*, October 29, 1832, Kilpatrick and Kilpatrick, *New Echota Letters*, p. 115.

252 **"Should the legislature of Georgia repeal"** Ross to William Wirt, October 7, 1831, Moulton, *Papers of Chief John Ross*, vol. 1, p. 224.

252 **William Wirt appealed . . . February 20, 1832** Marshall et al., *Worcester v. Georgia*, p. 6.

252 **"This duty, however unpleasant, cannot be avoided"** Ibid., p. 9.

253 **"America, separated from Europe"** Ibid., p. 10.

253 **"who could not write, and most probably could not read"** Ibid., p. 15.

254 **"the actual state of things"** Ibid., p. 10.

254 **"these powerful considerations . . . We think they will"** Ibid., p. 20.

Chapter Twenty-five: Executive

255 **"every Indian knows now that he stands upon a solid foundation"** Elijah Hicks to Cherokee delegation, March 24, 1832, reprinted in *Niles' Weekly Register*, May 12, 1832, vol. 42, March–August 1832, p. 201.

255 **"Our adversaries . . . enemies are seeking places where to hide their heads"** Ross to Cherokee delegates, Moulton, *Papers of Chief John Ross*, vol. 1, p. 241.

256 **"Georgia . . . has commenced her survey"** *Cherokee Phoenix*, April 21, 1832; reprinted in *Niles' Weekly Register*, May 12, 1832, vol. 42, March–August 1832, p. 201.

256 **"It was [McLean's] firm belief . . . unburden itself by a removal"** Ross to Wirt, June 8, 1832, Moulton, *Papers of Chief John Ross*, vol. 1, p. 245.

257 **Only after the Georgia courts failed would Marshall be in a position** Miles, "After John Marshall's Decision," pp. 528–29, 537.

257 **"and the President refuses to enforce"** Meacham, *American Lion*, p. 204.

257 **"Justice Marshall has made his decision; now let him enforce it"** The claim is found in Greeley, *American Conflict*, p. 106.

258 **"would not aid" "sportively said in private conversation"** Miles, "After John Marshall's Decision," pp. 528–29, 537.

258 **"The decision of the Supreme Court has fell still born"** Jackson to Coffee, April 7, 1832, Bassett, ed., *Correspondence of Andrew Jackson*, vol. IV, pp. 429–31.

258 **sent Ridge away in "despair"** Jackson to Coffee, April 9, 1832, quoted in Wilkins, *Cherokee Tragedy*, p. 229.

260 "Other important considerations" Cass to Lumpkin, December 24, 1832, cited in Miles, "After John Marshall's Decision," p. 537.

260 the governor had dined with the wives of Worcester and Butler Ibid., p. 535.

260 "considerations of a public nature" Ibid., p. 540.

260 Governor Lumpkin freed the missionaries on January 14, 1833 Ibid., p. 541.

260 negotiate a generous treaty Ibid., pp. 529–30.

260 Elisha Chester . . . infuriated John Ross Ross to Wirt, June 8, 1832, Moulton, *Papers of Chief John Ross*, vol. 1, p. 244.

261 "best good" Miles, "After John Marshall's Decision," p. 539.

261 "While the Union lasts" Peterson, The Great Triumvirate, p. 178.

Part Eight: Democracy in America, 1833–1835
Chapter Twenty-six: The Purest Love of Formalities

265 June 6, 1833 . . . Jackson became the first president to board a train Stover, *History of the Baltimore and Ohio Railroad*, p. 38.

265 Stephen A. Douglas of Vermont, age twenty, moved to Illinois Quitt, *Stephen A. Douglas and Antebellum Democracy*, pp. 38–39.

265 "too insignificant, to make [my] politics an objection" Lincoln, *Speeches and Writings, 1859–1865*, p. 164.

265 personal friends . . . included politically active Jackson Democrats David Donald, in *Lincoln*, p. 52, reports that many of Lincoln's friends, such as a gang of local toughs known as the Clary's Grove Boys, were Jackson men who "favored Lincoln purely on personal grounds."

266 "After I had retired to my room" Van Buren, *Autobiography*, p. 293.

267 Men raised giant hickory poles Parton, *Life of Andrew Jackson*, vol. 3, p. 424.

267 "nearly a mile long" M. Chevalier, a French traveler, quoted in ibid., p. 425.

267 unprecedented fall tour from the Hermitage to Washington Meacham, *American Lion*, pp. 218–19.

267 "aristocratic monopoly" Stiles, *First Tycoon*, p. 101.

268 offering an extortion payment of $100,000 Ibid., p. 103.

268 "Birth, condition, or profession" Tocqueville, *Democracy in America*, p. 279.

268 "They call for equality in freedom" Ibid., p. 203.

268 "I do not think that there is any other country" Ibid., p. 59.

268 "singular mildness . . . an evil which does not affect them" Ibid., p. 203.

269 "By contrast . . . respect for the laws of humanity would be impossible" Ibid., p. 391.

270 Lincoln volunteered . . . mosquitoes An account of his 1848 speech spells it "musquetoes." Donald, *Lincoln*, p. 45.

270 He was driven in a carriage "The President's Visit," *Niles' Weekly Register*, June 15, 1833, vol. 44, p. 256.

270 on June 6, 1833, he sat through a performance Trask, *Black Hawk*, p. 300.

270 the Indian leader chatted with . . . the Great Father of the nation Ibid.

270 "You will see" . . . "my people have suffered a great deal" "The President's Visit," *Niles' Weekly Register*, June 15, 1833, vol. 44, p. 256.

270 Black Hawk had to be taken out of the center city Ibid.

271 "Long before the climax was reached" Cited in Lepore, *In the Name of War*, p. 202.

Chapter Twenty-seven: I Have the Right to Address You

273   **"speculating tribe . . . anihilation"** Jackson to William Berkeley Lewis, August 25, 1830, Moulton, *Papers of Andrew Jackson*, vol. 8, pp. 500–501.

273   **The president offered $2.5 million** Moulton, *John Ross, Cherokee Chief*, p. 51.

273   **Jackson was offering something close to 50 cents** Wiley Thompson to Lewis Cass, February 2, 1833. Senate Document 512, no. 247, vol. 4, p. 68.

273   **United States should spend its money *relocating white settlers*** Ross letter in the American State Papers, Brown's Hotel, Washington City, January 28, 1833. Ibid., p. 65.

274   **"The usual scenes which our afflicted people experience"** John Ridge to Ross, quoted in Moulton, *John Ross, Cherokee Chief*, p. 51.

275   **Ross had relied on the younger man** John Ridge to Ross, April 3, 1832, Moulton, *Papers of Chief John Ross*, vol. 1, p. 241.

275   **"Were I to continue as editor local and sectional interests"** Boudinot to Ross, August 1, 1832, ibid., pp. 247–48.

276   **"the evil effects of their intercourse"** Speech reprinted in Gabriel, *Elias Boudinot*, pp. 106–7.

276   **"almost a dreary waste"** Boudinot, quoted in Smith, *American Betrayal*, p. 183.

276   **"moral degradation," yet.it seemed that Ross worried only about money** Smith, *An American Betrayal*, is particularly useful on this point, pp. 142–43.

276   **Men such as Boudinot openly admitted** Ibid., p. 143.

277   **"donned feathered headdresses"** Woodward, *The Cherokees*, p. 173.

277   **soon to be known as the Whigs** The Whig label emerged in the spring of 1834. Howe, *What Hath God Wrought*, p. 390.

Chapter Twenty-eight: We Are Yet Your Friends

278   **"The undersigned Principal Chief"** Ross to Jackson, February 3, 1834, Andrew Jackson Papers, 1775–1874, reel 44.

279   **Jackson would see them at noon on February 5** Endorsement on Ross letter requesting the appointment, February 3, 1834, Moulton, *Papers of Chief John Ross*, vol. 1, p. 273.

279   **about ten blocks up Pennsylvania Avenue** The Indian Queen was at 600 Pennsylvania Avenue NW, ten blocks from the White House at 1600 Pennsylvania. Photograph Record, "Sketch of Indian Queen Hotel," Washington Historical Society online archive.

279   **"quite unwell, with pain in my left breast & shoulder"** Jackson to Andrew Jackson Jr., February 5, 1834, Andrew Jackson Papers 1775–1874, reel 44.

280   **"be of great use in accomplishing the objects of the government"** William Carroll to Cass, February 2, 1834, Cherokee Agency East Papers, National Archives, reel 74.

281   **"Twenty years have now elapsed"** All text of this letter from Ross to Jackson, March 28, 1834, Moulton, *Papers of Chief John Ross*, vol. 1, p. 284.

282   **a disapproving note came from an aide** Moulton, *John Ross, Cherokee Chief*, p. 55.

Chapter Twenty-nine: Should They Be Satisfied with the Character of That Country

283   **A branch of the trail also led to Jacksonville** The trail is mapped in Mahon, *History of the Second Seminole War*, pp. 390–91.

283 **fighting the war against the Creeks in 1813–14** Ibid., p. 87.

283 **cast his vote in favor of the Indian Removal Act** House Journal, 21st Cong., 1st Sess., May 26, 1830, from American State Papers, p. 723.

283 **"deep regret" at the "sudden and unaccountable" resistance** Thompson to Cass, February 2, 1833, Senate Document 512, no. 247, p. 68.

284 **$1,500 a year** Mahon, *History of the Second Seminole War*, p. 87.

284 **"should they be satisfied with the character of that country"** Kappler, "Treaty with the Seminole, May 9, 1832," *Indian Affairs: Laws and Treaties*, vol. 2, p. 344. http://digital.library.okstate.edu/kappler/Vol2/treaties/sem0344.htm; also Mahon, *History of the Second Seminole War*, p. 64.

284 **Seminole leaders . . . apparently illiterate, began denying** The treaty text showed all fifteen men made X marks, not signatures, and even one of the interpreters signed with an X mark. Mahon, *History of the Second Seminole War*, pp. 75–76.

284 **descendants of generations of migrants, survivors, and refugees** The origins of the Seminoles are discussed in detail in ibid., chap. 1, and Wright, *Creeks and Seminoles*.

285 **Thompson's scalp was cut into pieces** Mahon, *History of the Second Seminole War*, p. 104.

286 **the Seminoles opened fire** The attack on Dade's force is described in Roberts, "The Dade Massacre," pp. 123–28.

286 **The number of U.S. military deaths** Mahon, *History of the Second Seminole War*, p. 325. Based on the population of the day, 1,535 military deaths amounted to roughly 1 out of every 8,000 Americans; the Iraq War U.S. military death toll of about 4,400, out of a far larger population, amounted to roughly 1 out of every 70,000 Americans.

Part Nine: Tears, 1835–1838
Chapter Thirty: Five Millions of Dollars

291 **he was by then demanding $20 million** Moulton, *John Ross, Cherokee Chief*, p. 60.

291 **they took up residence in a two-room cabin** Undated Payne letter copied in collection of Museum of the Cherokee Indian, part of the Hargrett Collection, p. 1.

292 **the Georgia Guard reached New Echota first** Moulton, *John Ross, Cherokee Chief*, p. 65.

292 **about fifteen hundred pieces of old type** This according to David Gomez, the site manager of the New Echota historic site, September 24, 2014.

292 **"You are to consider yourself a prisoner"** John Howard Payne's story from *Knoxville Register*, December 2, 1835, reprinted in Battey, *History of Rome and Floyd County*, pp. 55–74.

292 **"Well, gentlemen, I shall not resist"** Ibid.

292 **"A wild storm arose" . . . "Home, Sweet Home"** Ibid., p. 59.

292 **"to raise an insurrection among the negroes, who are to join the Indians"** Ibid., p. 65.

293 **"of middle size—rather under than over . . . represented to be"** Undated Payne letter copied in collection of Museum of the Cherokee Indian, part of the Hargrett Collection, pp. 1–2.

293 **"mob extraordinary"** *Niles' Weekly Register*, January 2, 1836.

293 **governor of Tennessee wrote his counterpart** Letter from Tennessee governor N. Cannon, reprinted in *Niles' Weekly Register*, January 16, 1836.

293 **"common street rumor"** Ibid., January 2, 1836, p. 308.

293 **Major Benjamin F. Currey . . . more extreme measures** Valliere, "Benjamin Currey, Tennessean Among the Cherokees," p. 252.

293 **member "of the whig party, and rumor makes him an abolitionist"** Currey letter to the *Federal Union*, reprinted in *Niles' Weekly Register*, January 30, 1836.

294 **"the native Indian has but little part"** Moulton, *John Ross, Cherokee Chief*, p. 47.

295 **388 in favor . . . only one single Cherokee voting to pay individuals** Ibid., p. 59.

295 **regarding Ross as the "devil"** Ibid.

295 **Ross won, 2,225–114** Ibid., p. 64.

295 **"The strange results of this council"** Currey letter reprinted in *Niles' Weekly Register*, December 1, 1835, vol. 49, p. 375.

296 **the roof caught fire** Wilkins, *Cherokee Tragedy*, p. 276.

297 **eighty-two men were counted** Moulton, *John Ross, Cherokee Chief*, p. 74.

297 **"The Georgians have shown a grasping spirit"** Wilkins, *Cherokee Tragedy*, p. 286.

297 **"If one hundred persons are ignorant . . . moral degradation"** Boudinot quoted in Smith, *American Betrayal*, p. 143.

298 **"five millions of dollars"** Treaty of New Echota, Kappler, *Indian Affairs: Laws and Treaties*, p. 439.

298 **compensation for houses and fences and other improvements on the land** Treaty of New Echota, article 15, includes a phrase saying that the $5 million would be paid only "after deducting the amount which shall be actually expended for the payment for improvements, ferries, claims, for spoliations, removal subsistence and debts and claims." Ibid., p. 446.

Chapter Thirty-one: The War Department Does Not Understand These People

300 **hair elaborately combed forward** A portrait of Wool is reprinted in Hauptman, "General John E. Wool in Cherokee Country," p. 5.

301 **In the early days he met with Major Ridge** Ibid., p. 8.

301 **arrested the principal chief** Ibid., p. 14.

301 **"The War Department does not understand these people"** Wool to C. A. Harris, August 27, 1836, American State Papers, Military Affairs, vol. 7, House of Representatives, 25th Cong., 1st Sess., p. 552.

302 **"I advised [Ross], however, to be careful"** Ibid., p. 553.

302 **"huts for the accommodation of strangers . . . huts, booths and stores"** Visitor to 1838 council meeting quoted in Butler, "Red Clay Council Ground," p. 147.

302 **"an unceasing current of . . . men, women, youths, and children"** Ibid.

302 **People might linger for days . . . freshly killed beef** Ibid.

302 **horns would echo through the woods** Snell, "Councils at Red Clay Council Ground," p. 352.

303 **the crowd already numbered three thousand** Wool to Cass, September 18, 1836, American State Papers, Military Affairs, vol. 7, House of Representatives, 25th Cong., 1st Sess., p. 557.

303 **attendance grew to between four and five thousand** Butler, "Red Clay Council Ground," p. 145.

303 "peaceful," operating with "order and decorum" Ibid.

303 "upwards of twenty-one hundred male adults" According to Cherokee memorial to Wool, September 30, 1836, American State Papers, Military Affairs, vol. 7, House of Representatives, 25th Cong., 1st Sess., p. 567.

303 Cherokee population of about 16,500 All figures from McLoughlin and Conser, "Cherokees in Transition," pp. 678–703; Table 3, p. 682.

303 "streaked with gray . . . a dark, brown, brilliant eye" Wilkins, *Cherokee Tragedy*, p. 199.

303 translated sentence by sentence into Cherokee This was the practice at the 1837 Red Clay meeting described in Snell, "Councils at Red Clay Council Ground," p. 351.

303 On the last day of the session According to General Wool, quoted in ibid., p. 350.

303 "a fraud upon the government of the United States and an act of oppression" Cherokee memorial to Wool, September 30, 1836, American State Papers, Military Affairs, vol. 7, House of Representatives, 25th Cong., 1st Sess., p. 566.

304 Here were men who went by their English names Ibid., p. 567.

304 "good faith" and "magnanimity" of "the President and the Congress" John Ross et al. to Wool, ibid., p. 567.

304 "immediately return it . . . in regard to the treaty" C. A. Harris to Wool, October 17, 1836, ibid., p. 564.

304 The president also criticized his general Lewis Cass to Wool, October 12, 1836, ibid., p. 557.

304 "The people are opposed to the treaty" Wool to Lewis Cass, September 12, 1836, ibid., p. 554.

304 "dragged like so many beasts to the emigration camp" Wool to Cass, September 18, 1836, ibid., p. 557.

305 "If any officer of the army should countenance resistance" Cass to Wool, October 12, 1836, ibid., pp. 556–57.

305 he thought Cherokees should move west for their own good Wool's view is clear from his letters, and is supported by Hauptman, "General John E. Wool in Cherokee Country," pp. 1–26.

305 "the shedding of human blood" Wool to Cass, September 18, 1836, American State Papers, Military Affairs, vol. 7, House of Representatives, 25th Cong., 1st Sess., p. 564.

305 Alabamans were upset when he interfered Hauptman, "General John E. Wool in Cherokee Country," p. 21.

305 State authorities complained to Washington Defense of Brigadier General Wool, American State Papers, Military Affairs, vol. 7, pp. 567–71.

305 Supposedly he was recalled from command at his "own request" Wool to Joel R. Poinsett, August 11, 1837, ibid., p. 565.

Chapter Thirty-two: Perchance, You May Have Heard That the Cherokees Are in Trouble

306 He had staggered . . . "severe illness" B. F. Butler to Wool, November 23, 1836, American State Papers, Military Affairs, vol. 7, House of Representatives, 25th Cong., 1st Sess., p. 562.

306 "advanced age and a broken frame" Jackson, farewell address, March 4, 1837, as reproduced in Woolley and Peters, Messages and Papers of the Presidents, http://www.presidency.ucsb.edu/ws/?pid=67087.

307 Jackson declined Long, *Duel of Eagles*, p. 329.

307 **expressed regret . . . cried when a crowd greeted his carriage** Parton, *Life of Andrew Jackson*, vol. 3, p. 630.

308 **explanations and excuses for the soaring expense** Joel R. Poinsett's annual message to Congress, December 5, 1837, American State Papers, Military Affairs, vol. 7, pp. 571–72.

308 **if they could not recapture slaves, they would rather continue the war** Mahon, *History of the Second Seminole War*, p. 201.

308 **turned out hundreds of Seminoles being held in a detention camp** Ibid., p. 204.

309 **250 soldiers surrounded him and took him prisoner** Ibid., pp. 214–16.

309 **fifty thousand tons of granite and cut stone** Ferguson, "An Overview of the Events at Fort Sumter, 1829–1991," p. 6.

309 **"twenty towns, three counties"** Mahon, *History of the Second Seminole War*, p. 218.

310 **Would Ross be willing to appeal to the Seminoles:** Moulton, "Cherokees and the Second Seminole War."

310 **stories of savages . . . contributed to prejudice** Fiorato, "Cherokee Mediation in Florida," p. 115.

310 **"I am of the aboriginal race"** John Ross to Seminoles, October 7, 1837, Moulton, *Papers of Chief John Ross*, vol. 1, pp. 523–24.

310 **Ross did not go along with a War Department suggestion** Fiorato, "Cherokee Mediation in Florida," p. 116.

311 **including their leader Micanopy** Ibid., pp. 113–14.

311 **The Seminoles believed them** Moulton, *John Ross, Cherokee Chief*, p. 88.

Chapter Thirty-three: The Thunder Often Sounding in the Distance

312 **They cast off from the Cherokee Nation on March 3, 1837** Wilkins, *Cherokee Tragedy*, p. 290.

312 **A steam locomotive arrived, pulling a string of open freight cars** Ibid., p. 291.

312 **watching the countryside blurring past in the dark** Grant Foreman describes it as a night journey in *Indian Removal*, p. 275.

313 **no reported deaths** According to Wilkins, *Cherokee Tragedy*, p. 293.

313 **365 emigrants loaded their wagons** The number is from Foreman, *Indian Removal*, p. 280.

313 **paid a call on white-haired General Jackson** Journal of B. B. Cannon, reprinted as "An Overland Journey to the West (October–December 1837)" in *Journal of Cherokee Studies*, vol. 3, no. 3, Summer 1978, p. 168.

313 **"Nov. 1st 1837 . . . Marched at 8 O'C A.M. buried Ducks child"** Ibid.

314 *"Nov 29th 1837 . . . child last night"* Ibid.

315 **"We will not attempt to describe the evils . . . deceived himself"** Address by federal commissioners John Kennedy and Thomas W. Wilson, and Nathaniel Smith, Superintendent of Indian Removal, December 28, 1837, reprinted in *Journal of Cherokee Studies*, vol. 3, no. 3, Summer 1978, pp. 134–35.

315 **The last census of the eastern Cherokees** All figures from McLoughlin and Conser, "Cherokees in Transition," pp. 678–703.

316 **"had a long talk . . . he will weep!"** John Ross to Lewis Ross, April 5, 1838, Moulton, *Papers of Chief John Ross*, vol. 1, p. 622.

316 **The War Department assured him** General Alexander Macomb to Scott, April 6, 1838, reprinted in Exec. Doc. 453, 25th Cong., 2nd Sess., July 4, 1838, pp. 1–2.

316 **cadets at . . . West Point were being ordered that spring** *Army and Navy Chronicle*, reprinted in *Boston Courier*, June 21, 1838.

316 **vowing "never to return without having killed at least one Indian"** Scott, "If Not Rejoicing, at Least in Comfort: General Scott's Version of Removal," *Journal of Cherokee Studies*.

317 **Arriving at Athens, Tennessee, fifteen days before the deadline** He arrived May 8. Scott to Poinsett, May 18, 1838, reprinted in Exec. Doc. 453, 25th Cong., 2nd Sess., July 4, 1838, p. 7.

317 **"powerful army . . . whole people of America"** Scott's address, reprinted in *Journal of Cherokee Studies*, vol. 3, no. 3, Summer 1978, p. 145.

317 **"a company of volunteers marched through Morganton"** *Fayetteville Observer*, May 16, 1838.

317 **North Carolina also announced its plan** *Raleigh Register* and *North Carolina Gazette*, May 7, 1838.

317 **"Nothing but destruction"** Lewis Ross to John Ross, April 6, 1838, Moulton, *Papers of Chief John Ross*, vol. 1, p. 625.

318 **He had seen Cherokees serenely planting their corn** John Ross to Lewis Ross, April 5, 1838, ibid., p. 622.

318 **twenty-three military posts throughout the Cherokee Nation** Scott to Poinsett, May 18, 1838, reprinted in Exec. Doc. 453, 25th Cong., 2nd Sess., July 4, 1838, p. 7.

318 **enrolled so many volunteer soldiers** Scott to Poinsett, May 18, 1838: "I shall be trammelled by an understanding, mounting almost to a compact, which had been entered into with the Governor of Georgia, in respect to eleven such companies." Ibid.

318 **"Whilst writing the foregoing"** Ibid.

319 **"were evidently deluded"** John Ross to Lewis Ross, April 5, 1838, Moulton, *Papers of Chief John Ross*, vol. 1, pp. 622–23.

320 **"I replied that I had never deluded the Cherokees"** Ibid., p. 623.

320 **the depression had forced the closure of thirty-three thousand businesses** Study cited in Roberts, *America's First Great Depression*, p. 22.

320 **Once again, religious groups led the way** Moulton, *John Ross, Cherokee Chief*, p. 93.

321 **"My friend Mr. Payne and myself"** Ross to Elizabeth Milligan, April 10, 1838, Moulton, *Papers of Chief John Ross*, vol. 1, p. 626.

321 **"Catlin's Indian Gallery," as it was called in an advertisement** *National Intelligencer*, April 17, 1838, p. 3.

321 **"The interests of your people cannot be dearer to you, than those of mine"** Ross to Martin Van Buren, April 1838 (exact date uncertain), Moulton, *Papers of Chief John Ross*, vol. 1, pp. 633–34.

321 **"You can expel us by force"** Ross to Samuel Cooper, April 17, 1838, ibid., p. 631.

321 **"The presence in this city of the chiefs"** Poinsett to Scott, June 1, 1838, reprinted in Exec. Doc. 453, 25th Cong., 2nd Sess., July 4, 1838, p. 4.

322 **"No communication has reached me"** Scott to R. Jones, May 22, 1838, ibid., pp. 12–13.

323 **"When the soldier came to our house"** Rebecca Neugin to Grant Foreman, reprinted in *Journal of Cherokee Studies*, vol. 3, no. 3, Summer 1978, p. 176.

323 **"as we were going from school"** From *Journal of Commerce*, reprinted in *Liberator*, July 20, 1838, p. 116.

324 **"Many of our friends are troubling themselves"** Ibid.

324 **"Families at dinner were startled by the sudden gleam of bayonets"** Mooney, *Myths of the Cherokee*, p. 130.

324 **"to rob them of the silver pendants"** Ibid.

325 **"I experienced no difficulty in getting them along"** Reprinted in *Journal of Cherokee Studies*, vol. 3, no. 3, Summer 1978, p. 154.

325 **"happily chosen," a "well shaded" area** Scott autobiographical fragment, reprinted in ibid., p. 139.

325 **"scattered and dispersed" in "family camps"** Quoted in Rozema, *Voices from the Trail of Tears*, pp. 128–29.

325 **"consequent upon the hurry of capture and removal"** Scott to N. Smith, cited in Evans, "Fort Marr Blockhouse," p. 259.

325 **"they are the most quiet people you ever saw"** Reprinted in *Journal of Cherokee Studies*, vol. 3, no. 3, Summer 1978, p. 155.

326 **In two follow-up letters** Poinsett to Scott, June 25 and 27, 1838, reprinted in Exec. Doc. 453, 25th Cong., 2nd Sess., July 4, 1838, pp. 5–6.

326 **"and the *squatters* . . . are as likely to annoy, to dispossess, and make war"** Scott to Poinsett, June 7, 1838, ibid., p. 18.

327 **"Not only the comfort, but the safety of the Indians"** Scott to Poinsett, June 18, 1838, ibid., p. 26.

327 **"a high grade of Diarrhea . . . heat that has prevailed in this country"** Quoted in Rozema, *Voices from the Trail of Tears*, p. 129.

327 **"two thousand" people had died** *Missionary Herald*, 1838, quoted in ibid., p. 29.

328 **"The loss was the fault of the Cherokees"** Quoted in Brown, *Old Frontiers*, p. 509.

329 **"Paid to John Ross . . . 25,000.00"** Receipt, June 25, 1838, Moulton, *Papers of Chief John Ross*, vol. 1, p. 647.

329 **$7,000 for two seasons in Washington** Travel expense receipt, June 26, 1838, ibid., p. 648.

329 **"thrilling news"** Ross to John Howard Payne, July 5 and 9, 1838, ibid., p. 648.

329 **"suddenly terminated"** Ross to the Cherokees, July 21, 1838, ibid., p. 649.

330 **"I shall not stop here to complain"** Scott to Poinsett, June 7, 1838, reprinted in "On the Removal of the Cherokees," Exec. Doc. 453, 25th Cong., 2nd Sess., July 4, 1838, p. 20.

330 **"extremely unwilling to delay the emigration"** Scott to John Ross et al., August 25, 1838, *Journal of Cherokee Studies*, vol. 3, no. 3, Summer 1978, p. 152.

331 **"I am still in the land of the living"** Jackson to Blair, August 9, 1838, Andrew Jackson Papers, 1775–1874, reel 51.

331 **"Benton is safe beyond a doubt"** A. G. Harrison to Jackson, August 15, 1838, ibid.

331 **"It is *indispensable* for us to have a new candidate for the Vice Presidency"** C. Johnson to Jackson, August 1838, ibid.

331 **"to be placed at West Point"** Amanda P. Craig to Jackson, August 22, 1838, ibid.

331 **"Col. Walker has just shown me"** Jackson to Felix Grundy, August 23, 1838, Moser et al., *Papers of Andrew Jackson*, reel 34.

333 **He had left out an allowance for soap . . . total cost should be $66.24** "Moneys Due the Cherokee Nation," clarifies this, p. 10. House Report no. 288, in 1843, gives the

money figures and specifies that it was an allowance for soap. "Moneys Due the Cherokee Nation," p. 10, also says that Scott asked for a reduction and that Ross countered with an increase.

333 **John Ross took no actual salary** Moulton, *John Ross, Cherokee Chief,* p. 106.

333 **$1.357 million** "Moneys Due the Cherokee Nation," p. 11.

333 **"accomplished with a much less expense to the United States"** Ibid.

334 **"At dawn of day the Emigrants were in readiness"** Ross to Scott, November. 12, 1838, Moulton, *Papers of Chief John Ross,* vol. 1, pp. 691–93.

334 **"at least Two third are in a destitute condition"** John Benge et al. to John Ross, September 29, 1838, ibid., p. 673.

335 **Another party . . . "the payment of unjust & just Demands"** George Hicks to Ross, November 4, 1838, ibid., p. 687.

335 **"The Ice on the Mississippi"** Thomas N. Clark to Ross, December 28, 1838, ibid., p. 696.

335 **around 600** "Moneys Due the Cherokee Nation," p. 11.

335 **one Cherokee list recorded 324** "Emigration Detachments," *Journal of Cherokee Studies,* vol. 3, no. 3, Summer 1977, p. 187.

335 **Cherokee population may have been reduced by as many as eight thousand** Thornton, "Cherokee Population Losses during the Trail of Tears," pp. 289–300.

335 **"excepting sickness"** Ross to Winfield Scott, November 12, 1838, Moulton, *Papers of Chief John Ross,* vol. 1, p. 691.

336 **"I wish I could have your influence for a few days"** Thomas N. Clark to Ross, November 15, 1838, ibid., p. 695.

Epilogue

342 **A glance at a modern census map** For example, "American Indians and Alaska Natives," produced by the U.S. Census Bureau, based on 2010 census data, www.census.gov.

342 **reservations are in southeastern Alabama . . . Chickasaw and Choctaw** Census maps, ibid.

342 **their numbers dwindled to as little as a hundred** Mahon, *History of the Second Seminole War,* p. 321.

343 **it was apparently on a riverboat that Ross's wife, Quatie, died** Worthen, "Quatie Ross Gravestone Given to Museum."

343 **She was buried after the boat tied up at Little Rock, Arkansas** An alternative version of Quatie's death, conveyed in a supposed letter by one John Burnett, was discredited in ibid.

343 **"The clouds vanished and the rain ceased to fall"** John Ross to Mary B. Ross, March 5, 1865, Moulton, *Papers of Chief John Ross,* vol. 1, pp. 631–32.

343 **cede some of the land that had previously been granted** Kappler, Article 31, "Treaty with the Cherokee, 1866," *Indian Affairs: Laws and Treaties,* p. 947.

344 **"he had been treated so bad by the whites life had lost all its endearments"** The wife's account was found by the scholar William Martin Jurgelski, who transcribed it in Pluckhahn and Ethridge, *Light on the Path,* pp. 137–39.

344 **"one of those unfortunate individual occurrences"** Ross to Winfield Scott, November 4, 1838, Moulton, *Papers of Chief John Ross,* vol. 1, p. 687.

344 Cherokees on trial themselves put Tsali Pluckhahn and Ethridge, *Light on the Path*, pp. 148–50.

345 several hundred thousand people, on and off reservations U.S. Census Bureau, "American Indians and Alaska Natives," based on 2010 census data, www.census.gov.

Sources and Acknowledgments

349 "endure . . . as long as the government itself" Van Buren, *Autobiography*, p. 295.

349 "wise and humane" Parton, *Life of Andrew Jackson*, vol. 3, p. 279.

349 white men "very naturally" would not tolerate Wilson, *Division and Reunion, 1829– 1889*, p. 37.

349 "were as religious, moral, high-minded a race of men who ever lived" Brooks, *History of Georgia*, pp. 225–26.

350 many Indians viewed him as "the devil" The video, narrated by Martin Sheen, was excerpted from *Andrew Jackson: Good, Evil and the Presidency*, a documentary released on DVD in 2008, and viewed at the Hermitage, August 17, 2013.

350 formal apology for the Trail of Tears Public Law 111-118 describes "years of official depredations, ill-conceived policies, and the breaking of covenants by the Federal Government regarding Indian tribes," and apologizes for "the many instances of violence, maltreatment, and neglect," p. 45.

350 "paternalist" Wilentz, *Rise of American Democracy*, p. 324.

350 "harried without ruth" Roosevelt, *Winning of the West*, vol. 4, p. 53.

350 the "race-importance" of the work Ibid., p. 52.

BIBLIOGRAPHY

Archives, Bound Letters, Pamphlets, and Other Documents

Adams, John Quincy. *Memoirs of John Quincy Adams Comprising Portions of His Diary from 1795–1848*. 12 vols. Edited by Charles Francis Adams. Philadelphia: J. B. Lippincott, 1875.

Alabama Department of Archives and History: miscellaneous letters.

American State Papers, Library of Congress.

Anderson, William, et al., eds. *The Payne-Butrick Papers*. 6 vols. in 2-vol. set. Lincoln: University of Nebraska Press, 2010.

Andrew, John III. *From Revivals to Removal: Jeremiah Evarts, the Cherokee Nation, and the Search for the Soul of America*. Athens: University of Georgia Press, 1992.

Austill, Margaret Eades. "Memories of Journeying through Creek Country and of Childhood in Clarke County, 1811–1814." Alabama Department of Archives and History, pages unnumbered.

Barrett, John S., ed. Correspondence of Andrew Jackson. 7 vols. Washington, DC: Carnegie Institute, 1926–35.

Beecher, Catharine. *Essay on Slavery and Abolitionism, with Reference to the Duty of American Females*. Philadelphia: Henry Perkins, 1837.

Bureau of Land Management, General Land Office Records database.

Cherokee Agency East Papers, National Archives, Microfilm Series M234, reels 71–76, 113, 115.

Clay, Henry. *An Address to the Colonization Society of Kentucky*. Lexington: Thomas Smith, 1829.

———. *Speech of the Hon. Henry Clay Before the American Colonization Society*. Washington, DC: The Columbian, 1827.

Coffee, John. Dyas Collection—John Coffee Papers, 1770–1917. Tennessee State Library and Archives, Nashville. Microfilm copy at Florence-Lauderdale Public Library.

Evarts, Jeremiah, ed. *Speeches on the Passage of the Bill for the Removal of the Indians*. Boston: Perkins and Marvin, 1830.

Gales, Joseph, and William Seaton. Joseph Gales Jr. and William Winston Seaton Papers, 1811–1867, Library of Congress.

Grimké, Angelina. *Letters to Catharine E. Beecher in Reply to an Essay on Slavery and Abolitionism.* Boston: Isaac Knapp, 1838.

Hargrett Collection, Museum of the Cherokee Indian: miscellaneous letters.

Hopkins, James F., et al., eds. *The Papers of Henry Clay.* 10 vols. plus Supplement. Lexington: University Press of Kentucky, 1959-1992.

Horseshoe Bend National Military Park: transcripts of letters and Cherokee muster roll.

House Committee on Military Affairs. *Proceedings of a Court Martial Ordered for the trial of certain Tennessee Militiamen.* Washington: Gales and Seaton, 1828.

Jackson, Andrew. Andrew Jackson Papers. Chicago History Museum.

Jackson, Andrew. Andrew Jackson Papers, 1775–1874. Library of Congress Manuscript Division.

Jackson, Shelby, et al. *"Secret" Journal on Negotiations of the Chickasaw Treaty, 1818.* New Haven: Avalon Project, Yale Law School. http://avalon.law.yale.edu/19th_century/nt005.asp.

Johnson, Herbert A., et al., eds. *The Papers of John Marshall.* 12 vols. Chapel Hill: University of North Carolina Press, 1974–2006.

Kilpatrick, Jack Frederick, and Anna Gritts Kilpatrick, eds. *New Echota Letters.* Dallas: Southern Methodist University Press, 1968.

Library of Congress Manuscript Division. *Index to the Andrew Jackson Papers.* Washington: Library of Congress, 1967.

Long, Ellen Call. Letter to her son Richard Call Long, August 16, 1853. Call and Brevard Family Papers, box 5, folder 19, item 1. Digitally posted by Florida Library and Information Services. http://www.floridamemory.com/items/show/180858?id=1.

Meriwether, Robert L., et al., eds. *The Papers of John C. Calhoun.* 28 vols. Columbia: University of South Carolina Press, 1959–2003.

Monroe, Haskell, and James McIntosh. *The Papers of Jefferson Davis*, vol. 1, 1808–1840. Baton Rouge: Louisiana State University Press, 1971.

Moser, Harold D., Sharon Macpherson, John H. Reinbold, and Daniel Feller, eds. *The Papers of Andrew Jackson: A Microfilm Supplement.* Wilmington, DE: Scholarly Resources, 1986.

———. *The Papers of Andrew Jackson: Guide and Index to the Microfilm Editions.* Wilmington, DE: Scholarly Resources, 1987.

Owsley, Harriet, Sam Smith, Robert Remini, Daniel Feller et al., eds. *The Papers of Andrew Jackson.* 9 vols. to date. Knoxville: University of Tennessee Press, 1980–.

Peters, Richard, ed. *The Case of the Cherokee Nation against the State of Georgia.* Philadelphia: Grigg, 1831.

Prucha, Francis Paul. *Documents of United States Indian Policy, Third Edition.* Lincoln: University of Nebraska Press, 2000.

Woolley, John, and Gerhard Peters. Messages and Papers of the Presidents. American Presidency Project, University of California, Santa Barbara.

Public Documents

Committee on Indian Affairs, Petitions on Indian Removal. Box HR 21A-G8.2, Box HR 21A-G8.2 (cont'd), Box HR 21A-G7.1 to HR 21A-G8.2, Box HR 21A-G9.1. Washington, DC: National Archives, 1830–31.

Coxe, Trench. *A Statement of the Arts and Manufactures of the United States of America for the Year 1810, Prepared in Execution of an Instruction by Albert Gallatin, Secretary of the Treasury.* Philadelphia: A. Cornman, 1814.

Ferguson, James N., supervising architect. "An Overview of the Events at Fort Sumter, 1829–1991." HABS Recording Team, 1991, National Park Service. http://www.nps .gov/fosu/historyculture/upload/392-D61---392_D61_Numeric-44636.pdf.

Lauderdale County Deed Records. Lauderdale County Courthouse, Florence, AL.

Marshall, John, et al. *Worcester v. Georgia.* Washington, DC: Gales & Seaton, 1832.

"Moneys Due the Cherokee Nation." Executive Document 182, 53rd Congress, 3rd Session, January 9, 1895.

Office of the Historian and Clerk of the House. "Old Hall of the House of Representatives." *History, Art & Archives, United States House of Representatives.* history.house.gov.

"On the Removal of the Cherokees." Executive Document 453, 25th Congress, 2nd Session, July 4, 1838.

Public Law 111–118. December 19, 2009, 123 stat. 3453. http://www.gpo.gov/fdsys/pkg/ PLAW-111publ118/html/PLAW-111publ118.htm.

Senate Document 512, no. 247.

Troup, George M. *Governor's Message to the General Assembly of the State of Georgia, at the Opening of the Extra Session, May 23, 1825, with a Part of the Documents Accompanying the Same.* Milledgeville, GA: Camak & Ragland, 1825.

U.S. Census Bureau. "Following the Frontier Line, 1790 to 1890." September 6, 2012. https://www.census.gov/dataviz/visualizations/001/.

———. "American Indians and Alaska Natives," based on 2010 census data. http://www2 .census.gov/geo/maps/special/AIANWall2010/AIAN_US_2010.pdf.

Contemporary Newspapers

Cherokee Phoenix. Library of Congress.

Gazette of the United States (single issue). Museum of the Cherokee Indian.

Harrisburg Democratic Union (single issue). Museum of the Cherokee Indian.

Nashville Whig. Tennessee State Library and Archives

National Intelligencer. Library of Congress.

Niles' Weekly Register. Hathi Trust database.

Truth's Advocate and Monthly Anti-Jackson Expositor, by "An Association of Individuals." Cincinnati: Lodge et al., 1828. Library of Congress.

The Tuscumbian. Florence-Lauderdale Public Library.

United States Telegraph. Library of Congress.

The War (single copy). Alabama Department of Archives and History.

Memoirs and Histories

Adair, James. *The History of the American Indians.* London: Edward and Charles Dilly, 1775.

Adams, Henry. *The Formative Years.* 2 vols. New York: Houghton Mifflin, 1947. First published 1889–90.

Ball, Timothy Horton, and Henry Sale Halbert. *The Creek War of 1813 and 1814.* Montgomery, AL: White, Woodruff & Fowler, 1895.

Banner, Stuart. *How the Indians Lost Their Land: Law and Power on the Frontier.* Cambridge: Harvard University Press, 2005.

Bass, Althea. *Cherokee Messenger.* Norman: University of Oklahoma Press, 1936.

Battey, George Magruder. *A History of Rome and Floyd County.* Atlanta: Webb and Vary, 1922.

Beecher, Catharine. *Educational Reminiscences and Suggestions.* New York: J. B. Ford and Co., 1874.

Benton, Jeffrey. *The Very Worst Road: Travellers' Accounts of Crossing Alabama's Old Creek Indian Territory.* Tuscaloosa: University of Alabama Press, 2009.

Boudinot, Elias. *A Star in the West.* Trenton: D. Fenton et al., 1816.

Brands, H. W. *Andrew Jackson: His Life and Times.* New York: Random House, 2005.

Braund, Kathryn E. Holland, ed. *Tohopeka: Rethinking the Creek War and the War of 1812.* Tuscaloosa: University of Alabama Press, 2012.

Brooks, Robert Preston. *A History of Georgia.* Boston, New York: Atkinson, Mentzer, 1913.

Brown, John P. *Old Frontiers.* Kingsport, TN: Southern Publishers, 1938.

Burstein, Andrew. *The Passions of Andrew Jackson.* New York: Vintage, 2003.

Cave, Alfred A. *Prophets of the Great Spirit.* Lincoln: University of Nebraska Press, 2006.

Clary, David A. *Eagles and Empire: The United States, Mexico, and the Struggle for a Continent.* New York: Bantam, 2009.

Clay, Henry. *Speeches of Henry Clay.* Philadelphia: Carey & Lea, 1827.

Cohen, Paul E. *Mapping the West: America's Westward Movement 1524–1890.* New York: Rizzoli, 2002.

Cole, Donald B. *A Jackson Man: Amos Kendall and the Rise of American Democracy.* Baton Rouge: Louisiana State University Press, 2004.

Crockett, David. *Narrative of the Life of David Crockett, by Himself.* Lincoln: University of Nebraska Press, 1987.

Dickens, Roy S. Jr. *Archaeological Investigations at Horseshoe Bend National Military Park, Alabama.* Tuscaloosa: Alabama Archaeological Society, 1979.

Dinkin, Robert J. *Campaigning in America: A History of Election Practices.* Westport, CT: Greenwood Press, 1989.

Donald, David Herbert. *Lincoln.* New York: Simon and Schuster, 1995.

Drake, Samuel G. *Biography and History of the Indians of North America.* Boston: Sanborn, Carter and Bazin, 1857.

Duncan, Barbara. *Cherokee Clothing in the 1700's* (forthcoming). Cherokee, NC: Museum of the Cherokee Indian Press.

———, ed. *Living Stories of the Cherokee.* Chapel Hill: University of North Carolina Press, 1998.

Eaton, John, and John Reid. *The Life of Andrew Jackson.* Philadelphia: M. Carey and Son, 1817.

Ehle, John. *Trail of Tears: The Rise and Fall of the Cherokee Nation.* New York: Anchor Books, 1988.

Ellis, Joseph J. *His Excellency: George Washington.* New York: Vintage Books, 2005.

Fischer, David Hackett. *Albion's Seed: Four British Folkways in America.* New York: Oxford University Press, 1989.

Foreman, Grant. *Indian Removal.* Norman: University of Oklahoma Press, 1932.

Freehling, William H. *The Road to Disunion, Vol. 1, 1776–1854.* New York: Oxford, 1990.

Gabriel, Ralph Henry. *Elias Boudinot, Cherokee, and His America.* Norman: University of Oklahoma Press, 1941.

Garrett, Jill Knight. *A History of Florence, Alabama.* Columbia, TN: J. K. Garrett, 1968.

Gaul, Theresa Strouth. *To Marry an Indian: The Marriage of Harriett Gold and Elias Boudinot in Letters 1823–1839.* Chapel Hill: University of North Carolina Press, 2005.

Gedney, Matt. *Living on the Unicoi Road: Helen's Pioneer Century and Tales from the Georgia Gold Rush.* Marietta: Little Star Press, 1996.

Graham, Paul K. *Georgia Land Lottery Research.* Atlanta: Georgia Genealogical Society, 2010.

Greeley, Horace. *The American Conflict.* Vol. 1. Chicago: Geo. & C. W. Sherwood, 1864.

Grund, Francis J. *Aristocracy in America.* London: Richard Bentley, 1839.

Harden, Edward J. *Life of George M. Troup.* Savannah: E. J. Purse, 1859.

Hayward, Edward Ferrell. *Lyman Beecher.* Boston: Pilgrim Press, 1904.

Haywood, John. *The Civil and Political History of the State of Tennessee.* Nashville: W. H. Haywood, 1891 (reprinted 1999, Overmountain Press).

Heidler, David S., and Jeanne T. Heidler. *Henry Clay: The Essential American.* New York: Random House, 2010.

Hicks, Brian. *Toward the Setting Sun: John Ross, the Cherokees, and the Trail of Tears.* New York: Grove, 2011.

Howe, Daniel Walker. *What Hath God Wrought: The Transformation of America, 1815–1848.* New York: Oxford University Press, 2007.

James, Marquis. *Andrew Jackson: Portrait of a President.* Indianapolis: Bobbs-Merrill, 1937.

Kennedy, John P. *Memoirs of the Life of William Wirt, Attorney-General of the United States.* 2 vols. Philadelphia: Lippincott, 1860.

King, Duane H., ed. *The Memoirs of Lt. Henry Timberlake.* Cherokee, NC: Museum of the Cherokee Indian Press, 2007.

Lepore, Jill. *In the Name of War: King Philip's War and the Origin of American Identity.* New York: Knopf, 1998.

———. *The Story of America: Essays on Origins.* Princeton: Princeton University Press, 2012.

Levasseur, Auguste. *Lafayette in America 1824 and 1825; or, a Journal of a Voyage to the United States.* 2 vols. Philadelphia: Carney and Lea, 1829.

Lincoln, Abraham. *Speeches and Writings, 1832–1858.* Edited by Don E. Fehrenbacher. New York: Library of America, 1989.

———. *Speeches and Writings, 1859–1865.* Edited by Don E. Fehrenbacher. New York: Library of America, 1989.

Long, Jeff. *Duel of Eagles: The Mexican and U.S. Fight for the Alamo.* New York: William Morrow, 1990.

Lumpkin, Wilson. *The Removal of the Cherokees from Georgia, 1827–1841.* Vol. 1. Manuscripts published by Wymberley Jones De Renne. Savannah: Savannah Morning News Print, 1907.

Mahon, John K. *History of the Second Seminole War, 1835–1842.* Revised edition. Gainesville: University Press of Florida, 1985.

McKenney, Thomas, and James Hall. *History of the Indian Tribes of North America.* 3 vols. Philadelphia: E. C. Biddle, 1836–1844.

McLoughlin, William G. *Cherokee Renascence in the New Republic.* Princeton: Princeton University Press, 1986.

Meacham, Jon. *American Lion: Andrew Jackson in the White House.* New York: Random House, 2008.

Miles, Tiya. *Ties That Bind: The Story of an Afro-Cherokee Family in Slavery and Freedom.* Berkeley: University of California Press, 2005.

Mooney, James. *Myths of the Cherokee.* 1900. Reprinted with Mooney's *Sacred Formulas of the Cherokee.* Cherokee, NC: Cherokee Publications, 2006.

Moore, Burton. *History of Alabama and Her People.* Chicago: American Historical Society, 1927.

Moulton, Gary E. *John Ross, Cherokee Chief.* Athens: University of Georgia Press, 1978.

———, ed. *The Papers of Chief John Ross.* 2 vols. Norman: University of Oklahoma Press, 1985.

Norgren, Jill. *The Cherokee Cases.* Norman: University of Oklahoma Press, 1996.

Oliphant, J. Orin, ed. *Through the South and West with Jeremiah Evarts in 1826.* Lewisburg: Bucknell University Press, 1956.

Parton, James. *Life of Andrew Jackson, in Three Volumes.* New York: Mason Brothers, 1860.

Perdue, Theda. *Cherokee Editor: The Writings of Elias Boudinot.* Knoxville: University of Tennessee Press, 1983.

———. *Cherokee Women.* Lincoln: University of Nebraska Press, 1998.

Peterson, Merrill D. *The Great Triumvirate: Webster, Clay, and Calhoun.* New York: Oxford University Press, 1987.

Philip, Cynthia Owen. *Robert Fulton: A Biography.* New York: F. Watts, 1985.

Pluckhahn, Thomas J., and Robbie Ethridge, eds. *Light on the Path: The Anthropology and History of the Southern Indians.* Tuscaloosa: University of Alabama Press, 2006.

Portnoy, Alisse. *Their Right to Speak: Women's Activism in the Indian and Slave Debates.* Cambridge: Harvard University Press, 2005.

Quitt, Martin H. *Stephen A. Douglas and Antebellum Democracy.* New York: Cambridge University Press, 2012.

Ramsey, J. G. *Annals of Tennessee to the Eighteenth Century.* Charleston, SC: Walker and James, 1853.

Raphael, Ray. *Founding Myths: Stories That Hide Our Patriotic Past.* New York: MJF Books, 2007.

Reid, Brian Holden. *The Origins of the American Civil War.* London: Longman, 1996.

Remini, Robert. *Andrew Jackson and the Course of American Empire, 1767–1821.* Vol. 1. New York: Harper & Row, 1977.

———. *Andrew Jackson and the Course of American Freedom, 1822–1832.* Vol. 2. New York: Harper & Row, 1981.

———. *Andrew Jackson and the Course of American Democracy, 1833–1845.* Vol. 3. New York: Harper & Row, 1984

Reynolds, David S. *Waking Giant: America in the Age of Jackson.* New York: Harper Collins, 2008.

Roberts, Alasdair. *America's First Great Depression: Economic Crisis and Political Disorder After the Panic of 1837.* Ithaca, NY: Cornell University Press, 2012.

Robertson, David. *Denmark Vesey: The Buried Story of America's Largest Slave Rebellion and the Man Who Led It.* New York: Knopf Doubleday, 2009.

Rohrbough, Malcolm. *The Land Office Business: The Settlement and Administration of American Public Lands, 1789–1837.* New York: Oxford, 1968.

Roosevelt, Theodore. *Thomas Hart Benton.* New York: Houghton Mifflin, 1887.

———. *The Winning of the West: An Account of the Exploration and Settlement of Our Country from the Alleghenies to the Pacific.* 4 vols. Philadelphia: Gebbie, 1903.

Royall, Anne. *Letters from Alabama.* Washington: [publisher unknown], 1830.

Rozema, Vicki, ed. *Voices from the Trail of Tears.* Winston-Salem, NC: J. F. Blair, 2003.

Schlesinger, Arthur M. Jr. *The Age of Jackson.* Boston: Little, Brown, 1946.

Smith, Daniel Blake. *An American Betrayal: Cherokee Patriots and the Trail of Tears*. New York: Henry Holt, 2011.

Smith, James F. *The Cherokee Land Lottery, Containing a Numerical List of the Names of the Fortunate Drawers in Said Lottery*. New York, 1838. Republished, Baltimore: Genealogical Publishing, 1969.

Smith, Margaret Bayard. *The First Forty Years of Washington Society*. New York: Frederick Ungar, 1965.

Starr, Edward C. *A History of Cornwall, Connecticut*. New Haven: Tuttle, Morehouse & Taylor, 1926.

Stiggins, George. *Creek Indian History*. Birmingham, AL: Birmingham Public Library Press, 1989.

Stiles, T. J. *The First Tycoon: The Epic Life of Cornelius Vanderbilt*. New York: Knopf, 2009.

Stover, John F. *History of the Baltimore and Ohio Railroad*. West Lafayette, IN: Purdue University Press, 1987.

Stuart, James. *Three Years in North America, in Two Volumes*. Vol. 2. London: Whitaker, 1833.

Takaki, Ronald. *A Different Mirror: A History of Multicultural America*. New York: Little, Brown, 1993.

Tocqueville, Alexis de. *Democracy in America*. New York: Library of America, 2004. First published 1835.

Tracy, E. C. *Memoir of the Life of Jeremiah Evarts, Esq*. Boston: Crocker and Brewster, 1845.

Trask, Kerry A. *Black Hawk: The Battle for the Heart of America*. New York: Henry Holt, 2006.

Treat, Payson Jackson. *The National Land System, 1785–1820*. New York: E. B. Treat, 1910.

Unknown. *Life of Lafayette*. Boston: Light & Horton, 1835.

Van Buren, Martin. *Autobiography*. Washington, DC: Library of Congress, 1918. First published 1854.

Van Every, Dale. *Disinherited: The Lost Birthright of the American Indian*. New York: William Morrow, 1966.

Wallis, Michael. *David Crockett: The Lion of the West*. New York: Norton, 2011.

White, Barbara A. *The Beecher Sisters*. New Haven: Yale University Press, 2003.

Wilentz, Sean. *The Rise of American Democracy*. New York: Norton, 2005.

Wilkins, Thurman. *Cherokee Tragedy*. New York: Macmillan, 1970.

Williams, David. *The Georgia Gold Rush: Twenty-Niners, Cherokees, and Gold Fever*. Columbia: University of South Carolina Press, 1993.

Wilson, Woodrow. *Division and Reunion, 1829–1889*. New York: Longmans, Green, 1893.

Wood, Betty, ed. *Mary Telfair to Mary Few: Selected Letters 1802–1844*. Athens: University of Georgia Press, 2007.

Woodward, Grace Steele. *The Cherokees*. Norman: University of Oklahoma Press, 1963.

Wright, James Leitch. *Creeks and Seminoles: The Destruction and Regeneration of the Muscogulge People*. Lincoln: University of Nebraska Press, 1986.

Journals and Articles

Bacon, Jacqueline, "The History of *Freedom's Journal*," *Journal of African-American History*, vol. 88, no. 1, Winter 2003.

Berutti, Ronald A., "The Cherokee Cases: The Fight to Save the Supreme Court and the Indians," *American Indian Law Review*, vol. 17, no. 1, 1992, p. 300.

Breyer, Stephen, "The Cherokee Indians and the Supreme Court," *Georgia Historical Quarterly*, vol. 87, no. 3/4, Fall/Winter 2003, pp. 408–26.

Butler, Brian M., "The Red Clay Council Ground," *Journal of Cherokee Studies*, vol. 2, no. 1, Winter 1977, pp. 140–53.

Cass, Lewis, "Removal of the Indians," *North American Review*, January 1830, vol. 30, pp. 62–121.

Chappell, Gordon T., "Some Patterns of Land Speculation in the Old Southwest," *Journal of Southern History*, vol. 15, no. 4, November 1949, pp. 463–77.

Cole, Arthur H., *Wholesale Commodity Prices in the United States, 1700–1861.* 2 vols. Cambridge: Harvard University Press, 1938. Republished by Centers for International Price Research.

Conser, Walter H., "John Ross and the Cherokee Resistance Campaign, 1833–1838," *Journal of Southern History*, vol. 44, no. 2, May 1978, pp. 191–212.

DeWeese, Georgina G., W. Jeff Bishop, Henri D. Grissino-Mayer, Brian K. Parrish, and S. Michael Edwards. "Dendrochronological Dating of the Chief John Ross House," *Southeastern Archaeology*, Winter 2012, pp. 221–30.

Dupre, Daniel, "Ambivalent Capitalists on the Cotton Frontier: Settlement and Development in the Tennessee Valley of Alabama," *Journal of Southern History*, vol. 56, no. 2, May 1990, p. 215.

Evans, E. Raymond, "Fort Marr Blockhouse," *Journal of Cherokee Studies*, Spring 1977, pp. 256–62.

Fiorato, Jacqueline, "The Cherokee Mediation in Florida," *Journal of Cherokee Studies*, vol. 3, no. 2, Spring 1978, pp. 111–19.

Glaeser, Edward, "A Nation of Gamblers," NBER Working Paper 18825, Cambridge: National Bureau of Economic Research, 2013.

Hauptman, Laurence M., "General John E. Wool in Cherokee Country, 1836–1837: A Reinterpretation," *Georgia Historical Quarterly*, vol. 85, no. 1, Spring 2001, pp. 1–26.

Hershberger, Mary, "Mobilizing Women, Anticipating Abolition: The Struggle against Indian Removal in the 1830s," *Journal of American History*, vol. 86, no. 1, June 1999, pp. 15–40.

"James Jackson, Thomas Kirkman and the Chickasaw Treaty of 1818," unpublished paper.

Jenkins, Jeffrey A., and Brian R. Sala, "The Spatial Theory of Voting and the Presidential Election of 1824," *American Journal of Political Science*, vol. 42, no. 4, October 1998, pp. 1157–79.

King, Duane H., and Raymond, Evans, eds., *Journal of Cherokee Studies*, special issue, "The Trail of Tears: Primary Documents of the Cherokee Removal," vol. 3, no. 3, Summer 1978.

Magliocca, Gerard N., "The Cherokee Removal and the Fourteenth Amendment," *Duke Law Journal*, vol. 53, no. 3, December 2003, pp. 875–965.

Malone, Henry T. "The Cherokee Phoenix: Supreme Expression of Cherokee Nationalism," *Georgia Historical Quarterly*, vol. 34, no. 3, Sept. 1950, pp. 163–88.

McLoughlin, William G., "Experiment in Cherokee Citizenship, 1817–1829," *American Quarterly*, vol. 33, no. 1, Spring 1981, pp. 3–25.

————, and Walter H. Conser, "The Cherokees in Transition: A Statistical Analysis of the Federal Cherokee Census of 1835," *Journal of American History*, vol. 64, no. 3, December 1977, pp. 678–703.

Miles, Edwin A., "After John Marshall's Decision: *Worcester v. Georgia* and the Nullification Crisis," *Journal of Southern History*, vol. 39, no. 4, 1973, pp. 519–44.

Moulton, Gary, "Cherokees and the Second Seminole War," *Florida Historical Quarterly*, vol. 53, no. 3, January 1975, pp. 296–305.

Olmstead, Alan L., and Paul W. Rhode, "Slave Productivity in Cotton Production by Gender, Age, Season, and Scale," unpublished paper, Harvard University, October 2010.

Prucha, Francis Paul, "Andrew Jackson's Indian Policy: A Reassessment," *Journal of American History*, vol. 56, no. 3, December 1969, pp. 527–39.

Quaife, M. M., and Thomas Forsyth, "The Story of James Corbin, A Soldier of Fort Dearborn," *Mississippi Valley Historical Review*, vol. 3, no. 2, September 1916, pp. 219–28.

Quaife, Milo M., "The Fort Dearborn Massacre," *Mississippi Valley Historical Review*, vol. 1, no. 4, March 1915, pp. 561–73.

Remini, Robert, "Andrew Jackson Takes an Oath of Allegiance to Spain," *Tennessee Historical Quarterly*, vol. 54, no. 1, Spring 1995, p. 9.

Rezneck, Samuel, "The Depression of 1819–1822, A Social History," *American Historical Review*, vol. 39, no. 1, October 1933, pp. 28–47.

Roberts, Albert Hubbard, "The Dade Massacre," *Florida Historical Society Quarterly*, vol. 5, no. 3, January 1927, pp. 123–38.

Scott, Winfield, "If Not Rejoicing, At Least in Comfort: General Scott's Version of Removal," 1864 autobiographical fragment, *Journal of Cherokee Studies*, vol. 3, no. 3, Summer 1978, pp. 138–40.

Simmonds, P. L., "Statistics of Newspapers in Various Countries," *Journal of the Statistical Society of London*, July 1841, collected in *Journal of the Statistical Society of London*, Vol. 4. London: Charles Knight & Co., 1841, pp. 111–36.

Sioussat, St. George L., "Letters of General John Coffee to His Wife, 1813–1815," *Tennessee Historical Magazine*, December 1916.

Snell, William R., "The Councils at Red Clay Council Ground, Bradley County, Tennessee, 1832–37," *Journal of Cherokee Studies*, vol. 2, no. 4, Fall 1977, pp. 344–55.

Thornton, Russell, "Cherokee Population Losses during the Trail of Tears: A New Perspective and a New Estimate," *Ethnohistory*, vol. 31, no. 4, Autumn 1984, pp. 289–300.

Unser, Daniel H., "American Indians on the Cotton Frontier: Changing Economic Relations with Citizens and Slaves in the Mississippi Territory," *Journal of American History*, vol. 72, no. 2, September 1985, pp. 297–317.

Valliere, Kenneth L., "Benjamin Currey, Tennessean Among the Cherokees: A Study of the Removal Policy of Andrew Jackson, Part 2," *Tennessee Historical Quarterly*, vol. 41, no. 3, Fall 1982, pp. 239–56.

White, Flint H. "A Memorial of Rev. Samuel Austin Worcester," *Congregational Quarterly*, July 1861.

Williams, H. David, "Gambling Away the Inheritance: The Cherokee Nation and Georgia's Gold and Land Lotteries of 1832–33," *Georgia Historical Quarterly*, vol. 73, no. 3, Fall 1989.

Worthen, Bill, "Quatie Ross Gravestone Given to Museum: Evidence Clarifies Her Tragic Story," *Newsletter of the Mount Holly Cemetery Association*, Little Rock, Fall 2003.

Yarbrough, Fay, "Legislating Women's Sexuality: Cherokee Marriage Laws in the Nineteenth Century," *Journal of Social History*, vol. 38, no. 2, Winter 2004, pp. 385–406.

Young, Mary E., "Indian Removal and Land Allotment: The Civilized Tribes and Jacksonian Justice," *American Historical Review*, vol. 64, no. 1, October 1958, pp. 31–45.

Indian Treaties

The principal authority consulted for treaty texts is:

Kappler, Charles J., ed., *Indian Affairs: Laws and Treaties*. Washington, DC: Government Printing Office, 1904. 7 vols. Vol. 2, *Treaties, 1778–1883*. Oklahoma State University Digital Library. http://digital.library.okstate.edu/kappler/index.htm.

INDEX